Revolutionary Politics in the Long Parliament

Revolutionary Politics
in the Long Parliament

JOHN R. MacCORMACK

Harvard University Press   Cambridge, Massachusetts   1973

To Ann Vibeke

. . . I know not what this Parliament may produce;
it is like to set long, and so must needs hatch much.

—William Montague to Lord Montague, 1641

Contents

Preface

Nearly three and a half centuries have passed since that November day in 1640 when the Parliament men took their places in St. Stephen's Chapel to form the most revolutionary Commons in English history. One of their number—Edward Hyde—was to be both a central actor in the events that followed and their first historian. The flaws in his great study are well known, yet it is one of the very few works to have survived time's test and remains indispensable to the student of the period.

It was not until the late nineteenth century that a historian appeared who was to begin the process of penetrating the mists of legend and prejudice that obscured any clear picture of that prolonged, painful upheaval. The first volume of S. R. Gardiner's monumental *History of the Great Civil War* appeared in 1886, and it has been rightly regarded as the first scientific history of the period. Certainly no one can follow in that historian's footsteps without appreciating the magnitude of his achievement. But it is the common fate of pioneers to be superseded, and Gardiner has been more fortunate than most in this regard. There is now general agreement that the scope of his work, and the pace at which it was written, precluded any systematic treatment of parliamentary politics.

As early as 1916 the late Professor Wallace Notestein criticized the widespread assumption among historians of the seventeenth century that there was "poor gleaning after Gardiner" and pointed out that, despite that historian's achievements, much still needed to be done. A substantial amount of material remained untapped, particularly in the field of parliamentary history, and more especially for a study of the Long Parliament itself.

Since that time Professor Notestein and his students have done much to remedy the situation. The parliamentary debates of 1610 and those of the Commons in 1621 and 1629 have been edited, and two volumes of the diary of Sir Symonds D'Ewes have appeared in print. Much work has been done on the earlier Stuart Parliaments, and the manner in which the Commons strengthened their hand in the reign of James I has been revealed.

A number of important works have now appeared on the Long

Parliament. The first to be published was J. H. Hexter's well-known pioneering study, *The Reign of King Pym,* which analyzed the party structure in the Parliament between Edgehill and the death of John Pym in December 1643. This was followed by the valuable study of individuals and groups carried out by Messrs. Brunton and Pennington. A giant stride was taken with the publication of Mary F. Keeler's *The Long Parliament,* which was supplemented by George Yule's study, *The Independents in the English Civil War.* Articles on various aspects of the Parliament have been produced by such scholars as David Underdown, Valerie Pearl, Lotte Mulligan, and Lawrence Kaplan. Dame Veronica Wedgwood has provided us with her useful and readable general study, *The King's War.* More recently Professor Perez Zagorin has produced his analysis of the early stage of the revolution in *The Court and the Country,* and just before the present work went to press, Underdown's solid study, *Pride's Purge,* appeared.

All of these writers have contributed to our knowledge of the Long Parliament; indeed any student of the Parliament cannot avoid the sense of being part of a cooperative venture. This is not to say that bland consensus on the subject is called for. Vigorous and healthy debate on this most critical period in the history of liberty is both necessary and desirable if its full impact is to be experienced.

All of the authors mentioned above restricted themselves to portions of what is an extremely complicated and unwieldy subject. There was thus room for a study of the struggle for power that went on within the Parliament between rival groups in the five years between Pym's death and Pride's Purge. One of the objectives of this work has been to determine as exactly as possible the extent to which there may be said to have been true "party" conflict in the period, and a delineation of the party structure has been attempted. The degree to which the division between parties was religious or political has been explored as has the question as to whether or not the "radicals" can be said to have been a truly popular party. I have dealt with the character of the leadership of the two major groups and the manner in which the aims and objects of the parties changed in the period. Particular emphasis has been laid on the contrast between the radicals in 1644, when they put themselves forward as a revolutionary group and maintained close relations with Lilburne and his followers, and the same party in 1647 and 1648, when their essentially oligarchic outlook was revealed in sharp contrast to the genuine populism of the Levellers. This latter group is now placed firmly in the political context of the Revolution.

The work contains new interpretations of the role of Oliver Cromwell in the period, especially in 1647 and 1648 when he emerged as the central figure. The complicated, indeed almost Byzantine, character of his dealings with the antipathetic groups into which the political nation was at that time divided have been explored and, it is hoped, clarified.

It would be tedious to detail all the points where my interpretation of events differs from that of Gardiner. A few examples may suffice. The significance of the struggle for control of the army in 1644, which was the prelude to the Self-Denying Ordinance and the establishment of the New Model, seems to have completely escaped that historian. He was also uncertain as to which group was in the commanding position in 1644 and even assumed that it was the Presbyterians who held sway and who dominated affairs at the Treaty of Uxbridge in early 1645. The significance of the Irish Adventurer group and their influence on parliamentary policies, and above all on negotiations with the King, is now revealed for the first time. There are also new interpretations concerning such matters as the impact of the "recruiting" of the Commons on the balance of power within the House in 1646 and 1647 as well as the curious alliance that emerged in 1648 between the Presbyterian Scots led by Argyle and the English radicals under Cromwell. Such instances could be multiplied, but perhaps it will be sufficient to say that the work constitutes a complete reinterpretation of the five years between the death of Pym and Pride's Purge.

This study has been based, in the main, on manuscript material in the British Museum, the Public Record Office, and the Bodleian Library, Oxford. The unpublished parliamentary diaries of Sir Symonds D'Ewes, Lawrence Whitaker, Walter Yonge, and John Harrington have been particularly useful. The parliamentary diary of John Boys, recently brought to light by Underdown, contains valuable items, particularly on Cromwell. Although Gardiner made extensive use of most of these sources, he appears to have overlooked much significant information contained in them.

A word should be said about the political predilections of the diarists. Whitaker, Yonge, and Harrington leaned in the radical direction, and all escaped Pride's Purge. Boys was purged, but before that was often on the radical side of the fence. D'Ewes was anything but a radical and was on many issues closer to royalist feeling than to the "violent ones." Despite his very shockable temperament, his diary, which comes to an end in late 1645, remains one of the most valuable sources for this period. Parts of it were written up at a later date but, as became a good antiquarian, on the basis of notes made at the time. His objectivity can be questioned but not his veracity, nor, on the whole, his accuracy. Yonge's shorthand notes often provide valuable quotations from speakers in particular debates.

The Journals of the House of Lords and House of Commons, when used in conjunction with the diaries, yielded a large amount of important material. The dispatches of the French, Venetian, Florentine, and Dutch ambassadors, as well as the Vatican correspondent, preserved in the British Museum and the Public Record Office, were also very useful. The diaries peter out by mid-1647. After that date, the major source, apart from those named above, were the letters of intelligence from London in the Clarendon State Papers in the Bodleian and the Thomason Tracts. Though, of course, most of the letter writers in the Clarendon collection had a royalist bias, their letters provide valuable evidence on the party struggles in late 1647 and 1648. The value of newspaper and pamphlet material is uneven, but these sources, when critically handled, sometimes produce evidence of the first importance.

I must now pay tribute to those whose advice, encouragement, and cooperation have helped to make this book possible. Four scholars, two Canadians, an Englishman, and an American, have been particularly involved in its genesis and production. George E. Wilson, emeritus professor of history, Dalhousie University, first introduced me to the discipline. His wise counsel, encouragement, and sound criticism have been invaluable. My doctoral research was carried out under the direction of Donald J. McDougall, emeritus professor of history, University of Toronto, who first suggested a study of the Long Parliament. His standards of scholarship and unfailing support leave me permanently in his debt. During my years in England I attended the late Professor R. H. Tawney's seminar at the Institute of Historical Research. His characteristically generous interest in my research was vital to its continuance. In 1962 I became acquainted with the late Professor Wallace Notestein. He read early drafts of the present work and encouraged its publication. The late Professor Walter Love also read portions of the manuscript, and I benefited greatly from his criticism.

I should also like to express my gratitude to the staffs of the libraries of the Universities of Toronto, Dalhousie, Saint Mary's; Worcester College and Christ Church, Oxford; the Beineke Library of Yale University; the Institute of Historical Research, University of London; the Nova Scotia Legislative Library, Marsh's Library, Dublin; the Manuscript Room and North Library of the British Museum; the Public Record Office and the Bodleian Library, Oxford. Others for whose assistance I am very grateful include my uncles, the late Mr. C. I. Cameron and Dr. A. H. Cameron, Wyandotte, Michigan; my mother-in-law, Mrs. S. H. Bailey; Mr. G. A. MacKay, Ottawa; Dr. Arthur P. Monahan, Mrs. Jean Monahan, Dr. Franklin A. Walker, Loyola University, Chicago; Professor Michael Howard, University of

London; Professor David Underdown, Brown University; Professor John Lynch, University of London; Professor Murray Tolmie, University of British Columbia; Professor George Yule, University of Melbourne; Mrs. Dorothy Whitney, Cambridge, Massachusetts; Mrs. F. Mercer, London, England; Mrs. W. Mosher, Halifax, Nova Scotia; Miss Barbara Spence, Fredricton, New Brunswick; and Mr. Mark Teehan, Halifax, Nova Scotia. The research for this work was greatly assisted by Canada Council Post-Doctoral Fellowships in 1962 and 1969 and a Canada Council grant in 1967. My debt to my immediate family can be more easily mentioned than adequately expressed.

My wife, Ann Vibeke, has lived with this work from the early research stages to the final published form. Her constancy and faith have made all possible. She has, moreover, acted as a most capable and experienced research assistant in the preparation of the appendix and in the compilation of the index.

Halifax, Nova Scotia   John R. MacCormack
August 1972

Revolutionary Politics in the Long Parliament

I] The Radical Power Structure

The death of John Pym in December 1643 robbed the parliamentary cause of one of history's great revolutionaries. Three years had passed since Charles I had called his most formidable Parliament into being, years during which Pym's ascendancy at Westminster had never been seriously challenged. A brilliant political strategist with a masterly sense of timing, Pym had been able to strike a kind of balance between the extremes of parliamentary opinion. But those who praise Pym as a "moderate" do him both more and less than justice. That section of the House of Commons that remained in Westminster after the spring of 1642 were themselves a revolutionary group, and Pym, more than any other man, had made them so. If, by 1643, he was the leader of a "middle party," it is quite evident that he was on much better terms with men like Sir Henry Vane, Jr., and Oliver St. John, who represented "violent" opinion, than with their opponents, the "peace party" men. Yet Pym's sense of the possible had exercised quite discernible restraint on the extremists, and the polarization of hostile groups that followed hard upon his death was the measure of that influence. Sir Henry Vane, Jr., and St. John, the avowed enemies of the Earl of Essex and of any compromise with Charles I, promptly stepped forward as the leaders of the radicals. They soon locked horns with their rivals, Denzil Holles and Sir Philip Stapleton, the spokesmen of the moderates.

Throughout the five years between Pym's death and Pride's Purge the two major political groups struggled for supremacy. By December 6, 1648, when Colonel Pride stood at the door of the House of Commons holding his famous list of proscribed members, the radicals had suffered many defections, but the leadership was still recognizably the same. By that date, too, although Stapleton lay buried in Calais, Holles still led those who favored the moderate course. It may then be well to review the careers of the four men who not only had been in the forefront of revolutionary activity in the early days of the Long Parliament, but who were to personify the divisions in the Parliament in the critical years after Pym's death.

Of the four main protagonists, Sir Henry Vane remains one of the most interesting and mysterious. A born rebel, he began to have conflicts with authority when, as a young student, he refused to take the oath of allegiance, a stand that necessitated his withdrawal from Oxford University. From that time until June 14, 1662, when, from the scaffold, he shouted his speech to the crowd above the blare of the sheriffs' strategically placed trumpets, his career was strenuous and hectic. More often than not he was "odd man out." His short term as governor of Massachusetts was notable for its turbulence, and the lucrative post obtained for him on his return to England did nothing to endear him to the regime, or it to him. In 1640 the English political situation once again came to a furious boil after a lull of eleven years, and Sir Henry was soon at the storm center. Assisted by the patronage of the Earl of Northumberland, he held seats in both the Short and Long Parliaments and played a key role in the attainder of Strafford. With Cromwell and St. John he sponsored the Root and Branch bill, and in January 1642, after the attempt on the "five members," he led the Commons during the temporary absence of Pym and John Hampden.

During the "reign of King Pym" he was one of the leaders of the "war party," or in Sir Symonds D'Ewes's terms, the "violent spirits." A steady opponent of negotiation with the King, Vane frequently displayed extreme hostility toward the House of Lords. But his "violence" does not appear to have alienated Pym, and that supple tactician could not have given greater evidence of his regard for Vane than by appointing him to negotiate the vital alliance with the Scots in the autumn of 1643. Of attractive appearance, Vane displayed a certain personal magnetism and a quality that "made men think there was something in him of extraordinary."[1]

Vane was to share the leadership of the radical party with St. John. In many ways a less sympathetic figure than Vane, "the Solicitor" was a dour person whose political actions were often characterized by a harshness of spirit unrelieved by that largeness of view that sometimes gave to Vane's revolutionary ardor something of the tone of a crusade.

A Cambridge man and a barrister of Lincoln's Inn, St. John found his path to the centers of power and influence smoothed by his association with the Earl of Bedford. His later career was no less furthered by his marriage to a favorite cousin of Cromwell. As the grandson of the first Lord St. John of Bletsho, he had an assured social position, but he was not, like Vane, a man of means and could ill afford collisions

1. Edward Hyde, Earl of Clarendon, *The History of the Rebellion and Civil Wars in England*, ed. W. D. Macray, 6 vols. (Oxford, 1888) [hereafter cited as Clarendon, *Rebellion*], III, 34. The best biography of Vane and one that supersedes previous works is Violet Rowe's recent monograph, *Sir Henry Vane The Younger* (London, Athlone Press, 1970).

with the government. His first encounter with the Crown came in 1629 when he was imprisoned in the Tower on a charge of sending to the Earl of Bedford "a seditious document."

The charges were eventually dropped, but not before St. John had spent some time in the Tower, been threatened with the rack, and hauled before the Court of Star Chamber. It was treatment that he neither forgot nor forgave. In the 1630's he was closely associated with the Providence Company and became increasingly sympathetic with both the political and religious attitudes of that group. In 1637 his papers were seized when the government suspected him of assisting Henry Burton with his defense in the Star Chamber. Hampden's ship money case was St. John's great legal opportunity, and he made the most of it. The notoriety accruing from the case, together with the judicious assistance of the Earl of Bedford, assured him seats in the Short and Long Parliaments. Although seldom seen to smile, St. John "could not conceal his cheerfulness" at the dissolution of the Short Parliament because, it was said, he believed that "so moderate a body of men would never have done what was necessary to be done."[2]

Charles I, never a good judge of men, accepted the Earl of Bedford's suggestion and named St. John to the post of solicitor general. St. John now became, if anything, more implacable, which was demonstrated during Strafford's trial when he put forward the notorious argument that "it was never accounted either cruelty or foul play to knock foxes and wolves on the head."[3]

During the Pym era St. John continued to demonstrate his penchant for the extreme measure. When the Earl of Northumberland, who was later to become a pillar of the radical cause in the House of Lords, was accused of complicity in Edmund Waller's plot in June 1643, St. John demanded his immediate arrest. He was at the same time one of the leading supporters of the ambitions to supreme military command of Essex's rival Sir William Waller. A consistent advocate of harsh measures against suspected traitors, he successfully pressed for charges by a court of martial law against the two Hothams, and when the Earl of Holland sought readmission to Parliament after having formerly deserted to Oxford, he led the attacks on him and favored his immediate arrest. A few days after Pym's death he introduced an ordinance providing for harsh measures against fellows and other members of Cambridge colleges who were regarded as "disaffected" by Parliament.[4] By

2. Clarendon, *Rebellion*, II, 78; III, 32.
3. *Dictionary of National Biography*, ed. Leslie Stephen and Sydney Lee, 22 vols. (Oxford, 1908–1909) [hereafter cited as *DNB*], XVII, 641.
4. Sir Symonds D'Ewes, "Journal of the Parliament begun November, 1640," British Museum, Harleian MS. 165 [hereafter cited as D'Ewes, "Journal," BM, Harl.], fols. 103b, 207a, 241a.

the autumn of 1643, he had already taken over the leadership from the ailing Pym and was later one of Pym's pallbearers.

Holles was in his vigorous early forties when the Civil War broke out. A younger son of the Earl of Clare, he was by then a veteran parliamentarian with a record in the House of Commons comparable to that of Pym himself. In the 1620's, with his brother-in-law Sir Thomas Wentworth and his friend Sir John Eliot, he had bitterly opposed the all-pervading influence of the Duke of Buckingham, and he was one of the central figures in that dramatic scene in the Parliament of 1629 when the Speaker, in obedience to the royal command, was about to dissolve the House. "Gods wounds," Holles had shouted, "you shall sit till we please to rise,"[5] and with the help of another member, he had held the Speaker in his chair by force. For his part in that day's work, Holles found himself heavily fined and faced with imprisonment during the King's pleasure. Holles chose exile and lived outside England for the next seven years.

In both the Short and Long Parliaments he was one of the leading members of the opposition and balked only at the attainder of his brother-in-law, Strafford. In this period he was distinctly hostile to the bishops, and, although Clarendon regarded him as not opposed to the Church itself, he was, nevertheless, one of the tellers for the second reading of the Root and Branch Bill. There was little sign of future moderation in the Holles of 1641. He supported the Grand Remonstrance as well as the declaration against Catholics at the outbreak of the Irish rebellion.

A man of considerable means, Holles was able to subscribe £1,300 to the cause at the outbreak of war as well as maintaining four horses for the defense of Parliament.[6] As the commander of a regiment at Edgehill, he distinguished himself on that field and in later battles. By December 1642, however, his attitude had changed radically; the erstwhile fire-eater had become a man of peace. No one ever questioned Holles's personal courage, but the cathartic experience of battle may have purged him of that all-consuming hatred of the enemy sometimes observed in the occupants of more sedentary posts.

By the summer of 1643 Holles was deeply involved in defending the position of the Earl of Essex against the "war party's" scheme—which enjoyed some support from Pym—to oust Essex as commander in chief and to make Sir William Waller the head of a "new modelled army."[7]

5. *DNB*, IX, 1056.
6. Mary F. Keeler, *The Long Parliament, 1640–1641: A Biographical Study of Its Members* (Philadelphia, American Philosophical Society, 1954), p. 220.
7. Sir William Waller, *Vindication of the Character and Conduct of Sir William Waller* (London, 1680), pp. 13–16. See also Vernon F. Snow's recent monograph,

The conflict reached its climax in August 1643 when Isaac Pennington, who was both lord mayor of London and a member for the City, planned a coup, the object of which was the seizure of Holles and other peace party leaders in both houses. Holles escaped arrest, but seriously considered leaving the country.

Holles's closest friend and strongest supporter was to be Sir Philip Stapleton, a doughty Yorkshireman, who had made a name for himself in the campaigns of 1642 and 1643, in the capacity of commander of the life guard of the Earl of Essex. Born into a well-established family in comfortable circumstances, Stapleton began his political career with his election to the Long Parliament as member for Boroughbridge. With characteristic vigor, he soon joined the other "northern beagles" in the pursuit of the Earl of Strafford. That he was highly regarded by Pym and his associates is attested by the fact that he was chosen as one of the parliamentary watchdogs who accompanied the King on his journey to Scotland in the summer of 1641. In January 1642, when Charles attempted to arrest the "five members," Stapleton was one of the Commons delegation that conveyed the reply of the House to the King. A short time later, when Charles tried to gain access to the munitions of Hull, Stapleton was among those dispatched by Parliament to stiffen the spine of his father-in-law, Sir John Hotham.[8]

Stapleton's close association and loyalty to both Essex and Pym were to create problems for him in 1643 when relations between the two leaders became strained. Down to August 1643 Stapleton could still be counted as one of Pym's supporters, and earlier in that year he had opposed peace negotiations with enough vigor to be included among D'Ewes's *bêtes noires*.[9]

His basic conservatism was, however, demonstrated by his defense of the House of Lords against the attacks of Vane, and by July 1643 he was wavering on the issue of a negotiated peace. Early in that month Essex had put the cat among the pigeons by a letter to Parliament in which he urged a peace overture. Pym had opposed the suggestion, but Stapleton, although he was persuaded by Pym to oppose it in the Commons, privately supported Essex's suggestion.

The growing hostility to Essex of many in Pym's group may have acted as a kind of catalyst for Stapleton's confused state of mind. In that same debate, when the younger Vane made some sarcastic remarks

---

Essex the Rebel, the Life of Robert Devereaux, the Third Earl of Essex, 1591–1646 (Lincoln, University of Nebraska Press, 1970), a work that is particularly useful for the military aspects of Essex's career.

8. *DNB*, XVIII, 986.

9. J. L. Sanford, *Studies and Illustrations of the Great Rebellion* (London, 1858), pp. 541–544.

at Essex's expense, Stapleton angrily attacked Vane. It was a foretaste
of what was to become a recurring theme in the bitter exchanges on
the floor of the House in 1644. Vane hastily backtracked, but in the
following weeks it became increasingly clear to the friends of Essex
that a plan to supplant him as commander in chief was afoot and that
Pym, if he was not actively furthering the scheme, was doing nothing
to oppose it. By August 5 Stapleton was strongly supporting further
consideration of peace proposals.[10]

A few days later, Pym, with the assistance of Isaac Pennington and
the London mob, had defeated the peace party. He followed this victory by a strategic retreat from the anti-Essex position and abandoned,
at least temporarily, the attack on the parliamentary commander.

In the autumn of 1643, the ailing Pym, faced by setbacks in the field
and the pressing necessity to ensure that Scottish promises of military
aid be translated into reality, was more concerned to present a united
front to the royalists than to exacerbate tensions in the Commons. Yet
Vane's key role in the Scottish negotiations and St. John's increasing
prominence in the House were signs that Pym's political heirs were to
be the leaders of the "war party" and that Pym's role as a kind of balance wheel between the factions would disappear.

Between Pym's death in December 1643 and the spring of 1647 only
two recognizable parties existed in the Long Parliament. There is no
evidence of a "middle party" in this period.[11] Most of those whom

10. J. H. Hexter, *The Reign of King Pym* (Cambridge, Mass., Harvard University
Press, 1941), p. 145, n. 35.
11. In her article, "Oliver St. John and the 'middle group' in the Long Parliament: August 1643–May 1644" (*English Historical Review*, LXXXI [July 1966]), Dr.
Valerie Pearl contends that a "middle party" led by St. John persisted after Pym's
death. It is, of course, true that men like John Glyn, Bulstrode Whitelocke, and
William Pierrepont were not always consistent in 1644, but there is a great difference between a "floating vote" and the self-conscious corporate entity, complete
with leaders and policies, that Pearl presents to us. Contemporary witnesses are
awkwardly silent on the subject, and far from suggesting some kind of division
between Vane and St. John, which the existence of such a "middle party" would
imply, they couple their names constantly as leaders of the radicals. Pearl's view of
St. John as an irenic, conciliatory figure is difficult to reconcile with the facts; nor
does he seem to meet her own specifications for a "middle party" man. She identi-
fies such an individual in part by his attitude toward Essex. If, she writes, St. John
were in fact the leader of the middle party, "we would expect him to support the
Earl of Essex as commander in chief . . . " (p. 507), and she finds that St. John was,
in fact, the friend of the lord general (p. 504). But if this is true, Essex was indeed
an ingrate, for in late January 1644 he was said to have made strenuous efforts to
impeach the same Oliver St. John on a charge of corresponding with the enemy.
(See *The Letters and Journals of Robert Baillie, Principal of the University of
Glasgow, 1637–1662*, ed. David Laing, 3 vols. [Edinburgh, 1841–1842] [hereafter
cited as Baillie, *Letters*], II, 135.) The fact is that St. John and his radical friends
were consistent in their opposition to Essex throughout the whole of 1644 and until
they ousted him in favor of Sir Thomas Fairfax in 1645.

J. H. Hexter placed in that category can, by 1644, be put firmly in the camp of either Vane and St. John or Holles and Stapleton. The former group had their origins as the "war party" of 1642 and 1643 and later come to be known as the "Independents" despite the fact that there were many genuine religious Presbyterians among them. Many of the followers of Holles and Stapleton had been numbered among the "peace party" of 1643. By 1645 they were beginning to be known as the "Presbyterians" although they included many individuals who were potential, if not actual, supporters of limited episcopacy. These religious labels, misnomers from the start, have actually done more to obscure the issues than to clarify them. For that reason I have used the terms "radicals" to describe the party of Vane and St. John and "moderates" to designate the group led by Holles and Stapleton.

There are, of course, difficulties with these terms as well. "Radical" is an accurate description of the policies pursued by the Vane-St. John group down to 1647. They were ruthless and single-minded in their determination to wrest control of the parliamentary forces from the moderates, and throughout 1644 they mounted an assiduous and systematic campaign against Essex and like-minded commanders. By April 1645 they had reached the long-sought goal by means of two well-timed strokes. The passage of the Self-Denying Ordinance forced the resignation of all commanders in either House (the majority of whom were moderates), while the almost simultaneous parliamentary approval of the slate of officers for the New Model assured the radicals of effective control of the new force. The victory at Naseby placed them in almost undisputed mastery of Parliament. In the same period their political radicalism helped to inspire John Lilburne with the conviction that a genuine social and democratic revolution was both desirable and feasible. Their decision to "recruit" the House of Commons, or to fill the vacancies left by expelled royalists, although it failed to win them any kind of permanent majority, did bring into the House a number of members whose extremism was eventually to prove decidedly awkward. By 1647 it was abundantly clear that Vane and St. John were no longer in the van of the revolution, but had in truth become a "middle party" sandwiched between the moderates and the extreme radicals who tended to make common cause with Lilburne. The resultant disintegration of the "old" radicals helped to create a vacuum that was eventually filled by the army.

Although they were a coherent, recognizable party, the radicals were by no means homogeneous, and time would reveal the cracks so assiduously papered over in 1644. At the extreme left were those whom we may call the "popular" as opposed to the "oligarchic" republicans, men like the temporarily expelled Henry Marten, who combined republicanism with a genuine desire for political and social reform. To the right of this group were the oligarchical republicans like Vane and Sir Arthur Haselrig who, although they were later to retain enough political radicalism to be thorns in the Cromwellian flesh, were also to exhibit enough social conservatism to earn the cordial dislike of Lilburne. To the right of the republicans were men like St. John, who, although much more "bloody minded" than Vane in 1644 and 1645, was no ideologue. His extremism was directed more against the government and person of Charles I than against monarchy itself. To these may be added persons such as William Strode and Sir Henry Mildmay whose past record had committed them, virtually irrevocably, to parliamentary supremacy.

The religious spectrum of the party was even more varied than the political, ranging from a relatively small group of genuine sectarians through the more conservative Independents, cool Erastians, and genuine Presbyterians. But despite these differences, the latent discord was submerged by a common determination to gain control of the army, push the war to a clear-cut decision, and impose a peace settlement that would secure that victory. The radicals united behind the leadership of Vane and St. John because they were confident of their ability to achieve those goals.

The term "moderate" creates some difficulties. It sounds suspiciously like a "value judgment," something that, until recently, all good historians were accustomed to avoid. The term has been employed in this case because it was, in fact, used by contemporaries to describe this group and because for most of the period it is a reasonably accurate description of the policies pursued by Holles and Stapleton and their followers.[12] It is certainly to be preferred to the label "Presbyterian" which the party earned for no better reason than their alliance with the Presbyterian Scots. But by 1647 its use, too, is less satisfactory. During the first six months of that year, when Holles shaped parliamentary policies, his attitude toward Charles I was almost reminiscent of that of Vane and St. John in 1644. On the other hand, after his re-

12. "Were we not called the moderate party? Branded with that title, for they [the radicals] held it a crime . . . " (*Memoirs of Denzil, Lord Holles, Baron of Ifield, from the year 1641 to 1648* [London, 1699] [hereafter cited as Holles, *Memoirs*], p. 130.) For other examples of the use of the term, see *The Diplomatic Correspondence of Jean de Montereul and the Brothers de Bellièvre, French Ambassadors in England and Scotland, 1645–1648*, ed. J. G. Fotheringham, 2 vols. (Edinburgh, 1898–1899) [hereafter cited as *MC*], II, 17; *Mercurius Pragmaticus* [hereafter cited as *Merc. Prag.*], July 25–Aug. 1, 1648, BM, E.456; Clarendon State Papers (Bodleian) [hereafter cited as Clar.SPB], 31, fol. 4b; *The Hamilton Papers; being selections from original letters in the possession of His Grace the Duke of Hamilton and Brandon relating to the years 1638–1650*, ed. S. R. Gardiner (London, 1880), p. 190.

turn from exile in 1648, and again in 1660, he demonstrated a fundamental parliamentary conservatism, both in politics and religion.

The fact that Holles and Stapleton could so seldom bring their full strength to bear on divisions in the House is perhaps evidence that they suffered from the disabilities of most moderate groups in revolutionary times. They lacked a positive program and were united only in their opposition to the extremism of Vane and his supporters. If the term "war party" is too unimaginative to characterize accurately the revolutionary policy of the Vane-St. John group, "peace party," however flaccid the phrase may sound, more adequately describes the outlook of Holles, Stapleton, and their followers. They were as opposed to the republican tendencies of Vane and his friends as they were to the increasingly powerful religious radicalism. But in politics as in religion they were more certain about what they disliked than what they favored. They abhorred republicanism, but were by no means sure of the kind of monarchy they wanted. They were horrified by the proliferating sects of London and the army, but were not really enthusiastic about the activities of the determined clerics of the Westminster Assembly.

The radical leaders, by contrast, had clear-cut goals from the outset. When they took over the reins of power from Pym in December 1643, Vane and St. John were determined to clear all obstacles from their path, not the least of which was the Earl of Essex. They had been deprived of Essex's scalp in August 1643 and were now determined to succeed where Pym had failed. Essex was certainly not the only target. Equally important was the task of ending the hegemony of the moderate parliamentarians, which they exercised through a wide variety of army commanders on the local level, such as Willoughby of Parham, the Earl of Denbigh, and Sir Edward Massey.

Radical success thus depended upon the support of as many allies as possible. Vane and St. John were, accordingly, soon hard at work building up alliances, not only with the Scots but with the City of London, anti-Essex elements in the armies, and political radicals among the general populace.

The City of London was still a key factor in parliamentary politics, and the radicals succeeded both in strengthening the hand of their cohorts in the City, especially in the Common Council, and in gaining the support of more conservative elements as represented by the great joint stock companies as well as the powerful Irish interest.

Actual or potential rivals of Essex and the other moderate commanders could now be given their head. The hostility between Essex and Sir William Waller was to be shrewdly exploited to Essex's disadvantage. The Earl of Manchester, commander of the Eastern Association, was temporarily favored as a rival of Essex. The support of radicals in the county committees was also effectively enlisted in a systematic campaign carried on against the less prominent moderate commanders on the local level. Finally, the radical policy toward the King, the Queen, Archbishop William Laud, the House of Lords, and the ancient constitution itself was one calculated to appeal to extremists of all shades of opinion.

Backed by London, the Scots, and army supporters like Cromwell, Vane and St. John were able to take a giant step forward when they won executive control of the parliamentary war effort through the establishment of the committee of both kingdoms. This step not only immensely strengthened their position vis-à-vis the Earl of Essex, but also provided them with a convenient instrument for the influencing of Parliament itself.

Pym's last main contribution to the parliamentary cause had been the arrangement, shortly before his death, of the vital if ill-starred alliance with the Presbyterian Scots. The link between the Pym group and the Scottish opponents of the Crown had been strong since 1640, when, with considerable finesse, they had cooperated to make the position of Charles I increasingly untenable. It had been further strengthened by close collaboration following the outbreak of the Irish rebellion in late 1641, when large quantities of arms had been shipped to Scotland by order of the House of Commons. The alliance had been made explicit in September 1643 with the signing of the Solemn League and Covenant, an act that, on the face of it, solemnly bound the parliamentarians to the extirpation of episcopacy. The religious aspects of this agreement have been sufficiently stressed by historians, but the pact had its more mundane side. The Scots exhibited a definite interest in the financial problems involved, and even managed to effect a rather neat fusion of the economic and religious aspects of the alliance by a clause in the agreement that provided that the Scots "shall . . . have due recompense made unto them by the kingdom of England, and that out of such lands and estates of the papists, prelates, malignants, and their adherents, as the two houses of the Parliament of England shall think fit . . . "[13]

The lands of the English bishops were thus involved in the religious question from the outset and, in the event, were to be sold to provide payment for the Scots in 1646. The name of the Marquis of Argyle headed the list of signatories, and the chief of the Campbells continued his close cooperation with the radicals down to the pivotal meeting with Cromwell in the autumn of 1648.

13. John Thurloe, *A Collection of the State Papers of John Thurloe, Esq.*, ed. Thomas Birch, 7 vols. (London, 1742), I, 29–30.

The Scots demanded that the churches of the three kingdoms be brought into "the nearest conjunction" with each other, but rather cannily insisted that the Church of Scotland was not to be tampered with. On Vane's suggestion, the qualification was added that this reformation should be "according to the word of God." Doubtless Argyle did not view this as much of a concession and felt confident that the presence of the Scottish army would be the most effective argument in support of northern theology.

Whatever the reservations held by the English, the Scots—and, more especially, the Scottish Kirk—viewed the Solemn League and Covenant as the guarantee that Presbyterianism would be established in England, and the English radicals, despite the religious scruples of many of their followers, demonstrated their support of the Scots by pressing the oath to the covenant on all and sundry.

English enthusiasm for the oath appears to have been restrained, to say the least. Sir Henry Heyman wrote of the cool reception accorded it in Sussex and Surrey, and the radicals were even accused of padding the list of covenant takers with the names of persons long since deceased.[14] For the moment at least, the Scots could afford to ignore such rumblings. The Scottish army was needed in England, and the readiness of the Commons to vote that a presbytery in the church was according to the will of God was the measure of that need. The Scots in London engaged in some rather smug self-congratulations. The future Church of England, they told themselves, would be organized on the rugged Scottish model. They had even succeeded in persuading the radical leaders to abolish the traditional holy day of Christmas and reported cheerfully that the Commons sat on Christmas Day itself. The Londoners, who had been ordered to remain open for business, were not so pleased, and the volatile apprentices, angered by the loss of the traditional holiday, rioted and forced many of the merchants to close up shop.

According to the royalist William Ogle, the signing of the covenant with the Scots had provoked a strong reaction among the "lovers of the Book of Common Prayer" in Parliament, whom he regarded as more numerous than either Presbyterians or Independents. Despite their early opposition to bishops, in part springing from nonreligious motives, this group, he wrote, now felt that "tis better for them to live under episcopacy . . . than under the tyranny of the militia and malicious Presbyterian."[15]

14. *Mercurius Aulicus* [hereafter cited as *Merc. Aul.*], Feb. 9–12, 1644, BM, E.35/27, pp. 829–830.

15. Thomas Ogle to the Earl of Bristol, London, Nov. 24, 1643 (apparently written Oct. 17, 1643), *Camden Miscellany*, 22 vols. [London, 1847–1964], VIII, 1–8.

The military impact of the alliance was at first disappointing. The Scots were "always pressing for money, without any sign of results from what has already been sent," wrote Agostini, the astringent and perceptive representative of the republic of Venice. The English, he thought, "cannot hope to hold out without their assistance" and, accordingly, would do their best to please the northerners. He contrasted the attitude of the rival parliamentary groups toward the Scots with the words: "those who are less rabid are afraid of them, but the desperate do not care."[16]

For a time the Scots turned a blind eye to radical policies designed to appeal to those who saw the Civil War and revolution in equalitarian terms. Thus the radicals were often vocal in their hostility not only to Charles I but to the House of Lords and to the monarchy itself. The charge of republicanism was frequently made, and neither Vane nor St. John felt obliged to clear himself of such accusations. They appear indeed to have deliberately adopted a kind of "popular front" policy through which they could win the support of radicals of every stripe.

The most conservative policy envisaged by the parliamentary radicals in 1644 was the deposition of Charles I and the installation of a puppet of their own making; the most revolutionary was the abolition of the monarchy and the establishment of a republic. Such "war aims" presupposed a fight to the finish with the King and a settled hostility toward any proposals for a compromise peace.

Vane and St. John soon made their opposition to any serious negotiations with the King abundantly clear. The insulting treatment of the French intermediary Count de Harcourt in December 1643 was underlined in January 1644 by the institution of impeachment proceedings against Queen Henrietta Maria. The trial of Archbishop Laud was pressed with renewed vigor, and observers regarded the chances for peace as dim. Some held that only a military disaster or strong pressure from London could change things because those in power would "never consent to a reasonable adjustment of their own accord."[17]

The cold reception accorded another Oxford peace move at the end of January 1644 further dampened hopes of a settlement. The Scots strongly supported the "war policy." That busy and opinionated Scottish divine, Robert Baillie, recently come to London with the Scottish commissioners, provided a certain insight into events as seen through

16. Agostini to Doge, Jan. 1, 1644, *Calendar of state papers and manuscripts relating to English affairs existing in the archives and collections of Venice and in other libraries of northern Italy,* vols. 10–38 (1603–1675) [London, H. M. Stationery Office, 1900–1940] [hereafter cited as *CSPV,*] *1643–1647,* pp. 58, 65.
17. Agostini to Doge, Jan. 12, 1644, *ibid.,* p. 65.

his minatory and somewhat myopic eyes. Although he was soon to become thoroughly disillusioned with both the religious and political attitudes of the radicals, he was as yet almost completely uncritical in his admiration. He agreed that nothing less than complete defeat could force Charles I to accept the religious settlement that Baillie (but not the radicals) regarded as necessary. Nor did this Presbyterian cleric entertain the slightest sympathy for Holles and Stapleton and the party that was soon to be known as "Presbyterian." If "the strong lurking party," as he termed them, had succeeded in opening negotiations with the King before the intervention of the Scots, it would have "undone all."[18]

By September 1644 many Scots were to regard Vane and St. John not only as betrayers of the trust placed in them but as most dangerous opponents. For the moment, however, all was serene, and Baillie was pleased to refer to St. John as "the sweet man, Mr. Pym's successor." Vane and St. John had apparently flattered the Scots into regarding themselves as the true masters of the situation. They also had succeeded in implanting in their minds a deep distrust of the Earl of Essex, Denzil Holles, and the whole moderate group. It was thus that the natural community of interest between that party and the Scots was effectively obscured for some nine months.

By the end of January 1644 Vane and St. John had laid the foundations of an alliance with the City radicals as preliminary to moves against Essex. The connection between the radicals in the City and the Commons was, of course, nothing new and had had an important effect on events during Pym's tenure. St. John led the way in further cementing this relationship. On December 20 he took steps designed to ensure that the impending elections to the London Common Council would yield a body that would be politically reliable. He introduced an ordinance to disfranchise electors to the Common Council who had been "questioned for malignancy" or who refused to take the covenant. He also urged that persons who refused the covenant should be barred from the Common Council.[19] The Common Council that emerged was to St. John's taste and was dominated by John Fowke who, throughout 1644, was to prove a willing worker in the radical cause. The radicals were described as having "contrived to continue their friends in the Common Council and to draw in none but . . . are approved and tried in the cause."[20]

18. Baillie to William Spang, Feb. 18, 1644, Baillie, *Letters*, II, 138.
19. D'Ewes, "Journal," BM, Harl. 165, fol. 249b; Walter Yonge, "Journal of Proceedings in the House of Commons" [hereafter cited as Yonge, "Journal"], BM, Add. MS. 18,799, fol. 34b.
20. *Merc. Aul.*, Dec. 25, 1643, BM, E.81/19, p. 736.

The City moderates had been effectively checkmated by the revelation of "Brooke's plot," in the breaking of which, Vane, St. John, and Lord Wharton played key roles. Many arrests were made in the City, and, although the mayor and aldermen were spared, their power had been effectively broken and was not to become effective again until late 1645. The Common Council was under Fowke's influence and was described as beginning "to engross all the City to themselves."[21]

Important elements in the City were willing to support the Parliament financially—for a price. The most powerful of these were companies like the Merchant Adventurers and the Levant Company. The party of Vane and St. John, despite the protests of parliamentary veterans like D'Ewes and Harbottle Grimston, now revived the old royal policy of granting monopolies to these powerful groups in return for financial support. The Merchant Adventurers had won confirmation of their monopoly in the previous October and had even succeeded in gaining concessions more favorable than those enjoyed under the royal government. In return, Parliament had obtained a loan of £30,000, and on January 12, 1644, a further loan of £10,000 was negotiated with that company. Parliament borrowed £6,000 from the East India Company on January 24, and at the same time an ordinance granting trading privileges to these companies was drawn up. The Levant Company agreed to an £8,000 loan on January 29, 1644, and, about a month later a grateful Commons confirmed that Company's monopoly.[22] St. John continued to play a key role in squeezing money out of the London companies, sometimes with the carrot, sometimes with the stick. By early 1644 the parliamentarians were in serious financial straits. In expectation of a short war, Parliament had decided on high pay for officers and soldiers, but had neglected to create a systematic financial organization. By this time the necessity for the support of the Scots in England and Ireland had vastly increased the burden. On March 4, 1644, the radical leader urged a policy of large-scale borrowing and mortgaging of real estate. He had pointed out that some merchants "might be dealt withal to borrow two hundred thousand pounds . . . ," and three weeks later negotiations were begun to persuade "some of the richest merchants" to borrow £300,000 in Holland. Security for this loan was to be provided from the estates of delinquents, Catholics, bishops, deans, and chapters. On April 13, 1644, a special committee headed by the radical Thomas Pury was to go so

21. *Ibid.*, Jan. 26, 1644, BM, E.32/17, p. 796.
22. W. R. Scott, *The Constitution and Finance of English, Scottish and Irish Joint Stock Companies to 1720*, 3 vols. (New York, Peter Smith, 1951), II, 237; *Journals of the House of Commons* [hereafter cited as *CJ*], III, 376, 413.

far as to urge the revival of that ill-famed device, the forced loan.[23]

Various other expedients were tried. A Committee of Accounts was set up to supervise finance and to reduce the widespread peculation. A new tax on all households was introduced in March 1644; the customs were farmed out for longer terms; and the hated excise tax was extended. Despite these measures, parliamentary finance tended to remain a hand-to-mouth affair.

The atmosphere in which loans to Parliament were made was not without an element of duress, as was evident when the Levant Company was somewhat behind in providing the promised funds. On April 16, 1644, the Commons ordered that the Company be directed to pay up and that the names of persons refusing to contribute should be reported. Company members whose contributions were not made within eight days were to be "disfranchised of their privileges." Giles Green, the chairman of the Navy Committee which supervised loan arrangements, demonstrated the rather crass character of these transactions when he declared that the Levant Company "had received their monopoly . . . and therefore should have lent £8,000."[24]

If the radicals could bully uncooperative companies, they could be benevolent toward those whose financial support could be relied upon, even if the interests of the "meaner sort" of citizens had to be sacrificed. Thus the favors granted to the Merchant Adventurers had been so harmful to the interests of the smaller clothiers of Essex and Suffolk that they vigorously protested to the Commons. On May 9, 1644, the clothiers of Essex asked for the restitution of their former privileges and complained bitterly of the "high demands made of them by the Merchant Adventurers." A short time later, Harbottle Grimston, member for Colchester and a Holles supporter, came to the defense of his constituents and declared that the small clothiers "were like to be undone" by the great London company and asked that the old privileges be restored to the small operators. He was seconded by an indignant D'Ewes, who maintained that the small clothiers had enjoyed these privileges for the previous eighty years. Despite the best efforts of men like Grimston and D'Ewes, the Commons, by a vote of seventy-four to fifty-three, ended the debate on the grievance of the Essex men; it would seem that the decision was affected by pressure from

23. D'Ewes, "Journal," BM, Harl. 166, fol. 23b; *CJ*, III, 415, 458, 468, 489; Lawrence Whitaker, "Diary of Proceedings in the House of Commons" BM, Add. MS. 31,116 [hereafter cited as Whitaker, "Diary," BM, Add. MS. 31,116], fols. 140b, 141a.

24. *CJ*, III, 486; Whitaker, "Diary," BM, Add. MS. 31,116, fols. 136b, 142b; D'Ewes, "Journal," BM, Harl. 166, fol. 69a.

the Company itself. Whitaker made the interesting note: "the Merchant Adventurers opposing it, it was recommitted."[25]

A similar desire to cultivate good relations with the London money men can be observed in the policy of St. John and the radicals with respect to the powerful Irish interest group in London. The outbreak of the Irish rebellion in 1641 and the resultant adoption by Parliament of the London-sponsored "Irish Adventurer" scheme for its suppression had greatly strengthened the vested interest that the Londoners had long held in Ireland.[26]

The sixteenth century background is instructive. In that era the fact that Ireland had remained Catholic greatly intensified old animosities. The policy of large-scale confiscation of the lands of rebellious Irishmen, initiated by Mary Tudor, was greatly extended under Elizabeth. By the end of the century many Englishmen were involved in the actual government of Ireland; others had taken up residence on their lands; still more had become absentee landlords. James I further complicated the picture with his project for pacifying Ulster by settling a Scottish Presbyterian colony on still more confiscated lands. About the same time the merchants of the City of London became deeply involved in the economic exploitation of Ulster and acquired extensive privileges in the region of Derry, now renamed Londonderry.

To all these groups—Londoners, landowners, and Scots—the rule of Strafford in Ireland in the 1630's was distinctly unpalatable, and in 1640 they combined against him to ensure his downfall. In late 1641, at a time when Charles I was striving to win back the alienated Scots and Londoners, the Irish rebellion in October of that year was almost a godsend to Pym, restoring, as it did, a common focus of interest to Parliament, London, and Scots. In the Commons itself, the Irish interest was strong and was well represented by men like Sir John Clotworthy, William Jephson, the brothers Goodwin, Lord Lisle, Robert Reynolds, and Robert Wallop.

These men welcomed, if they did not inspire, a plan brought forward by the citizens of London in February 1642. It was a proposal of great historic consequence because it was to lay the foundation for the future Cromwellian settlement in Ireland. It provided for the confiscation of 2,500,000 acres of Irish land and for the subscription by individuals and groups of sums of money for future acquisition of that

25. Whitaker, "Diary," BM, Add. MS. 31,116, fol. 142b.
26. See J. R. MacCormack, "The Irish Adventurers and the English Civil War," *Irish Historical Studies*, X (Mar. 1956), 21–58; Karl S. Bottigheimer, "English Money and Irish Land: The 'Adventurers' in the Cromwellian Settlement in Ireland," *Journal of British Studies*, VII (Nov. 1967), 12–27; T. W. Moody, *The Londonderry Plantation* (Belfast, W. Mullan & Son, 1939).

land. The money was to be used in the first instance to raise and equip a force under parliamentary control, which would put down the rebellion; that force was actually first employed at Edgehill. The long-range importance of the scheme was that it created a vested interest within Parliament and the City of London in favor of a certain type of settlement in Ireland. It was to bedevil negotiations between Crown and Parliament from the Treaty of Oxford in 1643 to the Treaty of Newport in 1648. Some 136 members subscribed, 98 of whom were original parliamentarians, as distinct from "recruiters," and they formed a high proportion of the active members in the period 1643–1648.

"Irish Adventurers," as subscribers were called, could be found all over England, but chiefly in the south and southwest, and above all in the City of London where the great livery companies and merchants invested heavily. The interests of the London group were protected and furthered by a Committee of London Adventurers that met regularly at Grocers' Hall and acted as a pressure group, the purpose of which was to win from Parliament ever more lucrative economic concessions in Ireland.[27]

Sir John Clotworthy was almost the personal embodiment of the Irish interest in the Commons. An old enemy of Strafford and a Presbyterian in religion, he had come from Antrim to become one of the leaders in the attack on "Black Tom," and after the outbreak of the Irish rebellion he was a key figure in parliamentary committees on Irish affairs. Aggressive and unwearying in the pursuit of his enemies, Clotworthy was to harry his *bête noire,* Archbishop Laud, to the edge of the grave and was credited with the declaration that he was prepared to convert the Catholic Irish with a Bible in one hand and a sword in the other. During the regime of Pym, with whom he was connected by marriage, Clotworthy enjoyed great power and influence in Irish affairs and was able to further his own interests, particularly in the matter of lucrative contracts to supply the parliamentary forces in Ulster.[28]

Prominent among the London Irish Adventurers were men like Sir David Watkins and William Hawkins, aggressive businessmen who tended to look upon economic rivals with a distinctly baleful eye. Their hostility to Clotworthy grew steadily more intense throughout 1643 and by the death of Pym had reached the flash point. The acces-

27. A notable example was the passage of the "doubling ordinance" in July 1643. This provided that Adventurers, on subscribing a further quarter of their original investment, would be credited with double the original subscription. In addition, the cities of Limerick, Waterford, Galway, and Wexford were put up for sale. (*CJ,* III, 141.)

28. See *A Regal Tyranny Discovered* (London, 1647), BM, E.370(12), pp. 103–107.

sion to power of Vane and St. John was, for them, a distinct boon, and it was soon clear that Clotworthy was to be thrust into the background and parliamentary favor accorded the Londoners.

The Scots too received significant benefits in Ireland as a result of the policy of Vane and St. John. Both the radicals and the London Adventurers now professed great enthusiasm for the support of the Scottish forces in Ulster. Clotworthy, on the other hand, seems to have regarded the Scots as rivals in his own home territory. On December 22, 1643, St. John defeated Clotworthy over the question of acceding to Scottish demands for military control of Ulster.[29]

Clotworthy's position as chairman of the Commons Committee on Irish Affairs was to be further undermined in March 1644 by the formation of a subcommittee of the committee of both kingdoms, the charter members of which were St. John, Vane, and Robert Wallop. It soon became apparent that Vane and St. John intended to use the subcommittee to bypass the Commons' committee and to further the interests of the Watkins group at Clotworthy's expense.

By September 1644 the quarrel was out in the open, with Clotworthy castigating Watkins as a "mean beggarly fellow" who had not lived up to his obligations. The radicals, notably the firebrand William Strode, sprang to the defense of Watkins, and the result was a resolution of the Commons to convey its thanks to Watkins for his services. The victory of the City group was assured by an order of the committee of both kingdoms of September 26, 1644, by which the Grocers' Hall men were designated as one of its subcommittees "for the better managing of the war in Ireland."[30]

Vane and St. John were to be well rewarded for their support of the Londoners. In the factional struggles throughout 1644 with the moderates led by Holles, the House of Lords, and the Earl of Essex, they enjoyed the consistent support of the City men led by John Fowke.

At the beginning of 1644, the radicals were in a strong position. In Vane and St. John they had shrewd and determined leaders who enjoyed the support of powerful elements in both the parliamentary forces and the City of London as well as substantial numbers of the "meaner sort" in the capital and elsewhere. The next twelve months were to demonstrate the effectiveness with which they could marshal these forces against those who still barred the way to supreme control of the parliamentary war effort.

29. *Tanner Letters*, ed. Charles McNeill (Dublin, Irish Manuscripts Commission, 1943), p. 171; *CJ*, III, 349–350.
30. *Calendar of State Papers, Domestic Series, 1603–1704*, 81 vols. (1857–1947+) [hereafter cited as *CSPD*], *1644*, pp. 61–62, 123–124, 227, 346, 453, 535–536; *CJ*, III, 364; Public Record Office, State Papers Domestic, 16 [hereafter cited as PRO, SP 16], 539, pt. ii/173/40, 41, 44, 223.

The factors that would eventually bring about the disintegration of their party were present in 1644, but were not yet apparent: their potential minority status in Parliament, and their oligarchic approach to politics, which was to become steadily more marked. Three years would pass before they would find themselves trapped between the genuine populism of Lilburne and the religious and political conservatism of the parliamentary majority.

But in January 1644 all this was far in the future. Vane and St. John had every reason to be confident as they addressed themselves to the agreeable task of settling accounts with those parliamentarians whom they regarded as "neuters" or worse.

II] The Attack on the Lord General

The firstfruits of the radical alliances with the Scots and London appeared in mid-January 1644 when the London Common Councillors, under Fowke's leadership, began to prepare a petition to the Commons. It called for a purge of the officers of Essex's army which, according to one publicist, was now to be "weeded and mangled at the citizens pleasure." The petition, wrote Bulstrode Whitelocke, gave "a stroke of jealousy and discontent to Essex and his friends."[1]

Shortly before this St. John had once again demonstrated his support of Waller as against Essex when, together with strong radicals like Sir Arthur Haselrig and Sir Peter Wentworth, he had demanded that Essex issue a more liberal commission to Waller.[2] About two weeks later St. John's right-hand man, Samuel Browne, delivered an indirect attack on Essex by suggesting that the Earl of Holland—whom Essex was attempting to have readmitted to the House of Lords—should rather be impeached for high treason. Essex countered by moving that Vane and St. John should themselves be impeached on a charge of correspondence with royalists arising out of their contacts with Lord Lovelace.[3]

It is against this background that the moves to set up the committee of both kingdoms must be viewed.[4] The committee has been called the forerunner of the modern cabinet and, as such, has been of more than passing interest to constitutional historians. Its significance in 1644 lay rather in the sweeping powers granted it by Parliament to "order and direct" the war. Vane and St. John, with the support of the Scots, succeeded in "packing" the committee with their friends and were thus able to make effective use of it as a lever against Essex

1. Bulstrode Whitelocke, "Annals" BM, Add. MS. 37,343 [hereafter cited as Whitelocke, "Annals," BM, Add. MS. 37,343], fol. 28b.
2. Sir Symonds D'Ewes, "Journal of the Parliament begun November, 1640," BM, Harleian 165 [hereafter cited as D'Ewes, "Journal," BM, Harl. 165], fol. 266a, b.
3. See S. R. Gardiner, *History of the Great Civil War, 1642–1649*, 4 vols. (London, 1893) [hereafter cited as Gardiner, *GCW*], I, 274; *The Letters and Journals of Robert Baillie, Principal of the University of Glasgow, 1637–1662*, ed. David Laing, 3 vols. (Edinburgh, 1841–1842) [hereafter cited as Baillie, *Letters*], II, 136; "Journal of Occurrences," Jan. 21, 1644, BM, Add. MS. 25,465, fol. 4a, b.
4. Wallace B. Notestein, "The Establishment of the Committee of Both Kingdoms," *American Historical Review*, XVII (Apr. 1912), 477–495.

and his allies in the Commons. The first ordinance, after consultations among Vane, St. John, Lord Saye and Sele, and the Scots, had been introduced and piloted through the upper house by Saye, strongly supported by Northumberland.[5] When, however, the original ordinance ran into strong opposition in the Commons the radicals backtracked. On February 7 they introduced a new ordinance, which, although it stripped the committee of its authority over peace negotiations, retained for it the vital power to "order and direct" the war and thus to control Essex and his army.

An analysis of the membership of the committee reveals that Vane and St. John were assured of an anti-Essex majority. The peers appointed were, besides Essex himself, Warwick, Wharton, Manchester, Saye, Robartes, and Northumberland. Of these, the last five could be counted on to support Vane and St. John against Essex. Northumberland and Saye had already made their position clear by their collusion with the radicals on the first ordinance. Almost a year later they again ranged themselves on the same side by their support of the first Self-Denying Ordinance. In the crisis of August 1647 both were among the nine peers who committed themselves to the support of the New Model by signing the "Engagement" with the army.[6] That Wharton had the firm confidence of Vane and St. John is demonstrated by his close collaboration with them in the matter of the discovery of Brooke's plot in late December 1643.[7] He continued to be a close supporter of the radicals throughout the Revolution, even assisting in the election of Henry Ireton. He remained a confidant of Cromwell into the years of the Protectorate.[8] The bitter rivalry between Manchester and Essex was a prominent feature of the parliamentary political scene in the first nine months of 1644. Lord Robartes, a close associate of Vane, was practically foisted on Essex as field marshal by the radicals and was widely believed to have been at least partly responsible for Essex's debacle at Lostwithiel in September 1644.

Of the fourteen members of the Commons on the committee, the overwhelming majority were in the Vane-St. John camp. Waller, Has-

5. Baillie, *Letters,* II, 141.
6. C. H. Firth, *The House of Lords during the Civil War* (London, Longmans, Green & Co., 1910), pp. 147, 170.
7. Baillie, *Letters,* II, 130, 133.
8. David Underdown, "Party Management in the Recruiter Elections, 1645–1648," *English Historical Review,* LXXXIII (Apr. 1968), 242–243; Cromwell to Wharton, Jan. 1, 1650, Thomas Carlyle, *Oliver Cromwell's Letters and Speeches,* with elucidations, 4 vols. (London, 1849), II, 108–109; Baillie, *Letters,* II, 107, 115, 117, 120, 130, 146, 220, 236, 298; Lawrence Whitaker, "Diary of Proceedings in the House of Commons" [hereafter cited as Whitaker, "Diary"], BM, Add. MS. 31,116, fol. 291b; Edward Hyde, Earl of Clarendon, *The History of the Rebellion and Civil Wars in England,* 2 vols. (Oxford, 1843), II, 686–687.

elrig, Cromwell, Vane, Robert Wallop, St. John, and Samuel Browne were firmly anti-Essex. Sir Henry Vane, Sr., although more conservative than his son, supported his policy in this respect. John Crewe was to lead the Commons' radicals in their assault on the Lords over the authority of the Earl of Essex in May 1644,[9] while William Pierrepont had shown his hand by his strong support in the Commons of the first (and more extreme) ordinance of the committee of both kingdoms. Vane and St. John demonstrated their confidence in Pierrepont by entrusting him with the management of the thorny peace propositions in the Commons. Both Crewe and Pierrepont supported the Self-Denying Ordinance.[10] Of the remaining four members, Stapleton alone could be regarded as a firm Essex man. John Glyn and Sir Gilbert Gerard were dubious supporters at best. Armine's politics in 1644 remain obscure. Contemporary witnesses like Baillie, Agostini, and Holles agreed that the committee was controlled by the enemies of Essex, and the lord general himself heartily concurred.[11]

Holles's anger and resentment at his exclusion from the committee can be seen in his bitter opposition to the enabling ordinance introduced by the radicals. But he could fight no more than a delaying action, and in spite of the support of influential persons like Robert Reynolds and Sir John Meyrick he was defeated by sixty-five votes to fifty-one, and, as the radicals wished, the committee was given power to "advise and consult, order and direct, concerning the carrying on the war."[12]

In the House of Lords the friends of Essex interpreted the words "order and direct" as a distinct threat to the authority of the lord gen-

9. Whitaker, "Diary," BM, Add. MS. 31,116, fol. 135a, b; D'Ewes, "Journal," BM, Harl. 166, fols. 55b, 56a.

10. Walter Yonge, "Journal of Proceedings in the House of Commons," BM, Add. MS. 18,799 [hereafter cited as Yonge, "Journal," BM, Add. MS. 18,799], fols. 62b, 98b; Whitaker, "Diary," BM, Add. MS. 31,116, fol. 134a; D'Ewes, "Journal," BM, Harl. 166, fols. 55a, 108a; *Journals of the House of Commons* [hereafter cited as *CJ*], III, 477; Edward Hyde, Earl of Clarendon, *The History of the Rebellion and Civil Wars in England*, ed. W. D. Macray, 6 vols. (Oxford, 1888) [hereafter cited as Clarendon, *Rebellion*], III, 508.

11. *Memoirs of Denzil, Lord Holles, Baron of Ifield, from the year 1641 to 1648* (London, 1699) [hereafter cited as Holles, *Memoirs*], pp. 24–25; Baillie, *Letters*, II, 178. For reasons stated above, I cannot accept the view that the committee was dominated by moderates. See Lotte Mulligan, "Peace Negotiations, Politics and the Committee of Both Kingdoms, 1644–1646," *Historical Journal*, XII (no. 1, 1969), 3–32. Mrs. Mulligan, by categorizing such persons as Oliver St. John, Sir Henry Vane, Sr., Samuel Browne, Northumberland, and Wharton as moderates, comes to this conclusion. It remains true, however, that by 1645 Manchester, Robartes, and Waller had grown considerably more conservative. This, together with the breakdown of the Scottish-radical alliance, substantially altered the political complexion of the committee.

12. *CJ*, III, 492.

eral and substituted for them the words "consult and advise." The Commons, under Vane and St. John, rejected the amendment, and in a conference between the Houses, Vane led the radical assault on the Lords.

The outnumbered Lords wilted and on February 16, 1644, passed the ordinance in the original form. Holles and his supporters saw the measure as a direct threat to the position of Essex, and D'Ewes noted gloomily that "the Lord General did hereby receive much discontent and discouragement." It was an important victory for the radicals but not a final one, and conflict over the committee and its powers continued well into the summer of 1644. As Agostini forecast at the time, "it may not prove easy to unite so many wills to deprive themselves of power for ever, which is what the others are trying for."[13]

While the Commons stubbornly opposed the attempts of the radicals to give the committee power to sit in judgment over peace proposals, the Lords vigorously opposed the imposition of an oath of secrecy on its members. But the vital issue was the Earl of Essex and his authority, and on this the upper house was particularly intransigent. The radicals, increasingly restive over the opposition in the Lords, pointedly warned the tiny knot of peers that "if any inconvenience did happen by their disagreement with us, we did remove the guilt thereof from our door."[14] The Lords ignored the implied threat, and when Essex forwarded on March 5 another peace overture from the King, they succeeded in setting up a joint committee to consider the letter and, by so doing, bypassed the committee of both kingdoms.[15]

If Vane and St. John were surprised by the Lords' move, they soon recovered the initiative. In so doing, however, they provoked the first political disagreement between themselves and their Scottish friends. They were now to realize that the Scots did not share their implacable hostility to Charles Stuart, much less any desire to alter the funda-

13. D'Ewes, "Journal," BM, Harl. 166, fol. 23a; Agostini to Doge, Feb. 16, 1644, *Calendar of state papers and manuscripts relating to English affairs existing in the archives and collections of Venice and in other libraries of northern Italy*, vols. 10–38 (1603–1675) [London, H. M. Stationery Office, 1900–1940] [hereafter cited as *CSPV*], *1643–1647*, pp. 74–75.

14. Whitaker, "Diary," BM, Add. MS. 31,116, fol. 117b.

15. During the debates on the committee of both kingdoms the following members favored the establishment of the committee: St. John, Pierrepont, Glyn, Sir Henry Vane, Jr., Edmund Prideaux, Sir Peter Wentworth, Francis Rous, William Strode, Thomas Hodges, John Lisle, Zouch Tate. Those against it included Robert Reynolds, Whitelocke, Sir William Lewis, Sir Benjamin Rudyard, Sir John Clotworthy. (Yonge, "Journal," BM, Add. MS. 18,799, fols. 61a, b, 62b, 65b, 66a, 70b; D'Ewes, "Journal," BM, Harl. 165, fols. 3b, 38a, b; Whitaker, "Diary," BM, Add. MS. 31,116, fols. 113b, 126a, b; *CJ*, III, 411, 412, 443; *Mercurius Aulicus* [hereafter cited as *Merc. Aul.*], BM, E.34/12, pp. 826, 828, 864–865; Baillie, *Letters*, II, 154–155.)

mental constitution. When the radicals amended the resolution of the Lords and produced a note to Charles I that was extremely hostile in tone, the shocked Scots refused to give it their assent. Vane, anxious to avoid a rift, quickly backtracked and agreed to draw up a message that both groups could approve. The matter was temporarily dropped, but to the watchful Agostini it was a portent. The Scots, he reflected, did not wish "to lose totally a Scottish King leaving themselves . . . dependent upon the democratic force of a nation which has always been inimicable to them."[16] But the alliance held firm when it was tested on March 30, 1644. The moderates, led by Pembroke and Salisbury in the Lords and by Holles and Robert Reynolds in the Commons, attempted to set up a special committee for peace negotiations and thus deprive the committee of both kingdoms of any authority to deal directly with Oxford. The issue forced a division in the Commons, and the deadlock was broken only by Speaker William Lenthall's casting vote in favor of the policy backed by Vane, St. John, and the Scots.

By April 1644 the true nature of the radical opposition to the Scottish religious ambitions was beginning to be more apparent. About this time Vane, St. John, and Lord Wharton attended a meeting at Baillie's lodgings which, it was hoped, would result in a kind of agreement between the granitic Scots and that tough group of Independent ministers whose presence in the Westminster Assembly Baillie and his friends had found so obnoxious. The evening does not appear to have been an unqualified success. According to the indignant Baillie, there were "very fair appearances of a pretty argument." Philip Nye, one of the outstanding Independents in the assembly, was particularly difficult and, Baillie complained, "was like to spoil all our play."[17] As we have seen, the radical leaders, themselves of Independent sympathies, had already gone to dangerous lengths in an effort to please the Scots on the religious question. They had risked the alienation of many potential and actual supporters among the sectaries by their support of the covenant and by the adoption by Parliament of the Presbyterian form of church government. Vane and St. John appear to have felt that there was some danger of dropping the Independent bone for the Scottish shadow.

The radical leaders were acutely aware that the alliance with the Scots was tenuous at best, and they knew too that it was necessary because the Holles group, through the Earl of Essex and other commanders, still held effective control of the parliamentary armies. They were also conscious of the fact that the Scottish connection tended to

---

16. Agostini to Doge, Mar. 15, 1644, *CSPV, 1643–1647*, p. 83.
17. Baillie, *Letters*, p. 145.

weaken their ties with important groups of Independents in the army, particularly those in the Eastern Association under the command of Cromwell.

Cromwell had been an active opponent of Essex as early as the summer of 1643 and was prominent in the campaign against him and other moderate commanders in 1644. He had, in fact, demanded the dismissal of Lord Willoughby of Parham in late January. Two months later the charge of incompetence was revived by Colonel Edward King, and the quarrel became part of the general conflict between radicals and moderates for control of the army.

Lord Willoughby saw elements of class conflict in the quarrels within the parliamentary ranks. "Here we are all hasting to an early ruin," he complained in a letter to the Earl of Denbigh. "Nobility and gentry are going down apace . . . till I saw their free concurrence in writing you a letter of thanks, I thought it a crime to be a nobleman."[18] Denbigh, another parliamentary commander of moderate leanings, was himself to be a target of the radical elements in the parliamentary committee at Coventry. William Purefoy, a republican-minded supporter of Vane and St. John, led the attack on Denbigh.[19]

By March 1644 the radicals were ready to employ their newfound authority in the committee of both kingdoms in the congenial task of breaking the Earl of Essex. They began with a project to purge his army of officers who were "unreliable." A committee in the Commons consisting, according to D'Ewes, of "all violent spirits," was named to investigate the officers and to make a list of those who should be removed. Zouch Tate was chairman of the sixteen-man committee which included at least twelve strong radicals.[20]

This attempt to eliminate the radicals' opponents in the army met strong opposition in the Commons. Holles, Stapleton, and their supporters, fully conscious of the threat to their position, fought so bitterly to preserve it that the project was quietly dropped. The most important change made in Essex's army was the appointment, in the face of strong opposition, of a close friend of Vane, Lord John Robartes, to be field marshal.[21]

The auspices under which the appointment was made are of some

18. *Fourth Report of the Royal Commission on Historical Manuscripts, Part I, Report and Appendix* (London, H.M. Stationery Office, 1874), p. 268.

19. *Dictionary of National Biography,* ed. Leslie Stephen and Sidney Lee, 22 vols. (Oxford, 1908–1909) [hereafter cited as *DNB*], XVI, 490.

20. D'Ewes, "Journal," BM, Harl. 166, fol. 40a. The twelve were John Gurdon, Edmund Prideaux, St. John, Sir Peter Wentworth, Roger Hill, Denis Bond, Edward Baynton, Lisle, John Blakiston, Cornelius Holland, Thomas Hoyle, and Tate himself, who was Presbyterian in religion but politically a radical. (*CJ*, III, 408.)

21. Clarendon, *Rebellion*, III, 387.

interest. On March 21 Tate recommended to the House, on behalf of
his committee, that Manchester be made a lieutenant general and Lord
Robartes a field marshal in Essex's army. Neither of these moves could
have been congenial to Essex, and it was probably with this in mind
that Sir Walter Erle questioned whether the committee was not now
exceeding its authority. The House compromised by suggesting that
Tate's committee indicate to Essex that he find a "place of honour" for
Robartes. This, however, did not satisfy the radicals. That afternoon
Vane insisted that the Commons specify the rank Robartes would hold
and, backed by Sir Arthur Haselrig, urged that it be that of field marshal. Essex eventually complied, but he must have felt deeply suspicious at the spectacle of Vane and Haselrig working so hard to see
Robartes promoted. According to Whitelocke, it was as a result of "the
over-ruling counsel of the Lord Roberts [sic]" that Essex was "persuaded into the narrow noose of Cornwall." Whether Essex later regarded himself as having been betrayed by Robartes is uncertain, but,
according to Clarendon, he broke with him after Lostwithiel.[22]

The frontal attack on Essex and his supporters was now abandoned
in favor of a flanking movement. Waller's forces were to be reinforced
at Essex's expense. "The Council is devoting itself to strengthening
the armies, but with partiality towards Waller," wrote Agostini. "To
this end they neglect no means of making Essex feel that they would
like him to resign his commission . . . "[23] Radicals like Haselrig, Prideaux, and Vane now demanded that Waller be freed from Essex's
control, and on March 16, 1644, an ordinance was brought in, the
terms of which gave Waller virtual autonomy.

The radicals next attempted to bring Essex more directly under the
control of the committee of both kingdoms, and on March 20, 1644,
Lisle, one of their fiery supporters, brought in an amendment to this
effect. The attempt was frustrated by the vigorous opposition of the
Holles group led by Glyn and Stapleton, and Vane, who had been
strongly supported by St. John and Haselrig, was forced to accept a
compromise, by which Essex was made subject to the committee, or "to
the orders and directions of both Houses . . . "[24] The disgruntled Essex
now took the field at the head of a greatly reduced army. Even Baillie,
no friend of Essex, conceded that "it was no ways his fault but he had

22. Edward Hyde, Earl of Clarendon, *The Life of Edward, Earl of Clarendon.
Being a continuation of the History of the Great Rebellion from the restoration to
his banishment in 1667* (Oxford, 1843) [hereafter cited as Clarendon, *Life*], p. 1030;
D'Ewes, "Journal," BM, Harl. 166, fols. 36b, 37a; Whitaker, "Diary," BM, Add. MS.
31,116, fol. 126a; *Memoirs of Edmund Ludlow*, ed. C. H. Firth, 2 vols. (Oxford,
1894), I, 100; Whitelocke, "Annals," BM, Add. MS. 37,343, fol. 320a.
23. Agostini to Doge, Apr. 21, 1644, *CSPV, 1643–1647*, p. 78.
24. D'Ewes, "Journal," BM, Harl. 166, fol. 36a; *CJ*, III, 432–433.

been recruited long ago."[25] The general complained bitterly of partiality to Manchester in the matter of recruitment. " . . . you have pleased," he wrote, "to reduce my army to 7000 foot, and 3000 horse, when Manchester is allowed an army of 14,000 and receives £34,000 a month for the pay of it."[26]

A whispering campaign against Essex gave rise to further party conflict within the House. An unnamed person, perhaps a member, had publicly asserted that there was no reason to recruit Essex's army because "he meant to betray those forces to the enemy and to join with them in the cutting of our throats."[27] The Lords promptly ordered an investigation, but apparently hesitated to press charges. Though the matter was smoothed over, it was illustrative of the suspicion with which the radicals viewed the moderates. Nor were their suspicions entirely unfounded. In the summer of 1644 a group of Essex's officers actually carried on secret negotiations with the royalists, but it seems certain that the much-abused commander in chief was himself completely loyal to Parliament.

In early April St. John demonstrated his support for two of Essex's leading enemies: Waller and Haselrig. In a move to strengthen the hand of Fowke as well as to reinforce Waller's army, he introduced an ordinance that would have given the London militia subcommittee sweeping powers and, at the same time, have raised 700 men for Waller. In the face of violent opposition from the moderates, St. John drew in his horns, and the ordinance was amended, but the recruits went to Waller rather than to Essex. St. John's close links with Haselrig were demonstrated on April 10 when the latter complained that he had been slandered by a Colonel Carr. During the ensuing debate the solicitor strongly defended Haselrig, claiming that Carr's action was a breach of privilege and urging that he be sent for as a delinquent. Carr soon found himself a prisoner in the compter.[28]

The radicals now attempted to render Manchester's army independent of Essex's authority, and once again the rival parties clashed in the Commons. A radical-sponsored ordinance dealing with Manchester's command made no mention of his subordination to Essex, and

---

25. Baillie, *Letters*, pp. 158–159.

26. *Journal of the House of Lords, 1578–1714* (1767+), [hereafter cited as *LJ*], VI, 505. In the Commons' debates over the position of Essex's army, supporters of Essex included D'Ewes, Sir Henry Cholmley, Stapleton, Sir William Lewis, Glyn, Sir Walter Erle. Anti-Essex speakers included Tate, Sir Peter Wentworth, Prideaux, Vane, Haselrig, St. John, Lisle, and Robert Scawen. (D'Ewes, "Journal," BM, Harl. 166, fols. 26, 32a, b, 34b, 36a, b, 37a, 40a; Whitaker, "Diary," BM, Add. MS. 31,116, fol. 127a; *CJ*, III, 431, 439.)

27. Whitaker, "Diary," BM, Add. MS. 31,116, fol. 133b.

28. *Ibid.*, fols. 130a, 131a; *CJ*, III, 450, 455; *Merc. Aul.*, Apr. 7, 1644, BM, Burney Collection, 13, p. 927; Yonge, "Journal," BM, Add. MS. 18,799, fol. 91.

the Lords, alive to the significance of the omission, amended the ordinance to supply the deficiency. The quarrel shifted to the floor of the Commons where Vane and St. John strongly opposed any change, and hostility toward the upper house reached new heights. On May 2, 1644, the radicals "with desperate and high language [said] they would give them [the Lords] no answer . . . but Mr. Glyn, Mr. Rouse and other discreet men did put this off from passing . . . "

St. John was particularly aggressive during this debate and accused the moderates of maintaining that the authority of Essex was supreme even over Parliament itself. D'Ewes heard "this strange logic and grammar" with some indignation, and, supported by other moderates, he read St. John one of his schoolmasterish lessons. "Some heat of words grew," and Vane, having jumped into the fray with some cutting remarks about Essex, was himself promptly attacked by Holles and Stapleton. The debate was indecisive but sufficiently explosive to send the gentle D'Ewes home early, "irritated to see this violent carriage of things."[29]

The radicals now stepped up the pressure on the Lords, and more than a hint of force was introduced on May 8, 1644, when the Commons appeared en masse at the door of the upper house. The Vane-St. John group, who had almost certainly organized the demonstration,[30] demanded that the Lords pass three ordinances, each of which was calculated to undermine the power of the moderates: the ordinances for Manchester's army, for the renewal of the committee of both kingdoms, and for the granting to the Commons of a veto on the admittance of former royalists to the House of Lords. If, as D'Ewes asserted, the radicals had intended "to terrify the Lords," they succeeded inasmuch as the ordinance for Manchester's army was passed substantially as the radicals had framed it. But although the moderate group had once again lost ground they continued to defend Essex with a stubbornness born of desperation, because, as Agostini pointed out, they would see in his removal "the disappearance of the last shadow" they possessed.[31]

By mid-May the harassed lord general was once more in the field, but in London his enemies were preparing new miseries for him. Haselrig, who could be described as the hatchet man of the Vane-St. John

29. D'Ewes, "Journal," BM, Harl. 166, fols. 54b, 55b, 56a.

30. A year later it was on St. John's motion that the Commons again appeared en masse at the door of the Lords. (*Ibid.*, fol. 196a.)

31. Agostini to Doge, May 10, 1644, *CSPV, 1643–1647*, p. 102. During the debates over the Essex-Manchester question, pro-Essex speakers included Sir Dudley North, Holles, and Stapleton; anti-Essex or pro-Manchester speakers included Haselrig, Edward Baynton, Jr., Crewe, St. John, and Sir Thomas Barrington. (D'Ewes, "Journal," BM, Harl. 166, fols. 53a, 54a, b, 55b, 56a; Whitaker, "Diary," BM, Add. MS. 31,116, fol. 134a, b.)

party, was working assiduously against Essex both in the Commons and in the committee of both kingdoms. The effect of his work was soon to become apparent.

Of the three ordinances that the radicals had thrust on the Lords, by far the most important was that for the extension of the life of the committee of both kingdoms. The moderates in both Houses deeply resented the extent to which the radicals were able to control Essex and Parliament itself through the committee and were determined to gain greater representation. Accordingly, when the radicals had sent their ordinance for the continuation of the committee to the Lords, the peers had retaliated with an ordinance of their own that contained the names of five additional Lords and ten Commons men, including Holles and Reynolds. This gave the radicals the opportunity of accusing the peers of a breach of privilege, and they made the most of it. It is probable that they were able to swing some of the "floating vote" in their favor; at any rate they succeeded in gaining a vote of eighty-two to sixty-nine against even reading the Lords' ordinance,[32] and it was on the following day that they staged the demonstration at the door of the Lords. "They will have to give way in the end, as they have always done, through fear," predicted the mordant Agostini.[33]

The Venetian had gauged the situation with his customary acumen. The Lords hastily agreed that the Commons had the right to appoint their own members to the committee, but insisted on their own right to name the five peers. This too received rough treatment in the Commons. Some of the radicals moved that the report on the dispute be presented between eleven A.M. and noon, "when they knew many men engaged to their dinner would go out."[34] The maneuver succeeded, and a thin House voted that the step taken by the Lords had been an unparliamentary one. D'Ewes, ever alive to constitutional issues, challenged the whole radical concept of the power of the committee of both kingdoms. It was no more, he argued, than "a select number of both Houses appointed to join their counsels with those of another nation."

But the times were not congenial to such views, and the radicals pressed on. Threatening now to exclude the Lords completely from the direction of affairs, they succeeded in passing a resolution calling for the establishment of a Commons' committee to carry on the work of the committee of both kingdoms, pending the passage by the Lords of the radical-sponsored ordinance. "Some violent spirits would have gone

32. Clotworthy and Haselrig were tellers for the majority; Sir John Maynard and Sir John Corbet for the minority. (*CJ*, III, 483.)

33. Agostini to Doge, May 3, 1644, *CSPV, 1643–1647*, p. 99.

34. D'Ewes, "Journal," BM, Harl. 166, fol. 58a, b.

higher," noted the shocked D'Ewes.[35] Unconditional surrender was the least the radicals demanded of the Lords. In their own ordinance, they not only ignored the names of peers put forward by the Lords, but, with a fine disdain for the privileges of the upper house, themselves specified the names of those five peers who were to be appointed. The Lords still had enough spirit to insist on their own privileges, but the Commons blandly refused to admit any breach of the Lords' rights.[36]

The weight of the City of London was now to be thrown on the scales. On May 16 Vane and St. John brought up strong reinforcements in the form of a delegation of sheriffs and aldermen from London; they were led by Fowke and were distinctly hostile to the Lords. They were resolved, they declared, "to live and die with the House of Commons."[37] Their demands were neatly tailored to suit the policy of Vane and St. John and included the reconvening of the committee of both kingdoms; the nonadmittance of members (that is, former royalists) to either House without the consent of both Houses; and the execution of justice upon "delinquents" (royalists). During the debate following the withdrawal of the delegation, Sir Henry Vane, Sr., piously observed that the arrival of the Londoners at the door of the House was a "wonderful providence of God." Not all agreed. The disgusted D'Ewes termed the incident "a mere plot and contrived by Young Vane, [and the] Solicitor . . . "[38]

The deadlock between the two Houses over the committee of both kingdoms was finally broken on May 22 when the aggressive William Strode proposed that the Commons simply take up for the committee the original ordinance that had first passed the Lords and been shelved by the Commons in February. The idea, which, in D'Ewes's view, was "invented certainly not in his [Strode's] . . . brain but by Vane and Solicitor etc.," was taken up, and the ordinance was passed by a large majority.[39]

Vane and St. John frequently used the petitions of their London friends as stalking-horses for future policy. The London demand for "justice on delinquents" foreshadowed the move to apply martial law and to establish special courts to try political offenders.

35. *Ibid.*, fols. 58b, 61a.

36. Whitaker, "Diary," BM. Add. MS. 31,116, fols. 137b, 138; D'Ewes, "Journal," BM, Harl. 166, fol. 61b. The leaders of the Lords in the dispute were Grey of Warke and the Earl of Stamford; Vane, St. John, Sir Gilbert Gerard, and Glyn were prominent opponents of the Lords. (D'Ewes, "Journal," BM, Harl. 166, fol. 61b.)

37. D'Ewes, "Journal," BM, Harl. 166, fol. 62a.

38. D'Ewes also regarded Vane and St. John as the organizers of a London delegation to the House of Lords a few days before. (*Ibid.*, fol. 62a; see also *Merc. Aul.*, May 16, 1644, BM, Burney Collection 13, p. 983.)

39. D'Ewes, "Journal," BM, Harl. 166, fol. 64b.

The effect of this new pressure on the Lords was soon evident. By May 17 they were ready to surrender and mildly assured the Commons that, if a new ordinance for the committee of both kingdoms was sent up to them, they would do "that which shall be fit . . . " The confident radicals exploited their victory with an ordinance for the establishment of a special tribunal for the trial of delinquents, a step that had also been urged in the Fowke petition. This measure was fiercely debated in the Commons because, as some members argued, "it was to establish martial law, which in the Petition of Right had been cried down."[40] Holles and Whitelocke were particularly vehement in their opposition to the measure, but despite their efforts the ordinance was read twice and was referred to a committee.

The radicals were able to rely on Fowke and his followers, but they did not, on that basis, feel really confident of the City. By mid-May 1644 there was considerable fear of a moderate or even royalist coup in London, and on May 8 Glyn brought in another ordinance to increase the power of the controversial London Militia Committee. A few days later the City was swept by rumors that the King intended to come to London and was confident of the support of the Lords, of "a great part of the other [House] and of many in the City."[41] The Commons nervously ordered Essex to receive no messages from the King without first informing Parliament.

The general assault on the Lords was now to be supplemented by attacks on individual peers.[42] Singled out for special attention were those Lords who had opposed the radical policy on the committee of both kingdoms, for example, Willoughby of Parham and Henry Grey, Lord Stamford. Anthony Nichols, a prominent radical, charged Stamford with dereliction of duty during the campaign in the west. The matter was referred to a radical-dominated committee, and two days later the proceedings against Willoughby of Parham were renewed. St. John wanted Stamford charged with treason and, with Nichols "and some other violent spirits, maintained it strongly, though all knew he [Stamford] had . . . failed through inadvertance."[43] On June 29 the

40. *CJ*, III, 495, 498; D'Ewes, "Journal," BM, Harl. 166, fol. 62b; Whitaker, "Diary," BM, Add. MS. 31,116, fols. 138b, 139a.

41. Baillie, *Letters*, II, 182.

42. During the May debates on the controversy between the Houses the following may be regarded as supporters of the Lords: Holles, Whitelocke, Clotworthy, D'Ewes, Reynolds, Rous, John Maynard, and Sir John Corbet. Those speaking or acting against the Lords included St. John, Sir Henry Vane, Jr., Thomas, Lord Grey of Groby, Sir Gilbert Gerard, Haselrig, Sir Thomas Barrington, Sir Peter Wentworth, Prideaux, Lisle, Strode. (D'Ewes, "Journal," BM, Harl. 166, fols. 58a, b, 61a, b, 64a, b; Whitaker, "Diary," BM, Add. MS. 31,116, fols. 139a, 140a; *CJ*, III, 483, 500, 503.)

43. D'Ewes, "Journal," BM, Harl. 166, fol. 73b.

Lords gave way to the relentless radical pressure and passed the ordinance against the reentry of former royalist peers into the House of Lords.[44]

After the victory at Marston Moor the radicals apparently felt that they could afford to be conciliatory. The pressure on the Lords was, at any rate, relaxed. Pembroke, who had opposed Vane and St. John in the spring, was made lord lieutenant of Cornwall, and the sequestrations of the estates of the Earls of Holland, Clare, and Bedford were suddenly lifted. There was some resentment among the more extreme radicals at this sudden leniency. John Blakiston was especially annoyed to see Holland accorded such treatment. Holland, he declared, had lied when he denied having borne arms against Parliament. "The Lords had been suffered too long to domineer," he declared, "and we see . . . how often they have been defective."[45]

Some letters found in the Earl of Newcastle's coach after Marston Moor gave the radicals an additional hold over the beleagured Lords. On the basis of this evidence, impeachment proceedings were instituted against Lord Rochford and Baron Hunsdon, bringing the total of threatened Lords to five. None of these charges, however, were pressed, and even Stamford, who in late June seemed a certain victim, was two months later voted £1,000 by the two Houses.[46]

As we have seen, the radicals were able to count on important elements in the City of London for support in their campaign against the Lords. The extent to which their policies originated with the Londoners, and the degree to which they were inspired by the parliamentary radicals themselves, is a problem easier to pose than to solve. Agostini asserted that "pressure from the commissioners in the Common Council of this City . . . " was behind some of the more extreme of the radicals' demands on the King.[47] There may have been considerable truth in the remark of a royalist writer that the radicals in Parliament were "directed by the wit, because supported by the wealth of the City."[48]

The hostility exhibited by the radicals toward the House of Lords, Charles I, and even monarchy itself was vitally important in uniting conservative opinion against them. The radical leaders toyed with several drastic solutions to England's problems, the least extreme of which envisaged the deposition of Charles I and the crowning of the Elector Palatine. Essex's hostility toward them was attributed partly to his love of "monarchy and nobility, which he suspected some designed to de-

44. *CJ*, III, 546–547.
45. *Merc. Aul.*, July 15, 1644, BM, Burney Collection, 13, pp. 1088–1089.
46. D'Ewes, "Journal," BM, Harl. 166, fol. 109b.
47. Agostini to Doge, May 20, 1644, *CSPV, 1643–1647*, p. 101.
48. *Merc. Aul.*, May 27, 1644, BM, Burney Collection, 13, p. 998.

stroy." Waller, too, who broke with the radicals in late 1644 or early 1645, recalled that it was because they had deviated from what they had publicly professed "into impious, disloyal, antimonarchical ends." Many others had turned against them for the same reason, Waller declared, "members of both the Houses who . . . did at the same time bid them farewell as I." Earlier in 1644, the Scots had been described as having become cool toward the party of Vane and St. John because they (the Scots) were not prepared "to do away with monarchy altogether."[49]

In June 1644 Vane shocked both moderates and Scots by boldly proposing the overthrow of the monarchy and the establishment of a republic. The proposal was made to Lord Fairfax, the Earl of Leven, and the Earl of Manchester who were, at that time, commanding the forces besieging York. If he expected such titled gentlemen to look kindly on republicanism, he received a rude shock. They not only told Vane that the monarchy must be retained, but declared that, provided proper safeguards were established, Charles himself should be restored to the throne. Far from agreeing with Vane, they angrily accused him of demagogic attempts to curry favor with the common people.[50] Undaunted, the radical leader went on to Edinburgh where he found "an equal opposition to the proposal to depose the King, the Scots being quite determined to keep at least the shadow of monarchy in the person of this King and his heirs."[51]

49. Bulstrode Whitelocke, *Memorials of English Affairs* (London, 1682), p. 103; Sir William Waller, *Vindication of the character and conduct of Sir William Waller* (London, 1793), pp. 11, 12; Agostini to Doge, c. Feb. 1644, *CSPV, 1643–1647*, p. 77.

50. Sabran described Vane as one of the group who aimed "renverser l'État." (Sabran to Brienne, London, June 1644, PRO, 31/3/75, fol. 17a, b.)

51. Agostini to Doge, July 5, 1644, *CSPV, 1643–1647*, p. 77. Dr. Lawrence Kaplan argues that the idea that Vane proposed the deposition of the King is "a historical myth which cannot survive serious examination." ("The Plot to Depose Charles I in 1644," *Bulletin of the Institute of Historical Research*, XLIV [Nov. 1971].) Kaplan is, however, mistaken in his contention that the evidence is restricted to two diplomatic reports. He has apparently overlooked the Sabran correspondence in the Public Record Office, which adds greatly to the collection in the British Museum. Three additional dispatches of Sabran contain references to Vane's journey. (See PRO, 31/3/75, fol. 17a, b; PRO, 31/3/74, fols. 149, 161.) Nor are Agostini's remarks on the subject restricted to the dispatches cited by Kaplan. On June 21 he reported that Vane had gone to Scotland after conferring with the generals at York (Agostini to Doge, June 21, 1644, *CSPV, 1643–1647*, pp. 112, 113). Again, on July 5, he describes Vane's pessimistic mood on his return from Scotland. (Agostini to Doge, July 5, 1644, *CSPV, 1643–1647*, p. 116.) According to Vane his discussions with the generals took place on June 10. He presumably left York a few days later for Scotland and stopped briefly on his return on June 28. Thus Kaplan's problem as to how Vane could carry out the visit to Scotland and return to London all between June 28 and July 1 does not really arise. Kaplan is also mistaken in his assertion that no other mention was ever made of Vane's trip and its character. David Bu-

The extent to which the generals at York were right to accuse Vane and his party of a demagogic appeal to the masses is one of the more important problems of the period. Neither Vane nor St. John considered himself common clay, and when vital interests were involved, as in the case of the Merchant Adventurers, they did not hesitate to side with power and pelf. Nonetheless, their hostility toward the monarchy and the House of Lords and their liberalism in religion could not but appeal to those who regarded the constitutional reforms of the early stages of the revolution as a mere prelude to more fundamental social and economic changes.

On the local level, the radicals appear frequently to have allied themselves with the "meaner sort." The county committees, set up by Parliament in each county, provided such persons with an avenue to positions of considerable power and influence. This silent revolution in the counties was more than once viewed with alarm by the more conservative members, but the radicals consistently defended it. Haselrig, an old schoolmate of Vane, argued strongly on May 27, 1644, in favor of an ordinance designed to strengthen the authority of the Leicestershire committee. D'Ewes opposed it and was supported by Sir Martin Lister who characterized most of the committee as "mean men in birth and fortune and some also strangers in that county . . . "

Some weeks later Sir Thomas Dacres, the substantial knight of the shire for Hertfordshire, protested against the appointment of men to committees in the eastern counties "that had no estates in the county." Once again D'Ewes sympathized and made a contemptuous reference to men of "mean rank." Sabran, the French ambassador, was scandalized by his impression that the parliamentary committees were "filled with artisans." Support of such practices appears to have been re-

---

chanan, writing a year later, recalled that "while the Forces of Manchester and Fairfax . . . are about the siege of York, unanimously; there is one who goes from hence to sow some dissension betwixt the Generals, Leslie, Fairfax and Manchester; which design is disappointed by God's mercy . . . " (*A Short and true relation of Some main passages of things* [London, 1645], BM, E.1174(4).) I must also take issue with Kaplan's statement that "from the very outset the Scots made it clear that they regarded themselves as loyal subjects of Charles I." As early as the summer of 1640 Argyle and others discussed the possibility of deposing the King. (See S. R. Gardiner, *History of England . . . 1603–1642*, 10 vols. [London, 1899], IX, 149, n. 2, 166.) The truth is that, although many Scots were alienated by the policies of the English radicals, there was a party in Scotland quite willing to co-operate with them, and they amply demonstrated this in the following years. Finally, why should it seem odd, or smacking of "conspiracy theories of history," that persons who had felt themselves obliged to take up arms against the King should contemplate his deposition? And after all, Vane did have pronounced republican leanings. For the date of Vane's conversation with the generals, see *Calendar of State Papers, Domestic Series, 1603–1704*, 81 vols. (1857–1947+) [hereafter cited as *CSPD*], *1644*, p. 223.

stricted to the radicals and, in particular, to fire-eaters like John Gurdon and Sir Henry Mildmay, both of whom were well established in their own counties.[52]

In Kent the county committee was dominated by the moderates until the formation of the New Model in the spring of 1645, after which the committee was reorganized. The result was a heavy influx of lesser gentry with more radical views, more dependent on the central government and less county minded. In Staffordshire the more active and aggressive recruits to the committee tended to be "new men."[53]

The radicals made effective use of their supporters on the county committees, particularly in their drive to win control of the parliamentary army. In the autumn of 1644, after Essex had been eliminated by the disaster at Lostwithiel, there remained a number of other moderates with important commands. The Earl of Denbigh and Colonel Edward Massey were two officers who found themselves the targets of a systematic campaign of obstruction and abuse at the local level preparatory to the Self-Denying Ordinance of December 1644.

After his unsuccessful attempt to convert the Scots to his own brand of radicalism, Vane returned to London in late June 1644 in a depressed state of mind and pessimistic about the future relations between his own party and that of the Scots. He singled out for particular criticism the Scottish General Lawrence Crawford, whom he blamed for the failure to capture York. Some weeks later the enmity between Cromwell and Crawford was to be made public. Cromwell's role in the victory at Marston Moor was another source of dissension between the Scots and the Vane-St. John party. The Scots complained that London had been filled with reports of the battle in which "the great Independent," Cromwell, had been made the hero of the action. The Scots argued, at least among themselves, that Cromwell would have fled if, at a critical moment after Rupert's charge, he had not been supported strongly by David Leslie. Baillie, increasingly dissatisfied with the radicals, noted gloomily that the victory had greatly strengthened the religious Independents and pointed out that in Parliament "the politic part . . . is the stronger."[54]

52. D'Ewes, "Journal," BM, Harl. 166, fols. 67a, 74b; Whitaker, "Diary," BM, Add. MS. 31,116, fol. 145b; *CJ*, III, 533; Sabran to Brienne, London, Aug. 4, 1644, PRO, 31/3/74, fol. 155a; Mary F. Keeler, *The Long Parliament, 1640–1641: A Biographical Study of Its Members* (Philadelphia, American Philosophical Society, 1954), pp. 200, 274.

53. A. M. Everitt, *The County Committee of Kent in the Civil War* (Leicester, University College of Leicester, 1957), pp. 20, 30; D. H. Pennington and I. A. Roots, *The Committee at Stafford, 1643–45* (Manchester, Manchester University Press, 1957), pp. 17–23, 74–83.

54. Baillie, *Letters*, II, 211.

After Marston Moor the radicals had been described as "more averse from peace than ever," and Holles recalled that it was after this that they began to "spit out their venom against Monarchy, against Nobility and Gentry . . . "[55] Their intention to strengthen their hold on the country was indicated by the reappearance of the ordinance for martial law, under which special courts were to be set up to try persons for political offenses. "The Kingdom will be losing the great privilege it enjoys that no person soever shall be condemned unless he had first been tried and found guilty by twelve of the same rank . . . " was the interesting criticism of the Venetian ambassador.[56] The ordinance had a rough passage in the Commons. The moderates protested against "certain dreadful articles" that provided the death penalty for holding intelligence with the royalists, and D'Ewes, basing his protest on the "higher law" theory, argued that the measure was "contrary to the Common Law of England."

St. John was the most active defender of the controversial ordinance, but when he demanded that persons convicted of contributing to the royalist cause should be executed, he met strong opposition from John Maynard, Sir Thomas Withrington, and D'Ewes, all of whom, wrote the diarist, were "not a little astonished to think that a shambles should be set up amongst us."[57]

The Lords had refused to pass the ordinance and had demanded that the two Houses retain the prerogative of mercy. During the ensuing deadlock a number of radicals recommended making use of the covenant as a stick with which to beat the Lords into line. Mildmay declared that certain Lords had before then "obstructed" the measures of the Commons and demanded that, if there were any such now, the Commons should "look after them." He urged further that any members of the Lords who had not taken the covenant should be expelled. Mildmay was strongly supported by other radicals including Strode, Prideaux, and William Ellis, and, in spite of the opposition of the party that was to be called "Presbyterian," he was ordered to demand of the Lords that they pass the martial law ordinance and to tell them that they were all to take the covenant and "that justice may be done upon such as shall refuse to take it."[58]

Here is an interesting example of the difficulty of using religion as a criterion of party allegiance. The "Independents," as they were to be

55. Agostini to Doge, July 26, 1644, *CSPV, 1643–1647*, p. 124; Holles, *Memoirs*, p. 18.

56. Agostini to Doge, July 26, 1644, *CSPV, 1643–1647*, p. 124

57. D'Ewes, "Journal," BM, Harl. 166, fol. 98a. Radical plans to impeach Staple-Burney Collection, 13, p. 1089.)
ton and Essex were rumored about this time. (See *Merc. Aul.*, July 16, 1644, BM,

58. *CJ*, III, 586.

known, apparently felt no embarrassment about forcing the covenant on the Lords, despite the fact that one of those Lords who had not taken it was said to be Lord Robartes, a close friend of Vane.

The summer of 1644 was dominated by a continuation of radical efforts to win control of the army. They exploited the rivalry between Waller and Essex and made good use of the suspected treason of some of Essex's officers. Holles and Stapleton, on the other hand, accused the radicals of a deliberate plan to bring about the defeat and disintegration of Essex's army. By September 1644 both Waller and Essex had been eliminated as factors in the struggle; the army of the Eastern Association, of which Manchester was general and Cromwell commander of the horse, emerged as the most important of Parliament's military formations.

A fierce dispute had arisen between Essex and Waller in June 1644 over the tasks to be given their respective armies. Both men wished to campaign in the western counties, and Waller, who regarded the west as his own preserve, may have hoped to gain a de facto independence from Essex's authority by moving his army into that area. The committee of both kingdoms, in spite of Essex's opposition, ordered Waller westward and Essex in pursuit of the royalist army led by the King. Essex countermanded this order and himself proceeded west, leaving an angry Waller to follow the King. Essex's action, wrote Baillie, who still backed the radicals, "was to enter in the heart of Waller's association and really to subvert his army."[59]

Essex not only defied the committee, but accused the radicals of an intention to make Waller commander in chief. The quarrel split the House of Commons along the usual lines. Glyn was attacked by the "violent spirits" when he moved that Essex be permitted to proceed west, and Lord Lisle was particularly vocal in his criticism of Essex. According to Holles, some of the radicals "did not stick to say it were better that . . . Essex and his whole army were lost . . . than the parliament not obeyed" and urged that neither Essex nor his army should receive any more aid from Parliament. The Vane-St. John party, Holles argued, deliberately allowed the "General and the army to be lost and the whole west further out of Parliament's reach than before." Haselrig, Waller's most aggressive advocate, was quoted as predicting that he would "ruin" Essex "or be ruined himself." A plan to impeach the lord general was reportedly abandoned in favor of allowing Essex to go west, "but with a resolution to let him perish."[60]

In June and July 1644 Essex marched into Devon pursued by strong

59. Baillie, *Letters*, II, 193.
60. D'Ewes, "Journal," BM, Harl. 166, fol. 74a, b; Holles, *Memoirs*, pp. 24, 25.

royalist forces which were soon threatening his communications with
London. As early as July 17 the moderates in the Commons had perceived Essex's peril, and, when Vane had urged the House to permit
Waller to remain near London to reorganize after his defeat at Crop-
redy Bridge, they had protested that such a course would expose Essex
to "unnecessary danger."[61] A month later the situation was even worse,
and Holles, Sir Walter Erle, and others were vehement in their criticism of Waller and were predicting that his delaying tactics "would
ruin the west."[62] Essex himself was warning the Commons by August 2
that, unless he received immediate help, the forces of the King were
"like to shut him up in Cornwall."[63] But if the moderates suspected
treachery on the part of the radicals, the latter had reason to think the
worst of Essex and his officers. By this time secret agents of the committee of both kingdoms had reported evidence of a plot among some
of the officers to go over to the royalist side and to take a large part of
the army with them. Late in September 1644 General Philip Skippon
revealed the reality of the plot before a Commons' investigating committee.[64] The scheme seems to have had its origin in a letter to Essex
from the King on August 6, 1644.

In this letter Charles, who apparently hoped that Essex's bad relations with the radicals had put him in the mood to make some kind
of agreement with the royalists, promised Essex future preferments if
he would abandon Parliament. One of the bearers of the letter, a Mr.
Harding, was instructed to speak to Essex alone and to point out to
him that "if either the Scots or the other violent party at London prevail," he would be in danger, but that if both armies joined forces,
the "violent party" would be incapable of opposing their will. If Essex
insisted that Parliament be informed, he should be told that "the temper and engagement of those of the House of Commons is such, that
there is no hope that the honest men amongst them dare appear against
the declared sense of the House, until they shall see a power on foot
sufficient to protect them. But then it is to be hoped that the major

61. D'Ewes, "Journal," BM, Harl. 166, fol. 98b. Waller later became a leading
moderate and was one of the "eleven members" in 1647. In a conversation with
D'Ewes he recalled that when he and Essex realized that the radicals had played
them off against one another they became good friends. Waller went on to assure
D'Ewes that he had never knowingly done a disservice to Essex. When D'Ewes
asked him why he had not moved to help Essex in the summer of 1644, he replied
that he had had "express orders from the Committee of Both Kingdoms not to
stir." (D'Ewes, "Journal," BM, Harl. 165, fol. 179a.)
62. D'Ewes, "Journal," BM, Harl. 166, fol. 100b.
63. Whitaker, "Diary," BM, Add. MS. 31,116, fol. 153a.
64. John Rushworth, *Historical Collections,* 7 vols. (London, 1654–1701) [hereafter
cited as Rushworth, *Hist. Coll.*], II, pt. iii, 710.

part of the members at Westminster will give a good approbation . . . "[65]
Essex received the King's letter, delivered by Lord Beauchamp, but refused to see Harding on the grounds that he had no authorization to
do so from Parliament.

Charles was now ready to drop the matter, but some of his officers,
arguing that Essex might yet be convinced, obtained Charles's permission to write another letter to Essex in which they proposed that Essex
meet their general accompanied by six officers of his choosing. This
was sent to Essex on August 9. The parliamentary lord general justified his reputation for probity, if not military brilliance, when he answered " . . . I having no authority from the Parliament, who have
employed me, to treat, cannot give way to it without a breach of trust."[66]

In spite of Essex's loyalty, he and his officers were viewed with understandable suspicion by the radicals who must, in any case, have welcomed any news of disaffection in the army which they so wished to
eliminate as a factor in the continuing struggle for power.

Essex's army, cooped up and beleaguered in Cornwall, surrendered
on September 2, 1644. The negotiations with the royalists were carried
on by a Colonel Butler, the same man who subsequently confessed to
having led the plot to join the army with that of the King. Few tears
were shed by the radicals at the news of the disaster. Cromwell, who
was described as hating Essex because he was "but half an Enemy" to
the King, managed to write that it was "with grief of heart" that he
viewed Essex's plight and that "truly had we wings, we would fly
thither."[67] He may have added to himself that since they did not have
wings, they would stay where they were. According to Manchester, the
Independent element in his army, of which Cromwell was the leading
spirit, was as joyful at the news of Essex's defeat as if they themselves
and not the royalists had gained the victory.[68] In the House of Commons, too, Cromwell's friends appeared singularly unmoved. During
polite expressions of sympathy, the lord general's old enemy Haselrig,
"laughing and jeering to himself, gave offence to many."[69] The radi-

65. Edward Walker, *Historical Discourses upon several occasions* (London, 1705),
pp. 52–61.

66. *Ibid.;* see also Philip Warwick, *Memoirs of the Reign of Charles I* (London,
1701), p. 272.

67. Laurence Eachard, *A History of England* (London, 1718), p. 609; W. C.
Abbott, *The Writings and Speeches of Oliver Cromwell*, 4 vols. (Cambridge, Mass.,
Harvard University Press, 1937–1947), I, 292.

68. *The Quarrel between the Earl of Manchester and Oliver Cromwell*, ed. J.
Bruce and D. Masson, Camden Society, New Ser., vol. XII (Westminster, 1875),
p. 76.

69. D'Ewes, "Journal," BM, Harl. 166, fol. 113a. During the Essex-Waller dispute
in the summer of 1644 the pro-Waller forces in the Commons included St. John,

cals had good cause to be pleased. One of the most formidable obstacles blocking their control of the parliamentary forces had been eliminated.

The news of Lostwithiel was not a week old before Cromwell, Manchester, and Crawford were in London. Cromwell was intent on two objectives: the dismissal of his old *bête noire*, the Scottish General Crawford; and the extraction from Parliament of a promise of toleration for the religious radicals in his army. Scottish opposition to him was strong enough to keep Crawford in his post, but the point concerning toleration was won.

The price of pleasing Cromwell was to prove a high one. The accommodation order, which his representations produced, placed an intolerable strain on the already shaky structure of the radical-Scottish alliance.

By the summer of 1644 relations between the radicals and the Scots had deteriorated to the point where Baillie could assure his friends in Edinburgh that if they "tasted the sauce wherein we dip our venison at London, their teeth would not water so fast to be here . . . "[70] Moreover, with the arrival of the Scottish Chancellor Loudon, a Scottish moderate party, which was soon to link up with the Holles-Stapleton group in London, made its appearance. Loudon was a Campbell and a relative of Argyle, but despite this connection he was in political opposition to the Marquis until January 1648 when, for reasons that remain somewhat mysterious, he began to support Argyle, the Kirk, and the English Cromwellian radicals.

Vane and his friends had, in fact, gone to remarkable lengths in the summer of 1644 in order to please their allies. Some of the sects had been prosecuted with considerable vigor; even Vane's friend Roger Williams did not escape. Williams had fallen under Baillie's censure because of his alleged statement that "there is no church, no sacraments, no pastors, no church officers, or ordinance in the world, nor has been since a few years after the apostles." A few weeks later, the Commons ordered "the public burning of one Williams his books . . . concerning the Tolerating of all sorts of religion."[71] On the same day the Westminster Assembly, prompted by the Scots, complained to the House about the activities of Anabaptists and Antinomians and named

Vane, Bond, Haselrig, Pierrepont, Lord Lisle, Strode, and J. Trenchard. The pro-Essex members included Holles, Stapleton, Glyn, Sir W. Erle, Henry Herbert, and D'Ewes. (*Ibid.*, fols. 72a, 74a, b, 77a, b, 98b, 99a, 100b, 106a, 107a, 109b; Whitaker, "Diary," BM, Add. MS. 31,116, fol. 145b; *CSPD, 1644,* p. 323; Whitelocke, "Annals," BM, Add. MS. 37, 343, fol. 313a, b.)

70. Baillie to Porterfield, July 16, 1644, Baillie, *Letters,* II, 207.

71. *CJ,* III, 585.

four ministers as the ringleaders. After a "long debate" the House ordered the arrest of the four. The Scots were duly gratified, and Baillie became more optimistic. The radicals, he thought, "will not own their way so much as to tolerate it, if once they found themselves masters. For the time they are loath to cast them off, and to put their party into despair, lest they desert them." He was soon cheerfully reporting that the next business was "to give our advice what to do for the suppressing of Anabaptists, Antinomians, and other sectaries."[72]

By early September, however, it was clear that the Erastian and even anticlerical spirit of the Commons was not to be denied. Strong objections were raised to the ministers' assertion that the manner of ordination they proposed was the "ordinance of Christ," and the Commons were even more reluctant to agree that the ministers "were set over us as rulers . . . "[73]

The debate was ended by the report of the defeat and dispersal of the army of Essex at Lostwithiel. If the news was disastrous for the Holles-Stapleton group, implying as it did the effective end of the power and authority of Essex, it was quite the reverse for the radicals. Vane and St. John were now freed from their dependence on the Scots and from the necessity of pursuing policies, particularly in the religious sphere, that threatened to alienate some of their most powerful English friends. For them and their party the "moment of truth" had come. They could no longer hope to continue to ride two horses, and although the espousal of the principle of toleration of "tender consciences" would temporarily alienate some of their own supporters, such as Tate and Prideaux, and virtually destroy their alliance with the Scots, they had little choice but to adopt it. Cromwell's star was fast rising, and with Essex out of the way the time was ripe for closer links with the army of the Eastern Association. The Scottish connection had, in any event, become almost a liability. There were deep political as well as religious differences between them, and, although some attempt had been made to gloss over such things and to mollify the Scots by repression of the sects, this policy had reached the point of diminishing returns. Any hope for accord with the Scots in religious matters had vanished when the irresistible Presbyterianism of the Kirk had collided with the immovable Erastianism of the lawyers of the Inns of Court. There was danger, moreover, that conciliation of the Scots could be bought only at the price of the loss of support of more liberal elements both in the religious and political spheres. Cromwell's presence in London in early September was a warning of just such an

72. Baillie, *Letters*, II, 218, 223–224.
73. D'Ewes, "Journal," BM, Harl. 166, fol. 111a; Whitaker, "Diary," BM, Add. MS. 31,116, fol. 158a.

eventuality. In the summer and autumn of 1644 influential voices were being raised on all sides in favor of a policy of religious toleration, and the radicals were now in a position to satisfy that demand.

William Walwyn, that most interesting and mysterious gray eminence of the Revolution, in his pamphlet "The Power of Love," had argued one year before in favor of toleration for Anabaptists, Brownists, and Separatists. In mid-1644 he had returned to the attack with the publication of "The Compassionate Samaritane" and had been ably seconded by Williams' "Bloody Tenet." In November 1644 John Milton brought forth his classic *Areopagitica*. The opinions of such men could neither be ignored nor ridiculed. They spoke for important elements in London, and some of their ideas were congenial to Vane himself. The result was the accommodation order of September 13, 1644, which, although gratifying to Cromwell and his buffcoats, was doubtless framed with more sophisticated groups also in mind, whose support was no less vital to the radicals.

The Scots reacted as if stung. In a bitter reference to the accommodation order, Baillie grumbled that "our greatest friends Sir Henry Vane and the Solicitor are the main procurers of all this and that without any regard to us, who have . . . brought these two persons to the height of the power now they enjoy, and use to our prejudice . . . We had much need of your prayers." "We must see for new friends," he concluded significantly, " . . . when our old ones . . . have deserted and half betrayed us."[74]

The accommodation order marked the final abandonment of a policy that had been carried on, with varying degrees of success, since the death of Pym. Many of the Scots were now so hostile to the radicals that the alliance, in its old form at least, was no longer viable.

The time between the death of Pym and the accommodation order was one of the great formative periods of the Puritan Revolution. Vane's key role in the negotiations with the Scots in late 1643 had enabled him to use their support in seizing and retaining the initiative in Parliament in the critical months following Pym's death. While Holles and Stapleton could do little more than fight a rearguard action, Vane and St. John had set up the committee of both kingdoms and, by filling it with their own supporters, had created a most formidable engine for the implementation of their policies and the frustra-

74. Baillie, *Letters*, II, 230. It should be pointed out, however, that from the point of view of the true Separatists—those who wanted no part of a national church—the measure was a distinctly conservative one. I am indebted to Dr. Murray Tolmie of the University of British Columbia for bringing this point to my attention.

tion of their opponents' plans. From the outset the radicals appear to have perceived that their ascendancy could be but temporary if it depended on the essentially dubious support of the Scots. Undisputed mastery of the army could alone give them assured supremacy at Westminster, and with a certain ruthless efficiency they had set about the task of gaining that control. With the committee of both kingdoms as the central instrument and the county committees as useful adjuncts, a general assault on all moderate-minded parliamentary commanders had been launched. Essex was, of course, the main target, and the disintegration of his army at Lostwithiel was an important milestone on the road leading to the Self-Denying Ordinance and the New Model.

If Pym had tended to vacillate between radical and moderate policies, his successors made a striking contrast. Far from trying to lead a "middle party," Vane and St. John boldly identified themselves with the most revolutionary factions and ideas. They made little attempt to conceal their hostility toward Charles I, the House of Lords, and even the monarchy itself, and on the local level they actively promoted the "new men" on the county committees. They maintained good relations with and received strong support from the most radical party in London and brought forward measures designed to suspend due process of law in the treatment of "delinquents." Their growing awareness that many of the Scots did not share their attitude toward the King and the monarchy seems to have led them to ideas of compromise and to proposals for a kind of puppet monarchy. In economic affairs, however, they did not permit notions of social justice unduly to impair good relations with powerful and monopolistic companies like the Merchant Adventurers.

But just as they had been forced to choose between the claims of Scottish Presbyterians and English Independents, so too would they be called upon to choose between power complexes like the Merchant Adventurers and the aspirations of the "meaner sort" and to answer outraged demands that the Revolution should mean more to them than a mere change of masters. There can be little doubt that the policies espoused in 1643 and 1644 by men like Vane, St. John, and Cromwell did much to promote that powerful extension and intensification of the revolution which was to be known as the Leveller movement. As yet those who made up the movement were an indistinguishable part of the general radical grouping in Parliament, City, and army. That it became a separate movement at all was the measure of the failure of the radical leaders to respond creatively to the challenges their own policies had called forth. In any case, loyalty to class and the rights of property triumphed, and the moral leadership of the Revolution was forfeited.

The policies of Holles, Stapleton, and their followers can be delineated more in negative than in positive terms. Their opposition was vigorous but, on the whole, rather ineffectual. They were most sensitive to the threat to Essex, and, although they defended him with energy and spirit in the Commons, they were not able to save his army. They opposed radical attempts to suspend the law and defended the position of the small clothiers of Essex as against the great Londoners. On the other hand, they were loud in their contempt of the "meaner sort" and strongly protested against their presence on the county committees. From what were perhaps mixed motives of principle and expediency, they were stout defenders of the rights and privileges of the House of Lords whenever the upper house came under the fire of the radicals. Their attitude toward religion remains rather obscure. Clearly they were by no means all "Presbyterians," and there is good reason to think that a high proportion of them would not have been adverse to a tamed episcopacy. They also included many hearty Erastians, but had no monopoly on that approach.

Their effectiveness as a political force was much reduced by their failure to enunciate definite policies, as well as by their tardiness in exploiting the obvious anomalies in the radical-Scottish alliance. It was not until the defeat of Essex had robbed them of their main prop that they began to investigate the possibilities of a link with Chancellor Loudon and his supporters. In sum, they suffered from the disabilities of most moderate groups: lack of clear-cut goals and the disciplined will to achieve them.

September 1644 was a critical period for both major groupings in the Long Parliament. The moderates were on the brink of becoming, through their Scottish alliance, "Presbyterians." The radicals, by the policy of toleration and the break with the Scots, had strengthened their links with both the political and religious "left wing." For them, the next months would be particularly crucial. Though the power of Essex was now virtually extinguished, they had yet to win complete control of the parliamentary forces. Circumstances dictated a détente with their parliamentary opponents preparatory to the virtual elimination of their military influence by the Self-Denying Ordinance and the formation of the New Model army.

III] The Treaty of Uxbridge

The winter of 1644–1645 was highly significant for the future course of the Puritan Revolution. The defeat of the Earl of Essex virtually ended the connection of the Holles-Stapleton party with the army and provided the radicals with their long-sought opportunity to make the armed forces of Parliament peculiarly their own. In this period the radicals appear to have adopted a policy of strategic withdrawal in the political and religious fields, in favor of a gradual strengthening of their position in the parliamentary armies. A coordinated attack on the remaining moderate military commanders culminated in the passage in December, by the Commons, of the first Self-Denying Ordinance which, if it had been passed by the Lords, would have destroyed moderate military influence. By April 1645 this was in fact achieved by the passage of the second Self-Denying Ordinance. The military ascendancy of the radicals had likewise been ensured by the appointment of a large number of radical sympathizers as officers of the New Model and by reason of the fact that one notable exception was made to the operation of the ordinance in the person of Oliver Cromwell.

Thus the goal that the radicals had set themselves two years before —control of the army—was achieved. This was the all-important development in the winter of 1644–1645, and the political and religious policies of the radicals in the period can only be regarded as subsidiary to it. Judging by their actions, Vane and St. John appear to have decided in September 1644 that, if the main objective was to be achieved, it was necessary to rid themselves of the "war party" image and also to attempt to mollify the Scots by soft-pedaling the toleration issue. At the same time the trial and execution of Archbishop Laud were to be pushed forward as evidence of their good intentions.

After a brief flare-up the issue of treason in the army of Essex was allowed to die, and the Commons under radical leadership considered with seeming seriousness the question of peace negotiations with the King. This activity culminated in the abortive Treaty of Uxbridge, in early 1645, which did more to embitter relations between King and Parliament than to ameliorate them. It did gain time, however, time during which, under Cromwell's leadership, major steps were taken toward the formation of the New Model.

In the religious field the Scots, especially after their capture of Newcastle, found the parliamentary policy much more to their taste. The parliamentary committee that had been set up to implement the accommodation order together with its subcommittee from the Westminster Assembly was ordered to suspend its activities. The assembly was told, moreover, to proceed with the establishment of a national church government and a directory of worship. By November Robert Baillie was once again hopeful that he would hear no more from the Independents.

But the relaxation of tension in politics and religion served only to underline the continuing conflict in the military formations. Manchester, who only a few months before had been favored at the expense of Essex, now found himself under heavy attack from Cromwell, assisted by extremists like Haselrig and John Lilburne. At the same time, radical-dominated county committees launched coordinated attacks on moderate commanders like the Earl of Denbigh and Edward Massey. By December 1644 the radicals were ready to administer what they hoped would be the *coup de grâce* to such rivals. But although they won a significant victory when the Commons passed the first Self-Denying Ordinance, the intransigence of the Lords forced them to wait until April 1645 before their goal was achieved.

The moderates, although in serious disarray after the eclipse of Essex, managed to recover their equilibrium by working out an alliance with the Scots under their pragmatic chancellor, the Earl of Loudon. The difficulty was that a political entente with Loudon was impossible without a corresponding link with the aggressive Scottish Kirk. Holles was willing to pay the price, but it would prove a high one.

By late September 1644 Essex's army was no longer a factor, and the radicals saw to it that it remained but a paper command. Their contemptuous handling of Essex's suggestion that he join the remnants of his army with that of Manchester made this abundantly clear. The survivors of the Lostwithiel disaster were straggling toward London, and the radicals saw an obvious opportunity to allow these soldiers to be absorbed into other formations, leaving Essex with little more than the hollow title of lord general. The moderates, no doubt aware of the radicals' intentions, gave Essex strong support, and there were lively scenes in the Commons. The committee of both kingdoms relayed Essex's suggestion to the Commons without comment, and despite angry speeches from Holles, Stapleton, and an aroused D'Ewes, "[the] violent . . . hindered it, so it would not be hearkened unto."[1]

Essex was to be further discredited a few days later by the sensa-

1. Sir Symonds D'Ewes, "Journal of the Parliament begun November, 1640," BM, Harleian 166 [hereafter cited as D'Ewes, "Journal," BM, Harl. 166], fols. 123b, 124a.

tional revelation of a plot among his officers to place his army under the King's orders. The radical leaders, who had penetrated the plotters' defenses some weeks before, exploited their opportunity and now made strenuous efforts to tar the moderates in the Commons with the same brush. The leader of the accused officers, a Colonel Butler, confessed that the hopes of the conspirators rested mainly on their belief that "there was a strong party in both houses for the King, and that if Essex would join his army with the King's, they would vote for a good and settled peace, and carry it being backed by such a power." Colonel Thomas Tyrell, who seems to have acted as an *agent provocateur* for the radicals, had revealed the plot to General Skippon, the veteran parliamentary commander who often contrived to have a foot in both parliamentary camps. Tyrell had also sent a letter to Stapleton, enclosing the treasonous instructions, apparently with the intention of testing Stapleton's reaction, and seems also to have kept the radicals in London well informed. One of these, Anthony Nichols, member for Bodmin, told the Commons that he had heard about the letter and had taken occasion to ask Stapleton if he had heard "anything from Colonel Butler concerning dangerous instructions . . . who answered me no . . . " This was the signal for uproar in the Commons, and, in D'Ewes's words, "many violent fellows fell very foul upon that noble and gallant gentleman [Stapleton]." Sir Philip protested that he had received Tyrell's letter only after the defeat of Essex in Cornwall. Holles and Sir William Lewis, to whom he had shown the letter, supported his statement.[2]

The radicals failed, however, to obtain concrete evidence of collusion between the moderate parliamentarians and the dissident army officers. Essex was certainly not implicated, and it is improbable that Holles and Stapleton were seriously involved. Certainly no attempt was made to prosecute any of the Holles party. The affair was, in fact, the prelude to a kind of détente in the relations between the rival groups, which, with some interruptions, lasted until the clash over the Self-Denying Ordinance in December 1644.

The new conciliatory policy of the radicals was apparent soon after the reception of a peace overture from the King that Charles had sent shortly after his victory at Lostwithiel. The first reaction appears to have been negative, and the committee of both kingdoms deliberately delayed passing on the King's message to the House. When it finally appeared it was greeted with the usual hostility of the more fiery members. John Blakiston's objection, that the form of the note cast doubt on the validity of Parliament, would have heretofore been sufficient to bring about its summary rejection. On this occasion, however, the Com-

2. *Ibid.,* fol. 125a.

mons appointed a committee to consider it, upon which moderates were well represented. Holles suggested a middle course. While conceding the unsatisfactory form of the message, he nevertheless urged that Parliament complete its peace propositions and send them to the King as soon as possible.

A change of tone was also to be noted in the treatment envisaged for former royalists. On September 19, 1644, some eleven royalists had been proscribed as beyond pardon. They included Archbishop Laud, Bishop Wren, Lord Digby, George Goring, and Edward, Lord Littleton. D'Ewes's attempt to put in a word for Littleton was "to no avail . . . [the] violent . . . carried it upon the question . . . "[3] On the following day, however, there was a marked change. In a debate on the treatment that former members of the House who had attended the Oxford Parliament could expect, a rather puzzled D'Ewes recorded that "the very violent among them [the radicals] seemed mild, and most men were passed on without exception." A few days later the House passed another resolution of moderate tenor to the effect that no additions could be made to the list of proscribed royalists except between the hours of ten and twelve A.M., that is, when the House was well attended. On the same day the Commons reviewed this list, and, according to D'Ewes, the proposal to do so "first proceeded from some of the violent themselves."[4]

Certain of the rank and file of the radicals appear to have experienced some difficulty in following the flexible policy of their leaders. When the question of amnesty for the Princes Rupert and Maurice came up, Denis Bond, a spirited woolen draper and member for Dorchester, bluntly declared "that if we could get them we would hang them up . . ." Such talk was not to D'Ewes's taste. Indeed he took occasion to speak on behalf of the two sons of Elizabeth of Bohemia urging that Parliament content itself with refusing to aid them in the recovery of the Palatinate. To his disgust, "the violent" carried the resolution against the princes without a division. "These Princes," the class-conscious D'Ewes exclaimed, "were no further regarded than the meanest . . . soldier in the King's army."[5] But despite the extremism of a Bond, the change to more moderate courses could be seen in the fact that out of ten cases reviewed the House granted pardons to five royalists.

The radicals had certainly not lost control of the House. They were, indeed, able to defeat the moderates in almost every important division between mid-September and December 1, 1644. The moderates,

3. *Ibid.*, fol. 123a.
4. *Ibid.*, fols. 123b, 125a.
5. *Ibid.*, fol. 125b.

moreover, suffered a decline both in morale and numbers. Essex's army had been liquidated, and the Scottish alliance was still tenuous. Holles and Stapleton themselves had been in some danger of prosecution in connection with the Butler plot. The swing to a more conciliatory policy was thus a tactical shift on the part of Vane and St. John rather than the result of a sudden acquisition of strength on the part of the moderates.

Agostini remained skeptical about radical intentions. They were more concerned "to obliterate the opinion, which has become universal, that Parliament abhors any treaty" than to make a genuine effort for peace. He felt, nevertheless, that the popular demand for peace was so strong that a treaty once begun might produce a settlement despite the terms with which it started.[6]

Holles and Stapleton, with the assistance of the French ambassador, were, meanwhile, taking the first steps toward the alliance with the Scots. The Earl of Loudon, recently arrived in London, was now the main spokesman for the Scottish commissioners and was in a mood to look for new friends. It was to be the beginning of a connection that, with some interruptions and vicissitudes, was to persist until December 1647 when Loudon went over to the side of his radical relative, the Marquis of Argyle. Loudon, at this point, was described as very disappointed with the radicals, "finding them very far from the disposition which he hoped."[7] Loudon, it should be noted, was much more the *politique* than the Kirk man, and it was on political rather than religious grounds that he opposed the radicals and made common cause with the Holles-Stapleton group.

Despite the suspension of open hostilities on the floor of the House, there was much intrigue going on behind the scenes in which Sabran, the French ambassador, was deeply involved. A meeting of Holles, Stapleton, and Sabran was arranged on October 29, 1644, probably at the home of the Countess of Carlisle, the purpose of which was to lay the groundwork for a rapprochement between the Scots and English moderates. The connection, which was to saddle the parliamentary group with the name "Presbyterian," was described by Sabran as primarily political in character. Its object, he wrote, was "the preservation of the monarchy against those who have seized authority in Parliament."[8] Holles and Stapleton had suggested in this interview that they join

6. Agostini to Doge, Sept. 27, Oct. 11, 1644, *Calendar of state papers and manuscripts relating to English affairs existing in the archives and collections of Venice and in other libraries of northern Italy*, vols. 10–38 (1603–1675), [London, H. M. Stationery Office, 1900–1940] [hereafter cited as *CSPV*], *1643–1647*, pp, 142, 146.

7. Agostini to Doge, Sept. 13, 1644, *ibid.*, p. 138.

8. Sabran to Brienne, London, Oct. 31, 1644, Public Record Office, Paris Transcripts, 31/3/75 [hereafter cited as PRO, 31/3/75], fols. 145b, 146a.

with the Scots in support of the King on condition that Charles would agree to abolish episcopacy and to establish Presbyterianism. It is significant that they justified this policy to Sabran, not on grounds of religious principle, but because they felt that major concessions in this area were the minimum price of Scottish support, without which they dared not give open support to the monarchy. Sabran argued unsuccessfully against this point of view. The pragmatic Frenchman found it difficult to believe that the Scots would make their support of the King conditional on the establishment of their religion in England and, moreover, doubted that the King would abandon his own religion for such support.[9] Sabran was, of course, insufficiently aware of the Kirk's power in Scotland and of the determination of that body to block any policy that seemed to sacrifice the interest of the church to the state.

Sabran's comments give us the first concrete indication of the newly formed alliance between moderates and Scots. We are also given a glimpse of its character. Although abolition of episcopacy was a policy that both the Scots and the Holles party felt they could safely avow, we need not conclude that antiepiscopal feeling was strong among the moderates. Holles presented the policy as a Scottish one that had been adopted to serve political ends. In other circumstances, he, Stapleton, and many of their followers might well have been persuaded to accept a limited episcopacy; as things stood, however, they were quite prepared to jettison the bishops in return for Scottish support. The alternative was political suicide. By late 1644, moreover, the proliferation of sects was scandalizing conservatives of all stripes, and there was increased agitation for some kind of enforced religious uniformity.

The alliance began to bear fruit when Holles went to Oxford in late November as one of the parliamentary commissioners conveying the peace terms. The King took the opportunity of visiting Holles and Whitelocke privately and soliciting their opinions as to his best course in dealing with the parliamentary demands. Holles admitted that he did not himself agree with all the propositions, whereupon Charles rejoined that he was confident that Holles and his friends in the House "endeavoured to have them otherwise."[10] Holles later recalled that he had assured the King that his party had been forced to agree to the propositions in order to retain their credit in the City and among the people, but he pointed out that the Scottish army was desirous of peace and argued that once peace was established it would be much easier to repeal "hard laws" than to change the character of the propo-

9. Sabran to Brienne, Oct. 31, 1644, *ibid.*, PRO, 31/3/75, fols. 145b–146b.
10. Bulstrode Whitelocke, *Memorials of the English affairs (1620–1660)* [London, 1732], p. 113.

sitions in time of war.[11] There appears to have been no direct reference to religion, but Holles' emphasis on the attitude of the Scottish army may indicate that he was hinting at the possibility of divisions among the Scots that might make it possible to repeal the Presbyterian aspects of the proposed settlement.

There was, however, little indication at Westminster of any relaxation of the Scottish position on religion. If anything, the Scots increased their demands for more discipline in such matters. The Scottish commissioner, Lord Maitland, was especially bitter about the blocking of Scottish religious ambitions by "the Independent party" who, he complained, "carry themselves far otherwise to us than they did; . . . even those who were then [early in 1644] activist for us do turn their cloak quite on the other shoulder." They urged the Commons to speed the formation of the new church government, "to prevent the great numbers of Sects and Schisms which did grow up so high . . ." The House resolved to spur the Westminster Assembly to greater efforts, and a Scottish commissioner reported that the motion was well received by all "but [Lord] Saye and Vane and some few Independents." In the debates that followed the idea of toleration was not confined to this last group. D'Ewes, a moderate Puritan whose conservative nature must have been perturbed by the sectaries, nevertheless told the House that the "persecuting Church is the malignant Church and the persecuted Church maintains the truth . . ." Sir Samuel Luke, the alleged prototype of Butler's *Hudibras,* is closer to the stereotype of the Long Parliament "Presbyterian." He had been extremely disturbed by persons in the vicinity of Newport who "deny our Church and condemn our Ministers." He had attempted to stop their meetings, but reported that they held them "twice or thrice a week . . . they are now grown so insolent . . ."[12]

Religion was suddenly assuming greater significance on the floor of the House. What, in one observer's opinion, had previously served "as a pretext for the war" was becoming an important issue, and he reported that there was not only "division in the army . . . but in the synod, and in Parliament itself."[13]

Once again, as in September 1644, when the resistance to the accom-

11. *Burnet's History of My Own Time,* ed. O. Airy, 2 vols. (Oxford, 1897–1900), I, 64–65.

12. Maitland to Earl of Lothian, Oct. 31, 1644, *Correspondence of Sir Robert Kerr and his son William,* ed. D. Laing, 2 vols. (Edinburgh, 1875), I, 176; D'Ewes, "Journal," BM, Harl. 166, fol. 152b; Sir Samuel Luke to Mr. Marshall, Nov. 13, 1644, BM, Stowe MS. 190, fol. 280a.

13. Agostini to Doge, Nov. 15, 1644, *CSPV, 1643–1647,* pp. 154–155. See also W. K. Jordan, *The Development of Religious Toleration in England,* 4 vols. (London, Allen & Unwin, 1938), III, 56–57.

modation order among certain radicals had indicated that by no means
all of that party could be called "Independents," the religious issue
appears to have produced a division in their ranks. On November 15,
after what D'Ewes termed *"acriter disputatum,"* the Commons passed
a resolution condemning unauthorized preaching. The vote was preceded by active petitioning on both sides. Sir Nathaniel Barnardiston,
the wealthy knight of the shire for Suffolk, led the citizens of Norfolk
in their demand for the settlement of church government and the
imposition of the covenant. This was countered on the following day
by an Independent petition,[14] after which the Commons set a day for
the presentation of dissenting opinions. The vote of November 15 may
be regarded either as a defeat for Vane and St. John or as evidence
that they were reluctant at this stage to alienate the Scots completely.

But if there was dissension on certain questions of religion there
was apparent unanimity on one: the disposition of the case of Laud,
late archbishop of Canterbury, who, since that day in November 1640
when he had been clapped up in the Tower, had awaited his fate.
Scottish Kirk man, English Independent, and anticlerical Erastian
found a common bond in their hatred of Laud, and, if there were
those in the Long Parliament who had a sneaking sympathy for the
aging prelate, they remained prudently silent. The lengthy trial was
now rushed to a conclusion. On October 28 a petition allegedly signed
by 10,000 Londoners demanded that justice be done on traitors like
Laud and Bishop Mathew Wren. Five days later the archbishop was
brought to the bar of the House to hear Samuel Browne, St. John's
first cousin, and in D'Ewes's terms "the Solicitor's ape," read the
charge. D'Ewes himself was not without some regard for the old *bête
noire* of the Puritans; during the reading of the charge Laud "wrote
all the while without Spectacles reasonable fair, he being about 70
years old, which caused me much admiration." When Browne had
finished, Laud rose and "without any change of countenance or show
of fear" asked for time to prepare his answer.[15] His efforts failed to
impede the ordinance of attainder, which on November 13 passed
without difficulty in the Commons. Considerable support for Laud
now developed in the upper house. Once again one of the more extreme radicals—William Strode—was chosen to whip the Lords into
line. Strode threatened the peers with the wrath of the London mob
if they refused to pass the attainder. The radicals were also alleged to
have circulated a petition among the Londoners calling for Laud's

14. *Journals of the House of Commons* [hereafter cited as *CJ*], III, 692–693; Mary
F. Keeler, *The Long Parliament, 1640–1641: A Biographical Study of Its Members*
(Philadelphia, American Philosophical Society, 1954), p. 96.
15. D'Ewes, "Journal," BM, Harl. 166, fol. 152a.

execution. "Everyone is eager to do this," observed Agostini dryly, "without knowing anything about the trial . . . in the firm belief that all the evils from which they suffer proceed from this individual."[16]

If, as Sabran thought, the blood of Laud was intended as a propitiatory sacrifice to the Scots,[17] the latter group, far from being appeased, grew more aggressive. The capture of Newcastle gave them control of London's coal supply, and, aware of their strengthened bargaining position, they coolly informed Parliament that they intended to use the coal to satisfy their debts. The imminence of winter appears to have given point to their religious demands; at any rate Baillie was soon happily reporting that the Scottish letters from the northern coal mining center had "moved the Houses to call once, twice, thrice to the Assembly for expedition." By December 1, 1644, he was confident that the Independents "will be gotten contented to submit themselves to the Assembly . . . their plots are so broken . . ."[18] Baillie was, of course, referring to the religious Independents in the assembly and Parliament rather than to the political followers of Vane and St. John in the Commons, who were not only strong but were on the threshold of their greatest triumph: the Self-Denying Ordinance.

The religious factor remains the most difficult to isolate in the politics of the Long Parliament. As we have seen, the radical leaders Vane and St. John, although personally sympathetic to the Independents, were not always able to persuade their followers to pursue an Independent religious policy. We may surmise that the true Independents among their supporters in the Commons were a distinct minority. Apart from this it seems probable that they were concerned that the Scots be not unduly alienated. Holles and Stapleton appear to have been in a similar position with regard to the imposition of a "Scottish" religious policy on their followers. Thus when a division took place on November 26, 1644, on the question as to whether the words "as in the Church of Scotland" should be included in a clause relating to the administration of the Lord's Supper, the House voted fifty-seven to thirty-four against their inclusion. The tellers for the insertion of the phrase were Sir Robert Harley and Sir Anthony Irby, both of whom may be presumed to be supporters of Holles and Stapleton at this time. Of the opposing tellers, Walter Long and Richard

16. *CJ*, III, 707–708; Lawrence Whitaker, "Diary of Proceedings in the House of Commons," BM, Add. MS. 31,116 [hereafter cited as Whitaker, "Diary," BM, Add. MS. 31,116], fol. 176b; Agostini to Doge, c. Nov. 25, 1644, *CSPV, 1643–1647*, p. 158.

17. PRO, 31/3/75, fol. 166a, b.

18. *The Letters and Journals of Robert Baillie*, ed. David Laing, 3 vols. (Edinburgh, 1841–1842) [hereafter cited as Baillie, *Letters*], II, 242, 243.

Knightley, the former may also be included among the moderates. No evidence exists as to the views of Holles and Stapleton, but if, in support of their embryonic alliance with the Scots they favored the inclusion of the clause, they were unable to carry their party with them.[19]

Disputes over the finer points of liturgy faded into the background during December 1644. They were abruptly pushed to one side by the renewal of the bitter struggle for control of the parliamentary armies. The conspiracy issue was revived on October 21 when a Colonel John Dalbier, who was being held by the Commons in connection with the plot, was sent for by the Earl of Essex. The matter was referred to the army committee under Zouch Tate who appears to have made an unfavorable report to the Commons on Dalbier. A fierce debate followed. The charges against Dalbier were "abundantly answered" by Stapleton, Holles, Sir John Clotworthy, and Sir Gilbert Gerard, but "divers [were] very violent on the contrary."[20] The waning prestige of the Earl of Essex can be seen in the small numbers that Holles and Stapleton could summon to their support. In a division they could count but a pitiful seventeen against forty-nine for Vane.[21]

Essex was not the only target of the radicals. Throughout 1644 something like a systematic campaign was carried on against a number of moderate commanders, and, in their attacks on officers like the Earl of Denbigh and Coloney Edward Massey, the radicals made effective use of the county committees.

In June 1643 Denbigh, the remainder of whose family was royalist, was given command of the parliamentary forces in the Midlands. He began operations in the spring of 1644, and from the first he met dogged opposition from the parliamentary committee of Coventry, which was headed by three well-known radicals, William Purefoy, Haselrig, and Sir William Brereton, the substantial knight for Cheshire. Purefoy, a well-to-do member for Warwick and a republican of long standing, was Denbigh's leading antagonist. In 1649 he was to sit on the High Court of Justice and was a signer of the King's death warrant.[22] He accused Denbigh of disaffection from the parliamentary cause, and the bitter quarrel came to a head on the floor of the House in November 1644. The Commons divided along the usual party lines.

When the joint committee of Lords and Commons, to whom the issue had been referred, decided in favor of Denbigh, there was an

19. *CJ*, III, 705.
20. D'Ewes, "Journal," BM, Harl. 166, fol. 154a.
21. *CJ*, III, 672.
22. *Dictionary of National Biography*, ed. Leslie Stephen and Sidney Lee, 22 vols. (Oxford, 1908–1909) [hereafter cited as *DNB*], XLVII, 47. See also Keeler, *Long Parliament*, pp. 165, 316.

immediate reaction from the radicals. William Strode was soon on his feet protesting "very impudently" that the Commons should never have referred the matter to a joint committee, adding what D'Ewes called "some more unsavoury stuff." In the debate that followed, St. John gave the impression that it would be some time before the issue would be put to the question. But after about twenty of the moderates had gone out to dinner (thinking of "their bellies," according to the outraged D'Ewes), St. John shortened the report and abruptly called for the question. By a vote of forty-eight to thirty-three the House decided that Denbigh was not clear of disaffection from the cause,[23] and a fortnight later, on November 20, he was relieved of his command. During the negotiations at Uxbridge he did not hesitate to unburden himself to Clarendon, telling him that he had "a full prospect of the vile condition himself and all the nobility should be reduced to" if the Vane-St. John group were to win control of the country.

Colonel Edward Massey had a somewhat similar experience with the county committee of Gloucestershire. In mid-October 1644 he complained of his ill usage by some of the members of that committee and accused them of making "false and scandalous complaints against me to the Parliament." The matter was aired in a conference between the Houses, where Massey found support from Lord Grey of Warke and the Earl of Pembroke. Thomas Pury, a prosperous solicitor and member for Gloucester and one of the more active radicals, was described by Massey as the "pole star" of the committee, whose "passions, envy and malice" were beyond all reason.[24] Luke saw a general pattern in this behavior and declared that "the committees in all places opposing themselves to the Governors who are so discontented, that they are either retired from those charges or little useful there." Gilbert Millington was reported to have performed the same kind of service for the radicals in the committee of Nottingham.[25]

But these quarrels were mere skirmishes compared to the conflict that came to a head about the same time between the Earl of Man-

---

23. *CJ*, III, 700. In a series of divisions, the pro-Denbigh tellers were Stapleton, Simon Thelwall, Sir John Potts, Reynolds, Sir William Strickland, and Henry Darley. The anti-Denbigh tellers were Strode, Vane, Sir Peter Wentworth, William Heveningham, Henry Heyman, and Sir R. Pye. (*Ibid.*)

24. Massey to the committee of both kingdoms, Oct. 11, 1644, *Calendar of State Papers, Domestic Series, 1603–1704*, 81 vols. (1857–1947+) [hereafter cited as *CSPD*], *1644–1645*, p. 31; Massey to Sir Samuel Luke, Nov. 6, 1644, BM, Stowe MS. 190, fol. 54a; Keeler, *Long Parliament*, pp. 316–317; Massey to the committee of both kingdoms, Nov. 11, 1644, *CSPD, 1644–1645*, p. 113.

25. Sir Samuel Luke to the Earl of Essex, Oct. 18, 1644, BM, Stowe MS. 190, fol. 32a.

chester and his subordinate, Oliver Cromwell. This dispute was transferred to the floor of the House on November 22 when Cromwell and Sir William Waller took their seats. According to D'Ewes, they were "not much welcomed" by the House, but Lenthall had accommodatingly paved the way for their appearance by his motion "to have to know what our armies had done and how they should move."[26] Three days later Cromwell and Waller made their reports. Both accused Manchester of unwillingness to engage the King's forces. Cromwell was opposed by George Montague, Manchester's half brother and one of the youngest members of the House.[27] Many members spoke in the debate, notably Tate, who, in support of Cromwell, "moved to proceed to vote upon suspicion . . ." The matter was finally referred to Tate's committee, although some members wished it to be handled by the committee of both kingdoms.

The underlying causes of the Cromwell-Manchester quarrel were variously ascribed by observers to religion and politics. Agostini regarded the fact that Cromwell was an Independent and Manchester a Presbyterian as "the chief reason for their mutual dislike . . ."[28] Baillie saw the whole affair as part of the general party struggle for control of the army. It was, he said, a "plot of the Independent party to have gotten an army for themselves under Cromwell . . . of dissolving the union of the nations, of abolishing the House of Lords . . ."[29] Manchester himself emphasized the political and social nature of the split between himself and his restive subordinate. He accused Cromwell of an excessive hostility toward the nobility and quoted him as having declared "that he hoped to live to see never a Nobleman in England." He also claimed that Cromwell was not only contemptuous of the assembly of divines, but that he had said that "he could as soon draw his sword" against the Scots as against any in the King's army. The character of the New Model was foreshadowed by Manchester's charge that Cromwell had declared that he wanted no soldiers in Manchester's army "but such as were of the Independent judgment" because if any attempts were made to make peace "such as might not stand with those ends that honest men should aim at, this army might prevent such mischief."[30]

26. D'Ewes, "Journal," BM, Harl. 166, fol. 166a; Whitaker, "Diary," BM, Add. MS. 31,116, fol. 175b; *CJ*, III, 703.
27. Whitaker, "Diary," BM, Add. MS. 31,116, fols. 175b, 176a; Douglas Brunton and D. H. Pennington, *Members of the Long Parliament* (London, Allen & Unwin, 1954), p. 115.
28. Agostini to Doge, Nov. 29, 1644, *CSPV, 1643–1647*, p. 159.
29. Baillie to Spang, Dec. 6, 1644, Baillie, *Letters*, II, 246.
30. Earl of Manchester to the House of Lords, Dec. 4, 1644, *Camden Miscellany*, 22 vols. [London, 1847–1964], VIII, (e), 1–3.

One of Cromwell's strongest supporters in his quarrel with Manchester was his old friend Lieutenant Colonel John Lilburne. The connection between the two men was of long standing, dating back at least to Cromwell's first speech in the Long Parliament in the autumn of 1640. At that time he had demanded Lilburne's release from prison where he had lain since his trial of strength with the Star Chamber in 1638. Lilburne was fond of recalling this act of Cromwell's which he described as having been engraved on his heart "as with the point of a diamond."[31]

In the first years of the Revolution the parliamentary radicals had continued to be on excellent terms with Lilburne and his friends in the London area. On May 4, 1641, they had led the way in persuading the Commons to declare Lilburne's imprisonment to have been tyrannical and illegal.[32] Later that year, during the crisis arising from the Irish rebellion and the Grand Remonstrance, Lilburne had reciprocated by helping to organize the large-scale demonstration of seamen and apprentices that culminated in the King's flight from London in January 1642. Again in July 1643, when parliamentary fortunes were at a low ebb and the "peace party" threatened to gain the upper hand, Lilburne's associates were called in to redress the balance.[33] Early in 1644 Lilburne had joined Cromwell in his attack on Colonel Edward King, whom both regarded as incompetent if not traitorous.

Lilburne's collision with Manchester himself was due to his own characteristic excess of zeal. Encouraged by Henry Ireton (Cromwell's future son-in-law) but against Manchester's express orders, Lilburne had ordered an assault on Tickhill Castle and had succeeded in capturing it. The enraged Manchester had threatened to hang Lilburne for his pains, and Lilburne, as a result, was only too eager to appear as one of Cromwell's star witnesses against Manchester.[34]

Like the other conflicts over the army, the dispute took on the character of a struggle between the two parties in the Commons, with the Lords throwing their weight into the balance on the side of the moderates. It was Holles who reported Manchester's countercharges against Cromwell. The radicals immediately claimed that the Lords

31. John Lilburne, *Jonah's Cry out of the Whale's Belly* (London, 1647), BM, E.400(5), p. 2.

32. John Lilburne, *The Resolved Man's Resolution* (London, 1647), BM, E.387(4), p. 9.

33. *A Key to the Cabinet of the Parliament*, BM, E.449(2), p. 5; William Walwyn, *A Whisper in the Ear of Mr. Thomas Edwards* (London, 1646), BM, E.328(2), p. 4.

34. *CSPD, 1644–1645*, pp. 148–149, 151–152; John Lilburne, *The Just Man's Justification* (London, 1647), BM, E.407(26), pp. 26–27; Lilburne to Cromwell, July 1, 1647, BM, E.400(5), p. 9; John Lilburne, *England's Weeping Spectacle* (London, 1647), BM, E.450(7), p. 5.

had breached the Commons' privilege, and Cromwell himself gave a "very large answer" in the House and appears to have won considerable support.[35]

It was at this point that an abortive project to checkmate the radicals was hatched by the Scots and the moderate leaders. Essex, Holles, Stapleton, Whitelocke, and some others met Loudon and the Scottish commissioners on the night of December 3. But their plan to charge Cromwell with acting as an incendiary was, after some discussion, rejected as impracticable, and the sway of the radicals continued unchecked.[36]

Vane and Cromwell were now ready for the stroke that was to give them ultimate control of the army, with all the consequences for the future course of the Puritan Revolution that the step implied. This was the famous Self-Denying Ordinance, by which all members of both Houses were to give up their military and civil commands. It was, superficially, an evenhanded measure from which neither party would gain since it would affect radicals like Cromwell as well as moderates like Essex. But the fact was that most of the commanders were supporters of the moderates. Both Holles and Stapleton had served actively, and Stapleton had actually been in the field with Essex in the summer of 1644. The radicals, however, still retained the initiative in the Commons, and since most of Cromwell's officers were radical supporters, there would be no difficulty in replacing the ousted commanders with the friends of "honest" men.

The decision to proceed with the ordinance had not been taken suddenly, but was foreshadowed by one of those convenient petitions from the radical groups in London, which Vane and St. John appear to have used as "trial balloons." A "seditious petition" (D'Ewes' description) was presented to the House on October 28, 1644, in which the House was thanked for a vote passed apparently some time before, "for the taking away of the offices both military and civil of the members of both Houses . . ."[37] The petitioners also urged new elections to the House to replace those members expelled as royalists, a policy

35. Whitaker, "Diary," BM, Add. MS. 31,116, fol. 178a; Agostini to Doge, Dec. 6, 1644, *CSPV, 1643–1647*, pp. 161–162.

36. The Committee of Estates at Edinburgh supported the move against Cromwell on the grounds of his "contempt for the . . . [crown?] of England whose just privileges we are sworn to maintain" and his alleged determination to have only Independents in Manchester's army in order that "they might be able to prevent . . . such a [peace] as might not stand with their ends." (Committee of Estates to commissioners at London, Dec. 17, 1644, *Correspondence of the Scottish Commissioners in London, 1644–1646*, ed. H. W. Meikle [London, Roxburghe Club, 1917], p. 52.)

37. D'Ewes, "Journal," BM, Harl. 166, fol. 151a; Whitaker, "Diary," BM, Add. MS. 31,116, fol. 170a.

that had been recommended by the radical Lisle about two weeks previously and that was eventually to be implemented by the radicals in 1645. There was a significant difference of opinion in the House as to whether the petition should be accepted. The radicals won the division on the issue by seventy-one votes to forty-four, with Tate being one of the tellers on the radical side. D'Ewes complained that "the violence of some transported them so far as to move to have public thanks given the petitioners, which the House did not yield unto."[38]

By December 9, 1644, the radicals were ready to make their move. Tate, chairman of the committee for the "purge" of the officers of the army of the Earl of Essex, was now chairman of the committee investigating the charges against Manchester and presented his report. He appears to have been content to declare merely that "the chief causes of our division are pride and covetousness." Tate was followed by Cromwell himself who urged his hearers to "deny themselves and their own private interests for the public good . . ." After some debate, Tate moved that no member of either House should "execute any office or command, military or civil . . ."[39] The motion was seconded by Vane.

Opinions on the significance of the Self-Denying Ordinance varied considerably. According to S. R. Gardiner, "those who wished to be rid of Cromwell were as ready to support it as those who wished to be rid of Manchester."[40] The implication is that it was not a party measure. Many contemporary observers would not have agreed with him. Whitelocke for one regarded it as disingenuous, to say the least. He told the House that the commanders who were to be dismissed would not be offended if it was done with honor. "But to do a business of this nature . . . by a side wind, is . . . not . . . becoming your honour . . ." The debate on the question lasted all night until, "envy and self ends prevailing," the ordinance passed. The Scot Alexander Henderson remarked on the following day that the "Secret and sudden contriving of it, is a matter of astonishment to many . . ." Whitelocke had no hesitation in calling it a partisan device of the radicals, some of whom had frankly admitted that Essex was the target. They opposed Essex, he thought, because he was too strong a supporter of "Monarchy and of Nobility . . . which they had a mind to alter." Agostini saw it as primarily aimed at Essex, while Salvetti, the Florentine ambassador, thought of it as the first step in a plan to abolish

38. D'Ewes, "Journal," BM, Harl. 166, fol. 151a; *CJ*, III, 680. Strode was the second teller for the radicals; Holles and Stapleton for the moderates. (*Ibid.*)

39. Whitaker, "Diary," BM, Add. MS. 31,116, fol. 178a; *CJ*, III, 718.

40. S. R. Gardiner, *History of the Great Civil War, 1642–1649*, 4 vols. (London, 1893) [hereafter cited as Gardiner, *GCW*], II, 90.

the House of Lords completely and "to reduce the whole government of the kingdom into the hands of the lower House and the people." Sabran regarded the ordinance as a blind to divert attention from the real aims of the radicals and characterized it as a most subtle artifice to place their supporters in positions of power.[41] The moderate group made various attempts to mitigate the effects of the ordinance. Sir John Potts's effort to impose the covenant on all army officers was rejected by the Commons on December 19. A more significant trial of strength took place two days later when the House divided on a motion to exempt the Earl of Essex from its terms. Both sides appear to have mustered close to their full strength for this historic vote, but, although Holles and Stapleton counted ninety-three supporters, their opponents numbered one hundred.[42] The division is a useful index of the relative strength of the two parties. Essex's rather dreary record as a military commander, and the unjustified suspicion of his loyalty, may have prompted ten to twenty uncommitted members to vote with the radicals. On the basis of this assumption, one may assume that the radicals would emerge with a voting strength of eighty to ninety members. The support for Essex is perhaps a slightly more accurate reflection of moderate strength. It is curious that the ordinance itself passed without a division of the House on December 19, 1644.

In the Lords Essex mustered enough strength to block the measure. The struggle reached its climax on January 13, 1645, when the Commons once again appeared en masse at the Lords' door and warned them that further delay would not only be "dangerous, but destructive to the Kingdom." The Lords had good reason to be nervous. Only a few weeks before the radicals had welcomed the petition of a group of Londoners who had pointedly proclaimed their loyalty to the Commons alone.[43] During the conflict over the ordinance, the Lords found that they had four "false brothers" in their midst, Northumberland, Nottingham, Saye, and Kent. Pembroke, angered by their failure to support Essex, is said to have remarked that he had not realized that they had "peasants" among them.

41. Bulstrode Whitelocke, "Annals," BM, Add. MS. 37,343 [hereafter cited as Whitelocke, "Annals," BM, Add. MS. 37,343], fols. 347a, 350a; Thomas Henderson to Robert Douglas, Dec. 10, 1644, Baillie, *Letters*, II, 486; Agostini to Doge, Dec. 13, 1644, *CSPV, 1643–1647*, p. 164; Salvetti to Gondi, London, Dec. 13, 1644, Salvetti Correspondence, Transcripts from archives at Florence of correspondence of Florentine ambassadors in England, 1616–1679, BM, Add. MS. 27,962L [hereafter cited as SC, BM, Add. MS. 27,962L], fol. 384a; Sabran to Brienne, Dec. 12, 1644, PRO, 31/3/75, fols. 240a, b, 241a.
42. *CJ*, III, 726.
43. Whitaker, "Diary," BM, Add. MS, 31,116, fol. 179a; Sabran to Brienne, Jan. 16, 1645, PRO, 31/3/75, fol. 420b.

Despite the internecine quarrels of Parliament, the general populace was cheered by the prospect of a peace conference. "Public joy" greeted the news of a possible end to hostilities.[44] But there was little in the behavior of the radicals to cheer those who wanted peace. The King's emissaries were received with studied and even insulting frigidity. In an age when the seating arrangements for visiting diplomats were regarded as highly significant, Parliament's representatives were seated on either side of a table while the royal envoys (one of whom was the King's cousin, the Duke of Richmond) were perched on a simple bench two yards from its lower end.[45] Despite the inauspicious beginning, it was agreed that a conference should be held, and the business of hammering out an agenda was begun. Sabran remained pessimistic about the outcome and felt that the parliamentarians had too much confidence in their military power to engage in any serious negotiations.[46]

While preparations were being made for the conference at Uxbridge, there was much intrigue behind the scenes. Sabran was particularly active and held a number of important talks with the Earl of Loudon. Loudon told Sabran that the Scots were willing to support the monarchy, which they felt to be in danger, on condition that the King would agree to abolish episcopacy. If Charles was willing to meet their demands on religion, he could expect to be restored in all his dignity with his revenue augmented. Even the return of the Queen was possible, "with more dignity and contentment for her and her dependents." Although previously skeptical about the possibility of such a concession from the King on religion, Sabran now began to regard it as a possibility. He reasoned that since episcopacy was not *de fide* for the English, Presbyterianism might be adopted without too much difficulty. The prospect of gains from the sale of bishops' lands, he thought, might also prove tempting to the Crown. He was perhaps unaware that these properties had already been earmarked by Parliament for payment for the Scottish "brotherly assistance."[47]

Further indications of Scottish disposition to support the King were provided by their conflicts with the radicals over the proposed conference agenda. The Scots demanded that religion be placed first, apparently intending, if the King proved conciliatory, to throw their support to him on Ireland and the militia. The radicals, reluctant to risk such an eventuality, pressed to have the Irish and militia questions

44. Sabran to Brienne, London, Dec. 12, 1644, PRO, 31/3/75, fols. 239, 240a.
45. Whitaker, "Diary," BM, Add. MS. 31,116, fol. 180a.
46. Sabran to Brienne, London, Dec. 19, 1644, PRO, 31/3/75, fol. 259a.
47. Sabran to Brienne, London, Jan. 30, 1645, PRO, 31/3/76, fol. 64a; Sabran to M. d'Avaux, London, Jan. 31, 1645, PRO, 31/3/76, fol. 74a.

placed first. They were aware that the Irish question involved the economic ambitions of powerful groups in the Commons and in London and that the King still looked to the Irish for potential military support. The control of the militia was, of course, the key to sovereignty and as such was the thorniest question of all. But although the Scots had their way and religion was discussed first, there was an immediate deadlock, which only became more rigid as the talks went on.[48]

The parliamentarians opened the proceedings with the flat demand that the King abolish episcopacy, take the covenant personally, and agree to the establishment of Presbyterianism. Neither party in the Commons was as enamored of Presbyterianism as this demand would indicate. The radical leaders favored its inclusion because they were confident that Charles would never consent to it. The moderates, on the other hand, were forced to support it because of their political dependence on the Scots. The Scottish *politiques* knew, in turn, that this was a necessity if they were to retain the support of the Kirk. But if the theological and political underpinning of the proposition was a bit loose, there was an economic aspect that was perhaps more real. In accordance with the agreement between Parliament and the Scots in 1643, the sale of bishops' lands had actually been made part of the parliamentary proposition on religion. The royalist commissioners objected at first that the resultant economic dislocation would cause many persons "to beg their bread . . ."[49] A few days later, however, they even appear to have been willing to sacrifice the bishops' lands in return for the retention of some form of episcopacy. This the Parliament rejected, and the first phase of the negotiations ended in deadlock.

In London, meanwhile, the Commons, still under radical control, were busily drafting bills for the abolition of bishops both in England and Ireland and for the confiscation of church lands in Ireland. Both measures were to be sent post-haste to Uxbridge for an increasingly doubtful royal assent.[50]

The negotiators returned to religion on February 13. Again the discussions were barren of any result. This was not, however, due to royalist intransigence. After observing that they failed to see that the alienation of bishops' lands was "necessary at all to the Reformation of religion," the King's representatives put forward a plan for a non-

---

48. Sabran to Brienne, London, Feb. 6, 1645, PRO, 31/3/76, fol. 76b; Sabran to Brienne, May 6, 1645, PRO, 31/3/76, fol. 112a, b.

49. John Rushworth, *Historical Collections*, 7 vols. (London, 1654–1701) [hereafter cited as Rushworth, *Hist.* Coll.], II, pt. iii, 868.

50. *CJ*, IV, 43; Whitaker, "Diary," BM, Add. MS. 31,116, fol. 191a.

coercive episcopacy, retention of the Book of Common Prayer, and freedom for all "in matters of ceremony."[51] The parliamentarians, unmoved, repeated their original demands. The King finally offered to call a national synod of divines that would include clergy from all the reformed churches of Europe to deliberate the question. This, too, met with no response, and the talks on religion dwindled to inconclusive bickerings on the historicity of the episcopal office.

A similar impasse took place over the vital question of the control of the militia. The parliamentary commissioners demanded no less than complete and permanent control of the armed forces by the two Houses of Parliament. The royalists countered with the suggestion that they be placed under a commission, half the members of which would be named by the King, half by Parliament. The proposal was rejected, the parliamentarians insisting on naming all the members of the proposed commission. They were willing, they said, to place a time limit of seven years on the tenure of such a body, but the royalists were aware that once the power of the sword was given up the decision was apt to be irreversible. They regarded Parliament's "concession" as more apparent than real.[52]

It was over the Irish question that animosity between the negotiators reached its height. Charles still hoped for help from the Irish and dared not appear to be abandoning them. The parliamentarians, on the other hand, had a vested interest in a Carthaginian peace and were determined tht the island should be completely at their disposal. "If he [the King] consent not to the suppressing of those rebels," wrote one parliamentary observer, "doubtless he frustrates all good intentions, and brings himself and all that side with him to ruin."[53] The parliamentarians were disarmingly frank about the financial interests involved; "several great sums of money were paid by particular persons and by corporations," they declared, and these interests had been endangered by the King's action in negotiating a "cessation" with the Irish in 1643. They demanded that this truce be disavowed and that the King agree to pass whatever bills they might submit to him for the reduction of Ireland.

This section of the treaty came to an end in an atmosphere made sulphurous by mutual charges of bad faith. Once more Charles was told that he had connived at the original Irish rebellion in 1641

51. Paper of the King's Commissioners, Rushworth, *Hist. Coll.*, II, pt. iii, 872–873.
52. *Ibid.*, 879–924.
53. H. Verney to Sir R. Verney, Feb. 13, 1645, Sir H. Verney Manuscripts, *Seventh Report of the Royal Commission on Historical Manuscripts, Part I, Report and Appendix* (London, H. M. Stationery Office, 1879), p. 450.

and had planned to bring an Irish army across the Irish Sea to fight in England. The King replied by accusing Parliament of converting a political rebellion into a war of religion by destroying the tacit toleration of Catholicism that had prevailed since the Reformation. Their threats "to eradicate the whole stock of the Irish," he declared, had forced the Catholic Anglo-Irish into an unwilling revolt and had made the rebellion a national war. As for the Irish Adventurer scheme, Charles, with some justice, characterized it as a device by which Parliament had been enabled "to raise a war in England." The parliamentarians angrily replied that there should be no peace "with such creatures as are not fit to live, no more than with wolves or tigers, or ravenous beasts." Apparently oblivious to any ironic overtones, they called upon the royalists "in the name of Him who is the Prince of Peace . . . give not your consent to this cessation of war in Ireland . . ." In return, the royalist commissioners dryly and rather provocatively observed that they wished it were in the King's power "to punish all rebellion with that severity that is due to it . . ."[54]

Before the conference ended the royalists attempted to extend the time limit, and although the suggestion was coldly received by the parliamentary commissioners, it seems to have had considerable support at Westminster. On February 22, 1645, the Commons extended their sitting into the afternoon "in expectation that some message might come for the continuance of the treaty."[55] The Lords went so far as to ask the Commons to agree to an extension of the treaty, and they might well have concurred had they not been interrupted by a letter from the Uxbridge commissioners in which, after complaining of the "little encouragement" they had received from the royalists, they announced the end of the treaty.[56] Both Houses, however, sat until nine P.M. "in expectation of some good news from Uxbridge." The end of the treaty, Whitelocke said, troubled "many honest men, lovers of their country's peace . . . , most sober men lamented the sudden breach of the treaty . . ." Richard Harman wrote that the course of the treaty "hath not been according to our hopes and expectations."[57] It seems clear that there was a much more conciliatory spirit at Westminster than in the radical-dominated delegation at Uxbridge.

Clarendon observed a deep division among the parliamentarians

54. Rushworth, *Hist. Coll.*, II, pt. iii, 863; Edward Hyde, Earl of Clarendon, *The History of the Rebellion and Civil Wars in England*, ed. W. D. Macray, 6 vols. (Oxford, 1888) [hereafter cited as Clarendon, *Rebellion*], III, 490.

55. Whitaker, "Diary," BM, Add. MS. 31,116, fol. 195a.

56. D'Ewes, "Journal," BM, Harl. 166, fol. 179b.

57. Whitelocke, "Annals," BM, Add. MS. 37,343, fol. 368b; Richard Harman to mayor of Norwich, Feb. 25, 1645, BM, Add. MS. 22,619, fol. 161a.

during the negotiations. In his eyes it was not Holles' group that was intransigent but the Vane-St. John faction "that would have no peace upon what conditions however, who did resolve to change the whole frame of the government, state as well as church . . ."[58] The Earl of Pembroke voiced the prevailing moderate opinion when he told Clarendon that if the radicals succeeded in breaking Essex "they would constitute such an army as should force the Parliament, as well as the King, to consent to whatsoever they demanded; which would end in the change of the government into that of a commonwealth."[59] The moderates, Clarendon thought, sincerely desired peace, but they lacked both courage and confidence in one another and could not bring themselves "to avow the receding from the most extravagant demands . . ."[60] They had agreed to the peace propositions, despite their extreme nature, because they had hoped to reach some accord at the actual conference. At Uxbridge they and the Scots clung to the illusory hope that, if the King would agree to the admittedly revolutionary terms of the radicals, the resultant peace would provide an opportunity for supporting him against the Vane-St. John party.

There appears to have been a significant amount of underhand negotiation between both parliamentary parties and the royalists. Holles and Whitelocke were in communication with the royalist Lord Lindsey, apparently with a view to convincing the royalists that the Scots were not completely intransigent on the subject of religion and that the King could expect to gain much support on his arrival in London. Holles may have argued that if the Scots relinquished the claim of Presbyterianism to be *jure divino,* any church government that Parliament might set up could be abolished, or at least modified by the same authority, thus leaving the door open for the restoration of some form of episcopacy. He may have suggested, too, that a continuation of the war could not but strengthen the hand of the radicals who were now in a position to win control of the army, while a settlement must almost certainly weaken them. These arguments were used more than once in the years ahead and to no better effect.

If a peace settlement would have been almost disastrous for Vane and St. John, another prospect was even less attractive: agreement between the King and their enemies. The fear of this eventuality may have prompted them to counter these moves by more realistic proposals of their own. On February 13, 1645, Sabran reported that both the Scots and the Independents were ready to join the party of the King, the former if he abolished the bishops and the latter if he re-

58. Clarendon, *Rebellion,* III, 492.
59. *Ibid.,* 494.
60. *Ibid.,* 492.

fused Presbyterianism, "such is the confusion of this Parliament and the uncertainty of events." Two weeks later he described the Independents as being attracted by the King's liberal religious policy.[61] We cannot know whether Sabran was referring to the religious sect or the political party in these remarks, but while we may doubt that the hardheaded leaders of the radical party would make such a political reversal on the sole grounds of toleration for tender consciences, there may have been, nevertheless, some dealings with the royalists that prefigured the secret negotiations that were to take place in the next two months.

Uxbridge had been a dismal failure. Englishmen on both sides had now to look forward to a renewal of the fratricidal struggle and a fight to the finish. Time was on the side of the parliamentarians, and the canalizing of their financial power into a reorganized army could not but tip the scales in their favor.

Why had the treaty failed? In the first place, the radical leaders who directed affairs wanted it to fail. The peace propositions at Uxbridge were, from the outset, framed and pushed through Parliament by the Vane-St. John party. After the parliamentary defeats suffered by Essex and the moderates in December 1644, the balance of power swung even more heavily to the radicals. Holles and Whitelocke were the only moderates in the Commons' delegation at Uxbridge, and Whitelocke was at best a weak reed. In any case, Vane and St. John kept a close watch on the remainder of the group.[62] Parliamentary policy at Uxbridge was, outwardly at least, only a continuation of what had been radical policy all through 1644.

Perhaps no moves on the part of the King could have made the negotiations succeed. It seems certain, however, that Charles might have made much more of the support that was offered him by Holles and the Scots. But Charles shared his father's deep detestation of Presbyterianism and of those saucy leaders of the Scottish Kirk who had once coolly informed James that he was no more than "God's silly vassal." Like James, he regarded their creed as inimical to monarchy. He seems, however, to have been insufficiently aware that the parliamentary moderates and the Scots like Loudon actually regarded themselves as defenders of the monarchy against a party that they— and not they alone—regarded as extremely hostile to Charles, if not to monarchy itself. Loudon's insistence on Presbyterianism was not so much a reflection of personal enthusiasm as a measure of the strength and influence of the Scottish Kirk. Publicly to relax the demand for

61. Sabran to Brienne, London, Feb. 13, 1645, PRO, 31/3/76, fol. 84a, b; Sabran to Brienne, Feb. 27, 1645, PRO, 31/3/76, fol. 104a, b.
62. Clarendon, *Rebellion*, III, 492.

thoroughgoing Presbyterianism was, for him, a political impossibility. The parliamentary moderates were virtually powerless without the support of the Scots, whose army was to become a makeweight against the New Model.

Charles's hopes for a religious rapprochement with the radicals tended to blind him to the implications of their political attitudes: "he thought nothing more impossible than that the English nation should submit to any other than monarchic government."[63] At the same time, Loudon and the moderates discovered that their demand for Presbyterianism had, in the King's mind, completely obscured the value of their political support. Their chagrin is reflected in Loudon's behavior after Clarendon had somewhat summarily rejected his offers. At that time, Clarendon recalled, "there was more contradiction" between himself and Loudon ". . . than between any other of the body of commissioners." Holles, too, was disappointed and pessimistic about the future. He foresaw a gradual weakening of his party and was described by Clarendon as predicting that "many of those who appeared most resolute to concur with him would by degrees, fall from him purely for want of courage, in which he [Holles] abounded."[64]

One of the last proposals made by the royalist commissioners was that there should be a general disbanding of the armies on both sides and a return of the expelled members to Parliament. Charles would then go in person to London to negotiate. The proposal fell on deaf ears. The radicals were well aware of their minority status, and not at all certain of London. Sabran commented that they also feared that it would be impossible to persuade men to resort to arms once they were laid down. In any case, the Vane-St. John group was now poised to consolidate their power in the New Model army, and against this formidable body neither the royalists, nor the moderates, nor indeed many of the radicals themselves would be able to prevail.

63. *Ibid.*
64. *Ibid.*

IV] The Saville Affair

Despite the overweening self-confidence displayed by the radical leaders at Uxbridge, the spring of 1645 was, for them, extremely uneasy and critical. June would bring the great victory of Naseby, which was to be a radical as well as a parliamentary triumph. They demonstrated, meanwhile, a distinct disposition to hedge their bets. They had good reason to be cautious. Relations with the Scots continued to deteriorate; the London merchants, despite the floating of an £80,000 loan, were increasingly open in their sympathy for the Holles group, and serious unrest in the counties culminated in an antiparliamentary rising in Kent. Although the second Self-Denying Ordinance virtually eliminated the influence of the moderates in the New Model, internal dissension plagued that force down to Naseby itself. The radicals must also have been aware that their parliamentary position was potentially a minority one. They also knew that a single great battle could still decide the issue of the war. Such considerations can be assumed to have prompted them to carry on secret negotiations with the King designed to guarantee their future security.

But while they put out feelers to the royalists, they were not deflected from their main objectives, the chief of which was the winning of complete control of the parliamentary armed forces. Even while the Uxbridge negotiations dragged on to their predetermined end, the work of reorganizing the army continued, and in the stormy debates that accompanied the changes Cromwell was an effective substitute for Vane and St. John.

The soldiers themselves were by no means unanimously in favor of the proposed changes that they knew had political as well as military objectives. Unrest among the officers and men of the forces under Essex and Manchester was soon evident, and petitions from concerned officers appeared as early as January 1645. By mid-February Waller was reporting insubordination in his army arising from "the discontents among the soldiery because their General Essex was laid aside . . . "[1] Three of Essex's old regiments, now under Waller's command, had

---

1. Bulstrode Whitelocke, "Annals," BM, Add. MS. 37,343 [hereafter cited as Whitelocke, "Annals," BM, Add. MS. 37,343], fol. 365a.

refused to march, and two troops of his horse had mutinied and had "snatched the colors from the Cornet . . . crying 'an Essex, an Essex!' "[2]

The appointment of Sir Thomas Fairfax as the New Model's commander was debated on January 21, 1645. Tate, still a key figure in the radicals' moves and chairman of the committee appointed to consider the slate of officers, presented the new list. After a "long debate" the radicals won a decisive victory with Vane and Cromwell counting 101 votes for Fairfax as against 69 mustered by Holles and Stapleton.[3]

John Pyne, M.P. for Poole, was enthusiastic about the radicals' plans for "our New Modell." There were, of course, obstacles: "the Great one [Essex?] looks big and black, and obstructs all good motions from us," he wrote, "but I hope to see him and his accomplices laid aside."[4] Pyne also noted that the Scots had joined "in a seeming confederacy . . . with Sir Philip Stapleton and his associates: viz., Holles, the Recorder [Glyn], Clotworthy, Reynolds, Whitelocke, Maynard, etc., and the Lords."[5]

The moderates, now fighting a delaying action, gained a minor victory on February 7, 1645, when they won an amendment that had the effect of giving either House a veto on the appointment of senior officers. In the division they were victorious by eighty-two votes to sixty-three for their opponents.[6] Religion was now to be pressed into the service of politics. The moderates, obviously hoping that the religious scruples of some of the Independents on the list might be used to eliminate them, pressed vigorously for the imposition of the covenant on both officers and men. The radicals strongly opposed the measure, but after an all-day debate the moderates, probably strengthened by a temporary defection of some religious Presbyterians from the radical ranks, obtained a resolution to the effect that all officers should take the covenant within twenty days of being commissioned. One overoptimistic moderate regarded it as the equivalent of voting the Independents "out of the New Model, or any part of the Army to be raised . . . "[7]

The balance of power in the House fluctuated between the contending factions. The radicals succeeded in voting down a proviso of the Lords that would have excluded commanders who refused the covenant, but two days later the moderates won an amendment that pre-

2. Sir Symonds D'Ewes, "Journal of the Parliament begun November, 1640," BM, Harleian 166 [hereafter cited as D'Ewes, "Journal," BM, Harl. 166], fol. 177b.

3. Lawrence Whitaker, "Diary of Proceedings in the House of Commons," BM, Add. MS. 31,116 [hereafter cited as Whitaker, "Diary," BM, Add. MS. 31,116], fol. 188a; *Journals of the House of Commons* [hereafter cited as *CJ*], IV, 26.

4. John Pyne to Colonel Popham, Feb. 3, 1645, *Mercurius Aulicus* [hereafter cited as *Merc. Aul.*], Feb. 27, 1645, BM, Burney Collection, 14, p. 1391.

5. *Ibid.*, p. 1392.

6. *CJ*, IV, 43.

7. "Wen: Oxford" to Sir S. Luke, Feb. 8, 1645, BM, Stowe MS. 190, fol. 11a.

vented all officers from assuming command until they had in fact taken the oath. The "Violent began to speak very highly on this," noted D'Ewes, but they were, perhaps, not as disturbed as they appeared to be and were doubtless pleased to see the Lords pass the ordinance for the New Model even with those reservations. Sir Samuel Luke was probably right when he wrote that "few of them will stick at the Covenant, so long as they may be their own interpreters."[8] The Independents in the House had been powerful enough to prevent the expulsion of their army commanders, but they were not able to persuade the Commons to tender the customary thanks to the Reverend Messrs. John Maynard and Nye who had delivered a strongly Independent sermon to the members.[9] On the other hand, a Scottish observer wrote a few days later that "the Independent faction [is] strong and like to do much, if God in his wisdom did not prevent it."[10]

At the conclusion of the Treaty of Uxbridge, Vane and St. John returned, and the radicals pressed for reform of the army with renewed vigor. Once again there was party division over the selection of officers. The debate on the preaching colonel, John Pickering, a brother of the radical-minded Sir Gilbert Pickering, "grew so hot . . . the time being far gone" that it had to be postponed. There were a number of divisions over these appointments, the significance of which is difficult to assess. After the failure of Uxbridge, attendance declined considerably, and both parties were far below the strength of the previous year. But in most instances a split along party lines is clearly discernible. The case of Colonel Nathaniel Rich caused "much debate." D'Ewes's opposition to Rich aroused some prominent radicals like Haselrig to "wanton" and "violent" language.[11] Rich had been a member of Essex's life guard and was to be an active Cromwellian until 1655 when he was imprisoned as a Fifth Monarchy Man.[12]

The Lords were aware of the dangers inherent in an army led by the friends and followers of Vane and Cromwell. They returned the list of officers to the Commons on March 10, 1645, having refused to approve of Colonels Edward Montague, John Pickering, and Thomas Rainsborough. Montague was to be a future member of Cromwell's Council of State and a leading figure in the period of the Protectorate. Rainsborough was of an extremely radical bent and was eventually to rival Cromwell himself for the leadership of the New Model. D'Ewes,

8. Sir S. Luke to Sir O. Luke, Feb. 12, 1645, *ibid.*, fol. 218a.
9. D'Ewes, "Journal," BM, Harl. 166, fol. 180a.
10. Correspondence of Sir Charles Erskine, 1644–1647, *Historical Manuscripts Commission, Fourth Report,* Mrs. Erskine-Murray Manuscripts, p. 522.
11. D'Ewes, "Journal," BM, Harl. 166, fols. 180b, 181a.
12. *Dictionary of National Biography,* ed. Leslie Stephen and Sidney Lee, 22 vols. (Oxford, 1908–1909) [hereafter cited as *DNB*], XVI, 1005–1006.

obviously in agreement with the upper house, recorded that the Lords had struck out the names of many other "young and little experienced commanders and named others in their stead . . . who were able and well experienced." The radicals were unbending. The Lords were not "to dispute them but to approve them . . . debate . . . would take up longer time than we could spare . . . " The Commons refused to agree to any of the Lords' alterations: "as it were, condemning the Lords . . . "[13] Finally, the delicate balance in the Lords was upset by Lord North's defection to the radical side, after which approval of the entire slate of officers followed swiftly. The radicals, assured now of control of the army, were not above a little mockery. In a needling message to the Lords the Commons sanctimoniously denied "that scandalous report that had been laid upon us, that we intended to attempt the taking away of the Peerage."[14] D'Ewes regarded the message as "cleanly sarcasm put on the Lords to yield thus at last . . . "[15]

Having broken the main core of resistance in both Houses, the radicals seemed determined to push their opponents to the wall. Their mood was exemplified by a change in the wording of Fairfax's commission, in which the customary clause safeguarding the actual person of the monarch was significantly omitted. The dispirited moderates in the Commons appear to have put up little opposition to the change, but the Lords were more stubborn. St. John decided to apply the old technique of mass pressure and on March 31 moved that the whole House accompany him with the message to the Lords.[16] Denbigh and Essex led a last-ditch fight in defense of their commands and "spoke gallantly and freely" against the radicals. Despite their best efforts, however, they were defeated when Bolingbroke, "pretending to be satisfied . . . altered his opinion . . . leaving the Earl of Essex party: and so the Lords yielded."[17]

The radicals now proceeded to clinch their victory by ramming through the second Self-Denying Ordinance. The Lords, apparently completely cowed, returned it to the Commons on April 4, 1645, having passed it without altering a word. The radical triumph was complete. Unlike the first ordinance, which had been thrown out by the Lords, the second did not prohibit the reemployment of members and was thus a broom to sweep Essex and his friends out of command but was not a barrier to the reemployment of his enemies.

13. D'Ewes, "Journal," BM, Harl. 166, fols. 183a, 184b.

14. Whitaker, "Diary," BM, Add. MS. 31,116, fol. 199b; Whitelocke, "Annals," BM, Add. MS. 37,343, fol. 375a; CJ, IV, 88.

15. D'Ewes, "Journal," BM, Harl. 166, fol. 193a.

16. Ibid., fol. 196a; Whitaker, "Diary," BM, Add. MS. 31,116, fol. 201b; CJ, IV, 94.

17. D'Ewes, "Journal," BM, Harl. 166, fols. 196b, 197a; CJ, IV, 95.

The failure of the moderates to put up more effective resistance to the radicals over these vital issues was probably due in part to their demoralization in the face of the King's rejection of their offers of support at Uxbridge. They were now more than ever eager to cement relations with their newfound allies. The Scots, for their part, bitterly resented the abrupt dismissal of numbers of Scottish professional officers who had joined the parliamentary armies as far back as 1642. What rankled even more deeply was the fact that they had been replaced by persons "not zealous to the reformation and uniformity of religion between the Kingdoms . . . "[18] They expressed their indignation to Parliament on March 3, 1645. The radicals, led by Vane, Prideaux, and William Strode, promptly claimed that their complaint was a breach of privilege, and the dispute gave rise to the first recorded instance of cooperation between the Holles party and the Scots on what could be called a politico-religious issue. Holles, Stapleton, and Glyn were moderate spokesmen, and were "for the paper and [tried] to justify it . . . "[19]

After this brief show of resistance, both the Scots and the moderates in the Commons tended to wilt; it may be that this was due, as Clarendon said, to the intervention of that strong Scottish ally of the English radicals, Archibald Campbell, Marquis of Argyle, who had just suffered a humiliating defeat at the hands of Montrose, at Inverlochy. According to Clarendon, Argyle arrived in London during the disputes over the New Model, and "from the time of his coming to the town, the Scots commissioners were less vehement in obstructing the ordinance for the new modelling the army . . . "[20] If Argyle did come to London, it is probable that such was his course of action, but there is no independent corroboration of Clarendon's statement. It is certain that many of the Scots in Edinburgh keenly resented the action of the radicals. As late as April 2, 1645, the Committee of Estates at Edinburgh was still writing angrily about the dismissal of the Scottish officers and their replacement by "men of less skill and experience, reputed to be of those who are called Independents . . . "[21]

The radicals owed something to London's support in the conflict over New Model officers. The London merchants were described as

18. Scottish commissioners to Committee of Estates, Mar. 22, 1645, *Correspondence of the Scottish Commissioners in London, 1644–1646*, ed. H. W. Meikle (London, Roxburghe Club, 1917), p. 64; *Journals of the House of Lords, 1578–1714* (1767+) [hereafter cited as *LJ*], VII, 261–262.

19. D'Ewes, "Journal," BM, Harl. 166, fol. 181b.

20. Edward Hyde, Earl of Clarendon, *The History of the Rebellion and Civil Wars in England*, ed. W. D. Macray, 6 vols. (Oxford, 1888) [hereafter cited as Clarendon, *Rebellion*], IV, 4–5.

21. Meikle, *Correspondence*, p. 71.

"ready to bring in money in case the list passed, or to offer their obedience, though the Lords dissented."[22] The desultory resistance of some of the Scots, the dwindling Commons moderates, and a handful of Lords could scarcely counterbalance the influence of London finance upon which the parliamentarians had relied so heavily from the earliest days of the Civil War.

Now that victory on the vital issue was assured, the radicals could afford to be magnanimous. Moreover, it was spring, and the campaigning season was at hand. All signs pointed to another great and decisive clash of the armies. It was important that at least a temporary closing of the ranks be effected. From April to early June 1645 the disposition to apply balm to old wounds and to distribute rewards for services rendered was very much in evidence; the Committee for Sequestrations, whose task it was to seek out and confiscate the income of royalist estates, usually rewarded informers with a certain percentage of the amount seized and was thus a convenient agency for the purpose.

Lord Willoughby of Parham, so long the *bête noire* of the radicals, was in early April voted half of all "Moneys as shall be discovered" by him.[23] Two weeks later the arrears owed to the Earl of Nottingham were ordered paid, and a committee formed to consider a scheme—implemented in early June—for regular pay for members of the House of Commons.[24] Colonel Edward Massey, who only a few months before had been a favorite target of the radical members on the Gloucestershire committee, was voted the "use, advantage and benefit" of the ironworks and mills formerly owned by Sir John Wyntor. A short time later, probably as a sop to the moderates, he was made commander in chief of the forces of the Western Association.[25]

The provision of further largess was foreshadowed by the preparation of an ordinance for the sale of royalist estates, and on May 20, 1645, the smarting Earl of Essex was voted £1,000 per annum as well as £4,310 back pay. Lord Grey of Groby was granted the "Two Assessments . . . discovered by him to the Committee at Haberdasher's Hall . . . " Lionel Copley, an old officer in Essex's army, had long been in prison on various charges pressed by the radicals. Such was the change in the political climate that, after some pressure by Holles, Stapleton, and Sir William Lewis, Copley was suddenly released on bail.[26]

The closing of ranks was perhaps partly occasioned by a growing

22. E. Bowles to Lord Fairfax, Mar. 18, 1645, *Memorials of the Civil War; correspondence of the Fairfax family*, ed. R. Bell, 2 vols. (London, 1849), I, 168.
23. *CJ*, IV, 101.
24. *Ibid.*, 115, 161–162.
25. *Ibid.*, 128, 145.
26. *Ibid.*, 146, 148, 166; Whitaker, "Diary," BM, Add. MS. 31,116, fol. 211a.

awareness of unrest in those counties which had been controlled by Parliament from the outset, and upon which they had tended to rely heavily for money and manpower. The unwelcome news of a revolt in Kent came to London on April 14, 1645. The rising was directed in the main against the unpopular county committee. Sir Thomas Walsingham, member for Rochester, urged that martial law be declared. On the following day the House was further jolted by the report of an insurrection in Westmoreland,[27] and a month later three members, headed by the minatory Miles Corbet, journeyed to Cambridge to investigate an alleged plot for betraying the Isle of Ely.[28]

Vigorous action was taken against the dissident elements. Roger Hill and John Lisle, two prominent radicals, were instructed to bring in an ordinance for martial law for Kent, under which a special court, empowered to execute anti-Parliament rebels, was to be set up.[29] But all members did not approve of such methods. John Maynard, an active moderate, protested against the mode of trial, which, he said, was one "to hang men before any articles are made."[30] Despite such protests, the Commons, on June 5, passed an ordinance for martial law in Kent.

With the summer campaigning season at hand, the Commons were increasingly disturbed by reports of mass desertions from the New Model. "Our pressed men run away to the king as fast as they are pressed," Walter Yonge had complained in late April, and at Robert Scawen's urging, the Commons had ordered all ranks to repair to the colors on pain of cashiering for the officers and "death without mercy" for the soldiers.[31] Scawen also began work on an ordinance for the punishment of deserters by martial law in all counties. This ordinance, however, was opposed vigorously by Vane and others and was finally defeated by a vote of sixty two to thirty five.[32] By early June a conscription ordinance was before Parliament. Once again there were vigorous protests, particularly against the clause in the measure that provided that such service could be avoided on the payment of £10. D'Ewes, in one of his more democratic moments, protested that "the burden would lie upon the poorer sort" and, recalling protests against such practices on the part of the Crown during the Bishops' Wars, urged that Parliament not be guilty of "the same oppression which we

27. Whitelocke, "Annals," BM, Add. MS. 37,343, fol. 379a.
28. Whitaker, "Diary," BM, Add. MS. 31,116, fol. 205a.
29. CJ, IV, 114.
30. Walter Yonge, "Journal of Proceedings in the House of Commons," BM, Add. MS. 18,780 [hereafter cited as Yonge, "Journal," BM, Add. MS. 18,780], fol. 6a.
31. D'Ewes, "Journal," BM, Harl. 166, fols. 205b, 206a; CJ, IV, 126; Yonge, "Journal," BM, Add. MS. 18,780, fol. 7b.
32. CJ, IV, 135; D'Ewes, "Journal," BM, Harl. 166, fol. 207b.

had formerly so unanimously condemned." The ordinance passed without a division. The atmosphere of crisis was such that even the loyalty of the counties of the Eastern Association was suspect. On the motion of Colonel Valentine Walton and Corbet, an ordinance for martial law in that region was introduced, despite the protests of members from the area like D'Ewes.[33] Prideaux had, a week before, brought in a similar measure for the city of Plymouth.

A kind of miasma of fear and uncertainty prevailed in the Parliament at this time and was accentuated by the loss of Leicester to the royalists on May 31, 1645, which may explain in some measure the willingness of the moderates to accept Cromwell as the commander of the horse in the New Model. As they had on other critical occasions, the radicals once again received important backing from their supporters in London. John Fowke led a group of aldermen and Common Councillors to the House on June 4 with a well-timed petition asking that Cromwell be made commander in chief of the associated counties. Many of the moderates protested that the petition was a breach of privilege, but after a "hot and long debate" the moderates gave way because, according to D'Ewes, "affairs of the parliament were now in doubtful condition . . . "[34] Six days later the House agreed without a division that Cromwell should command the horse, and the long struggle for control of the army had thus ended in a complete radical victory. The Scots, who had opposed Cromwell's reemployment, were greatly angered by the appointment and were now determined not to join their army with that of Fairfax.[35]

The radicals, acutely aware of the continued need for Scottish support, had actually gone to considerable lengths to please the Scots on the religious question in the hope that Leslie's army could still be counted on in what promised to be a decisive summer campaign. The Scots, in turn, had bluntly warned that if Parliament continued its dilatory, Erastian attitude toward the establishment of religious uniformity no such assistance would be forthcoming. On April 14, 1645, they had pointed out that progress toward Presbyterianism would result in a "nearer union" between the two kingdoms and that, as a result, they would be "more encouraged to assist [the Parliament]."[36]

They were not to be disappointed. During the next two months, in

33. D'Ewes, "Journal," BM, Harl. 166, fol. 216a, b.
34. *Ibid.*; R. R. Sharpe, *London and the Kingdom*, 3 vols. (London, 1894–1895), II, 218.
35. D'Ewes, "Journal," BM, Harl. 166, fol. 216a, b; *CJ*, IV, 169–170; Instructions from the Scottish commissioners to William Thomson, May 14, 1645, Meikle, *Correspondence*, p. 74; Sabran to Brienne, London, June 12, 1645, PRO, 31/3/77, fol. 75b.
36. D'Ewes, "Journal," BM, Harl. 166, fol. 201a.

spite of the continued dominance of the Vane-St. John party, the Commons displayed a remarkably Presbyterian spirit. Three days after the receipt of the Scottish message, the Commons had voted to implement the directory of worship as well as to abolish the Book of Common Prayer.[37] The radicals were apparently even willing to put a damper on some of their more enthusiastic followers. When it was reported to the House that the preaching of the Independent Colonel Pickering had caused "tumults," the Commons had agreed to forbid unauthorized preaching and requested Fairfax to report further infractions.[38]

It is true, on the other hand, that the ministers, in spite of the determined advocacy of one leading radical, Prideaux, had not been able to secure the right to excommunicate persons for matters of "scandal." After a long debate the House had adhered to their accustomed Erastian position and had voted that the eldership could suspend only such persons as had been "lawfully convicted."[39]

By May 1645, however, the armies were taking the field, and Erastian and Independent alike became suddenly more willing to bow to the Presbyterian will. Baillie, who had previously been rather pessimistic about the chances of establishing Presbyterianism in England, now became quite the opposite. The directory of worship, he exulted, was so far from being "cried down, as fools say . . . that there is an ordinance . . . of that severity . . . that . . . few shall dare to condemn, either that whole book, or any part of it." The strongly Presbyterian ministers of London, he wrote, had advised the establishment "just after our Scottish fashion, [of] an eldership in every congregation . . . "[40]

Presbyterian fervor in the House had perhaps reached its apogee on May 31 when that body actually considered a proposal to punish criticism of the directory with life imprisonment. It is worth noting that among those opposing the measure was that supposed paladin of the Presbyterians, D'Ewes himself, who pointed out that Parliament, by such a step, would make itself more intolerant than the King.[41] On the same day, with Naseby only a fortnight away, Vane was optimistically reporting that the Scottish army was moving south in support of the parliamentary forces.

The parliamentary victory at Naseby on June 14, in which Cromwell played such a prominent role and from which the Scots were

37. Whitaker, "Diary," BM, Add. MS. 31,116, fol. 205b; *CJ*, IV, 113–114.
38. D'Ewes, "Journal," BM, Harl. 166, fol. 205a; *CJ*, IV, 123; Whitaker, "Diary," BM, Add. MS. 31,116, fol. 207a; Yonge, "Journal," BM, Add. MS. 18,780, fol. 9a; *The Letters and Journals of Robert Baillie*, ed. David Laing, 3 vols. (Edinburgh, 1841–1842) [hereafter cited as Baillie, *Letters*], II, 265.
39. Whitaker, "Diary," BM, Add. MS. 31,116, fols. 206b, 207a.
40. Baillie to Mr. Ramsay, May 4, 1645, Baillie, *Letters*, II, 271–272.
41. D'Ewes, "Journal," BM, Harl. 166, fol. 214a.

conspicuously absent, not only ended the hopes of the royalists, but interfered with the cherished plans of the Scots for a "covenanted uniformity." By July 1, a gloomy Baillie was speculating darkly as to "what retardment we may have from this great victory, obtained most by the Independent partie . . . we expect a great assault, how soon we know not, for a toleration to we wot not what."[42]

The political picture in the spring and summer of 1645 is complicated by a tangled web of secret negotiations among rival groups of royalists, parliamentarians, and Scots. There is evidence of underhand dealings between the radical leaders and dissident royalists as well as serious proposals for a peace settlement between those same radicals and the King's representatives, including the Queen herself. The moderates, notably Holles, appear to have been in communication with Oxford in the period. The embarrassing details of Scottish "trinketting" were made known to their enemies after the capture of Digby's correspondence in the autumn of 1645.

The slippery and devious Lord Thomas Saville was a central figure in some of these negotiations. A leading member of the popular party in 1640, Saville had become a royalist, but by March of 1645 was no longer *persona grata* at Oxford, and after narrowly escaping a charge of treason he had obtained permission from the King to go to France. Although Charles I seemed pleased to be rid of Saville, as well as some other royalists who had led the clamor for a renewal of the Uxbridge negotiations,[43] he may have given him permission to sound out parliamentarian opinion. Instead of going to France, Saville turned up in London and was soon engaged in a baffling series of intrigues that left him highly suspect by both sides. Whether, as one observer thought, he was in London "with the King's leave"[44] and was a loyal royalist is as difficult for the historian as it was for contemporaries to decide.

Shortly after his arrival in London Saville went to see Scottish Chancellor Loudon, at that time confined to his bed. He found him suspicious, uncommunicative, and still bitter about the failure of the Treaty of Uxbridge. Saville claimed that he was in a position to negotiate through the Queen and let it be known that there was another group in London, the members of which would support the King if he would "make good what he had declared concerning Toleration in matters of

42. Baillie, *Letters,* II, 291.
43. *Letters of the Kings of England,* ed. J. O. Halliwell, 2 vols. (London, 1846), I, 369, 387.
44. A. Trevor to Earl of Ormonde, Apr. 9, 1645, Thomas Carte, *Ormonde Papers, a collection of original letters and papers concerning affairs of England, 1641–1660, found among the Duke of Ormonde's papers,* ed. T. Carte, 2 vols. (London, 1739), I, 80.

Religion."[45] Loudon, who knew the Saville of old, perhaps cast his mind back to the occasion in 1640 when Saville had forged the signatures of six English peers to a statement promising support of the invading Scots.[46] Loudon cautiously maintained his support of the parliamentary propositions at Uxbridge and told Saville that they were an essential part of any agreement with the King.

Saville now turned to the radicals and some weeks later reported to Oxford that he was on good terms with that party and asked for instructions from Digby.[47] By mid-May there had been an exchange between Digby and the radicals, which, though unproductive of concrete results, is not without interest.

The radicals appear to have been ready to make a significant retreat from the intransigence they displayed at Uxbridge. Their terms were outlined as follows. The control of the militia would be shared, as had been suggested by the royalists at Uxbridge, with the King naming one-quarter or one-third of the commissioners. In Ireland the losses of the Protestants were to be made good "without destroying the natives." It is significant that no specific proposal was made on religion; that problem was to be shelved until the King went to London. But partisan rather than parliamentary control of the executive was envisaged by the proposal that "the persons who treated would have the power to dispose of all places." Holles later claimed that some of the more important posts had tentatively been filled: "my Lord Saville to be Lord Treasurer, Mr. Solicitor to be Lord Keeper, and others of that faction to have several offices of honour and trust." When Saville reportedly asked what would happen if "the people here should grumble" at this kind of settlement, he was assured that there was an army in existence that was "sure against such."[48]

The Scots, who had rather mysteriously come into possession of documentary evidence of these dealings, declared in July that their information had been confirmed by intelligence from France, which had described the radicals as attempting to convince the King, through the Queen, that he should deal with them rather than with the moderates. The radicals had assured the Queen that the Scots were not only pow-

45. BM, Add. MS. 32,093, fol. 220b; Scottish commissioners to the committee of both kingdoms, c. July 14, 1645, Baillie, *Letters,* II, 487.

46. *DNB,* XVII, 864.

47. Saville to – – – – , n.d., Baillie, *Letters,* II, 487.

48. Scottish commissioners to the committee of both kingdoms, c. July 14, 1645, *ibid.* Holles asserted that he, Whitelocke, Stapleton, Essex, Willoughby, and Sir Christopher Wray had all seen the documentary evidence of the negotiation, some of which was in Saville's handwriting. (*Memoirs of Denzil, Lord Holles* [London, 1699] [hereafter cited as Holles, *Memoirs*], pp. 39–40.)

erless but opposed to peace; that the radicals were all powerful in Parliament, London, the army, and the navy. Particular stress was laid on the bogey of Presbyterianism, which was described as "prejudicial to Monarchy, and to the recovery of regal power in Church matters." It was pointed out, on the other hand, that the confusion resulting from a policy of toleration "would call quickly for a remedy, and open a way for the King to return to his own power . . . "[49] The Scots had made strenuous efforts to counter the radical intrigues in France. The radicals lacked the support of "the body [majority] of the English," they told the royalists, arguing that the Queen's dealing with them would make her more unpopular in England and Scotland and, moreover, that their avowed aims were to settle the state "without any King at all, and so they are for the ruin of the whole Royal family."[50]

Saville also appears to have convinced Lord Saye, St. John, and other leading radicals of the possibility of ending the war through the defection of George Goring, the royalist general, and William Legge, governor of Oxford. The failure of the Uxbridge negotiations, he said, had given rise to serious dissension among the leading royalists, some of whom felt that the King should have given way to the parliamentary demands. Two of these, Goring and the Earl of Newport,[51] were prepared to surrender a large part of Goring's cavalry, and even Oxford itself, in return for a guarantee of their own security and the restoration of their estates. They also wished to be satisfied "that there was no intention to destroy monarchy, nor to alter the government of the Kingdom."[52] The radicals were skeptical, but took the matter seriously enough to appoint a kind of informal subcommittee of the committee of both kingdoms, without, however, informing the whole committee of its true role. To further the project, Saye made it known that the betrayal of Oxford would be worth £10,000 to those who carried it out. The Scots, who had originally been excluded from the subcommittee, suspected that the radicals were attempting to make a secret peace agreement with the King and were using the device of the subcommittee to give their dealings a cloak of legality.

An opportunity to attack the radicals in a vulnerable area was provided in early June with the seizure of a letter from Digby to Colonel William Legge, containing guarded references to a negotiation with

49. Scottish commissioners to the committee of both kingdoms, c. July 14, 1645, Baillie, *Letters*, II, 487.

50. Paper for "Mr. Dickson," June 10, 1645, *ibid.*, 277–278.

51. "Information of Oliver St. John" [to parliamentary committee on Saville affair], c. June 18, 1645, Victoria Tower, Manuscripts of the House of Lords, June 24–July 9, 1645, fols. 229a, 232a.

52. Examination of Saville, June 12, 1645, BM, Add. MS. 32,093, fol. 213a.

the radicals.[53] The Scots made the most of it. About June 10, 1645, Baillie told his Presbyterian friend the Reverend Mr. James Cranford of Digby's letter[54] and apparently gave Cranford the impression that parliamentary forts were actually to be surrendered to the royalists rather than vice versa. Shortly afterward Cranford publicly accused the radicals of an intent to make peace and to surrender the parliamentary forts and told the same story to the lord mayor of London and some of the Common Councillors. The mayor suggested that John Glyn should be informed, and Cranford agreed on the grounds that Glyn "is none of them." The lord mayor, however, decided to send a copy to the Speaker, Lenthall, who promptly informed Vane and St. John. Cranford was summoned to the bar of the Commons, subjected to an examination, and released on bail.

The parliamentary moderates were also aware of the secret negotiations and anxious to frustrate them. On June 14, 1645, one Mr. Hillesley testified that the future leading moderate Sir John Maynard had also accused the radicals of underhand dealings. When Hillesley had expressed doubt that such persons as Northumberland, Saye, Vane, and St. John "should go to undo us," Maynard had reaffirmed the truth of his charges and had added that Cromwell too was implicated. When Hillesley argued that Cromwell could not be implicated since he was then in the field and that "it was contrary to his principles to do any such vile thing or horrid thing," Maynard conceded that he could not say for certain that Cromwell was involved, but observed that "it was not long since he was all one with them." On a second occasion, Maynard told Hillesley that the Scots had knowledge of the negotiation and that the previously named persons were involved, adding: "Aye and Cromwell too as before."[55]

The radicals apparently decided to counter these dangerous charges with some of their own against Holles. In this Saville was a willing helper since he regarded Holles as the source of information for some of the charges that had been brought against him at Oxford.[56] Another reason for Saville's cooperation may have been fear for his own life since the radicals had good reason to suspect that he had played them false with regard to the possibility of the surrender of Oxford.[57] He knew too that the Scots had obtained information that could only

53. "The letter to CCC contained nothing but a dislike of my answer to the propositions you wot of, as not at all satisfactory. All is villainy and juggling among them . . . " (*LJ*, VII, 416.)
54. Baillie to Lauderdale, June 17, 1645, Baillie, *Letters*, II, 279–280.
55. Information of Mr. Hillesley, June 14, 1645, Victoria Tower, Manuscripts of the House of Lords, June 24–July 9, 1645, fols. 211a–212a.
56. Information of Oliver St. John, *ibid.*, fols. 229a–232a.
57. Nathaniel Fiennes, *Vindiciae Veritatis* (London, 1654), BM, E.811, pp. 137–138.

have come from a royalist source. They were thus not disposed to protect him unduly, and when Holles complained to the House that he had been "scandalized" by Saville, who had accused him of treasonous correspondence with Digby, the Commons resolved to ask the Lords to arrest Saville and to carry out a formal examination of the charge.[58]

A few days later Sir Gilbert Gerard told the House that Saville had deliberately misled the members of the secret subcommittee in the matter of the surrender of royalist forts and garrisons. As a result, D'Ewes indignantly noted, "Sir Thomas Fairfax had been drawn to that unnecessary siege of Oxford, and . . . Colonel Cromwell also had been called back, which had occasioned the loss of Leicester."[59] But Gerard also reported that Saville had told Saye that "there was constant intelligence given of what was done in this House by Mr. Holles to the Lord Digby." A furious Holles protested that the charge was "utterly false" and was supported by Wray who declared that the letter, allegedly from Oxford, containing the accusations against Holles "was framed here in town."[60] When Whitelocke, who was the chairman of the committee investigating the Saville affair, reported that Saville had refused to name the source of his information, he was ordered to be committed to the Tower.

With the Battle of Naseby won, the position of the radicals was immeasurably strengthened, and they soon showed a disposition to exploit the charges against Holles. The assault began on July 2 when John Gurdon, one of D'Ewes's "fiery spirits," reported to the Commons that Saville had accused Holles and Whitelocke of treasonable behavior before and during the Treaty of Uxbridge. Holles, he alleged, had promised the King to persuade the Commons "to yield to such propositions as the King should make."[61] They had also assured the royalists, he said, that the Scots "were weary of that violent party [the radicals] and out of hope to establish their presbitery."[62] Gurdon rather naïvely revealed that Saye, Vane, and Sir Nathaniel Barnardiston had all seen Saville's letter and had suggested that he present it to the Commons.

The hard-pressed Holles admitted to the House that, at Uxbridge, the royalists and parliamentarians had "visited one another," but denied any disloyalty to the Parliament. With his usual frankness, Holles, in the words of the more politic Whitelocke, "confessed more than

58. Whitaker, "Diary," BM, Add. MS. 31,116, fol. 215a; Yonge, "Journal," BM, Add. MS. 18,780, fol. 35b.
59. D'Ewes, "Journal," BM, Harl. 166, fol. 219a.
60. *Ibid.*
61. Whitaker, "Diary," BM, Add. MS. 31,116, fol. 217a, b.
62. Yonge, "Journal," BM, Add. MS. 18,780, fols. 60, 61b.

he needed to have done."[63] Seizing the opportunity, some of the radicals loudly accused Holles and Whitelocke of treason and demanded that they be sent to the Tower. They were strenuously opposed by Sir William Lewis and other leading moderates. Lewis, after castigating Saville as a turncoat and his letter as a libel "against two worthy members of the House," moved that the letter be thrown out and Saville himself closely questioned as to "who set him on to promote this business."[64] The radical action was laid aside, but Whitelocke could sense his danger from the changed attitude of his fair-weather friends. Robert Reynolds, among others, "saluted me at a distance and as a stranger, and declined speech with me . . . "[65]

Holles, rather than Whitelocke, was the main target of the radicals who made strenuous efforts to isolate him.[66] Whitelocke and Holles admitted that at Uxbridge they had spoken to the Earl of Southhampton and Lindsay at the latter's lodgings, but disavowed any treasonable intent. Whitelocke denied that they had alluded to "any violent Independent party" in Parliament or that they had characterized the parliamentary propositions as unreasonable.[67] The committee met again on July 8 and was heavily attended by members of both parties. It was, however, dominated by the radicals and chaired by St. John's general factotum, Samuel Browne.

During the intervals between the sittings, Whitelocke's friends were working diligently for him. One of them, a Mr. Lambert Osbaldeston, attempted to persuade St. John to drop the charges. He came away with the impression that the radicals "were resolved to ruine" Holles if they could, and, although they had less animosity toward Whitelocke, it was impossible to separate them.[68] Whitelocke stated that he received many offers from the radicals of rewards and preferments in return for testimony against Holles, but, although he wavered perceptibly under questioning, he refused to turn on the moderate leader.

The Scottish commissioners, who had been watching the proceedings in silence, now determined to intervene. Their assistance probably saved Holles from disaster. The victory at Naseby had relieved the radicals of the necessity to please the Scots, and from that date relations between the two groups steadily deteriorated until, by the au-

---

63. Whitelocke, "Annals," BM, Add. MS. 37,343, fol. 394a.
64. *Ibid.*, fols. 394, 395a.
65. *Ibid.*
66. Holles later recalled that St. John had made such strenuous efforts to isolate him that "the eyes of many indifferent persons, Members of the House, were opened and their spirits raised in indignation . . . " (Holles, *Memoirs*, 40–41.)
67. Whitelocke, "Annals," BM, Add. MS. 37,343, fols. 396b, 397a; Yonge, "Journal," BM, Add. MS. 18,780, fol. 62b.
68. Whitelocke, "Annals," BM, Add. MS. 37,343, fol. 401a, b.

tumn of 1645, there was real danger of an armed clash between the
New Model and its erstwhile ally. The Scottish policy of installing garrisons in strategic northern cities like Carlisle was particularly galling
to the radicals, and peremptory orders had been issued for their immediate removal. The Scots, for their part, complained of lack of financial support and supplies as well as of the fact that they had not
yet been shown the King's letters captured at Naseby. In this strained
atmosphere the Scottish commissioners brought forward evidence that
caused the radical attack to boomerang.

On July 12 the Scots received a letter from an unnamed source together with an enclosure of three notes in Saville's hand. These last
contained clear evidence of Saville's royalist sympathies and of his role
in the negotiations between Digby and the radical leaders.[69] The Scots
quickly exploited their advantage. Word of the windfall was sent immediately to Holles and Whitelocke, and on July 14 Lord Warriston
appeared at the meeting of the committee, armed with the embarrassing documents. Whitaker noted sourly that the new evidence indicated that Saville was more loyal to the King than to the Parliament,
"notwithstanding his long protestation to the contrary."[70] The revelations effectively destroyed the credibility of the radicals' star witness
and weakened the position of the radicals as self-righteous accusers by
revealing, in Baillie's gleeful words, their own "real trinketting with
Oxford by Saville."[71] Whitelocke recalled that the exposure "took off
the edge of divers gentlemen, who thought this prosecution not in-
genious nor handsome against us."[72]

The Scottish commissioners declared that Saville was in truth working for the royalists and that his stories about the possibility of the defection of Goring and Legge were "but pretensions."[73] They emphasized, however, that there had been some serious "underhand dealing"
regarding peace propositions. After Loudon had refused to deal with
Saville, the Scottish chancellor, they declared, had heard from reliable
sources that he was meeting regularly with "others" and that with
their knowledge was sending messengers to Oxford. The Scots were, of
course, referring to the radicals, the awkward details of whose overtures were soon revealed.

The examination of the two accused members, whose position was
now greatly strengthened, took place on July 18. The two had agreed
beforehand on the general tenor of their answers "so as not easily to

69. Baillie, *Letters,* II, 487.
70. Whitaker, "Diary," BM, Add. MS. 31,116, fol. 220b; *CJ,* IV, 207.
71. Baillie to Lauderdale, July 15, 1645, Baillie, *Letters,* II, 303–304.
72. *Ibid.*
73. Whitelocke, "Annals," BM, Add. MS. 37,343, fols. 403b, 404a.

be taken contradicting one another," and, during Holles' examination, Whitelocke was given reports on its progress.

There were two charges against Holles. The first was that he corresponded with Digby and provided the royalists with continuous information of the deliberations of Parliament's inner counsels. St. John had testified some weeks before that Saville had told him that "the particular things that were done in the House of Commons and the names of the persons that speak here were sent in weekly intelligence and divers passages in the close committee." Saville had claimed to have often heard these things read out in the Privy Council at Oxford, of which he had for some time been a member. When Saville had been accused of disloyalty by Digby, the latter had supported his charges by evidence he claimed to have received from "those at Westminster." Saville demanded to know the informant's name, but Digby allegedly had said that the person concerned "had done the King so good and real service as that he had as good almost take the crown from the King's head" as name him.[74] Both Saville and Lady Temple claimed that a letter had come to Saville about May 12 from a person in Oxford in which Holles was named as the person who was in correspondence with Digby.[75] Saville also testified that when he went to London he carried with him a letter from Lord Lindsay for delivery to Holles.[76] Holles flatly denied that he had any underhand dealings with those at Oxford. That Digby should have any dealings with him, he said, was highly improbable since Digby hated him "as much as any man living." He denied that he had "meddled in any kind, had any traffic, or held any correspondence with any one that hath left the Parliament . . . "[77] As for the note from Lord Lindsay, Holles admitted that he had received a note without a signature recommending the bearer, who was in fact Saville himself, the latter having visited Holles during a period in which he was confined to bed for two weeks.

The second charge, that of treasonous relations with the royalists at Uxbridge, was more dangerous. Saville's letter to John Gurdon contained damaging accusations, such as that Holles had disavowed the parliamentary propositions, but had urged the King "to treat upon them" and to come to London. Saville claimed that Lord Lindsay had told him that Holles was "well affected to the King" and that the royalists were of the opinion that he could do the King better service at London than Oxford. Holles was also reported to have told the royal-

74. Information of Oliver St. John, c. June 18, 1645, Victoria Tower, Manuscripts of the House of Lords, June 24–July 9, 1645, fols. 229a–232a.

75. Information of Lady Temple, June 12, 1645, *ibid.*, fols. 196a–197a.

76. Examination of Saville, June 14, 1645, BM, Add. MS. 32,093, fol. 218b.

77. Information of Denzil Holles, June 26, 1645, BM, Add. MS. 32,093, fol. 227b.

ists that he regarded the parliamentary propositions as so absurd that he "could hardly forbeare laughing" when they were presented to the King. His own supporters and the Scots, he was alleged to have assured the royalists, would be able to overawe the "violent party."[78]

The text of Saville's letter to Gurdon has not survived, but the substance of it was given in the charge against Holles and the other eleven members in June 1647. The moderate leader was accused of having advised the King to overlook the extreme character of the propositions and to agree to a treaty, but that he should specify that the negotiation be held in London, "adding that there was nothing in the world that the violent party . . . did so much fear as his Majesty's coming to London, which would be a certain dissolution of their authority and power . . ." The radicals would oppose his coming, but he was confident "that he and his party . . . should carry it."[79] Holles was also accused of having drawn up, at the royalists' request, a paper setting out a suggested answer of the King to the propositions and of having advised the royalists that the Scottish commissioners were "very weary of that violent party; and that they, being desperate [without hope] to establish their Presbytery here as in Scotland, made their addresses to him and his party."[80]

Holles admitted having conversations with the royalists during the Uxbridge talks, but denied any disloyalty to Parliament. He had prepared a paper that, he said, had stressed the necessity of the royalists recognizing the validity of the Parliament at Westminster. He admitted discussing the attitude of the Scots, that they had been "for a rigid Presbitery but were taken off . . ."[81] He also admitted discussing religion, the militia, and Ireland, but denied advising an answer and declared that the project of the King's coming to London was "never in question." He claimed further that he had acquainted his brother commissioners at Uxbridge with the fact that he had drawn up the paper for the Earl of Lindsay. The other commissioners denied this, although Denbigh recalled that Holles had informed them of his visits to the royalists.

Whitelocke showed a distinct disposition to excuse himself during his interrogation. When asked whether he knew of the paper in question, he asserted that he had not written the paper and that it was read by Holles in his presence. Whitelocke had "never consented at the delivery nor dissented," but had "made some scruple of it." There had

78. Yonge, "Journal," BM, Add. MS. 18,780, fols. 78b, 79a.
79. *The Parliamentary and Constitutional History of England from the earliest times to the restoration of Charles II,* 24 vols. (London, 1751–1762), XVI, 70–92.
80. *Ibid.*
81. Yonge, "Journal," BM, Add. MS. 18,780, fol. 79b.

been some discussion of "presbytery *jure divino* which it was thought the Scots did not hold." The question of the King's coming to London had been discussed, he said, the Earl of Southhampton being particularly anxious that the King should do so.[82] But despite the fact that the royalists felt the parliamentary demands to be unreasonable, he and Holles had insisted on them. During the examination Whitelocke was particularly hounded by Wentworth, "a man fuller of envy than honor, [who] asked me about thirty questions only for his part."[83]

The moderates in the Commons gave the two accused members strong support. D'Ewes, as might be expected, declared Saville's statement to be a "meere libel" and opposed even putting the question as to their guilt.[84] The House debated the matter until seven P.M. with, as Whitelocke recalled, "the Earl of Essex his party and all our friends putting forth the utmost of their power and interest to rescue us from the malice and danger we were now under." The "other party of the House as earnestly labored to be rid of us both; either by cutting off our heads, or at least by expelling us . . . "[85]

Just as the House was ready to vote on the charges, a new element was introduced when Godfrey Bosvile declared that he had information from Lilburne bearing on the case. Lilburne, having been called to the bar, asserted that Holles, in July 1643, had asked the royalist Sir John Mounson to assist him in making his peace with the King. Lilburne's evidence was of a hopelessly hearsay character. He had heard of the matter from a Mr. Robinson who, in turn, had been told of it by a Mrs. Toye, a friend of the Mrs. Cotton, who as Mounson's sister had been the alleged messenger between London and Oxford.

Mounson was said to have replied to Holles' request for his intercession by telling him that he would be glad to assist Holles if the parliamentary leader would use his influence on behalf of royalists who went to London. It was claimed further that shortly after this Mrs. Cotton's property was relieved of sequestration.[86] Lilburne went on to state that when he had first heard of the affair (about April 1645) he had informed "Col. Cromwell" about it and a few days later had also told Vane, in "his own chamber as he was making it ready." Other members who were informed included John Trenchard, Gurdon, and Humphrey Salway.[87] But if Lilburne expected support from the radical

---

82. *Ibid.*
83. Whitelocke, "Annals," BM, Add. MS. 37,343, fol. 405a.
84. D'Ewes, "Journal," BM, Harl. 166, fol. 242a.
85. Whitelocke, "Annals," BM, Add. MS. 37,343, fol. 405a, b.
86. Manuscripts of the House of Lords, Victoria Tower, June 24–July 9, 1645, fols. 262b, 263a.
87. *Ibid.*, fols. 260a, 263a.

leaders, he must have been bitterly disappointed. Whatever may have been the degree of truth in the allegations—and Holles' behavior in August 1643 lends credence to them—the radicals, who by this juncture were apparently willing to concede victory to the moderates, seemed to find Lilburne's intervention embarrassing. At any rate Vane cut the ground from beneath Lilburne's feet by declaring that he had no recollection of any such conversation.[88] Holles denied that he had any hand in relieving Mrs. Cotton's sequestration, and the matter was referred to the committee on the Saville affair headed by Samuel Browne.[89]

The animosity of the radicals toward the Scots was now demonstrated by their demand that the Scottish divine, Robert Baillie, who had been instrumental in publicizing the charges against the radical subcommittee, should answer to the House for it. The Scots refused to permit this, and Baillie merely submitted a report on the affair to the House. The moderates, led by Stapleton, attempted to assist the Scots, but were unable to block a resolution to the effect that Cranford's accusations against John Crewe, Pierrepont, St. John, and Vane were "false and scandalous." Cranford was sent to the Tower and ordered to make financial reparation to the accused members.[90] Shortly after this, however, the moderates won a significant victory when by a vote of ninety-five to fifty-five the Commons cleared Holles of the charges of having engaged in treasonous correspondence with either Digby or Lindsay.[91]

But the charge against Holles and Whitelocke of treasonous behavior before Uxbridge still remained to be dealt with. The radicals were described as wishing to postpone the hearing, being apprehensive that "as the present constitution of the House was . . . Mr. Holles and I might be acquitted."[92] It was with considerable difficulty that the moderates succeeded in carrying a motion to proceed with the question on July 21. On the same day Lilburne, doubtless bitter at the lack of support he had encountered in the Commons, was ordered arrested in connection with charges of peculation and disloyalty that he had allegedly leveled against Speaker Lenthall.[93]

After a heated all-day debate on July 21, 1645, during which the radicals once more failed to isolate Holles, the House acquitted both of the accused members and even gave them permission to prosecute

88. Yonge, "Journal," BM, Add. MS. 18,780, fol. 79b.
89. D'Ewes, "Journal," BM, Harl. 166, fol. 245b; *CJ*, IV, 213.
90. Whitaker, "Diary," BM, Add. MS. 31,116, fol. 221b; *CJ*, IV, 213.
91. *CJ*, IV, 213.
92. Whitelocke, "Annals," BM, Add. MS. 37,343, fols. 405b, 406a.
93. *CJ*, IV, 213; Pauline Gregg, *Free-born John: A Biography of John Lilburne* (London, G. G. Harrap, 1961), pp. 119–121.

the now friendless Saville.[94] Throughout the affair the moderates maintained an unusual degree of party discipline. With typical self-satisfaction, Whitelocke recalled that "generally the gentlemen of best interest and quality in the House were all for the acquittal of us." But even "the gallants," who usually regarded their meals or "other of their refreshments" as more important than the business on the floor, remained in their seats. When they did leave they were confronted by the seventeenth-century equivalent of party whips "to solicit [them] . . . to return to the House."[95]

The attempt of the radicals to rid themselves of Holles had misfired, but the whole episode was revelatory of the policies of all three groups, radicals, moderates, and Scots. In the first half of 1645 they were all apparently negotiating secretly with the royalists with a view to making a "separate peace" to their own advantage. The most significant exchange of this type took place in March and April 1645 between the radicals and the King with Saville and Henrietta Maria as intermediaries.[96] This negotiation, if it can be called that, collapsed partly, it would seem, because of Digby's crushing of the "peace party" among the royalists and partly because of rising royalist expectations as a result of the spectacular victories of Montrose in Scotland. As late as May 23, 1645, however, Lord Jermyn wrote to Digby expressing his pleasure that the latter had approved "of the essay proposed concerning the Independents" and went on to allude to some "business" that was then to be "gone about."[97]

The peace feelers of the radicals may have been intended as no more than a further delaying action pending the completion of the preparations for the summer campaign. They are significant, however, in that they foreshadowed the much better known Heads of the Proposals in 1647. There was the same willingness to compromise over religion and the same insistence on partisan rather than parliamentary control of the army and of the highest offices of the state.

Evidence that the Scots and the moderates were not idle during the same period was provided as a kind of by-product of the investigation

---

94. *CJ*, IV, 214; Whitaker, "Diary," BM, Add. MS. 31,116, fol. 222a; D'Ewes, "Journal," BM, Harl. 166, fol. 243b.

95. Whitelocke, "Annals," BM, Add. MS. 37,343, fol. 406a, b.

96. *Letters of Queen Henrietta Maria*, ed. M. A. E. Green (London, 1857), p. 296; *Letters of the Kings of England*, ed. J. O. Halliwell, 2 vols. (London, 1848), I, 374; *Ormonde Papers, a collection of original letters and papers concerning affairs of England, 1641–1660, found among the Duke of Ormonde's papers*, ed. T. Carte, 2 vols. (London, 1739), I, 80; *Calendar of State Papers, Domestic Series, 1603–1704*, 81 vols. (1857–1947+) [hereafter cited as *CSPD*], *1644–1645*, pp. 373–483; Eliot Warburton, *Memoirs of Prince Rupert and the Cavaliers*, 3 vols. (London, 1849) [hereafter cited as Warburton, *Rupert*], III, 73.

97. Jermyn to Digby, May 23, 1645, *CSPD, 1644–1645*, p. 514.

into the charges arising out of the activities of Saville. Lord Saye testified on June 19 and 28, 1645, that Saville had told him that one Mullins, a "brother" of Sir William Raby, had come from Oxford and was suspected of carrying on some kind of secret negotiation. There had been "many meetings and consultations" at Lady Devonshire's home, which had been attended by the Scottish commissioners as well as by "divers Lords and divers of the House of Commons."[98] Saville was evasive when questioned about the matter, but asserted that when Mullins came to see him some time after the middle of May he had asked him "where Mr. Holles lay," and Saville had told him that he would find Holles in Covent Garden.[99] The matter was not pursued, but enough had been said to indicate some kind of dealings between the Scots and the moderates on the one hand and the royalists on the other. It should be noted, too, that in late May a royalist council of war was held during which the possibility of coming to terms with the Scottish army in the north was seriously considered.[100]

The Scots in London strenuously denied that there was any intention on their part to make a separate peace. They declared that those who feared "underhand dealing or correspondence with the King" were mistaken, and the Scots reaffirmed their allegiance to the Solemn League and Covenant.[101] This protest seems to have been disingenuous for these same Scottish commissioners appear to have made a firm offer to the King, through the Queen, sometime in June, of their complete support provided he agree to the establishment of a Presbyterian church government.[102] Evidence of this offer came to light after the capture of Digby's correspondence at the Battle of Sherborne. These letters revealed further that a group of Scottish leaders in the army, including the Earl of Callander and Lords Sinclair, Montgomery, and Lothian, had attempted to negotiate with the King through Callander's nephew, Sir William Fleming, who was at that time in the royalist army.[103] Though nothing came of these moves, they served to illustrate deepening disunity not only among the parliamentarians but among the Scots themselves.

The months after the collapse of the Uxbridge negotiations saw important and indeed decisive changes in the balance of power. The second Self-Denying Ordinance ended the military career of the Earl of Essex and the influence of many of his supporters in the parliamentary

98. Victoria Tower, Manuscripts of the House of Lords, June 24–July 9, 1645, fols. 233–247.
99. *Ibid.*, fols. 246a–247a.
100. Warburton, *Rupert*, III, 98.
101. Scottish commissioners to – – – – , n.d., Meikle, *Correspondence*, pp. 82–83.
102. Yonge, "Journal," BM, Add. MS. 18,780, fol. 160a, b.
103. *Ibid.*, fols. 157–160.

armed forces. Even more important was the fact that the radicals succeeded in officering the New Model with their friends and keen supporters. Their awareness of the significance of this step was made clear
when they assured the royalists that the army would be available to
enforce any settlement that they chose to make. Relations with the
Scots continued, meanwhile, to deteriorate despite efforts to placate
them by a rather spurious display of Presbyterian zeal. With Naseby
won and Cromwell's star at its zenith, the necessity for such charades
vanished, and the deep animosity between the followers of Vane and
St. John and the Scots was made abundantly clear during the attack
on Holles and Whitelocke. The Saville affair itself was the occasion of
one of the more effective demonstrations of the alliance that had been
concluded between Holles and the Scots in the autumn of 1644. Montrose had temporarily eclipsed the power of the Marquis of Argyle,
and members of the "peace party" among the Scots were able to show
bolder faces. With Argyle's recovery of power in late 1645 the alliance
between the English moderates and the Scots led by Loudon was largely
vitiated by deep divisions among the Scots themselves.

By August 1645 the radical leaders, despite their failure to impeach
Holles, had good reason to congratulate themselves. Naseby had broken
the royalist resistance, and in the New Model Cromwell was emerging
as the real power behind the unpolitical Fairfax. The animosity of the
Scots was a problem but not a real threat. The future settlement of
the kingdom could wait until mopping up operations had reduced the
King to the position of a supplicant. Meanwhile the ascendancy of the
radicals in the Commons could be assured by the "recruiting" of the
House, that is, by the replacement of expelled royalists by new and
carefully chosen members.

And yet there were clouds on the horizon. Future trouble could be
detected in the treatment accorded Lilburne in the Saville affair. Not
only had Vane rejected his support in the attack on Holles, but Lilburne, by the end of July, had found himself imprisoned in Newgate.
Unimportant as these events may have seemed to contemporary observers, they constituted a genuine turning point in the history of the
Revolution and may be regarded as marking the genesis of the Leveller party as a self-conscious entity, distinct from, and increasingly hostile to, the parliamentary radicals.

The iron appears to have entered Lilburne's soul in January 1645
when he returned to London fresh from his support of Cromwell against
Manchester and doubtless expecting a warm welcome from the parliamentary radicals. The reality was otherwise. His attacks on William
Prynne, the Presbyterian champion, were awkward at a time when the
radicals were supporting the demand for Presbyterianism at Ux-

bridge.[104] The loudly expressed hostility of Lilburne and his friends toward powerful interests like the Eastland Merchants and the Merchant Adventurers were, moreover, embarrassing to Vane and St. John who had already demonstrated their willingness to support the privileges of those companies in return for their financial support.[105] Far from being treated as a hero, Lilburne found himself harried by the parliamentary Committee of Examinations, presided over by the radical Miles Corbet, and by the summer of 1645 he was aware that of those who wielded power and influence in Parliament, Cromwell was one of his few remaining friends.[106] He had returned to London, he recalled bitterly, "expecting a joyful and cheerful entertainment . . . But to my exceeding grief and astonishment, I found a very sad and frowning countenance from most of those that had had us in great and good esteeme."[107] By the autumn and winter of 1645–1646 his hostility to Vane and St. John had become implacable.[108]

The Leveller threat was a real if distant one; a more immediate difficulty was the Scottish army which had become a formidable obstacle and had partly replaced the defunct force of the Earl of Essex as the mainstay of Holles and his English moderates. Accordingly, relations between the English radicals and the Scots worsened swiftly, and by late 1645 the erstwhile allies were close to open conflict.

104. John Lilburne, "A Copie of a Letter," printed in *Tracts on Liberty in the Puritan Revolution,* ed. William Haller, 3 vols. (New York, Octagon Books, 1965), III, 181–187.

105. *Ibid.,* I, 99–106; Joseph Frank, *The Levellers* (Cambridge, Mass., Harvard University Press, 1955), p. 46; John Lilburne, *London's Liberty in Chains Discovered* (London, 1646), BM, E.359(17), pp. 43–44.

106. *CJ,* IV, 22–23; W. C. Abbott, *The Writings and Speeches of Oliver Cromwell,* 4 vols. (Cambridge, Mass., Harvard University Press, 1937–1947), I, 363–364.

107. *The Reasons of Lieut. Col. Lilburne's sending his letter to Mr. Prin* (London, 1645), BM, E.288(12).

108. Lilburne to Cromwell, Dec. 9, 1645, BM, E.400(5), pp. 12–13.

V] The Flight of the King to the Scots

Through the winter of 1645–1646 the antagonism between the radicals, on the one hand, and the Scots and their London allies, on the other, smoldered and almost flared into open hostility. Holles and his followers were, for the time being, a spent force, but their role as a counterweight to the radicals was effectively taken up by a combination of the Scots, the conservative Londoners, and the Westminster Assembly. As the royalist garrisons were gradually winkled out, the King, cornered in Oxford, turned first to the Scots and then to the radicals for support. Some of his disgruntled followers, meanwhile, were attempting to salvage something from the wreck of their cause by secret overtures to Parliament. The radicals bided their time. Charles, after all, was the man whom they regarded as most responsible for the Civil War; he would, it seemed, soon be their prisoner. There was little reason for haste. Such offers as actually were to be made to the King by both radicals and Scots were actuated more by hostility and fear of one another than by any newfound affection for Charles.

Holles seems now to have regarded negotiations with the King as not only dangerous but unrewarding, and in view of Charles's penchant for dealing with Holles' enemies, his disenchantment is understandable. About two weeks after the failure of the attempt to impeach him, Whitelocke relayed to Holles a warning from William Pierrepont to the effect that the radicals had gathered further evidence against him. "Let them do their worst, we will not care a fig for them"[1] was the characteristic reply. But his mood of defiance was short lived. By late 1645 he and his followers had entered into a brief entente with the radicals.

Vane and St. John now attempted to create a kind of parliamentary "united front" as a prelude to the dictating of peace terms. They also hoped, through the "recruiting" of the House of Commons, to swamp the moderates with large numbers of newly elected members who, it was assumed, would support the radical cause. In an evident attempt to bury the hatchet, they judiciously distributed rewards from the

---

1. Bulstrode Whitelocke, "Annals," BM, Add. MS. 37,344 [hereafter cited as Whitelocke, "Annals," BM, Add. MS. 37,344], fol. 1b.

public purse to old friend and old foe alike. The policy was effective—
at least in the short run—and the political truce lasted until the spring
of 1646 when the moderates suddenly became aware that the new elections had given them, rather than the radicals, the advantage of numbers, and once again they went on the offensive.

While the party truce lasted, it was the Scots, supported by more
substantial Londoners and the divines at Westminster, who provided
the hard core of resistance to radical ambitions. Scottish support of
Holles in the Saville affair had provoked deep resentment among the
radicals, and, after Naseby, disputes over the projected peace terms
had flared up again. The tension between the Scots and the radicals
was only in part ideological in origin. The New Model army was a
political as well as a military factor in the power struggle, and the fact
that it was controlled by the parliamentary radicals was of the greatest significance. A complete victory by this group, and this army, could
not but be disastrous from the Scottish point of view. The most convenient way of avoiding such an eventuality appeared to lie in the direction of an understanding with the King. It is, of course, true that
Scots like Argyle were willing to concede a radical victory, and were
even anxious to bow to the rising sun, but, for men like Loudon, there
were other possibilities to be explored.

As early as July 8, 1645, it had been noted that "the best and most"
in London were anxious for a renewal of peace talks with the King on
the basis of the Uxbridge propositions. The Scots were well disposed
but the prospects were dim. Just as Charles was writing that he would
"go no less than was last offered . . . at Uxbridge," the radicals, brush-
ing aside Scottish protests, were demanding that he sign the parliamentary propositions without further parley.[2]

Far from being disposed to take advice from the Scots, the radicals
were increasingly angered and alarmed by their suspicious behavior in
the north of England. The Earl of Northumberland was disagreeably
startled to hear that the Scots intended to garrison his residence at
Cockermouth. Foreseeing his valuable rents lining Scottish pockets, he
warned that the Scots might squat indefinitely in the north of England.[3] The continued presence of the Scots in the north, the Commons declared, would destroy those counties. They underlined the
point by ordering the sale of the jewels of the Earl of Roxborough,

2. Charles I to Henrietta Maria, Droitwich, July 31, 1645, *Letters of the Kings of
England*, ed. J. O. Halliwell, 2 vols. (London, 1848), I, 384–385; *Journals of the
House of Commons* [hereafter cited as *CJ*], IV, 232.
3. Northumberland to Sir H. Vane, Sr., Sept. 2, 1645, *Calendar of State Papers,
Domestic Series, 1603–1704*, 81 vols. (1857–1947+) [hereafter cited as *CSPD*], *1645–
1647*, p. 105.

which had been the subject of dispute between the Scots and the English since 1644.[4]

By early October the radicals, as a result of the seizure of Digby's correspondence after the Battle of Sherborne, learned of Scottish negotiations with the King. "I fear," wrote the younger Vane, "there is a greater scourge hangs over our heads than we imagine."[5] A parliamentary resolution of October 13, 1645, roundly condemned the Scots' behavior as "prejudicial to those ends for which their assistance was desired, and destructive to those parts of the kingdom."[6] But the Scots had many influential supporters in England, who, they noted, were "exceedingly desirous that a considerable part of the [Scottish] army should be continued here." Any retreat of their army, they argued, would tend to undo the work of the previous two years resulting in the suppression of "these that are our friends and [who] have adhered to us in confidence of mutual assistance."[7] D'Ewes was perhaps one of them. He recorded his fear of the coming of "open force betwixt us and the Scots' army."[8]

Religion continued to be a source of bitter dissension between the Scots and the radicals. By contrast, it helped unite the disparate English elements who looked to the Scots for religious or political assistance. Yet it was not so much the positive force of doctrine as the negative fear of religious—and perhaps social—anarchy that provided the cement that bound Scots, Londoners, and assembly divines in a loose but significant alliance. By the autumn of 1645 London had become a rich, bubbling stew of conflicting religious opinions and sects. To the conservative, wealthy citizen, the whole development was repugnant and even frightening and was linked with the radical politics and social ideas of men like Lilburne and Walwyn. However vague his positive religious beliefs, the more substantial London gentleman tended to be sufficiently decisive in his declarations against the "tub preachers," and on this issue he enjoyed the fervent support of the majority of the divines of the Westminster Assembly. The increasingly arrogant

4. Advices from London, Aug. 23, 1645, *Calendar of state papers and manuscripts relating to English affairs existing in the archives and collections of Venice and in other libraries of northern Italy*, vols. 10–38 (1603–1675) [London, H. M. Stationery Office, 1900–1940] [hereafter cited as *CSPV*], *1643–1647*, p. 213; *CJ*, IV, 274–275.

5. S. R. Gardiner, *History of the Great Civil War, 1642–1649*, 4 vols. (London, 1893) [hereafter cited as Gardiner, *GCW*], III, 5; Sir H. Vane, Jr., to Sir H. Vane, Sr., *CSPD, 1645–1647*, pp. 191–192.

6. *CJ*, IV, 305; Whitelocke, "Annals," BM, Add. MS. 37,344, fol. 18b.

7. Scottish commissioners to the army, London, Sept. 16, 1645, *Correspondence of the Scottish Commissioners in London, 1644–1646*, ed. H. W. Meikle (London, Roxburghe Club, 1917), pp. 117–118.

8. Sir Symonds D'Ewes, "Journal of the Parliament begun November, 1640," BM, Harleian 166 [hereafter cited as D'Ewes, "Journal," BM, Harl. 166], fol. 269b.

Erastianism of the House of Commons, moreover, led by the very persons who were identified with the policy of toleration, served to drive the assembly into the arms of Scots and Londoners and even to prompt thoughts of overtures to the King himself.

The conservative forces in London, supported by the Scots and the divines, now launched a vigorous attack on Parliament's religious policy. The radicals, confident of their power in the army and of the support—on this issue at least—of the predominantly Erastian Commons, were ill disposed to make concessions. This is not to say that they had completely abandoned any idea of a national religious system. The consensus in the Commons seems to have favored both a national church and at least limited toleration of dissent. On one essential point virtually all were agreed: parliamentary supremacy.

Parliament's determination to control the church was indicated on July 25, 1645, when the Commons named a committee to supervise the choice of elders for the presbyteries of London and directed the county committees to take similar steps on the local level.[9] This coincided with a step in the direction of toleration. The penalty for nonconformity to the directory of worship was reduced from life imprisonment to a fine of £50. In the House of Lords a distinctly Anglican spirit now became evident. The peers demanded that their private chapels be exempt from the new jurisdiction and that in those places "God's worship . . . be used as formerly it had been."[10]

Such sentiments would hardly find favor among the ministers at Westminster. But it was the cool Erastianism of the Commons that they and their Scottish friends found especially galling. If, the ministers threatened, they were not given wide powers of excommunication, they would resign the ministry and "rather endure affliction than iniquity." The House was unmoved. "Most disliked their high language," noted D'Ewes.[11] And as usual the witty and urbane Mr. Selden led the anticlerical forces.

Once again the dissonance between religion and politics was evident. Moderates like Whitelocke, D'Ewes, and John Glyn, who were certainly opposed to the radicals in politics, saw no inconsistency in siding with them against the assembly. Political radicals like Zouch Tate, Sir John Evelyn, and John Wylde appear, at the same time, to have favored giving the ministers wider powers in the delicate area of

9. *CJ*, IV, 218.
10. Lawrence Whitaker, "Diary of Proceedings in the House of Commons," BM, Add. MS. 31,116 [hereafter cited as Whitaker, "Diary," BM, Add. MS. 31,116], fol. 226b; *CJ*, IV, 242.
11. Whitaker, "Diary," BM, Add. MS. 31,116, fol. 225a; D'Ewes, "Journal," BM, Harl. 166, fol. 250b.

excommunication.[12] Baillie regarded the genuine religious Independents as a minority group. "The most part of the House of Commons," he lamented, "especially the lawyers . . . are either half or whole Erastians."[13] Accordingly, when the Scots set about to make political capital out of the religious issue, it was not to the "Presbyterian" members of the House of Commons that they turned, but to the more substantial Londoners and the ministers of the assembly. "The underhand working of the Scots ministers" was widely, and doubtless correctly, regarded as the cause of the assembly's newfound truculence. Collusion among Scots, Londoners, and divines became even more apparent with a report by Sir Peter Wentworth to the Commons on September 20, 1645, that London clergy and laity were petitioning the Common Council in favor of more authority for the clergy. The petition was described as "so cunningly penned . . . [that] it was not doubted but some of the Assembly had a hand in it," and the Commons were stung by the charge that they had not "dealt sincerely" in setting up Presbyterianism.[14]

St. John led the attack on the petitioners and characteristically urged that a parliamentary committee investigate "the first setters on of it." He also suggested that Parliament publicize the fact that the divines, who had taken two years to finish their deliberation on the directory of worship, "would have us to dispatch it in two months." Due note should also be taken, he urged, of statements such as that "the kingdom of Scotland is amazed at our stay, and other like passages."[15] A committee dominated by radicals was appointed to investigate the matter, and Recorder Glyn was ordered to inform the Common Council of the wrath of the Commons. The resentment against the Scots increased when it was observed in the House that their commissioners had echoed the wording of the ministers' petition in their protest against the nonpayment of their troops and the delay in setting up Presbyterianism.[16]

Parliament made it increasingly evident, meanwhile, that the religious settlement was to be essentially Erastian. A Commons committee was set up to receive information about "scandalous persons" who

12. Walter Yonge, "Journal of Proceedings in the House of Commons," BM, Add. MS. 18,780 [hereafter cited as Yonge, "Journal," BM, Add. MS. 18,780], fols. 113a, b, 114a, 123a, b, 134a, 135b, 140a, 144a, b, 154a.

13. *The Letters and Journals of Robert Baillie,* ed. David Laing, 3 vols. (Edinburgh, 1841–1842) [hereafter cited as Baillie, *Letters*], II, 306–308.

14. Sir R. Honeywood to Sir H. Vane, Sr., London, Sept. 9, 1645, *CSPD, 1645–1647,* p. 128; Honeywood to Vane, Oct. 7, 1645, *ibid.,* pp. 179–180; D'Ewes, "Journal," BM, Harl. 166, fol. 265a, b; Whitaker, "Diary," BM, Add. MS. 31,116, fol. 233a.

15. Yonge, "Journal," BM, Add. MS. 18,780, fols. 123a, 124b.

16. Honeywood to Vane, London, Oct. 7, 1645, *CSPD, 1645–1647,* pp. 179–180.

might be denied the sacrament.[17] Steps were also taken to make members of Parliament ex officio participants in the government of the church on the local level. Thus the fact that a member might play an active role in the Presbyterian system was no guarantee that he sympathized with it. In many cases the reverse was probably true. To many a Presbyterian minister, the presence of the local Parliament man in the parish government must have been something less than welcome. For Independents, as for Erastians and even simple skeptics, participation in the system was a convenient method of maintaining control.

But the ministers had still a few cards to play. In addition to Scottish support, they received increasingly effective backing from the London aldermen and Common Council. The result was a further deterioration of the relations between Parliament and City. When, on November 19, 1645, the City fathers petitioned the Commons to grant the ministers wider powers in the matter of election of elders, they were frigidly received, and an open breach was averted only by the fiction that the City men had been misled and Parliament misrepresented. Lenthall contented himself with a blast at the ministers who, he indignantly declared, aimed at "independence upon the civil power."[18] But the mask of diplomacy was abruptly dropped when a delegation from the ministers themselves appeared at the door of the House. The unfortunate clerics received the full force of the Commons' fury. The fact that their petition agreed almost word for word with that of the City did nothing to mend matters. It was well, observed one member tartly, that "nothing is to be complained of in the City of London but want of jurisdiction in the ministry." Their tongue-lashing duly received, the humiliated "black coats" were peremptorily ordered home and told not to trouble themselves with further attendance. The inevitable committee was then set up to investigate the "promoters of this business."[19] The support that the ministers received from the City governors was probably actuated as much by political as by doctrinal motives. It is safe to say that however much the Londoners professed to oppose the Erastian spirit of the Commons they had even less sympathy for the Scottish model of church-state relations.

Relations between the radicals and the City men were further exacerbated by increasingly bitter rivalry between rival Irish interest groups

17. D'Ewes, "Journal," BM, Harl. 166, fol. 265b; Whitaker, "Diary," BM, Add. MS. 31,116, fol. 233b; *CJ*, IV, 288–290; Yonge, "Journal," BM, Add. MS. 18,780, fol. 144a.
18. Yonge, "Journal," BM, Add. MS. 18,780, fol. 168a.
19. *Ibid.*, fol. 169a; *CJ*, IV, 348; Whitelocke, "Annals," BM, Add. MS. 37,344, fol. 27a; Whitaker, "Diary," BM, Add. MS. 31,116, fols. 243b, 244a.

in the Commons and the City. In 1644, as we have seen, the radicals had supported both the Scots and the London Irish Adventurers against the Clotworthy group in the Commons. Since then, however, the alienation of both Scots and many Londoners from the political and religious policies of the radicals, and the evident desire of Vane and St. John for good relations with the moderates, provided Clotworthy and his followers with an opportunity for revenge; of this opportunity they took full advantage.

By mid-1645 Clotworthy had succeeded in consolidating his position by becoming chairman of a new joint committee of both Houses for Irish affairs. Under his direction the committee had become a formidable roadblock to the London interests. When the City men had proposed that the Irish cities of Cork, Kinsale, and Youghal be put up for sale, they had received a dusty answer, and their petition had been quietly shelved. The result was a settled hostility on the part of the London merchants to any attempt to raise money for the war in Ireland. The London Irish Adventurers committee at Grocers' Hall was strongly supported by the aldermen and Common Councillors, and, on November 11, 1645, amid the conflict with Parliament over religion and politics, they petitioned the Commons to consider the Adventurers' petition.[20]

On the same day, William Hawkins outlined the proposals to the Clotworthy committee. They were sweeping enough. Four cities in Ireland were to be handed over to the Adventurers with privileges similar to those of London. In addition, persons with bad debts in Ireland, on payment to Parliament of a portion of the debt, were to have the total amounts secured by grants of Irish land.

A few weeks later the London Adventurers again petitioned the Commons on the subject. They now offered to contribute £20,000 to the cause if their requests were granted. It is perhaps worth noting that the generosity that they expected from the Commons they were scarcely willing to accord to the native Irish. They appear, indeed, to have envisaged a wholesale expulsion or even extermination of the population. They were anxious, they explained, to effect a "speedy plantation of that Kingdom with a religious people, in the place . . . of that idolatrous Nation, the Irish rebels . . . and a fruitful and good land will thus again . . . be re-peopled to live under the Sunshine of the Gospel . . . "[21]

The Commons were apparently unimpressed by this roseate picture,

---

20. *Journals of the House of Lords* [hereafter cited as *LJ*], VII, 695; see also J. R. MacCormack, "Irish Land and the English Civil War," *Canadian Catholic Historical Association Report*, no. 25 (1958), pp. 53–66.

21. "Reasons delivered . . . , " BM, E.314(7), p. 13.

whereupon the exasperated Adventurers accused Clotworthy and his associate, John Davies, of collusion and dishonesty in connection with lucrative army supply contracts. The Commons reacted in turn by ordering the London Adventurers to surrender all their books and papers relating to Irish affairs since June 1643.[22] The Londoners prudently pulled in their horns, but for the next six months a kind of armed truce reigned between the contending interest groups.

In all these disputes the hand of the radicals was greatly strengthened by a significant change in the composition of the House of Commons itself. For the first time since 1640 elections were held to fill the many vacancies left by the expelled royalist members. The voting began in August 1645 and went on intermittently for the next three years. Some 275 new members were to be admitted in this fashion before Cromwell expelled the Rump in 1653.[23] From the beginning it was a distinctly radical project, and, initially, the hopes of Vane and St. John were justified by a substantial accession of voting strength. In the long run, however, the majority of "recruiters," as the new members were termed, threw their weight to the conservative side, and, by mid-1646, they were helping to give Holles the majority in the Commons that was to make possible the six-month reign of the moderates from January to June 1647. It was the character of this new radical support rather than its numerical strength that was to be of significance for the future. Men of a fanatical stripe, they were to provide a hard core of extreme radicalism that was soon to prove embarrassing to the radical leaders themselves.

The elections had been foreshadowed as early as October 1644, when the radical Lisle had moved that the vacant seats be filled before any peace was concluded. The matter was dropped, but in August 1645 it was revived when the radical voters of Southwark petitioned for new representatives.[24] The moderates once again opposed the move, but after a hot debate on August 21, 1645, they lost by three votes; the election was duly ordered.[25]

The Southwark election gave rise to considerable speculation as to the political impact of the recruiters. Jean de Montereul, lately arrived from France, advised Mazarin that the change would not bring about

22. *Ibid.*, pp. 14–16.
23. Douglas Brunton and D. H. Pennington, *Members of the Long Parliament* (London, Allen & Unwin, 1954), pp. 21–37.
24. D'Ewes, "Journal," BM, Harl. 166, fol. 149a; Whitaker, "Diary," BM, Add. MS. 31,116, fols. 167a, 170a, 226a.
25. Whitaker, "Diary," BM, Add. MS. 31,116, fols. 226a, 227a, b; D'Ewes, "Journal," BM, Harl. 166, fols. 253b, 256b; *CJ*, IV, 241. The radicals were not unanimous on the issue; St. John opposed the project. (*Memoirs of Denzil, Lord Holles* [London, 1699] [hereafter cited as Holles, *Memoirs*], pp. 41–42.)

a peace settlement, and the atrabilious Baillie put the scheme down to the "cunning and diligence" of the radicals.[26] Vane was soon reporting enthusiastically that "the new elections go on apace,"[27] and many of the new members were described as being "of the severer strain." The irrepressible Hugh Peters told the assembled Commons that he hoped that "the spirit of the Pyms, Hampdens, Strodes, might be redoubled upon the new elected members."[28]

Active electioneering was carried on by both moderates and radicals.[29] Whitelocke was urged to assist the cause of Colonel Tyrell in Buckinghamshire. Tyrell later complained to Whitelocke of the electioneering tactics of Thomas Scott and Edmund West. Scott was a candidate for Aylesbury, and he and his friends were accused of having assisted matters by gathering "divers of the inhabitants on the Lords Day into a cellar at drinking."[30] A new election was ordered, but with the same result. Scott was to become a vocal member of the extreme wing of the radicals, and his staunch republicanism was to plague Oliver Cromwell to the end of his days.

There was sharp criticism in the Commons about the undue influence of peers in elections, but despite the outcry against the Earl of Warwick, his second son, Charles Rich, was elected for Sandwich and served until Pride's Purge. There was more grumbling about irregularities in Buckinghamshire, concerned with the elections of West and George Fleetwood, both of whom enjoyed radical support.[31]

Holles accused the radicals of attempting to control the course of the elections by withholding writs from constituencies of which they were unsure; by employing their supporters in the county committees to influence elections; and by using the power of the New Model itself to intimidate electors.[32] He also charged them with frustrating appeals against such practices through their control of the Committee of Privi-

26. Montereul to Mazarin, London, Aug. 21, 1645, *The Diplomatic Correspondence of Jean de Montereul and the Brothers de Bellièvre, French Ambassadors in England and Scotland, 1645–1648,* ed. J. G. Fotheringham, 2 vols. (Edinburgh, 1898–1899) [hereafter cited as *MC*], II, 7; Baillie to Spang, Sept. 5, 1645, Baillie, *Letters,* II, 316.

27. Sir H. Vane, Jr., to Sir H. Vane, Sr., Sept. 30, 1645, *CSPD, 1645–1647,* p. 167.

28. Sir R. Honeywood to Sir H. Vane, Sr., Oct. 13, 1645, *ibid.,* p. 190.

29. For a thorough discussion of party influence in elections, particularly that of Edmund Prideaux, Sir Robert Harley, and Anthony Nicols, see David Underdown's valuable article, "Party Management in Recruiter Elections 1645–1648," *English Historical Review,* LXXXIII (Apr. 1968), 235–264.

30. Whitelocke, "Annals," BM, Add. MS. 37,344, fol. 15b; Brunton and Pennington, *Members of the Long Parliament,* p. 244. Whitelocke asserted that he had been opposed by Prideaux and Haselrig in the matter.

31. Whitelocke, "Annals," BM, Add. MS. 37,344, fol. 25a, b.

32. Both moderates and radicals benefited from the application of military pressure. See Underdown, "Party Management," pp. 243–247.

leges. Recent research tends to substantiate these charges, particularly with respect to Prideaux's use of his position as a commissioner of the great seal in the service of the radicals.

The radicals could reply with countercharges. Lionel Copley, a moderate, was accused of attempting to bribe the mayor of Castle Rising with £20 and the borough electors with £100.[33] Though this election was voided, Copley, who had already run into heavy weather as commissary general under Essex, managed to become the member for Bossiney. The election of Tanfield Vachell was also voided on grounds of irregularities, and a new election was ordered.[34]

John Corbett, a future supporter of the radicals, was elected in Bishop's Castle, as a result of personal and political influence. The son of the former member, a parliamentarian who died in 1643, writing on his behalf to the aldermen and burgesses of the town, pointed out that Corbett was not only a cousin of his, but had married the daughter of the redoubtable London alderman and member Isaac Pennington.[35] He also was described as "well beloved of the [County] Committee."

The radicals were soon to discover that the recruiting of the House, far from providing them with a guaranteed majority, actually had the reverse effect. The Commons' division figures for 1646 clearly support Holles's statement that, although most of the new members entered the House as radical sympathizers, the actual parliamentary experience "made them change their minds . . . "[36] As early as January 1646 Holles began to win significant divisions, and by May and June of that year he was able to count as many as 150 supporters on particular issues.

But all this was in the future. In the autumn of 1645 the radicals had seemingly little cause to worry. As they strengthened their military hold on the nation, they adroitly checkmated the Scottish overtures to Charles I with intrigues of their own. Toward their old parliamentary opponents they adopted a conciliatory, even a magnanimous, attitude that was pleasant enough while it lasted. Generous grants of cash and property were ladled out of the public pot to friend and old adversary alike. Holles himself was granted a twenty-one-year lease of the royal estates at Chepstow.[37] The Earl of Stamford, long a favorite

33. Holles, *Memoirs*, pp. 42–43; Underdown, "Party Management," pp. 253–258.
34. "Diary of the Corporation," in *The Records of Reading*, ed. J. M. Guilding, 4 vols. (London, 1892–1896), IV, 167–168.
35. Samuel More to the bailiff, aldermen, and burgesses of Bishop's Castle, Feb. 19, 1646, Report on the Bishop's Castle Manuscripts, *Tenth Report of the Royal Commission on Historical Manuscripts, Appendix, Part IV* (London, H. M. Stationery Office, 1885), p. 404.
36. Holles, *Memoirs*, pp. 43–44.
37. Whitaker, "Diary," BM, Add. MS. 31,116, fol. 231a.

whipping boy of the radicals, was, on the same day, listed among those
to be reimbursed. Giles Green was granted an annual pension of £500,
and Speaker Lenthall was rewarded for his loyal services to the radicals by a life grant of the mastership of the rolls. To top it all off, the
Earl of Essex, the old *bête noire* himself, was granted the handsome
pension of £10,000 per annum. Perhaps even more significant, in view
of the shaky position of Charles Stuart, was the fact that his nephew,
the Elector Palatine, who had hung on in London after his somewhat
vinegary reception in September 1644, was given a pension of £8,000
per annum.[38]

In the peace propositions drawn up in early December 1645 the
radicals were careful to maintain the same evenhanded balance between the old factions. Charles I was to be asked—perhaps ordered
would be the better word—to confer dukedoms on Essex, Northumberland, Warwick, and Pembroke and marquisates on Manchester and
Cecil. Robartes, Saye and Sele, Wharton, Willoughby of Parham, and
the elder Fairfax were to be made earls. Holles was to become a vis-
count, and Cromwell (who had by now apparently revised his earlier
equalitarian contempt for lords), the elder Vane, and Fairfax were to
be awarded baronies. Annual pensions of the order of £5,000, £2,500,
£1,500, and £1,000 were to be conferred on Sir Thomas Fairfax, Cromwell, Waller, Haselrig, Stapleton, Ireton, and Skippon, respectively.[39]

Such demands reflected the complacency with which the leading
parliamentarians viewed the military and political scene in late 1645.
The fall of Bristol and the defeat of Montrose at Philiphaugh had
virtually extinguished any lingering royalist hopes. Digby's defeat at
Sherborne drove another nail in the coffin, and by November 1645
such power as Charles had possessed after Naseby had been effectively
destroyed. He could now do little more than jockey for position between the Scots and the parliamentarian radicals who were themselves
more interested in preventing an agreement between the King and
their opponents than in any real settlement with Charles himself.

By late September Montereul predicted that they would depose the
King and would only come to terms with him as a last resort. "The
complete perdition of their King" was, in some Scottish eyes, the
logical end of radical policy, and Montereul argued that Charles could

---

38. *CJ*, IV, 271, 276, 287, 322.

39. *Ibid.*, 359. Lilburne viewed these proceedings with a jaundiced eye. ". . .
there are those that have no small influence on you," he told Cromwell, "that if
the wheel of honour and profit shall turn around every day of the week, they are
able to carry themselves so that they shall be no losers by it, and are able to give
the fairest words in the world to you, or any other honest man they deal with
when they intend to cut your throat." (Lilburne to Cromwell, Dec. 9, 1645, printed
in BM, E.400(5), pp. 12–13.)

avert ruin only by an alliance with the Scots.[40] But despite their apparent hostility toward the Crown, the radicals in the autumn of 1645 carried on certain negotiations, the exact significance of which remains cloudy. They involved at one time or another such personages as Cromwell, Prince Rupert, the Prince of Wales, and some of the leading Oxford Royalists.

A royalist agent later recalled that the radicals at this time were "influenced entirely by Cromwell."[41] He appears indeed to have played a role of some importance in these secret dealings and to have discussed the peace settlement with a royalist officer just after the fall of Bristol.[42] Since Rupert left for Oxford on September 11 reportedly carrying peace terms with "the English Independents,"[43] the question arises as to whether Sir William Vavasour, who was almost certainly the royalist officer concerned, was acting on behalf of Rupert and was, in fact, his ambassador to Cromwell. Another possibility is that Cromwell was negotiating with the royalist General George Goring who was later reported to have been dealing with "the heads of the army" with respect to a plan whereby he would seize the Prince of Wales and hand him over to Parliament.[44]

Rupert, since the spring of 1645, had been numbered among the royalist "peace party." When he surrendered Bristol, after what seemed to be but a token resistance, the King suspected his loyalty and ordered his arrest along with Colonel Legge, the Oxford commandant whose name was linked during the Saville affair with those said to have been ready to hand over Oxford to the parliamentarians. The King was no doubt also aware that Rupert's brother, the Elector Palatine, had just been granted a handsome pension by Parliament, and he had some reason to fear that other hands were now reaching out for the crown so precariously perched on his own head.

The intentions of the radicals with respect to the Prince of Wales were potentially a more serious threat to Charles than the ambitions of the Palatine house.[45] In late September the Prince was alleged to have asked Fairfax for permission to rejoin his father in order to

40. Advices from London enclosed in Nani to Doge, Paris, July 27, 1645, *CSPV, 1643–1647*, pp. 203–204; Montereul to Mazarin, London, Sept. 25, 1645, *MC*, I, 21–24; Advices from London, Oct. 16, 1645, *CSPV, 1643–1647*, p. 220; D'Ewes, "Journal," BM, Harl. 166, fol. 270a; Montereul to Mazarin, London, Oct. 30, 1645, *MC*, I, 45; Mazarin to Montereul, Paris, Nov. 21, 1645, *MC*, II, 577–578.

41. *Colonel Joseph Bamfield's Apologie written by himselfe and printed at his own desire* (The Hague? 1685) [hereafter cited as Bamfield, *Apologie*], p. 12.

42. Montereul to Brienne, Nov. 20, 1645, Bodleian Library, Carte MS. 83, fol. 87a.

43. Montereul to Mazarin, London, Sept. 18, 1645, *MC*, I, 16.

44. Montereul to Mazarin, London, Nov. 27, 1645, *ibid.*, 68.

45. C. V. Wedgwood, *The King's War, 1641–1647* (London, Collins, 1958), pp. 487–490.

work for an agreement between the King and the parliamentary radicals. According to reports, which the Scots and their English allies found very alarming, some of the radicals were to profit handsomely from the projected settlement. Northumberland was to be made lord admiral, while Saye, the veteran leader of the radicals in the House of Lords, was to become treasurer.[46] The King, alarmed by these rumors about his son, sent orders that the Prince be transported to France immediately. According to Clarendon, however, Goring ignored these instructions and neglected even to inform the Prince of Wales of the order.[47]

The intentions of the radicals concerning Prince Charles remain obscure at this time, but if the King was to be deposed and the monarchy preserved the legitimate heir could scarcely be ignored in the political calculations. Radical overtures in his direction were to be widely reported in the first half of 1646. The Holles' party was to demonstrate similar leanings in 1647.

An offer of the crown to Prince Charles was a policy upon which a number of otherwise disparate elements could unite. A truce between parliamentary moderates and radicals had been effected, and it was reported that some royalists in Oxford were so impatient for a settlement that they were even willing to see it accomplished by "Cromwell and the Independents" if there were no feasible alternatives. Montereul was disturbed to find that even the Earl of Holland and his friends were moving in this direction. He warned Holland that in such an eventuality the King would be in the power of "persons who hate the monarchy, and on whom it would devolve to destroy it in England . . . "[48] The royalist Colonel Bamfield—with the benefit of hindsight—recalled that the radicals, despite their links with leading royalists, were aiming at the destruction of the monarchy. "The bulk of the party, and the leading men . . . were resolved," he wrote, "upon an entire subversion of monarchy, and the establishment of a new government."[49]

The peace offer that the radicals reportedly made to the King in November must be viewed against this background. If Montereul was correctly informed, the radicals had offered control of religion to the King as well as the appointment of one-half the executive offices of the kingdom. But radical supremacy in the army and in Ireland was

46. Montereul to Mazarin, London, Sept. 25, 1645, *MC*, I, 23–24.

47. Edward Hyde, Earl of Clarendon, *The History of the Rebellion and Civil Wars in England*, ed. W. D. Macray, 6 vols. (Oxford, 1888) [hereafter cited as Clarendon, *Rebellion*], IV, 97–98.

48. Montereul to Mazarin, London, Dec. 4, 1645, *MC*, I, 74.

49. Bamfield, *Apologie*, p. 12.

implied in a proposal to supply the King with an army to conquer that country provided that they were given control of it and that Independency was tolerated in England. Once again, as in the secret proposals of the previous spring, the radicals envisaged factional rather than parliamentary supremacy. Once again they were prepared to use the army to force Parliament to accept such a settlement.[50]

Montereul was understandably skeptical about the offer and predicted that it would come to nothing. The radicals, he thought, had no genuine desire for a peace settlement and would, moreover, encounter great difficulties in attempting to implement such an agreement. They were also aware, he said, that Rupert had "formed a powerful party for them" in Oxford.[51] It seems clear that they felt no pressing need for an agreement with the increasingly isolated King and that their main concern was to frustrate any potential understanding between him and the Scots.

The deposition of Charles and the crowning of the Prince of Wales was the most lenient treatment that the House of Stuart could now expect from the radicals; the most severe was the abolition of the monarchy and the trial of the King. Charles could do little now but negotiate frantically with Irish and Scots, whose internal divisions and eccentric ambitions made alliances with them difficult and dangerous. The covenanting Scots were split along lines that mirrored to some extent the divisions among the English parliamentarians. But the brooding presence of the Kirk was a force of incalculable strength, and it is doubtful whether the King's distaste for Presbyterianism, which matched the Kirk's zeal for its propagation, permitted him to treat his negotiation with the Scots as anything more than a device to frighten the radicals into a settlement.

The Scottish commissioners in London with whom he dealt were not so much plenipotentiaries as a liaison group between the Scottish parliament or Committee of Estates and the English Parliament. They were also divided among themselves and, to that extent, unreliable. Chancellor Loudon was a moderate, but there were a number of dubious personages, such as Balmerino, who were close to Argyle and doubtless kept him informed of developments throughout the negotiation. The parliamentary radicals apparently knew what passed between the Scottish commissioners and the King; Balmerino may have been the source.

Scots were further handicapped by their growing unpopularity in England. As the moderates in the Commons drifted toward the radicals, the increasingly isolated Scots looked for support to the group of

50. Montereul to Brienne, Nov. 20, 1645, Bodleian Library, Carte MS. 83, fol. 111.
51. Montereul to Mazarin, London, Nov. 13, 1645, *MC*, I, 59–60.

peers centered around the Earl of Holland, declaring themselves ready
to dispense with the support of the Holles group and, if necessary, to
use force against all opponents of their projected settlement.[52]

Chancellor Loudon's influence can be clearly seen in the proposals
made by the Scottish commissioners to Montereul on October 16, 1645.
There was no mention of the dread word "covenant," and while it
would be difficult, they said, to change "what had been decided upon"
—Presbyterianism—points as yet unsettled could be submitted to a
new assembly in which Anglican ministers might take part.[53]

There were also interesting contrasts with the position taken by the
radicals with respect to the militia and to Ireland. At Uxbridge the
parliamentary demand, sponsored by the radicals, had been for complete parliamentary control of the militia. A short time later, however,
in their secret peace overture to the King, they had required that their
own party rather than Parliament have that power and had even envisaged use of the military to force the peace settlement on Parliament.
They were now taking a similar stand and, by implication, were demanding control of the executive of any new government. The Scots,
on the other hand, were prepared to accept the royalist Uxbridge
proposition on the militia, that is, that the King be permitted to name
one-half the commissioners controlling it. Partial royal control of
English forces was, in their minds, infinitely preferable to the military
supremacy of the parliamentary radicals.

They were determined, on the other hand, to protect their interests
in Ireland. At Uxbridge complete parliamentary control had been demanded. The radicals, in their secret overture after Uxbridge, had
softened this to the extent of disavowing any intent to exterminate the
Irish. Their position in November had changed to a demand for partisan rather than parliamentary control of that country. The relatively
strong Scottish position in the north of Ireland was viewed with some
jealousy, especially by parliamentarians with Irish interests. The radical proposal would have taken care of this problem. But the Scots, by
proposing that the Irish issue be settled by the parliaments of both
kingdoms, were protecting their own stake in Ireland.

Presbyterian church government was the biggest single stumbling
block in the way of any agreement, and this, despite the lack of enthusiasm felt by the English "Presbyterians" and some leading Scots
themselves for the system. The Earl of Holland assured Montereul
that English adherence to Presbyterianism was but a temporary phe-

52. Scottish commissioners to Montereul, London, Oct. 17, 1645, *ibid.*, II, 569–
570.
53. Memorandum from Montereul to the Scottish commissioners in London, Oct.
16, 1645, *ibid.*, 569–570.

nomenon. Parliament had resisted the claims of the ministers to a "divine right" presbytery, he said, in order that a future Parliament might more easily "do away" with Presbyterianism. We can picture Mazarin in Paris smiling as he read the addendum of the prudent Montereul: "it is, as you will perceive, not necessary to inform the Scots of this intention."[54]

But even among the Scots there were those who were not unduly disturbed by such a prospect. Loudon, while insisting that concessions on Presbyterianism were politically impossible for the Scots because of the power of the Kirk, nevertheless gave assurance that if the King knew how to take advantage of the times he could "restore a moderate Episcopacy in England, without trouble and before long."[55]

Neither Charles I nor his Queen was disposed to take such an optimistic view of things. Sir Robert Moray, who carried the Scottish proposals to Paris, found the Queen stubborn on religion, and his reports were discouraging to those who still hoped for an alternative to the triumph of the radicals. Holland complained that there was no hope of working through the Queen, and soon Balmerino was accusing the King of making use of the Scots only as a lever in his negotiations with the radicals.[56] The Queen had, in fact, been persuaded by Mazarin to advise her husband to concede the point of religion, but this was not known in London. But Charles was, in any case, adamant on the subject and was as impervious to Henrietta's arguments as he was to the increasing impatience of his own followers.[57]

The radicals could now sit back and regard, with a kind of cool detachment, the spectacle of a King of England, isolated and reduced to the role of a supplicant, almost pleading for the favor of men whom he would have more cheerfully seen hanging at Tyburn. Charles dispatched a steady stream of letters to Westminster between December 1645 and May 1646. They took the form mostly of almost embarrassingly humble requests for permission to remount his throne on practically any terms. His messages received little support in the radical-dominated Commons. St. John opposed his request for a safe-conduct for his emissaries on the grounds that in previous treaties with the King "there was always some dangerous design."[58] Scottish protests that this was tantamount to the complete rejection of negotiations were to no avail. It was shortly after this, in the cold December of 1645, that the Commons ordered that the hangings from the King's

54. Montereul to Mazarin, London, Oct. 16, 1645, *ibid.*, I, 32.

55. Montereul to Mazarin, London, Nov. 27, 1645, *ibid.*, 67.

56. Montereul to Mazarin, London, Dec. 18, 1645, *ibid.*, 79.

57. Montereul to Mazarin, London, Dec. 4, 1645, *ibid.*, 73–75.

58. Whitelocke, "Annals," BM, Add. MS. 37,344, fol. 29a; *CJ*, IV, 369–371; Whitaker, "Diary," BM, Add. MS. 31,116, fol. 247a, b.

wardrobe at Whitehall be used as curtains in front of the Commons windows "against the injury of this bitter weather."[59] The King's further offer to come to London in person to discuss peace terms and put the militia under a joint commission was summarily rejected. The House, pointedly ignoring the Scots, declared that the militia should be controlled by Parliament.[60]

Charles could no longer look to the moderates in the Commons for support. Indeed it was Stapleton himself who read the reply of the English members of the committee of both kingdoms to the royal overtures. The document was sufficiently menacing in tone. So much "innocent blood" had been shed by the King's commands and commissions, it read, that it was impossible to agree to his coming to London "until satisfaction and security be first given . . . "[61] The Scots perhaps gauged the mood correctly when they wondered aloud whether or not such words implied something more than a simple refusal to treat with the King. They were not empowered, they told Parliament, to agree to such a declaration.[62]

If the Scots suspected that the radicals had thoughts of bringing the King to trial, the reappearance of the witty and uninhibited Henry Marten did nothing to dispel the impression. If his reckless words with respect to the royal family had resulted in his expulsion from the House in 1643, the mood was far different now. That order was now erased, and Marten took his old seat as knight of the shire for Berkshire. Not only had the new elections brought in some kindred spirits, but there were those who argued that the war had, after all, been fought "in maintenance of as much in effect as Mr. Marten had said."[63] By mid-January 1646 the radicals were said to be preparing an apartment for the King in the Tower of London, and it was widely held that they intended "to destroy totally the monarchy in this country."[64] The future of the monarchy itself was becoming an issue between radicals and Scots who, in the words of one Scottish commissioner, wanted nothing but "the preservation of the King and the monarchy."[65]

Although the Scots received little support in the Commons, they were vigorously seconded by the City of London and the Westminster Assembly. The radicals had opposed Charles's coming to London perhaps as much from fear of future bloodshed as from indignation over the blood spilled in the past. The latent support available to Charles

59. *CJ*, IV, 381.
60. *Ibid.*, 392.
61. *LJ*, VIII, 81–82.
62. *Ibid.*, 85; Whitaker, "Diary," BM, Add. MS. 31,116, fol. 247a, b.
63. Whitaker, "Diary," BM, Add. MS. 31,116, fol. 247a, b.
64. Montereul to Mazarin, London, Jan. 11, 15, 1646, *MC*, I, 89, 109.
65. Public Record Office, Paris Transcripts, 31/3/78, fols. 47a, 48a.

in the City was now of formidable proportions. A group of influential Londoners assured the Earl of Holland in early January 1646 that if the King would agree to come to the City they would fight for him and "either die at his feet or place him in a position beyond the power of the Independents." Holland replied that all his friends would do like-wise.[66] Prince Rupert was said to have argued at Oxford that, if the King came to London with 300 men, he would soon find 9,000 more to assist him "to cut the throats of the Roundheads in the Parliament and City." Alarmed by these reports, the Commons pressed for martial law in London, and by mid-January Holland and his cohorts had thought better of the project.[67]

In London opposition to the radicals continued on a more prosaic level. The religious issue was at once real and convenient. But despite the increasing uneasiness of the more substantial Londoners, as the shouts of the religious and political zealots swelled ever louder in the streets, their alarmed protests to the Commons were virtually ignored.

The City's increasing dependence on the Scots was, at the same time, emphasized by their demand for a speedy church settlement according to "our most solemn League and Covenant."[68] A significant difference between Lords and Commons was observable in the reception accorded the Londoners. The peers, not otherwise noted for their enthusiasm for Presbyterianism, gave them a warm welcome and suggested that they suppress "unlawful courses." "Our last refuge is to God," intoned Robert Baillie, adding pragmatically, "and under him to the City." The Londoners, he felt, were understandably hostile to the demand of the religious Independents that toleration include Lutherans and even the despised Baptists. But Parliament must finally yield, he predicted, because they could not survive without the support of London.[69]

The strength of religious Independency in the Commons at this time is difficult to gauge. It is clear that the Independent ministers and their supporters outside the House regarded the radical leaders in Parliament as their friends and allies, but it is equally clear that the radical party as such was by no means wholly Independent in sym-pathy. The Independent ministers could exert sufficient influence in the Commons to delay parliamentary permission for the printing of a Presbyterian pamphlet in December 1645, but the numerical weakness of their genuine coreligionists in the Commons was revealed when the House divided. A division in October 1645 over the question of mak-

66. Montereul to Mazarin, London, Jan. 4, 1646, *MC*, I, 83–84.

67. Montereul to Mazarin, London, Jan. 11, 1646, *ibid.*, 89.

68. *CJ*, IV, 407; Whitaker, "Diary," BM, Add. MS. 31,116, fol. 254a, b.

69. Baillie to Ramsay, c. Jan. 17, 1646, Baillie, *Letters*, II, 336–337; Whitaker, "Diary," BM, Add. MS. 31,116, fol. 247b; *CJ*, IV, 372–373.

ing the covenant a condition of ordination was a case in point. After a debate during which one "Presbyterian" (D'Ewes) pointed out that no such impediment existed in any other Christian church the anti-covenant forces mustered only thirty-three votes as against eighty-eight for its supporters.[70] Baillie's view that the number of religious Independents in the House was "very small" seems accurate, as does his description of them as "prime men, active and diligent." He characterized the lawyers as a "strong party" and thoroughgoing Erastians in their approach. Still a third group was that of the "worldly, profane men" who were terrified at the thought of the minatory rule of an English version of the Kirk. These three groups, wrote Baillie, accounted for two-thirds of the Commons' membership.[71]

Until mid-March 1646, when London's opposition to the radicals collapsed like a pricked balloon, the City strongly supported both the Scots and the Westminster Assembly. The angered radicals responded with a number of steps designed to bring the Londoners to heel. The outspoken Lisle clashed with Glyn, the Recorder of London, after Lisle had declared that Londoners were on the point of doing as much harm to the kingdom as they had originally done good by their financial assistance. Glyn countered by accusing the radicals of an intention of bringing matters "to the last extremity."[72]

The radical-led Commons drew up a peace proposition that would have reduced the jurisdiction of the London militia to its old boundaries, depriving the City of military control of such important (and radical) suburbs as Southwark. The aroused City men replied with a delegation headed by that erstwhile friend of the radicals, Alderman John Fowke. If the proposition were not changed, they threatened, they would take action, "according to their conscience and . . . their covenant."[73]

The City then made a defiant decision to lend £31,000 to the Scots for which they were duly thanked by a Scottish delegation headed by Lauderdale. "Great signs of love," exulted Baillie, were expressed by the City fathers. Such signs were few in the House of Commons, and, when the radical Francis Allen gave the members an account of this affair, a serious dispute erupted. Once again the Lords supported the City even to the extent of voting to set aside three royalist houses for the use of the lord mayor and sheriffs. The moderates, too, newly aware of their voting strength, ventured some support, and in one

70. D'Ewes, "Journal," BM, Harl. 166, fol. 271a, b; *CJ*, IV, 319.
71. Baillie to Ramsay, London, Jan. 20, 1646, Baillie, *Letters*, II, 336.
72. Montereul to Mazarin, Jan. 29, 1646, *MC*, I, 125.
73. *Ibid.*; R. R. Sharpe, *London and the Kingdom*, 3 vols. (London, 1894–1895), II, 232.

division on an issue concerning London, they defeated the radicals by a vote of 120 to 72.[74]

The signal for renewed hostilities was the passage in March 1646 of an ordinance designed to give to parliamentary commissions direct jurisdiction over religious subjects, such as excommunication. The policy can be regarded as radical inspired, but it was Holles who carried it to the upper house. The City men reacted violently, very nearly condemning the measure as contrary to the covenant, and petitioned the Lords against it. Attributing its character to the Independents, they demanded safeguards against arbitrary power. But in contrast to their former cordiality, the Lords now turned a stony face to the Londoners and proceeded to vote their petition a breach of privilege. After waiting in vain on the Commons, the City men returned home and were soon made aware that more such petitions would also be considered a breach of privilege.[75]

The rulers of the City may have contemplated calling out the apprentices and the bully boys and the use of the techniques of mass pressure so well taught by John Pym and Isaac Pennington. They were rumored to be planning a mass demonstration outside the House of Commons and the use of slogans against both Independency and liberty of conscience. But the London policy makers were not cast in the heroic mold, and they shrank from a confrontation with the New Model. On March 19, 1646, they collapsed completely and even apologized for any breach of privilege they might have committed.[76] For the next six months the City was virtually eliminated as a factor in the political balance of power.

With London cowed, the Commons could now deal with the Westminster Assembly at their leisure. The ministers were still stubbornly resisting and even had the temerity to petition the Commons against the controversial church ordinance. By a vote of eighty-eight to seventy-six the Commons voted the petition to be a breach of privilege. In this case, despite the fact that he had carried the measure to the Lords, Holles joined Stapleton as a teller in support of the ministers.[77]

After a "long doubtful debate" a notable declaration, epitomizing the Erastian spirit, was passed. By it, the Commons proclaimed to the

74. Baillie to Spang, Feb. 20, 1646, Baillie, *Letters,* II, 345, 352–353; Whitaker, "Diary," BM, Add. MS. 31,116, fol. 256a; *CJ,* IV, 439, 444, 449.

75. Baillie to Roberts, c. Mar. 10, 1646, Baillie, *Letters,* II, 358; Report on the Manuscripts of House of Lords, *Sixth Report of the Royal Commission on Historical Manuscripts, Part I, Report and Appendix* (London, H. M. Stationery Office, 1877), pp. 104–105; Whitaker, "Diary," BM, Add. MS. 31,116, fol. 259b.

76. Whitaker, "Diary," BM, Add. MS. 31,116, fol. 260b; *CJ,* IV, 479.

77. *CJ,* IV, 506. Sir John Evelyn of Wilts. and Haselrig were tellers for the majority.

world that the Westminster Assembly was scarcely more than its rubber stamp. It had no powers other than those explicitly granted it and no authority even to debate whether a law was or was not agreeable to the word of God except on parliamentary demand. The church, protested one irate divine, had possessed a legitimate jurisdiction even before the supreme magistrate was a Christian, adding: "Why it should lose that under Constantine which it had under Nero, I know not."[78]

More gall was in store. The Commons referred the charge of breach of privilege against the clergy to the two members who could be expected to be least sympathetic: Sir Arthur Haselrig, whose almost blasphemous sallies had already shocked some members, and the notorious rake, Henry Marten.

Under Haselrig's guidance, the House drew up a list of nine questions to which the ministers were required to give written answers. They were remarkable for their sarcastic, not to say skeptical, tone, which the assembly understandably regarded as threatening and insulting. Nor were they without support in the Commons. Some members were reported to have encouraged the City to issue a declaration attacking Marten as a man "that never speaks in the House but when he is drunk, and yet speaks every day; yet being Independent, is thought the only fit man to present the queries . . . to the synod."[79]

The parliamentarians had thus managed to alienate some of their oldest supporters, and, in their extremity, the ministers began to think again even about Charles I. In early May 1646 they were described as having "prayed very zealously for his Majesty" and to have begun "to fumble and botch in the mention of the parliament."[80] The desperate King could ill afford to ignore support even from such an unlikely quarter. Nonetheless, as the dispute between the divines and the Commons reached its climax, he was making his last frantic appeals not to them, but to their enemies—the radicals.

Charles's hatred of Presbyterianism seems to have blinded him to the possibilities in these directions. Indeed, he regarded that creed as more dangerous to monarchy than the rumored republicanism of some of the parliamentary radicals. The monarchy, he maintained, would never be destroyed by Englishmen. But apart from the high arguments of principle, Charles recognized that the radicals held effective power, and he argued that, even if he were to make the concessions on Presbyterianism that the Scots so assiduously demanded, the measure could never be put into effect as long as the radicals were masters of the

78. W. Sancroft to F. Sancroft, Cambridge, May 4, 1646, *Memorials of the Great Civil War, 1646–1652,* ed. H. Cary, 2 vols. (London, 1842), I, 18.
79. W. Sancroft to F. Sancroft, May 11, 1646, *ibid.,* 32.
80. W. Sancroft to F. Sancroft, May 4, 1646, *ibid.,* 17–18.

situation. Principle and realpolitik were in rare agreement and seemed to dictate that the radicals must be courted and their opponents ignored. It is hardly surprising that the latter tended to lose interest in supporting the King.

By early 1646 even Holland and his group of peers were ready to capitulate to radical power. Charles was told that the Scots and "the moderate English" would now scarcely hear of coming to terms with him.[81] The Scots professed to be dissatisfied with his position on Presbyterianism despite his willingness to guarantee the system in Scotland and to permit but not enforce it in England.[82]

At the same time the King was losing the support of the moderates he was making little headway with the radicals. Observers found it difficult to see the ground upon which his hopes rested. They saw only a steady hardening of attitude in the Vane-St. John faction, who, by January 20, 1646, were arguing the impossibility of any further treaty with the King.[83] Montereul warned Charles that any overtures made by them were designed only to frustrate agreement between himself and the Scots and that they intended only to "ruin him." Charles replied that he was aware of the resolutions the "Independents" had taken "to destroy the monarchy."[84] He remained skeptical, however, as to the reality of those intentions.

For their part, the radicals continued to exploit the King's habit of losing incriminating correspondence. His secret negotiations with the Irish were revealed to an intent House on January 16, 1646, and produced the expected explosion. The House had the example of former Parliaments, declared one angry radical, and it knew "how they had acted towards Kings of England in similar circumstances."[85] John Gurdon, long numbered among the "violent" members, told the Commons that the King's hands were "red with the murder of . . . many of his subjects." Vane characterized the King's offer of toleration to the Independents as insincere. In any case, he said, they would prefer to receive that toleration from Parliament rather than from the King.[86] A radical plan to depose Charles, and to crown either the Duke of York or the Duke of Gloucester with Northumberland as Protector, was reported a few days later.[87]

Royalists like Secretary Edward Nicholas had few illusions about

81. Montereul to Mazarin, London, Jan. 29, 1646, *MC*, I, 123.
82. Clarendon, *Rebellion*, IV, 164.
83. Baillie to Ramsay, London, Jan. 20, 1646, Baillie, *Letters*, II, 337–338.
84. Montereul to Mazarin, London, Jan. 15, 1646, *MC*, I, 104.
85. Montereul to Mazarin, London, Jan. 22, 1646, *ibid.*, 117.
86. Montereul to Mazarin, London, Jan. 29, 1646, *ibid.*, 124–125.
87. Montereul to Mazarin, London, Jan. 22, 1646, *ibid.*, 117; Gardiner, *GCW*, III, 62, n. 3.

radical policy. "You cannot suppose the work is done," he told Vane in early March, "Though God should suffer you to destroy the King." Urging that the King be permitted to go to London, he promised Vane that even if Presbyterianism should be temporarily established, the radicals would have the King's full cooperation in the task of "rooting out of this Kingdom, that tyrannical government."[88] Vane may have given Charles some encouragement, if we can judge from the wording of a letter sent by the King to the radical leader a few weeks later. "Hasten my business all that possibly you can," entreated Charles, promising, if Vane cooperated, to "repay . . . to the full."[89]

The radicals could afford to remain detached in the face of these varied appeals. The resistance of London was collapsing; the opposition of the Scots was ineffective; the Westminster Assembly was cowed; and the parliamentary moderates were without a policy. Yet there were disquieting factors in the situation. The character of the new members was disappointing in that they evinced a disturbing tendency to conservatism. In four divisions in early 1645 the moderates, gradually feeling new strength and slightly emboldened by it, won significant victories.[90] Holles and Stapleton had as yet no intention of challenging the radical position, but it was a straw in the wind and gave point to Baillie's description of the radicals as "the small handful which guides all." His remark is supported by that of Montereul, who characterized radical policy as that of "opposing their small private interest to the general welfare of both kingdoms."[91] More and more painfully aware of their minority status, the radicals now took increased interest in their one trump card: the New Model army.

"The great business of some," noted Baillie suspiciously, was "to send recruits to Cromwell's army." The ostensible excuse—that of preparing for a French invasion—he described as a blind "to cover somewhat else." Six weeks later he was commenting acidly that "forty thousand men are a great army when there is not one man in the field against them." The purpose of the New Model he thought was now a political one to "keep the country in awe by a perpetual army and fall on us [the Scots], who have deserved so well of them."[92]

88. Nicholas to Vane, Mar. 2, 1646, in *Diary and Correspondence of Sir John Evelyn,* ed. William Bray, 4 vols. (London, 1895–1900), IV, 173.

89. Charles I to Vane, Mar. 2, 1646, *ibid.,* 174.

90. *CJ,* IV, 412, 428, 449, 471.

91. Baillie to Spang, London, c. Jan. 20, 1646, Baillie, *Letters,* II, 344–345; Montereul to Mazarin, London, Jan. 29, 1646, *MC,* I, 124.

92. Baillie to Roberts, London, Mar. 6, 1646, Baillie, *Letters,* II, 359; Baillie to Spang, Apr. 23, 1646, *ibid.,* 364–365; Meikle, *Correspondence,* p. 172. On the same day the Scots commissioners in London warned that the radicals might make a prisoner of the King and that the committee in Edinburgh should be prepared in order that they "might not be surprised if matters should turn to the worse."

The radicals appear to have aimed now, not so much at the extinction of monarchy, but at the deposition of Charles I and his replacement by a person more amenable to their influence. In 1644 and for a time in the autumn of 1645 they had leaned toward the Prince Elector or the Prince of Wales as possible candidates. By the spring of 1646 they were anxious to have the Prince of Wales come to London and may have considered offering him the crown. In mid-January a hostile note toward the younger Charles had been sounded. He had been told to disband his forces under pain of being declared an enemy of the state, and a scheme for crowning either the Duke of York or Gloucester had been discussed. By the end of January the radicals were in a more conciliatory mood, and had sent the Prince a "very respectful letter begging him to come here."[93] Six weeks later, the Commons, having contemptuously rejected the appeals of Charles I, agreed to write to his son in a "loving and tender way," inviting him to come over to the parliamentary side and to "have such counsellors about him as should be approved by both Houses."[94]

Speculation concerning a possible agreement between the Prince of Wales and the radicals continued through the summer of 1646. On July 22 Charles I, then virtually a prisoner of the Scots at Newcastle, made a rather enigmatic reference to "the prince of Wales treating with the Independents."[95] Whether the radicals wanted the Prince in London in order merely "to pretend to crown him," as some said, or whether they regarded him seriously as a future monarch who might heal the nation's deep divisions, it is, on the available evidence, impossible to say. But it is worth noting that a year later Holles revived the same policy and may even have been willing to support it in 1646. Such a prospect would also have had a strong appeal for many royalists, faced as they were by more unpleasant possibilities.

Charles I seems neither to have entertained the possibility of giving way to his son nor to have realized that a monarch who is forced to wage a civil war must regard his crown as the price of defeat. Instead, he offered on March 24 to dismiss his armies, go to London accom-

---

(Scottish commissioners to Committee of Estates, London, Apr. 23, 1646, Meikle, *Correspondence,* pp. 176–177.) Earlier, Loudon had been the unsuccessful advocate of an aggressive policy toward the radicals and complained that "too much scrupulosity hath lost a fit opportunity . . . we are in danger of being ruined." (Loudon to Lothian, Roystoun, Apr. 15, 1646, *Correspondence of Sir Robert Kerr, First Earl of Ancram and his son William, Third Earl of Lothian,* 2 vols. [Edinburgh, 1875], I, 182.)

93. *MC,* I, 109, 117, 124–125.

94. Whitelocke, "Annals," BM, Add. MS. 37,344, fol. 44a.

95. Charles I to Henry, Lord Jermyn *et al.,* Newcastle, July 22, 1646, *Letters of the Kings of England,* ed. Halliwell, I, 414; *MC,* I, 211.

panied only by his court, and permit Parliament to decide on the peace settlement.[96] The proposal, which amounted to unconditional surrender, received strong support in the Lords. The Commons, however, insisted that Charles agree first to such propositions as might be sent him. If he came to the City without permission, they bluntly warned, steps would be taken to "secure his person." Shocked by this threat, the Lords attempted to soften it by adding the words "from danger," to which the Commons agreed only after a fierce debate.[97] Whatever the phrasing, it seems clear that if Charles had gambled on an appearance in London he would have been unceremoniously hustled to the Tower. The "abolition of royal authority" was the aim of the radicals in the eyes of the Venetian representative, while Baillie believed that they intended "to have no shadow of a King."[98]

After Parliament's rejection of his offer Charles was ready to agree with Baillie. "Nothing will satisfy them," he wrote angrily, "but the ruin, not only of us, our posterity and friends, but even of monarchy itself."[99] He was now prepared, despite the risks, to consider throwing himself on the doubtful mercies of the Scots. The radicals' dislike and distrust of Charles were reinforced by their growing apprehension of a hostile London. For this reason, asserted one observer, there was nothing they feared more than the King's presence. The King would win strong support not only in the City, but in Parliament itself, many of the members of which would "appear for him with an open face, who now mask under a vizor, and sigh to see a party they like not, carry all before them."[100]

The charge that they were hostile, not only to Charles I, but to monarchy itself, was one that two years before the radicals would have shrugged off. But it had now become an embarrassment, particularly in view of their "loving and tender" overtures to the Prince of Wales. It was perhaps with a view to disarming such fears that in mid-April they publicly declared that there was no intention of altering the ancient constitution but only of obtaining the consent of the King to such powers as would prevent another civil war.[101]

But it was soon made clear that, abase himself as he might, Charles I

96. Advices from London, Mar. 19, 1646, *CSPV, 1643–1647*, pp. 251–253; Whitaker, "Diary," BM, Add. MS. 31,116, fol. 262a.

97. John Harrington, Parliamentary Diary, 1646–1647, BM, Add. MS. 10,114, fol. 11a.

98. Advices from London, Apr. 2, 1646, *CSPV, 1643–1647*, pp. 252–254; Baillie to Spang, London, Apr. 3, 1646, Baillie, *Letters*, II, 362–364.

99. Charles I to the Marquis of Ormonde, Apr. 3, 1646, *Letters of the Kings of England*, ed. Halliwell, I, 405.

100. W. Sancroft to F. Sancroft, Cambridge, May 4, 1646, *Memorials of the Great Civil War, 1646–1652*, ed. Cary, I, 17.

101. *CJ*, IV, 514.

was not acceptable on any terms to those who controlled the Long Parliament. Cromwell, now making one of his infrequent but significant appearances in the House, took the lead in stiffening the spines of any waverers. On April 25 his daughter's fiancé, Colonel Henry Ireton, forwarded another message from the King, the supplicatory tone of which aroused little sympathy. Charles seems to have made only one condition for his surrender to Parliament: that he might "continue King only, without being deposed for aught past."[102]

The opinion that the King would be treated "as Cromwell and his friends think it fittest for their affairs"[103] was borne out by Cromwell's handling of the incident. After reading Ireton's letter to the House he declared, perhaps somewhat disingenuously, that although Ireton had served Parliament well he deserved reproof for so much as forwarding the King's letter. After a long debate the lieutenant general had his way, and the Commons duly voted that commanders should receive no more such overtures.[104] Charles had now three choices open to him: fleeing the country; a desperate personal gamble in London; or the Scots. Two weeks later he was with the Scottish army.

The Battle of Naseby had assured parliamentary victory in the long struggle that had darkened life in England since the summer of 1642. After Naseby the royalists had done little more than postpone the inevitable day of reckoning. Through the autumn and winter Charles saw his support melt rapidly away until by March and April of 1646 he was an isolated figure whose only remaining expedients were the difficult and perilous ones of appealing for foreign military aid and exploiting the differences among his domestic enemies. It had become painfully clear, however, that whatever issues might divide them, on one point his adversaries were more and more united: Charles I could rule again, if at all, as no more than a titular monarch.

The parliamentary moderates had, it is true, supported Charles's interests on more than one occasion and at considerable personal risk. But they were concerned not so much to restore Charles I as to preserve monarchy itself from the real and imagined aims of the parliamentary radicals. Both Holles and Stapleton had a long record of pre-Civil War opposition to Charles I, and they had both personally fought the King's armies. Their efforts to offer a middle road between

102. Ireton to Cromwell, Apr. 23, 1646, *Memorials of the Great Civil War, 1646–1652*, ed. Cary, I, 2. On the same day the Venetian ambassador at Munster was making the following observation: "Confirmation is awaited with interest in the spectacle of a monarchy reduced to a republic in our day, upon which, with the passage of time, the French will have cause for reflection more than any others." (Contarini to Doge, Apr. 17, 1646, *CSPV, 1643–1647*, p. 255.)
103. Baillie, "Public Letter," Apr. 24, 1646, Baillie, *Letters*, II, 368–369.
104. Whitaker, "Diary," BM, Add. MS. 31,116, fol. 266b.

radicals and royalists had, moreover, brought them little thanks from either camp. By 1646, though their affection for Vane, St. John, and their friends had not appreciably deepened, they were now distinctly hesitant to act on whatever lukewarm feelings they may have had for Charles.

If radical policy had changed since the death of Pym in December 1643 it was with respect to the monarchy rather than to the King himself. They had, it is true, made secret overtures to him in the spring of 1645 just before Naseby and again in the autumn of that year. But it may be doubted if in either case there was a sincere attempt at a settlement. Their concomitant attempt to effect the desertion of royalist armies and garrisons throws considerable doubt on the good faith of the first negotiation; the second seems to have been little more than an attempt—and a largely successful one—to frustrate the negotiations between Charles and the Scots.

A more genuine alteration appears to have taken place with respect to the radicals' attitude toward the monarchy. Whereas in 1644 they had been widely regarded as hostile to that institution and republican in sympathy, by late 1645 they appear to have been more concerned to find a substitute for Charles than for the monarchy itself. The change coincided with the alienation of Lilburne and his followers from the parliamentary radicals. Henceforth the antimonarchical cry was to be taken up even more vociferously by the Levellers, and although Lilburne was to reconsider his position in 1647, many of his supporters continued to be ardent republicans.

It is perhaps not too much to say that by their declaration of April 1646 upholding the monarchy the parliamentary radicals unwittingly served notice that they were no longer in the vanguard of the forces of revolution in England. Leadership of this kind was passing rapidly to men who were determined that the grim struggle that had been going on in England since 1640 was not to end in the permanent ascendancy of a parliamentary oligarchy.

VI] The Genesis of the Newcastle Propositions

On April 27, 1646, the King slipped out of Oxford in disguise and headed for London. He appears to have entertained characteristically contradictory hopes of either a royalist coup in the City or an overture from the radical leaders in the Commons. Neither materialized, and he turned northward toward the Scots. When the Commons learned of his escape, the radicals, fearing that Charles might stake everything on a sudden personal appearance in the capital, took drastic counter-measures. They had only recently ordered a search of the house of the lord mayor himself; the King's escape was the signal for a general ransacking of suspected premises. Any person harboring the King, the Commons threatened, would "die without mercy." The doubtfully loyal London trainbands had been scheduled to muster in Hyde Park on May 4. This was now abruptly canceled, and stringent measures were ordered against Catholics and other suspected royalists in London and vicinity. In the general excitement one member drew some historical parallels for the guidance of the House. Kings John and Richard II had hidden themselves in the Isle of Wight and Wales, respectively, he pointed out, and warned that Charles I might well be hiding in London.[1]

On leaving the vicinity of the capital, the King headed first for King's Lynn with the apparent intention of escaping to the Continent should the Scots be unwilling to support him. Unfortunately for himself—and his country—he decided to clutch at the Scottish straw and to remain in England and make yet another bid to regain the throne.

Montereul had for some time been negotiating with the Scots in the hope of extracting a guarantee of support for the King. But although the Scots had produced some reasonably firm proposals and had claimed to be ready to back them by force of arms, they exhibited even

---

1. *Journals of the House of Commons* [hereafter cited as *CJ*], IV, 531–532; Bulstrode Whitelocke, "Annals," BM, Add. MS. 37,344 [hereafter cited as Whitelocke, "Annals," BM, Add. MS. 37,344], fol. 49b; Lawrence Whitaker, "Diary of Proceedings in the House of Commons," BM, Add. MS. 31,116 [hereafter cited as Whitaker, "Diary," BM, Add. MS. 31,116], fol. 268a; *Calendar of state papers and manuscripts relating to English affairs existing in the archives and collections of Venice and in other libraries of northern Italy*, vols. 10–38 (1603–1675) [London, H. M. Stationery Office, 1900–1940] [hereafter cited as *CSPV*], *1643–1647*, p. 259.

greater interest in offering the King the dubious hospitality of the Scottish army in the event that other avenues were closed to him. The notion seems first to have occurred to the Earl of Holland and was taken up eagerly by Balmerino who, of all the Scottish leaders, had one of the longest standing grudges against the House of Stuart. A close friend of the Marquis of Argyle, Balmerino doubtless saw possibilities in such a move that escaped Holland.[2]

By April 1646 Montereul had become distinctly uneasy; with the object of sounding out the Scottish military leaders, he had journeyed to Newark. He found the officers in no mood to give hard and fast promises, and very much under the influence of Balmerino, who seemed to be acting as a kind of political commissar. After much desperate negotiation, Montereul had to content himself with a vague verbal assurance of support for the King, which, actually, was to be honored more in the breach than in the observance.[3] Charles had not been long in the Scottish camp before discovering that his hosts were also his jailers.

The news from Newark produced a violent reaction at Westminster. Unimpressed by Scottish protests that the King's arrival had filled them with amazement and made them "like men that dream," the Commons, after a furious debate, peremptorily ordered that the King's person should be "disposed of" as the English Parliament should direct and that he should be placed in Warwick Castle.[4]

The use of words like "disposal" with respect to the person of the King did not sit well with the Scots and their allies, who now became distinctly more aggressive. A kind of pact among the City, the Lords, and "all the moderate members of Parliament" was said to have existed at this time to support an agreement between the King and the Scots "by force of arms."[5]

For the moment, however, the most strenuous opposition to the radicals came from the upper house, which, led by Essex, rejected the Commons' vote for the disposal of the King's person. Parliament, Essex declared, was bound by the covenant to defend the King's just rights. Now that he had deserted his evil counselors and had "freely offered himself," the main objective of the war had been gained. There

2. Montereul to Mazarin, Sept. 25, 1646, *The Diplomatic Correspondence of Jean de Montereul and the Brothers de Bellièvre, French Ambassadors in England and Scotland, 1645–1648*, ed. J. G. Fotheringham, 2 vols. (Edinburgh, 1898–1899) [hereafter cited as *MC*], I, 21.

3. *Ibid.*, 185–195.

4. *Calendar of State Papers, Domestic Series, 1603–1704*, 81 vols. (1857–1947+) [hereafter cited as *CSPD*], *1645–1647*, p. 433.

5. Sir Robert Moray to M. du Bosc, London, May 7, 1646, *MC*, II, 580–581; *CSPV, 1643–1647*, pp. 260–261.

was now nothing left to do, he urged, but to disband the armies and to make peace. He concluded by warning that the Lords would "all die in the place" before they would agree to imprison the King.[6] Stapleton was equally forthright, and the radicals reluctantly pulled in their horns. They dropped the Warwick Castle plan, but continued to insist that since the King was in England his disposition was a matter for the English Parliament alone.

Battle was again joined on May 13 when Sir John Evelyn, Jr., backed by the radicals, bluntly warned the peers that if they did not give way the Commons would proceed without them.[7] In the dispute that followed, Henry Marten, Nathaniel Fiennes, and Lisle were prominent as hammers of the Lords, with Marten insisting particularly on the Commons' right to act independently of the upper house.[8]

The open hostility between radicals and Scots was brought into sharp focus by the interception of the commissioners' mail by parliamentary agents. Doubtless the radicals hoped that the correspondence would reveal the true nature of the Scots' dealings with the King, but the moderates in the Commons took on new life and provided the Scots with some welcome support in a difficult and embarrassing situation. One of the uncoded letters contained a detailed account of the Commons' debate on the King's flight to the Scots, in which St. John, Samuel Browne, Vane, Marten, and William White were described as having "made bold with foul expressions." Another annoying item in the letter was the statement that news of the King's arrival in the Scottish army had caused "bonfires of joy through London."[9] When the radicals demanded that one of the intercepted letters be decoded, however, they were snowed under by an avalanche of moderate votes.

The Vane-St. John forces suffered another reverse a few days later when they attempted to exclude the Scots from any participation in peace proposals concerning England. In successive divisions they were defeated by seven and thirty-three votes, respectively. The moderates once again demonstrated their strength on May 21, 1646, when, in the face of determined radical opposition, they forced a debate on church government.[10]

6. W. Sancroft to F. Sancroft, Cambridge, May 11, 1646, *Memorials of the Great Civil War, 1646–1652*, ed. H. Cary, 2 vols. (London, 1842), I, 30.

7. *Journals of the House of Lords* [hereafter cited as *LJ*], VIII, 315; *CSPV, 1643–1647*, p. 262.

8. *CJ*, IV, 547–548; Whitaker, "Diary," BM, Add. MS. 31,116, fol. 270a; John Harrington, Parliamentary Diary, 1646–1647, BM, Add. MS. 10,114, fol. 15b; newsletter, London, May 21, 1646, Bodleian Library, Clarendon State Papers [hereafter cited as Clar.SPB], 28, fol. 40a.

9. John Harrington, Parliamentary Diary, 1646–1647, BM, Add. MS. 10,114, fol. 15a.

10. Whitaker, "Diary," BM, Add. MS. 31,116, fol. 269a; *CJ*, IV, 545, 552.

The radicals now proceeded to bring into play two factors that materially altered the situation in their favor: the New Model army and the Marquis of Argyle. The latter, recently returned from Ireland, was ready to use his great influence in the service of the radicals.

At this point, radical-Scots relations had reached a new low, and armed conflict appeared to be a real possibility. After reports of skirmishes between Scottish and English forces in Cumberland reached London, Fairfax moved north with 8,000 men and forced the Scots to retire hastily in order to avoid being outflanked.[11]

The radicals had long regarded both the behavior and character of the Scottish army with suspicion. As early as January 1646 they had accused the Scots of maintaining an illegally large force in England and of recruiting Englishmen and Ulstermen.[12] The proximity of the New Model may have prompted the Scots to be more careful. At any rate, shortly after the King's arrival all former royalist soldiers, of which there were a considerable number in the Scottish army, were barred from approaching him.

By the end of May there were definite signs both of the ascendancy of Argyle and of a policy designed to dovetail neatly with the aims and objectives of the English radicals. The latter, meanwhile, were quick to recognize that a financial settlement with the Scots was essential if the twin objectives of persuading the Scots to surrender the King and to return home were to be realized. On May 19, 1646, the House resolved that England had "no further use . . . of the Scotts army within . . . England" and that they should be paid the sum of £100,000, half to be forwarded on the surrender of the English towns that they still stubbornly held and the other half on their arrival in Scotland.[13] Almost immediately the attitude of the Scots toward the King changed significantly. They began to treat him with something like contempt, and their demands became suddenly much harsher. The covenant now became a *sine qua non,* and as early as May 20 the King suspected a germinating understanding between the Scots and the English radicals.[14] Particularly disquieting for him was the fact that the Scots, who had heretofore opposed complete parliamentary control of the militia,

11. Whitaker, "Diary," BM, Add. MS. 31,116, fol. 269a; Whitelocke, "Annals," BM, Add. MS. 37,344, fol. 50b; Baillie to Spang, London, May 15, 1646, Baillie, *Letters,* II, 370.

12. Montereul to Mazarin, London, Jan. 4, 1646, *MC,* I, 85; *CJ,* IV, 399, 402–403; *Calendar of the state papers relating to Ireland, 1603–1670,* ed. Robert P. Mahaffy, 13 vols. (London, H. M. Stationery Office, 1870–1910) [hereafter cited as *CSPI*], *1643–1647,* p. 448.

13. Whitaker, "Diary," BM, Add. MS. 31,116, fol. 270a; *CJ,* IV, 551.

14. Montereul to Mazarin, Newcastle, May 20, 1646, *MC,* I, 200.

were now pressing him to give way to the English demands on this point.[15]

At this juncture the Argyle faction appear to have been apprehensive that General David Leslie would throw his support to the King; Balmerino was one of the leading spirits in persuading him to remain uncommitted until Argyle himself arrived on the scene from Ireland.[16] The King, meanwhile, looked increasingly to the Earl of Lanark and his brother, the Duke of Hamilton, for support.

After Argyle's interview with the King on May 29, Loudon and Balmerino again obtained assurances from Leslie that he would make no decision until Argyle returned from his projected trip to London. It was perhaps in response to a word from Argyle that Sir Henry Mildmay, erstwhile master of the King's Jewel House, was asked by the Commons on June 8 to report on "the matter of the jewel to be given by the House to General Leven." Argyle was said to have made similar arrangements to secure the loyalty of David Leslie when he came to London in mid-June.[17] These efforts were not fruitless. By July 4 the Scottish commissioners were able to report that Leven and his officers had petitioned the King to take the covenant and to agree with his Parliament. They had, moreover, announced their determination to preserve the union between the two kingdoms and to discountenance both English and Scottish Royalists. They had also given assurances that the King's "unexpected" arrival among them had not given rise to any actions contrary to the covenant.[18]

The English radicals, meanwhile, had recovered quickly from the initial shock of the news of the King's flight. They were aware that, despite religious differences, there were many Scots with whom they could agree on political matters. If Argyle could win the ascendancy, Charles I was as good as in their own hands. In that event they appear to have been in a mood to adopt the most extreme measures against the King. "Nothing is left except to see them shed his blood," wrote the Venetian ambassador in Paris. Once the King was in their power, they would make an "example" of him, asserted Baillie, adding: "I abhor to think of it what they speak of execution."[19]

15. Charles I to Henrietta Maria, Newcastle, May 20, 1646, *Charles I in 1646*, ed. John Bruce (Westminster, 1856), p. 40.

16. *Memoirs of Henry Guthry, Bishop of Dunkeld*, ed. George Crawford (Glasgow, 1748) [hereafter cited as Guthry, *Memoirs*], pp. 219–221.

17. *CJ*, IV, 569; Guthry, *Memoirs*, pp. 223–224.

18. Whitelocke, "Annals," BM, Add. MS. 37,344, fols. 56b, 57a.

19. Nani to Doge, Paris, May 12, 1646, *CSPV, 1643–1647*, p. 258; Baillie to Henderson, London, May 19, 1646, *The Letters and Journals of Robert Baillie*, ed. David Laing, 3 vols. (Edinburgh, 1841–1842) [hereafter cited as Baillie, *Letters*], II, 372–373.

But the Vane-St. John group was encountering increasing difficulties in controlling the House. By the end of May and early June 1646, they were losing divisions on both religious and political issues. The moderates were now adopting a more "Presbyterian" policy, as part of the renewal of the alliance among themselves, the City, and the Scottish moderates. The vexed matter of lay commissioners for the control of excommunication was again raised, and during a two-day dispute the moderates seem to have favored abolition of the commissioners in order to strengthen the authority of the ministers. The radicals, by contrast, supported the extreme Erastianism of Browne who moved that such matters be directly controlled by a committee of Parliament.[20]

The weight of the City of London was once again thrown onto the scales: the City fathers drew up a remonstrance that was strongly in favor of negotiations with the King and bitterly anti-Independent in tone. The Londoners had already incurred the wrath of the radicals by their friendly reception of a letter from the King on May 19. The remonstrance, which condemned the "swarm of sectaries," praised the Scots and defended the King's "just power and greatness,"[21] was well received in the House of Lords. After a protracted struggle in the Commons on the question of the consideration of the paper, the moderates won a striking victory by a vote of 151 to 108.[22]

The King had by now made a number of important concessions. He was, he said, willing to accept parliamentary control of the militia and to make a serious attempt to satisfy their demands regarding Ireland. Although he was conciliatory on religion, he was also careful to nourish both the ministers' resentment against Parliament and their new-found loyalty to him, by blandly suggesting that the Houses should take direction from the assembly of divines on religious matters.

The voting strength of the moderates had become impressive; if they had continued to enjoy the backing of the Scots, they might have been able to defy the radicals on the crucial issue of the peace settlement. But Scottish support suddenly and mysteriously evaporated, and without it Holles was impotent. A "great debate" on the King's offer took place on May 28. Although the Lords supported the King's position, the Commons, dominated by the radicals, voted to adhere to their former positions on the militia and Ireland. "Many sober men"

20. *CJ*, IV, 552; Whitaker, "Diary," BM, Add. MS. 31,116, fol. 270b.
21. *LJ*, VIII, 332–333; *CJ*, IV, 555; Salvetti Correspondence, Transcripts from archives at Florence of correspondence of Florentine ambassadors in England, 1616–1679, BM, Add. MS. 27,962L [hereafter cited as SC, BM, Add. MS. 27,962L], fol. 182a.
22. *CJ*, IV, 556.

favored concessions to the King, but were overawed by the radicals.[23]

A key factor in the collapse of the moderates was the refusal of the Scottish commissioners in London to back them on the question of the militia.[24] The commissioners themselves hesitated to take a stand in the absence of any clear directive from Newcastle, itself the scene of a struggle for power between Hamilton and Argyle. As at Uxbridge, the covenant was now to be employed by Argyle and by the radicals in London to block any settlement. On June 2 the Commons resolved that all persons coming into Parliament's quarters should take the covenant, and one week later steps were taken to set up the Presbyterian system in London.[25] By June 10 Charles was reporting to the Queen that the Scots, apparently on instructions from London, were pressing him not only to enforce Presbyterianism on his subjects but to take the covenant himself and to abide by the directory even within his own family. The demand was certainly in the interests of both Argyle and the English radicals since it would not only please the Kirk but would also virtually preclude any agreement.

Holles and his supporters now adopted an attitude of almost studied passivity. Anxious to see propositions presented to the King, they preferred to agree to harsh terms rather than delay matters by attempting to ameliorate them. By mid-June they were advising the Scottish commissioners in London to follow the same line, arguing that if the Scots disputed the terms they would be labeled enemies of peace and the radicals would be provided with the excuse they sought to send the New Model against them. Meanwhile the commissioners themselves sought in vain for clear directives from their government.[26]

It was in this atmosphere that Argyle, accompanied by a watchful Hamilton, left Newcastle for London. Argyle had represented himself to the King as working in his interest, but Charles could hardly view the "great professions" of Montrose's most implacable enemy with anything but skepticism. Argyle had been "very civil and cunning," wrote Charles, adding that the results of his London visit would be a better indication of his true attitude. More might perhaps be hoped for from Hamilton, who, as the representative of the "politiques" among the Scottish nobility, might be expected to have little sympathy for either the Kirk or the English radicals.

23. Whitelocke, "Annals," BM, Add. MS. 37,344, fol. 53a, b.

24. Scottish commissioners to Committee of Estates, London, May 31, 1646, *Correspondence of the Scottish Commissioners in London, 1644–1646*, ed. H. W. Meikle (London, Roxburghe Club, 1917) [hereafter cited as Meikle, *Correspondence*], p. 188.

25. *CJ*, IV, 561, 569–570.

26. Scottish commissioners to Committee of Estates at Newcastle, London, June 16, 1646, Meikle, *Correspondence*, pp. 193–194.

Argyle's sympathies and the general outlines of his policy were sufficiently revealed in an address to the members of both Houses on June 25, 1646. He had had at least a week in which to confer with the radical leaders, and his words may be regarded as the outward expression of his agreement with them. He was particularly concerned to allay the widespread suspicion that the Scots were "too much affected with the King's interest." Any natural affection that the Scots had for the King, he pointed out, had never made them forget that "The safety of the people is the supreme law."[27] If Argyle seemed to be giving the radicals a blank check with respect to the fate of Charles, he was more conservative on the question of the monarchy itself, which, he suggested, should be "rather regulated than destroyed." Perhaps even more significant was his concession to the religious sects, which, in the prevailing atmosphere, could only be interpreted as a pledge of his intention to remain on good terms with the religious Independents and their political supporters in Parliament. Despite his close alliance with the Kirk, he was able to assure his hearers that persons "who cannot through scruple of conscience, come up in all things to the common rule" should not be persecuted.[28] Any doubts about the significance of Argyle's words and the extent of his influence must have been dispelled by the alacrity with which the Scottish commissioners now agreed to the peace propositions that they had recently so strenuously opposed.[29]

Argyle's role at this juncture formed the basis of one of the main charges against him during his trial in 1661. He was accused of having gone to London for the purpose of concluding an agreement with the "infamous party of the . . . army" for the surrender of the King and of having assured the English, at a meeting of the committee of both kingdoms, that his influence (and the generous financial settlement that was probably then agreed upon) would be sufficient to prevent the Scottish army officers from declaring for the King.[30]

In his defense Argyle rather inaccurately stated that the Independents were at that time powerless in Parliament, that the Houses had declared their support for the King's person and authority, and that the report of his remarks at the committee of both kingdoms was forged. Argyle's disclaimers aside, there seems little doubt that

27. Speech of the Marquis of Argyle to the Grand Committee of Both Houses, John Rushworth, *Historical Collections*, 7 vols. (London, 1654–1701) [hereafter cited as Rushworth, *Hist. Coll.*], I, pt. iv, 299.

28. *Ibid.*

29. Whitaker, "Diary," BM, Add. MS. 31,116, fol. 275b.

30. William Cobbett, Thomas B. Howell, and Thomas J. Howell, *Collection of state trials and proceedings for high treason and other crimes*, 34 vols. (London, 1809–1828), V, 1396; see also Guthry, *Memoirs*, pp. 219–221.

his alliance with the Vane-St. John group, which was to survive many vicissitudes, had its beginnings in June 1646, if not earlier. By bringing the Scottish Kirk and the English radicals into a working relationship Argyle squared the circle and won a place for himself as one of the more significant architects of the Puritan Revolution.

Contemporary Scottish opinion was at variance with Argyle's later views regarding the strength and policies of the English radicals. The day after Argyle's speech, Baillie asserted that if the King had remained in Oxford and given himself up to Parliament he would have been faced with either life imprisonment or execution, "which is the mind of too many here."[31] The judicious Sir Robert Moray had told the French on June 11 that the radicals, or "Independents," were on the point of charging Charles with the murder of his father and with the instigation of the Irish rebellion. Despite their repeated overtures to the Prince of Wales, he thought they had no intention of crowning him and indeed "wanted no King."[32] In this connection it may be observed that many influential members of the Scottish Kirk did not share Baillie's horror of radical policies. Ministers like George Gillespie (Argyle's friend) and Samuel Rutherford were much in tune with the radicals in political attitudes. It was the existence of this group that made possible the seemingly incongruous alliance between Presbyterian Scot and Independent-radical Englishman.

Now that Argyle had obliged the radicals by silencing Scottish opposition to the propositions, the peace terms were soon put into final shape and dispatched to Newcastle on July 13, 1646. They bore the stamp of radical policy and in the opinion of many observers had been deliberately designed to be unacceptable. The covenant was the centerpiece despite the fact that neither the leading English "Presbyterians" nor many of the Scottish "politiques" had any particular enthusiasm for it. A similar charade was to be repeated in 1648 when the traditional opponents of the covenant were once again to urge it upon Charles. The King was required to accept it himself and see it imposed on the nation, to concede the abolition of episcopacy and to agree to a parliamentarian church settlement. The effective direction of the militia and fleet was to pass to Parliament for at least twenty years and permanently if Parliament so desired; the Irish Cessation of 1643 was to be voided, and the settlement there was to be a parliamentary one.

Charles was aware that the propositions enjoyed the support neither of the moderate parliamentarians nor of that amorphous but

31. Baillie to Spang, London, June 26, 1646, Baillie, *Letters*, II, 375.
32. Bacon to Montereul, Newcastle, June 11, 1646, *MC*, I, 211–212.

significant group among the Scots led by Chancellor Loudon. But both English and Scottish moderates were agreed upon the necessity of Charles consenting to the propositions. Loudon, supported by Hamilton, appealed to the King to sign them, arguing that only by this means could he save his throne and even his life. He told him that if he signed the terms, and, as a consequence, returned to London and his throne, he could expect to enjoy strong support. If, on the other hand, he refused to sign them, all moderate support for him would collapse, and he would be brought to trial, deposed, and "another government" set up. Abolition of the monarchy itself was, he believed, the goal of the radicals, who would be able to achieve it even against the wishes of the more conservative populace if Charles remained intransigent.[33]

The moderates still hoped that with the help of London and the support of the King the power of the radicals could be broken and a reasonable peace settlement worked out. Bellièvre described the Holles party at this time as eager to support the King, if only to prevent the complete overthrow of monarchy, which, they feared, would put "absolute power into the hands of the people." If the King signed the propositions, they argued, they would be able to use their voting strength not only to disband the New Model but to dissolve the Long Parliament after having passed another "Self-Denying Ordinance," which would have barred sitting members from reelection. If, on the other hand, they did not receive the support of the King and Queen, they would have no alternative but to make their peace with the radicals.[34]

But would the radicals permit Charles to return to London on any conditions? This was the weak point in the moderates' argument. If they were unable to block the drawing up of such terms, could they prevent their implementation? The heart of the matter was that the radicals, who possessed overwhelming power in the shape of the New Model, were not likely to permit their position to be eroded as a result of any wave of popular support that might follow the King's return.

The New Model army was rightly regarded by all factions as the mainstay of radical power, and its political significance now came into sharp focus. To disband it was the devout wish of the Holles group; to maintain it in full battle array, the firm resolution of the radicals. The struggle over the army, usually associated with the year 1647, was clearly foreshadowed in 1646.

33. Rushworth, *Hist. Coll.*, I, pt. iv, 319–320.
34. Bellièvre to Mazarin, London, July 16, 1646, PRO, 31/3/80, fol. 69b.

Three groups, whose aims had become increasingly divergent, were now almost equally concerned to prevent the disbanding of the New Model: the parliamentary radicals who were fully aware that the "recruiting" of the Commons, far from guaranteeing their own supremacy, had actually provided Holles with a potentially overwhelming majority; the radical religious sects for whom the army was a shield against the rising tide of intolerance both in London and Parliament; and the Levellers. Lilburne and his supporters, now completely disillusioned with the parliamentary radicals, were looking increasingly to the army as an instrument of political and social reform.

Early in 1646, in a personal conversation with Cromwell, Lilburne had "anatomized the baseness" of Vane and St. John.[35] Cromwell's reliability also left something to be desired from Honest John's point of view. When the Leveller leader was arrested in April 1646 on a charge brought against him by Cromwell's old enemy, Colonel Edward King, Lilburne looked in vain to Cromwell and the radicals for support. With some bitterness, he recalled that he had been "left in the suds by L. G. Cromwell who first engaged me in it and promised to stand to me."[36] He fared no better in his clash with the Lords in July that resulted in a sentence of seven years in the Tower. "You plucked your head out of the collar," he later reminded Cromwell, "while I was catched in the briars." It was at this point that Lilburne made his far-reaching decision to turn to the "honest blades" of the army.[37]

Lilburne's keen sense of betrayal extended beyond mere personal considerations, and his embittered accusations reflect the close alliance that had once existed between the parliamentary radicals and the "meaner sort" in the early years of the revolution. In those days, Lilburne told the radicals, they had "seemed to abominate" the practices of great monopolies like the Merchant Adventurers who were now being "licensed to go on in their oppression."[38] The radicals had abandoned their old democratic attitudes: "Ye are extremely altered in demeanour towards us . . . " he charged, "in the beginning you seemed to know what freedom was . . . whether rich or poor, all were welcome to you . . . hardly would you permit men to stand

35. John Lilburne, *Jonah's Cry out of the Whale's Belly* (London, 1647), BM, E.400(5), p. 3.
36. John Lilburne, *The Just Man's Justification* (London, 1647), BM, E.407(26), p. 26.
37. Lilburne to Cromwell, July 1, 1647, BM, E.400(5), p. 9.
38. *A Remonstrance of many thousand Citizens of England to their own House of Commons, occasioned through the illegal imprisonment of John Lilburne* (London, 1647), BM, E.343(11), p. 15.

bare-headed before you." He concluded with a significant contrast between the timeserving politicians of the Long Parliament and "the faithfulness" of the New Model.[39]

The first rumblings of renewed conflict over the army could be seen in a petition from the Wiltshire county committee on June 19 in which the "robberies and cruelties" of the troops under the well-known moderate commander, Sir Edward Massey, were catalogued.[40] Massey had been a target of the radicals as far back as the autumn of 1644, and at the height of the army crisis of 1647 he was to play a key role in organizing the London opposition to Cromwell and Ireton. At this point the radicals seized upon the complaints against him and succeeded in passing an order designed to wipe out Massey's forces either by disbandment or by sending them to Ireland.[41]

The truth was that both parliamentary factions regarded Ireland as a convenient place to dispose of soldiers whose political views were uncongenial, and they were correspondingly determined to block the transfer of their own military allies. Colonel Michael Jones reported on July 14 that his attempts to raise a force for Ireland out of troops of the Eastern Association had met with strong resistance. The soldiers told him that when their arrears were paid they would give him an answer, but not before.[42] When the moderates seized the opportunity to attack the New Model, Cromwell himself, now in regular attendance in the House, delivered a long speech in which he vindicated the army "from an aspersion cast upon it."[43] On the same day the moderates, who favored the disbandment of the Exeter garrison, were defeated by a vote of ninety-six to seventy-three.[44] The possibility of an army revolt was again hinted at on July 24, 1646, when Robert Reynolds, now drifting over to the radicals, warned the peers that if, as a result of the refusal of the upper house to agree to the sale of royalist lands, "the Armies be not paid . . . and so not disbanded," the Commons would take no responsibility.[45]

Matters came to a head on July 30 when the moderates made a concerted attempt to divide the New Model and to send 5,000 of its soldiers to Ireland. Once again Cromwell led the radicals in a strong

39. *Ibid.*, pp. 16, 17.
40. Whitaker, "Diary," BM, Add. MS. 31,116, fol. 274b; Whitelocke, "Annals," BM, Add. MS. 37,344, fol. 55a.
41. Whitaker, "Diary," BM, Add. MS. 31,116, fol. 274b.
42. *CSPI, 1643–1647*, p. 475.
43. Whitaker, "Diary," BM, Add. MS. 31,116, fol. 277b.
44. *CJ*, IV, 617; Whitaker, "Diary," BM, Add. MS. fol. 277b. N. Fiennes and Haselrig and Holles and Stapleton were tellers for the majority and the minority, respectively. (*CJ*, IV, 617.)
45. *LJ*, VIII, 442.

resistance to the scheme. The debate was an acrimonious one, with some of the radicals indirectly admitting their dependence on the army by accusing their opponents of a plot to weaken it in order that they "may be forced to any conditions."[46] During the debate the next day the fiery Gurdon claimed that the idea of sending troops had been instigated by plotters outside Parliament. His accusations offended Holles who was in turn attacked by Cromwell who jumped into the debate "largely and passionately."[47] The moderates succeeded in winning one division by ninety-eight votes to seventy-eight, but they could not hold their advantage. On the vital question of the dispatch of the six New Model regiments to Ireland, they were defeated by one vote.[48] The radical victory was probably due in part to the reluctance of many members to reduce the strength of the New Model while the Scottish army yet remained in England.

As it turned out, the House followed the radical policy of sending to Ireland only soldiers from the dismantled garrisons and the counties. The subcommittee of the Committee for Irish Affairs, of which Cromwell was now a leading member, was empowered to supervise the recruiting and dispatch of troops for Ireland. The radicals had thus not only frustrated the threat to one of their main sources of power, but were now themselves in a stronger position to deal effectively with garrisons whose political complexion was not to their liking.[49]

The attack on Massey was now pressed with renewed vigor. On August 6, after hearing a new list of complaints against Massey's men, the House listened to a letter from Fairfax recommending the disbanding of those regiments. Despite Massey's protests, his forces were ordered either to be sent to Ireland or disbanded, and on August 11 the same policy was applied to all troops outside the New Model.[50]

The radicals' elation at their successful defense of the New Model

46. John Harrington, Parliamentary Diary, 1646–1647, BM, Add. MS. 10,114, fol. 16b.

47. *Ibid.*

48. *CJ*, IV, 631, 632. Holles and Stapleton were tellers for the majority; Haselrig and Cromwell for the minority. (*Ibid.*, 631.)

49. Whitelocke, "Annals," BM, Add. MS. 37,344, fol. 61a; *CSPI, 1643–1647,* p. 485.

50. "The Commonwealth party, taking advantage of the arguments used in the House for the relief of Ireland . . . procured an order for the disbanding of Col. Massey's brigade . . . " (Edmund Ludlow, *Memoirs of Edmund Ludlow*, ed. C. H. Firth, 2 vols. [Oxford, 1894], I, 141–142; see also *Selections from the papers of William Clarke, secretary to the council of the army 1647–9 and to General Monck and the commanders of the army in Scotland 1651–60,* ed. C. H. Firth, 4 vols. [Westminster, 1891–1901] [hereafter cited as *Clarke Papers*], I, 424–425.)

was further reinforced by the news of the King's refusal to sign the Newcastle propositions. They were as pleased by this development as the moderates and Scottish commissioners were angered and depressed. Baillie was particularly incensed at the temporizing of "that mad man," as he termed the King, and predicted that his stubbornness would not only bring about his own downfall but that of his family and of monarchy as well.[51] The parliamentary moderates, "exceedingly unsatisfied," were almost ready to give up any hope of preventing a vote for the King's deposition which they regarded as imminent.[52]

The radicals were in a particularly violent mood. In August, Bellièvre described them as persons who "are not assured of their own heads but by the loss of his [the King's]."[53] If they spared his life, he asserted, they would never again allow him the title of king. It seems clear that, at this juncture, the trial and execution of the King, followed by the establishment of a republic, were seriously considered by at least some of the radicals. But there were alternatives. The Prince of Wales, it was conjectured, could be offered the crown, or if he proved reluctant there remained the Duke of York and the Duke of Gloucester as possible candidates. James was apparently already regarded as somewhat stubborn, but his brother was too young to cause trouble and might make an acceptable figurehead with the Earl of Northumberland or some such personage as Protector.[54] A third possibility remained: that of offering to restore Charles as a titular ruler on condition that he hand over the reins of power to the chiefs of the radicals. This project was to be actively pursued in the coming autumn.

Members of the Holles party found themselves effectively checkmated by the King's continued reluctance to give them the necessary encouragement and by the gradual evaporation of any real hope of Scottish assistance, in which connection Argyle served the radicals well. His close connection with the Kirk enabled him effectively to vitiate the attempts of the moderates to strengthen their hand in England by appeals for Scottish support.

The King had refused to sign, or even to give a categorical answer to the Newcastle propositions; he had, indeed, demanded a treaty, and although this appeared to play directly into the hands of the radicals,

51. Baillie, *Letters*, II, 386–387.
52. Scottish commissioners to the Lord Chancellor, Argyle, *et al.*, London, Aug. 4, 1646, Meikle, *Correspondence*, p. 202.
53. Bellièvre to Mazarin, Aug. 4, 1646, Public Record Office, Paris Transcripts, 31/3/80, fols. 93, 94.
54. Cheylieu to Mazarin, Aug. 6, 1646, PRO, 31/3/80, fol. 100b; Brienne to Mazarin, London, Sept. 17, 1646, PRO, 31/3/81, fol. 30b.

the moderates did not give up hope. They had a potential majority in the House and were beginning to use it. The withdrawal of the Scots from England would, moreover, have the effect of making the New Model redundant and would afford them an opportunity of ending, at a stroke, the overweening power of their opponents in the Commons. There were, admittedly, already some disquieting signs that the army might choose to defy Parliament; against this, however, was the influence of London, the leading citizens of which were increasingly eager to see the army disbanded and willing to throw their financial power onto the scales to achieve this end.

The first concern of the moderates in mid-August was to prevent any precipitate vote in the House for the deposition of the King. Loudon, Dunfermline, and Argyle were on their way south with the English commissioners, and, with the object of preventing matters from coming to a head, the moderates had suggested that the Scottish emissaries arrive in London the day before the Newcastle commissioners in order that plans might be laid. After the King's answer was read the "Independent party" moved that no more addresses be made to Charles, that his person be demanded from the Scots, and that the army be sent northward to enforce the demand.[55] The Scots, however, frustrated the move by offering to withdraw their army from England and to join with the English Parliament in working out a peace settlement without further reference to Charles.[56]

An agreement between the Scots and the moderates was probably concluded at this point. In return for a large sum of London money the King would be handed over; the Scots would march out; and the Holles-Stapleton group, backed by a majority in the Commons, the wealth of London, and the Scots themselves, would disband the New Model and proceed to a peace settlement.[57]

Though it was an attractive plan, it contained a number of possible snags: it depended for success on a firm understanding between Charles and the parliamentary moderates as well as on the courage and constancy of the Londoners, the close support of the Scots, and the willingness of the New Model and its party in the Commons to depart

55. Gilbert Burnet, *Memoirs of the lives and actions of James and William, Dukes of Hamilton* (London, 1677) [hereafter cited as Burnet, *Memoirs of the Hamiltons*], p. 283.

56. Scottish commissioners to the Lord Chancellor *et al.*, London, Aug. 4, 1646, Meikle, *Correspondence*, p. 202; Baillie to Dickson, London, Aug. 18, 1646, Baillie, *Letters*, II, 390–391; Moray to the Duke of Hamilton, Aug. 8, 1646, *The Hamilton Papers; being selections from original letters in the possession of His Grace the Duke of Hamilton and Brandon relating to the years 1638–1650*, ed. S. R. Gardiner (London, 1880) [hereafter cited as *Hamilton Papers*], pp. 106–107.

57. Baillie to Spang, Edinburgh, Sept. 1, 1647, Baillie, *Letters*, III, 16; Robert Monteith, *History of the Troubles of Great Britain* (London, 1735), p. 260.

tamely from the scene of their triumphs. All of these conditions were, to say the least, doubtful. Charles had a tendency to exploit—not always skillfully—the differences between his opponents and to prefer to deal with the radicals, whose power he respected and with whom he hoped to make a more acceptable settlement of the religious question. The support of the Londoners was reasonably firm, but whether, in the last analysis, they would be willing to pit the trained bands against the battle-hardened New Model was a nice question. Scottish support was, if anything, less dependable. It is true that *politiques* like Loudon and Scottish army leaders like Callander and even David Leslie saw eye to eye with the English moderates, but they tended to be overawed by the Kirk, the leaders of which, in turn, were in the pocket of Argyle. Argyle was also in a position to furnish the radicals with the details of any agreement worked out between the moderates and the Scots. According to Burnet, the King instructed Dunfermline, Loudon, and Argyle to persuade "those who were best affected [the moderates]" to work for a personal treaty in or near London. Dunfermline, who was trusted by Charles more than his two colleagues, was particularly charged with the task of negotiating with the moderates. But despite the fact that secrecy was imposed on all three, Lauderdale later complained that the King's instructions were known in London before the three Scots arrived in the City.[58]

It is, indeed, highly probable that Argyle had already concluded an agreement with the radicals for handing over the King. It may be remembered that on May 19, with Argyle's star already in the ascendant at Newcastle, the Commons, without a division and presumably with the approval if not the prompting of the radicals, had agreed to pay the Scots £100,000 upon their withdrawal from England. When he visited London in June, Argyle must surely have discussed these terms and, judging by the friendly atmosphere, must have come to some firm agreement with the radicals on them. It would seem, accordingly, that the later agreement between the Holles party and the Scots had from the outset a certain air of unreality. The radicals were probably not averse to seeing the moderates doing their business for them, as long as they held a trump card in the form of Argyle and his influence with the Kirk.

Charles's gamble on the Scots had been a dismal failure, but he had not yet realized its extent. His days at Newcastle had been spent, not in relaxed leisure sustained by a reasoned hope of an early resumption of the throne, but in gritty disputations with the formidable champions of the Scottish Kirk. We may perhaps spare Charles a twinge of

---

58. Burnet, *Memoirs of the Hamiltons,* pp. 283–284; Bellièvre to Brienne, Newcastle, Sept. 7, 1646, *MC,* I, 261.

sympathy as we picture him facing the solemn Scottish ecclesiastics, steeled as they were in the school of George Buchanan and Andrew Melville, and only too willing to indicate to their royal auditor the error of his ways.

In the spring of 1646 it had been possible to believe that a combination of parliamentary moderates, Londoners, and Scots was sufficient to overawe the radicals and effect a settlement. This scheme had, however, been effectively checkmated by the radicals, working through Argyle. His influence had been sufficient to rob the moderates in both City and Parliament of the minimum support necessary to deal effectively with the radicals, backed as they were by the New Model. The result was the framing, following Argyle's London visit, of the extremist Newcastle propositions and the frantic appeals of the moderates to the King to agree to any conditions on the grounds that peace itself would be the radicals' undoing.

Holles and his supporters were the more desperate because their attempt to weaken the New Model had backfired and stripped them of their last substantial English military support. The ascendancy of Argyle meant that an understanding with him was a prerequisite of any agreement with the Scots and must take account of his hostility to Charles. It seems highly likely that the moderate policy of support for the Prince of Wales, which became so pronounced in the first months of 1647, after they had won control of the Commons and before the King was actually handed over by the Scots, had its beginnings in late August or early September 1646 in discussions with Argyle.

If the moderates were in difficulties, the picture was by no means a rosy one for the radicals. Their minority status in the Commons was even more pronounced than it had been before the new series of elections, and their position was further weakened both within and without Parliament by the alienation of the Levellers. The New Model itself, which was still their mainstay, was becoming suspect, even from their point of view, infected as it was by political and religious radicalism with which they found themselves increasingly unsympathetic. In such a situation it was to be expected that new, secret, and more realistic overtures would be made to the King and that both parties would begin to think in terms of a coalition in the face of the new, aggressive populism and of a program that envisaged the dissolution of the Long Parliament itself.

VII] Point and Counterpoint

The first parliamentary offer to the Scots was £100,000, which they promptly rejected, indicating that £600,000 was the least they could accept. Even that sum, wrote Baillie, hungrily, was only the first installment on the "huge sums which we crave to be paid afterward."[1] They lowered their sights considerably, however, in the face of the moderates' assurance that £200,000 was the most that could be expected.[2]

London was a key factor in all these dealings. Both Scots and moderates hoped to use the financial influence of the City to destroy the military power of their opponents. Baillie was confident that the Londoners would require the disbandment of the New Model as a quid pro quo, and the moderates were persuading the City to make just such a demand.[3] The radicals, for their part, were determined to block any threat to the army although they were pleased enough to speed the Scots home. The result was that on September 1, 1646, the moderates carried by a vote of 140 to 101 a resolution to pay the Scots a total of £400,000 on condition of their withdrawal from the country.

When the Scots, encouraged by Holles, demanded a down payment of £200,000, the Earl of Pembroke voiced the widespread resentment when he protested that it was not the Scots themselves but "some of us" who prompted the demands.[4] "Our private dealings with our friends in the Houses," Baillie admitted, had greatly assisted the proj-

1. Lawrence Whitaker, "Diary of Proceedings in the House of Commons," BM, Add. MS. 31,116 [hereafter cited as Whitaker, "Diary," BM, Add. MS. 31,116], fol. 281a; *Journals of the House of Commons* [hereafter cited as *CJ*], IV, 649; Baillie to Dickson, London, Aug. 18, 1646, *The Letters and Journals of Robert Baillie*, ed. David Laing, 3 vols. (Edinburgh, 1841–1842) [hereafter cited as Baillie, *Letters*], II, 390.

2. Scottish commissioners to Committee of Estates, London, Aug. 25, 1646, *Correspondence of the Scottish Commissioners in London, 1644–1646*, ed. H. W. Meikle (London, Roxburghe Club, 1917) [hereafter cited as Meikle, *Correspondence*], p. 206.

3. Baillie to Dickson, London, Aug. 18, 1646, Baillie, *Letters*, II, 390–391; Grignon to Brienne, London, Aug. 27, 1646, Public Record Office, Paris Transcripts, 31/3/81, fol. 6b.

4. John Harrington, Parliamentary Diary, 1646–1647, BM, Add. MS. 10,114, fol. 18a.

ect, and the Scottish commissioners themselves reported that they had made full use of their supporters both in the Commons and the City.[5] Their assiduous lobbying was rewarded on September 5 when, after an all-day debate, the moderates, by a majority of 112 to 102, carried a vote that the Scots should receive the requested payment.[6] A predominantly moderate committee which, however, included Cromwell, was then appointed to confer with the City about raising the money.

The Londoners suggested that the bishops' lands form part of the security. They further urged that persons who had already lent money to Parliament should be permitted interest at 8 percent and that those who lent a further sum for this purpose be permitted to secure the whole sum on bishops' lands and the excise. The radicals pressed to have royalists' estates substituted for the excise and won their point by a vote of 105 to 100. Repelled by the eagerness with which the London moneyed men reached for their rewards, some members criticized the generous terms to be accorded to those who had "lent of their superfluity," while the less affluent were neglected.[7]

If such policies were calculated to please the Londoners, they were scarcely likely to arouse the enthusiasm of Charles, with whom the moderates appear to have had little or no communication since the arrival of Loudon, Argyle, and Dunfermline in mid-August. Moreover, the episcopal land policy, as Bellièvre pointed out, would almost certainly swing London into the antiepiscopal camp "and consequently against their King."[8] The aims of the radicals were thus being furthered by policies carried out under the nominal direction of their opponents.

It was John Glyn, the Recorder of London and a prominent Holles supporter, who introduced the ordinance for the abolition of the "name, title and function" of archbishops and bishops and for the sur-

5. Baillie to Dickson, London, Aug. 18, 1646, Baillie, *Letters*, II, 390–391; Scottish commissioners to both committees, London, Sept. 9, 1646, Meikle, *Correspondence*, p. 211.

6. Bulstrode Whitelocke, "Annals," BM, Add. MS. 37,344 [hereafter cited as Whitelocke, "Annals," BM, Add. MS. 37,344], fol. 64b; *CJ*, IV, 663. Holles and Sir William Lewis were tellers for the majority; Haselrig and Evelyn of Wilts. for the minority.

7. John Harrington, Parliamentary Diary, 1646–1647, BM, Add. MS. 10,114, fol. 18b; Whitaker, "Diary," BM, Add. MS. 31,116, fol. 283b; Whitelocke, "Annals," BM, Add. MS. 37,344, fol. 65a; *CJ*, IV, 665. Haselrig and Evelyn of Wilts. were tellers for the majority; Holles and Stapleton for the minority.

8. Bellièvre to Brienne, Newcastle, Sept. 21, 1646, *The Diplomatic Correspondence of Jean de Montereul and the Brothers de Bellièvre, French Ambassadors in England and Scotland, 1645–1648*, ed. J. G. Fotheringham, 2 vols. (Edinburgh, 1898–1899 [hereafter cited as *MC*], I, 276.

veying and sale of their lands by London-nominated trustees. As Harrington so succinctly put it, "ye office of bishop must be abolished else the security of their lands will be the worse."[9]

Throughout these weeks the moderates were able to win divisions of the House with some consistency. This was due partially to a disposition on the part of leading radicals like Vane and Cromwell to cooperate on the Scottish and episcopal lands policy. But the forces led by Holles also won victories in the face of determined radical opposition over such questions as the custody of the great seal and the granting of permission to former royalist constituencies to return members to Westminster.[10] Encouraged by these successes, they now looked for firm concessions from the King. They were, according to Bellièvre, anxious that Charles grant "some of the proposals," arguing that if he indicated a willingness to come to terms they would be in a position to give him real support.

They were still demanding outwardly that the King sign the Newcastle propositions without further discussion, but their real position, as reported by Bellièvre, was significantly milder. They repeated the old demand for Presbyterianism—a political necessity if they were to retain Scottish support—and there was to be no compromise on Ireland. On the militia, however, they were considerably more flexible, and, although firmly in favor of parliamentary control during Charles's lifetime, they were willing to see it restored to the Crown thereafter. They were also more conciliatory in the matter of executive offices, which Parliament would approve only at Charles's restoration.

"Many persons," Bellièvre wrote, thought that the King's acceptance of these terms could not only produce a stable peace, but would, in case of a renewed war, provide him with strong support. If Charles failed to act quickly, however, this potential support would evaporate.[11] Charles saw things differently. Presbyterianism was anathema to him on political as well as religious grounds, and he still failed to appreciate the skin-deep nature of the "Presbyterianism" of many of the moderate parliamentarians. He was not, moreover, ready to give up Ireland and, despite the disastrous influence of the papal nuncio, Giovanni Rinuccini, still hoped to salvage something from the maelstrom of Irish, English, and Scottish factions that contended for control of that island. With regard to the militia, he was no longer alone in disliking the idea of parliamentary control of the armed forces. It had become increasingly clear that the parliamentary majority was not

9. John Harrington, Parliamentary Diary, 1646–1647, BM, Add. MS. 10,114, fol. 19b; Whitaker, "Diary," BM, Add. MS. 31,116, fol. 284a,b.
10. *CJ*, IV, 659, 662.
11. Bellièvre to Brienne, Sept. 10, 1646, *MC*, I, 266–267.

only moderate in sympathy, but increasingly hostile to the New Model. Parliamentary authority was a growing threat to the radicals, and to the sources of their strength, with the result that an unexpected but real communiy of interest developed between Charles and his old enemies. In addition to these considerations, the radicals were aware of the necessity to block any possibility of agreement between Charles and the moderates and were thus ready to make overtures to Charles on their own behalf. These took place about the time of the death of the Earl of Essex on September 16, which was itself a heavy blow to the morale of the moderates in both Houses, and may have been enough to deflect the King from any agreement with the Holles party.

The royalist agent Colonel Joseph Bamfield was in London at this time and was a close observer of affairs. Years later he wrote a remarkably circumstantial and apparently sound account of the radical overtures and of their effect on both the royalists and the "Presbyterians." The radicals were, according to Bamfield, greatly worried that the King might be persuaded to sign the propositions and to conclude an agreement with the "Presbyterians." At Cromwell's suggestion, they had decided to make him an offer. Bamfield heard about it from an exultant royalist who, "with joy even in his eyes," told him that the overtures had come from "some of the army and principal persons of their adherents" who had offered to restore the King on condition that he reject the propositions and grant them "such power in the militia as might secure all to them," as well as liberty of conscience.[12] Within three months, predicted the enthusiastic royalist, they would have the King back on the throne. Some of the most prominent royalists were involved in the scheme, he said, including "one of the wisest men who serves the King." Bamfield assured the royalists, however, that he had certain knowledge that the offer was a "manifest cheat" planned by Cromwell, Ireton, and some of their adherents in Parliament, whose real aim was not to make peace, but, by persuading the King to reject the propositions, to create a breach between him and the "Presbyterians." The effect of this would be the permanent alienation of the more rigid members of that party from the King and a fusion of the extreme Presbyterians with "the army's party." If this happened, Bamfield argued, both the monarchy and the King's person would be in great danger.

On the following day Bamfield went to see the royalist Marquis of Hertford who was also enthusiastic about the plan and warned Bamfield not to attempt to interfere with it, adding that he was already suspected of being too friendly with the Presbyterians. At this, Bam-

12. *Colonel Joseph Bamfield's Apologie written by himself and printed at his own desire* (The Hague? 1685) [hereafter cited as Bamfield, *Apologie*], p. 16.

field protested his loyalty to the King and again warned that the radicals aimed not at agreement but at "destruction of the King's person and monarchy."[13]

Contemporary evidence tends to confirm the general outlines of Bamfield's account. As early as August 20, Grignon, referring to a negotiation carried on in London with a view to the King's return, wrote that royalists believed that the move was "introduced by the Independents" for the purpose of diverting the King from signing the propositions and thereby providing Parliament with an excuse to "proceed against him with rigour."[14] By September 17 another observer was reporting that "the Independents . . . seem ever less averse from the royal name" and were, he thought, beginning to see the dangers of too much democracy.[15] Four days later, Sir Robert Moray in Newcastle informed Hamilton that letters had arrived from "the Independent party" that contained offers of a moderate episcopacy and a shelving of the Irish issue "till King and Parliament be agreed." He added that the King had been warned, apparently by William Moray, that the offers were "but snares."[16]

The radicals were by now becoming increasingly aware that their control of Parliament was shaky at best and that it was largely dependent on their close connection with the New Model. Cromwell made his views on the subject sufficiently clear in a conversation with Ludlow sometime in September.[17] As they walked through Sir Robert Cot-

13. *Ibid.*, pp. 17–18.
14. Grignon to Brienne, London, Aug. 20, 1646, PRO, 31/3/80, fol. 119b; Baillie, *Letters*, II, 390.
15. Advices from London, Sept. 17, 1646, *Calendar of state papers and manuscripts relating to English affairs existing in the archives and collections of Venice and in other libraries of northern Italy*, vols. 10–38 (1603–1675) [London, H. M. Stationery Office, 1900–1940] [hereafter cited as *CSPV*], *1643–1647*, p. 283.
16. Moray to the Duke of Hamilton, Newcastle, Sept. 21, 1646, *The Hamilton Papers: being selections from original letters in the possession of His Grace the Duke of Hamilton and Brandon relating to the years 1638–1650*, ed. S. R. Gardiner, (London, 1880) [hereafter cited as *Hamilton Papers*], p. 115. The radicals' emissary was almost certainly Dr. Stewart, dean of the King's Chapel, who had been allowed to escape from the Tower for the purpose. Bellièvre, in a letter from Newcastle on the same day, noting that the King seemed much firmer in his resolve to retain episcopacy and consequently cooler to any overtures from the English moderates, added: "I do not know whether or not this be the result of an interview he has had with one of his former chaplains, Dr. Stewart who has retired to France." (Bellièvre to Brienne, Newcastle, Sept. 21, 1646, *MC*, I, 276.)
17. Ludlow says that this conversation took place soon after the death of Essex. Gardiner has moved it to March 1647 on the highly questionable grounds that "In the autumn of 1646 Cromwell and his friends had a parliamentary majority." (*History of the Great Civil War, 1642–1649*, 4 vols. [London, 1893] [hereafter cited as Gardiner, *GCW*], III, 221, n. 6.) Since radical control of the House was by no means assured at this time, I see no reason for altering Ludlow's date.

ton's garden, he unburdened himself with respect to his parliamentary opponents. It was a miserable thing, he said, "to serve a Parliament, to whom let a man be never so faithful, if one pragmatical fellow amongst them rise up and asperse him, he shall never wipe it off. 'Whereas,' said he, 'When one serves under a General, he may do as much service, and yet be free from all blame and envy.'" Ludlow's opinion, which is borne out by the character of the radical propositions, was that Cromwell's eventual subjugation of the Long Parliament had its beginnings here.[18]

The attitude of the English moderates at this juncture was ambivalent to a degree. They still claimed to be but awaiting the opportunity to support the King and had even sent proposals to him. In the Commons, however, and in their conversations with the Scots, they made it plain that they were ready not only to abandon Charles, but to support harsh measures against him if he refused to accept some if not all of the propositions of Newcastle. By September 26 they had significantly stiffened their stand of two weeks before. Although they now required that Charles give up the militia for only ten years, they demanded that afterward it be controlled jointly by king and Parliament. They proposed, moreover, that offices of state be henceforth filled "with the participation and consent of Parliament."[19] They remained firm on Ireland—a necessary stance if they were to retain the backing of the Londoners—and continued to support the Newcastle demand for Presbyterianism. The radicals were able to offer Charles what was, on the surface at least, a much more attractive package: Irish issues would be shelved for the time being; limited episcopacy would be permitted; and a parliamentary faction, rather than Parliament itself, would be given control of the militia and, by implication, of the great offices of state.

If Bamfield knew of the radical proposals, Holles, too, must have been aware of them and of the threat they posed to his party and to himself. At any rate, a sudden hardening of the moderates' attitude toward Charles is apparent in the last half of September. For a time indeed, Holles worked in a seeming alliance with the radicals. As a result of moderate action the question of the "disposal" of the King's person was taken up on September 18. After the House had passed the radical-sounding and anti-Scottish vote that the King's person would be disposed of as the Parliament of England thought fit, it was none

18. *Memoirs of Edmund Ludlow*, ed. C. H. Firth, 2 vols. (Oxford, 1894) [hereafter cited as Ludlow, *Memoirs*], pp. 144–145.
19. *MC*, I, 283.

other than Holles who carried the vote to the upper house.[20] A few days later, under St. John's leadership, a House committee, chaired by the radical leader but with a moderate majority, was appointed to consider the matter.[21] This should have served notice on Charles that the support of the moderates could disappear and that there were limits to the possibilities of exploiting the differences among the parliamentarians.

The radicals, for their part, appear to have been anxious to clarify the alternatives that awaited the King should he choose to reject their offers. Some of their number were violently opposed to treating with him under any circumstances, and one of them (perhaps Henry Marten) was quoted as declaring that the King "could not be too far away" for the good of England.[22] By early October 1646 the Commons was described as debating whether the King should be deposed or merely imprisoned without any legal formality, and the Scottish commissioner Baillie was worried lest "their course with the King will be more summary than we can join in peace."[23]

The shift in moderate policy came as a surprise to the Scots. Only three days before the vote of September 18 relating to the "disposal" of the King's person, they had conferred with leading moderates and had received no warning of what was to come. When they protested against this treatment they were simply told that the votes had the unanimous support of the Commons and would also be approved by the Lords. The moderates were unresponsive to the possibility of the King's return to London and took the line that unless Charles agreed to the Newcastle propositions they would never consent to his coming to London "with freedom." Nor, they added, did they know any man in the Commons who thought differently. If the King did not give prompt satisfaction, they would ask the Scots to concur with them "for securing his Majesty . . . and to settle the government of the future without him."[24]

Not all the Scots in London would have been shocked by such sentiments. The Marquis of Argyle was, as Clarendon said, in matters of religion "purely Presbyterian" but in affairs of state "perfectly Inde-

20. CJ, IV, 672; John Harrington, Parliamentary Diary, 1646–1647, BM, Add. MS. 10,114, fol. 19a. The moderates won the division by ninety-one votes to eighty-three. Holles and Stapleton were tellers for the majority; Sir William Armine and Sir William Masham for the minority. (CJ, IV, 672.)

21. MC, I, 280; CJ, IV, 673.

22. Grignon to Mazarin, London, Sept. 24, 1646, Public Record Office, Paris Transcripts, 31/3/81, fol. 38a.

23. Baillie, Letters, II, 401–402; MC, I, 291.

24. Meikle, Correspondence, p. 216.

pendent."[25] On September 26 he suggested that the King agree to accept the protection of the New Model, which was probably a foreshadowing of the policy that resulted in the seizure of Charles by the army in June 1647. Montereul pretended not to be disturbed by the "pernicious" proposal. It is doubtful that Argyle made the suggestion without prior consultation with the radical leaders. By October 5 he was in Newcastle, where he was said to have been attempting to add "new rigour" to the proposals. *Persona grata* both to the English radicals and the Scottish Kirk, the nimble Marquis was in a uniquely influential position.

The Scottish commissioners in London were, meanwhile, reporting that the English Parliament was almost unanimously in favor of either imprisoning or deposing Charles if he refused the propositions. "Some few," they said, still preferred to send commissioners to the King once again, before taking action. Their English "friends," they said, were "altogether desperate" and had told the Scots that they had "neither strength to wrestle with the difficulties they meet with, nor [to] prevent the evils they see approaching, and therefore must give over all hopes of reconciliation."[26]

It may be that Holles' change of mind had its roots in some kind of understanding with Argyle and that the eventual agreement delivering the King into his hands had its beginnings here. We may discern, too, the first glimmerings of the rapprochement between Holles and the leading radicals, which was such a prominent feature of the same period.

But Loudon and the more moderate Scots were still not willing to give up without a struggle. In an important conference between the Scots and the parliamentarians on October 6, the Scottish chancellor, after insisting that the future of the King was of as much interest to the Scots as to the English, objected to the phrase "disposal of the King's person," as one that could be interpreted to mean "depose, or worse." He warned Parliament that if, in the face of demands inconsistent with his honor and safety, the King was forced to appeal to Scotland, he might receive such assistance that "the youngest amongst us [would] not live to see the end of these unnatural wars."[27] But Loudon was fighting a last-ditch struggle. The chief difference between the two parties at Westminster now seemed to lie, not in the conditions of

25. Edward Hyde, Earl of Clarendon, *The History of the Rebellion and Civil Wars in England*, ed. W. D. Macray, 6 vols. (Oxford, 1888) [hereafter cited as Clarendon, *Rebellion*], IV, 5.

26. Meikle, *Correspondence*, p. 218.

27. John Rushworth, *Historical Collections*, 7 vols. (London, 1654–1701) [hereafter cited as Rushworth, *Hist. Coll.*], I, pt. iv, 331–334.

peace to be offered to Charles, but in whether he should be placed in honorable retirement or simply deposed, and perhaps brought to trial.

The radicals, led now by Cromwell, were determined that the ground would not be cut from under them by a majority vote in the Commons. They were described as fearing nothing more than seeing themselves "without an army, in which all their credit consists."[28] On September 10 St. John had quoted letters from France advising the parliamentarians "not to disband the army of Fairfax, that all would thereby be lost . . . "[29] The moderates had been greatly weakened on September 16 by the sudden death of the Earl of Essex, whose influence, despite his loss of military command, had remained strong in the upper house. Party conflict had at once erupted over the choice of his successor as lord lieutenant of Yorkshire. The Lords announced that Northumberland had been appointed, but the radicals pressed for Lord Fairfax, and in the ensuing flare-up in the Commons Cromwell and Holles were "in some heat" upon it.[30]

By October 7 the moderates neglected even to contest an order for the maintenance of the New Model for a further six months. Two days later, when there was "some heat about the army," Cromwell took the lead in its defense and was described as pleading "for charity."[31] The moderates were certainly in no position to attempt to face down the army, and may even have begun to fear that it might be used against them. In early September the radical-minded John Harrington, after criticizing some elements among the Scots, had made the disquieting suggestion that "it would be happy for both nations if the bad [were] purged out."[32] Some such reflections may have prompted Sir John Clotworthy, a Holles man, to propose that a ballot box be used on questions concerning the granting of money or offices. Led by Cromwell, the radicals opposed this and won the division by fifty-six votes to fifty-four.[33]

The radicals were now pursuing two policies, which, on the surface at least, were mutually incompatible. They were widely regarded as not only ready to depose Charles I but to abolish the monarchy itself. There is equally clear evidence, on the other hand, that they contin-

28. *MC*, I, 267–268.
29. *Ibid.*
30. John Harrington, Parliamentary Diary, 1646–1647, BM, Add. MS. 10,114, fol. 19a.
31. Whitaker, "Diary," BM, Add. MS. 31,116, fol. 285a; John Harrington, Parliamentary Diary, 1646–1647, BM, Add. MS. 10,114, fol. 20b; *CJ*, IV, 687.
32. John Harrington, Parliamentary Diary, 1646–1647, BM, Add. MS. 10,114, fol. 18a.
33. Whitaker, "Diary," BM, Add. MS. 31,116, fol. 285b; *CJ*, IV, 690.

ued their secret dealings with the King that had been going on intermittently since the preceding August.

By mid-October, under St. John's leadership, the House had begun
the process of converting the Newcastle propositions into ordinances
that were to become law without the King's consent. In Baillie's view,
affairs were in a "marvellous ambiguity." He regarded the vote on the
New Model as maintaining "the sword, and moneys, and preferments
in the hands of the sectaries." He feared that the radicals were on the
point of declaring the King "for no scant of faults, incapable to gov-
ern while he lives."[34] The moderates' power was now at a very low
ebb. Ignored by the King for the previous two months, they were on
the point of dissolution as a party and were ready to make their peace
with the radicals as private individuals. London was also a question
mark. The heavy loans on the security of bishops' lands were creating
a vested interest in the abolition of episcopacy, while the Irish Adventurers still looked forward to a due return on their investments.[35]

By October 22 the moderates had lost another of their props with
the disbandment of the troops under the command of Sir Edward Massey. Cromwell appears to have played a key role in the final liquida-
tion of Massey's brigade which had been under radical attack for the
previous four months. Massey had attempted to stave off the disbandment by offering to take his troops to Ireland. Cromwell countered
this offer, however, by promising the Commons that he would himself
take as large a proportion of the New Model to Ireland as Parliament
thought fit and would "disband the rest if they [the Parliament]
pleased."[36] According to Colonel Wogan, the motion "took off all
jealousy from Cromwell and the rest of the army" and may have been
an important factor in smoothing the passage of the Commons' resolution of October 7 which extended the life of the New Model.[37]

Having blocked attempts to disband the army, the radicals appear
now to have contemplated its use against their parliamentary opponents. On October 21, 1646, with the support of Mildmay and Haselrig, St. John urged a mysterious scheme "for regulating both houses of
Parliament and their Committees."[38] One member reportedly declared

34. Baillie, *Letters*, II, 402–403.
35. *MC*, I, 299–300.
36. "Colonel Wogan's Narrative," *Selections from the papers of William Clarke,
secretary to the council of the army 1647–9 and to General Monck and the commanders of the army in Scotland 1651–60*, ed. C. H. Firth, 4 vols. (Westminster,
1891–1901) [hereafter cited as *Clarke Papers*], I, 424–425.
37. *Ibid.;* Whitelocke, "Annals," BM, Add. MS. 37,344, fol. 68a; John Harrington,
Parliamentary Diary, 1646–1647, BM, Add. MS. 10,114, fol. 21b; *MC*, I, 317.
38. John Harrington, Parliamentary Diary, 1646–1647, BM, Add. MS. 10,114, fol.
22a.

that "having won the kingdom by the sword they can dispose of it as a just conquest."[39] Henry Marten was soon urging the Commons to ignore the Lords if they refused to concur with the Commons. Three weeks later, and again on November 21, Lauderdale, the Scottish commissioner, reported from London that the radicals were about to adjourn the Parliament.[40]

Meanwhile, at Newcastle, Charles had been advised by the Scots to become a Presbyterian, by the royalists to give way to the Scots covenanters, and by the Frenchman Bellièvre to pin his hopes on one more attempt to win back his throne by an appeal to arms.[41] Charles rejected all these proposals in favor of a belated attempt to gain the support of the rapidly fading English moderates and on October 12 dispatched William Murray to London with his terms. The existing church settlement (that is, Presbyterianism) was to remain in force for three years. During this time a combined synod of Anglican, Presbyterian, and Independent divines was to attempt to come to a settlement, after which the King and Parliament would render the final decision. Charles was prepared to give up control of the militia for ten years or even for life provided that it return to the Crown on his death. By October 15 Charles was ready to permit Presbyterianism for five years and to abandon the idea of a synod if the English "Presbyterians" would agree to eventual restoration of a "regulated episcopacy." Although unwilling to abandon the Irish, his terms were reasonably close to the September proposals of the moderates themselves. There were, however, significant differences on the militia, the moderates having insisted that Parliament share authority with the Crown indefinitely.

The King's message was not official and was never recognized as such by Parliament, but the resultant debate in the Commons produced a dramatic scene reminiscent of the debate over the Grand Remonstrance five years before. The moderates supported the King's proposals "with all their might," while the radicals were "steadily rejecting them." Even bloodshed seemed imminent when some of the members drew their swords.[42]

Murray's attempt ended in failure, the reasons for which are complex but highly significant. The Scottish commissioners and the Scottish ministers in London appear to have been in large measure responsible for Parliament's rejection of the King's terms. Moderates like Holles, Stapleton, and Willoughby of Parham were reported to have

39. CSPV, 1643–1647, p. 289.
40. John Harrington, Parliamentary Diary, 1646–1647, BM, Add. MS. 10,114, fol. 22a; Hamilton Papers, pp. 126, 128–129.
41. Gardiner, GCW, III, 174–178.
42. CSPV, 1643–1647, pp. 389–390.

been satisfied with the offer, and it was later reported that "had it not been for the Scots" the Londoners also would have responded favorably.[43] "None of the English Presbyterians do care for the Covenant," Murray reported, despite the fact that the Scots were making it a *sine qua non*. He added that the English "Presbyterians" were in a much more yielding mood than were the Scots and that if sufficient concessions were made on religion and the militia "a considerable prevailing party" might declare in favor of the King's coming to London.[44]

A split in the moderate party developed at this time over the attitude to be taken toward the King's proposals. The more conciliatory section of the party—those actuated more by political than religious considerations—wished to treat the King's message as a basis for negotiation. The zealots—genuine Presbyterians—were worked upon to good effect by Scottish ministers like George Gillespie and Baillie, with the result that a substantial number of them deserted Holles for the "sectarian party."[45] Baillie had been greatly enraged by the rumors of the conditions offered by the King and by the alleged willingness of parliamentary leaders to compromise on the point of religion. "If the King grant satisfaction to all the propositions but that of religion and the covenant, as some whisper it will be," he wrote angrily, "then both his and their ingratitude to God will not pass without a just revenge."[46]

In this incident we can see how the insistence on the covenant and on thoroughgoing Presbyterianism was actually operating to further the ends of the radicals. Not only was it preventing agreement between the King and the English moderates, but it had weakened that party and strengthened their opponents. It is interesting to speculate on the role of George Gillespie in all this. The redoubtable "Galasp," the quintessential Scottish Presbyterian, had been one of the strongest fighters in the Westminster Assembly against English parliamentary Erastianism. As such, one might expect him to be poles apart from the English radicals and Independents. Yet the same could be said for Samuel Rutherford who had nevertheless written that, of all the English religious groups, the Independents were the nearest to "walkers with God."[47] The truth was that there was much religious, and more political, common ground between a certain type of Scots Presbyter and an English radical-Independent. Argyle had bridged the gap, and it is worth noting that Gillespie until his death in 1648 was closely

43. *MC*, I, 323, 341.
44. *Hamilton Papers*, p. 121.
45. Bamfield, *Apologie*, pp. 18–19; Baillie to Robert Blair, London, Nov. 3, 1646, Baillie, *Letters*, II, 408.
46. Baillie to Lord Warristone, Oct. 27, 1646, Baillie, *Letters*, II, 407.
47. Samuel Rutherford to Viscountess Kenmure, Mar. 4, 1645, *Letters of the Rev. Samuel Rutherford*, ed. J. Anderson (London, 1848), p. 630.

associated with the Marquis. His brother Patrick was to become one of Cromwell's favorite Scottish ministers.[48] Gillespie's key role in the rejection of the Murray proposals makes it seem likely that he was working in the interests of Argyle and the English radicals at this time. It was not the first nor the last occasion that the covenant would serve the turn of the party to which it was supposed to be anathema.

One of the lessons Holles learned from the incident must have been that he could support the restoration of a limited episcopacy only at the price of splitting his party and of completely alienating the Scottish Kirk. The rigorously Presbyterian policy that Holles was to pursue in the first half of 1647 was the result.

The radicals themselves appear to have been somewhat divided at this time. On November 3, 1646, Baillie asserted that the leaders of the party were willing to "welcome the King" under certain conditions. "The sectarian party," on the other hand, together with many others "who professed most to oppose them," was now ready to bring a charge against the King's person.[49] The truth seems to be that in both factions there was a real or potential cleavage between the leadership and the rank and file. The moderate leaders were quite willing to make use of genuine Presbyterian religious feeling, but were always ready to compromise on this very point in order to make political headway. The radical leaders, although prepared to fan the flames against Charles and even against monarchy itself, were at the same time willing to make secret offers to him even at the risk of a rift in their own ranks. The radicals pursued outwardly a policy in the Commons that appeared extremely hostile both to King and monarchy. In early November many Londoners were almost hourly awaiting the passage of a vote in the Commons "that never shall be recalled."[50] Scots like Lauderdale, who was then in London, attributed the most revolutionary aims to the radicals. They might cajole the King with smooth propositions, he wrote, but once he was in their power they intended to destroy him.[51] Warriston attacked them in the Scottish Parliament, claiming that their policy was "tending to up-root monarchy." On November 28, by a vote of 110 to 90, they carried a declaration through the Commons to the effect that it was the right of the English Parliament alone to dispose of the King's person as long as he

48. *Dictionary of National Biography,* ed. Leslie Stephen and Sydney Lee, 22 vols. (Oxford, 1908–1909), XXI, 361.

49. Baillie to Robert Blair, London, Nov. 3, 1646, Baillie, *Letters,* II, 408.

50. *Ibid.* 408–410.

51. Gilbert Burnet, *Memoirs of the lives and actions of James and William, Dukes of Hamilton* (London, 1677) [hereafter cited as Burnet, *Memoirs of the Hamiltons*], pp. 288–289.

was in England. The declaration, which had not been approved by the Lords, was then sent to the Scots, who refused to accept it.[52] Books were reportedly published in London in which it was contended that the Stuart line was spurious and that "the succession devolves legitimately upon others."[53] On December 10 the possibility of the deposition and even of the trial of the King was indicated when the House debated the question of "disposing" of Charles after the withdrawal of the Scots and of "giving satisfaction to the people touching the exercising of arbitrary power."[54]

Charles thus had little choice but to deal with one or the other of the parties at Westminster. By mid-December 1646 he was, typically enough, dickering with both. In choosing between them he was faced by the unpleasant fact that those who had been favorably inclined to him—the moderates—although able to dispose of impressive voting strength in Parliament, had been unable to deal effectively with the New Model. The radicals, although much more revolutionary in their reputation, possessed the undeniable advantage of power and, if they so wished, could restore Charles to his throne. Admittedly he would be a puppet, but he would have saved something from the wreckage by the restoration of a modified episcopacy and, given the temper of the country, he could hope to regain some, or perhaps much, of his lost authority. Although the moderates reflected the prevailing mood of the country much more accurately than did the radicals, they had, from Charles's point of view, serious shortcomings. The parliamentary nature of their power and the threat posed by the New Model to that authority forced them to insist on parliamentary control of the militia. Their links with the Scots and the need for unity within their own party were, moreover, obliging them to be more "Presbyterian."

In the first two weeks of December the King had a bewildering number of irons in the fire. His dealings with the moderates were serious enough to provoke disagreement with the Queen. On December 5 he had drafted a message to them in which he offered Presbyterianism for three years, the militia for ten, parliamentary control of appointments to the great offices of state, and an equivocal future for Ireland. In the face of opposition from the Queen, the French, and the Scots, Charles never sent the message, and Holles and his followers waited in vain for some sign of support. The King now turned much more seriously to the radicals, from whom he had received an overture as far back as September. Contemporary witnesses like Bamfield may have

52. *CJ*, IV, 730; Whitelocke, "Annals," BM, Add. MS. 37,344, fol. 71b.
53. *CSPV, 1643–1647*, p. 295.
54. Whitaker, "Diary," BM, Add. MS. 31,116, fol. 292b.

been right to characterize this merely as an attempt to persuade Charles to reject the Newcastle propositions in order to mobilize parliamentary opinion against him. Charles did not take the bait, and the hardening attitude of the radicals in October was perhaps a reflection of their chagrin. But Murray's mission in that month had come uncomfortably close to effecting an agreement between Charles and Holles. Accordingly, by late November, London was once again buzzing with rumors of secret dealings between the King and the radicals.

An agreement appeared possible if, in return for his restoration, Charles provided the radicals with the "principal offices" that would "deprive him of the will and even of the power of injuring them."[55] The radicals were aware of the growing unrest in the counties. The fact that the erstwhile bastion of parliamentarianism, the Eastern Association, could no longer be completely trusted was, moreover, a measure of the gap that separated the more extreme radicals from the substantial gentry of the home counties who had done so much to initiate the Revolution.

Had the radical leaders possessed the power, Bellièvre argued, they would have ruined the King, but they were discovering that it would not be easy to suppress the monarchy. There was evidence, too, that the zenith of republicanism and kindred doctrines among them had been reached and that they felt a growing uneasiness in the face of the developing social revolution led by the Levellers. They were now willing to concede much to the King in the realm of religion, if, in return, they were given control of the commanding heights of power. Bellièvre characterized them as more concerned to gain personal direction of the militia than to win for Parliament a greater share in its management.[56]

Two observers of considerable acumen have left interesting analyses of radical policy in this period. Sir Robert Moray, commenting on the fact that Charles had been receiving offers from the radicals to the effect that he could "satisfy England with little religion and without the Covenant," observed that "the leaders of them . . . will be apt enough to turn their sails another way . . . if they see themselves ready to be invested with the whole power of the State and King's person by offices and changes." He pointed out, moreover, that they had found the Scots and "many in England" to be strong supporters of monarchy. On the other hand, he did not rule out the possibility that their aim was simply to get the King into their hands after which it would be easier for them "to dispose of his person."[57]

---

55. Bellièvre to Brienne, Newcastle, Nov. 14, 1646, *MC*, I, 331.
56. *Ibid.,* 324.
57. Sir R. Moray to the Duke of Hamilton, Nov. 14, 1646, *Hamilton Papers,* pp. 123–126.

Clarendon agreed that the radicals were not as antimonarchical as they appeared to be. They had deliberately exaggerated this aspect of their policies because "they find their strength the greater by suffering men to believe they shall be subject to no law at all." They would not abolish the monarchy, he declared, because they knew that the English people would resist such a move. Its abolition, moreover, "would bring many unprofitable changes to any private man's condition that is worth anything." Clarendon feared, nevertheless, that the radicals intended to depose Charles and set up a puppet who would, in turn, give them effective control of the government. Perhaps thinking of the Prince Elector who was still living comfortably in London at Parliament's expense, Clarendon added: "I pray God they have not such a nose of wax ready for their impression; this it is makes me tremble more than all their discourse of destroying Monarchy." As for the Holles group, Clarendon thought that they would restore the King but only to the shadow of power, "which they would absolutely exercise."[58]

A number of observations may be made on the foregoing. Clarendon and Moray agreed that neither party would restore Charles to more than titular power. With respect to the antimonarchical reputation of the radicals, both observers make an interesting distinction between the leaders and the rank and file. For Moray, it was the "leaders of them" who would be willing to change direction. Clarendon also regarded the vaunted republicanism of the radicals as demagogic in character and implied that this was not the true opinion of the leadership of the party, who were too concerned with the rights of property to take such a revolutionary step. This may have been a foreshadowing of the open conflict between radicals and Levellers in 1647 and 1648 and even more specifically of Henry Ireton's well-known defense of the political privileges of property owners against the agitators during the Putney debates. The radicals' attitude toward the royal prerogative is also interesting, particularly with respect to offices of state and the militia. Both commentators saw the possibility of the radicals entrenching themselves, not behind extended parliamentary powers, but behind the Crown's prerogative, from which would come the offices and commands that would guarantee their future security.

"There is great noise in London of the King's treating with the Independents," wrote Lauderdale at the end of November. A few days later, however, Moray was of the opinion that there had been no "particular treaty" between that group and the King despite the alarm of "our friends of all kinds at London."[59] On the same day the King sent

---

58. Sir Edward Hyde to Sir Edward Nicholas, Dec. 12, 1646, Bodleian Library, Clarendon State Papers [hereafter cited as Clar.SPB], 29, fols. 4b, 5a.
59. *Hamilton Papers,* pp. 131–132, 133–134.

Lanark a copy of his projected overture to the moderates in which he carefully pointed out that, although he had included a concession to the "Independents" relating to freedom for tender consciences, he had done it simply in order that his message might "relish the better with that kind of people." He added that if the Scots would agree to support him he would not only expunge the clause, but would agree to make "what declarations I shall be desired against the Independents, and that really, without any reserve or equivocation."[60] In the grim struggle for survival in the British Isles at this time no one had a corner on "duplicity," but the Scots could be pardoned if they wondered why the person who had just admitted equivocation should have his next statement taken at face value. Charles was not really at his best when he assumed the role of Machiavellian politician.

In London, meanwhile, the financial agreement whereby the Scots undertook to hand Charles over to the English Parliament in return for £400,000 was nearing consummation. Both parties wanted to see the King in English hands: the moderates because they hoped to disband the army and rule England through a restored but hamstrung monarchy; the radicals because they were confident that their military power would be too much for either a defeated monarch or a parliamentary majority.

Argyle's party was now in the ascendancy at Edinburgh. Described as being composed of persons who wish "to destroy the King and the monarchy and profess it openly,"[61] this group, by December 17, had not only succeeded in reversing a statement favorable to Charles passed by Parliament on the previous day, but had pushed through a declaration stating that the Scots would never be satisfied by religious concessions alone. Charles could even take the covenant itself and still have no hope of Scottish support unless he also agreed to the whole of the Newcastle propositions. If he refused to do this, the statement went on, the Scots would look with equanimity even on his deposition. This attitude on the part of the Scottish Parliament accorded well with the plans of both major parliamentary parties in England. Both wanted to gain control of the King's person, and both had already displayed attitudes that boded ill for the political future of Charles.

By mid-December 1646 Holles was faced with the necessity for bold and decisive action. Agreement with the Scots was imminent, and the King would soon be in the hands of Parliament. Holles knew that if he, rather than his enemies, were to receive the King from the Scots, with all that implied, it was imperative that he win undisputed con-

60. Burnet, *Memoirs of the Hamiltons*, p. 290.
61. Montereul to Brienne, Edinburgh, Dec. 22, 1646, Bodleian Library, Carte MS. 83, fols. 118b–119a.

trol of the Commons. He made his first move only three days after the signing of the agreement with the Scots on December 16. His strategy was simply to bring all his potential strength to bear and to bury the radicals under an avalanche of votes. Holles demonstrated this power on December 19 by crushing the radicals in a division by 168 votes to 92.[62] The weight of London was almost simultaneously thrown onto the scale, in the form of a petition calling for the disbandment of the New Model.

There had been some difference of opinion as to the extent to which Charles could count on firm support from the City, and the petition did nothing to clear up the doubts. The civic government, it was noted, had readily complied with a parliamentary order for the expulsion of all royalists and Catholics. But the radicals were disturbed by the wave of antisectary feeling in the City and by the December elections to the Common Council, which produced a body described as "very partial against the Independent party."[63]

The London petition was, on the surface at least, rigorously Presbyterian. Parliament was asked to impose the covenant on all and to suppress unordained preachers. The crucial demand was, however, the fifth: that the army be disbanded. The King was not even mentioned, a clear indication that in the negotiations between Holles and the City that must have preceded these moves the restoration of Charles had no central place and may even have been ruled out.[64]

In the trial of strength between the two parties that followed, the moderates scored an overwhelming victory. After an all-day debate "till dark night," they defeated a radical motion by 156 votes to 99 that the petition be declared a breach of privilege.[65]

It is clear that the Holles-Stapleton party intended to be in control of affairs when the King arrived and to be in a position to deal boldly with the keystone of the radical structure, the New Model. With the army out of the way they could settle accounts with Charles at their leisure, provided, of course, that men like Vane, St. John, and Cromwell would stand quietly aside and watch the dissolution of the New Model and with it their hopes for the future. Holles and Cromwell had already clashed heatedly on the subject in the preceding summer and autumn, and there were indications that some of the radicals favored immediate use of the power of the army to redress the politi-

---

62. *CJ*, V, 25.
63. Newsletter, London, Clar.SPB 29, fol. 161b.
64. *CSPV, 1643–1647*, pp. 297–298; Sir E. Hyde to Cottington, Jan. 1, 1647, Clar.-SPB 29, fol. 42b.
65. *CJ*, V, 20–21; Whitaker, "Diary," BM, Add. MS. 31,116, fol. 293b. Stapleton and Sir W. Lewis were tellers for the majority; Haselrig and Evelyn of Wilts. for the minority. (*CJ*, V, 20–21.)

cal balance, one of them declaring that it was time "to send for the army, to curb the pride of the mechanic citizens." Two days after the debate on the London petitions, suspicious troop movements were nervously noted in the City.[66]

Apart from calling for the disbandment of the New Model, the Londoners had specifically attacked it in the section of their petition dealing with unlicensed preaching and were particularly incensed over the army's contemptuous handling of a case that involved a charge laid by a minister against a soldier accused of this offense. The Council of War, having blandly concluded that the trooper's only fault lay in his calling the cleric "a minister of anti-Christ," had sentenced him to a token imprisonment of one night.[67]

When the Commons debated the religious clauses of the petition on December 31, the hatred and fear felt by the conservative Londoners toward the sectaries (and Levellers) were amply demonstrated. A large and vociferous crowd shouted encouragement to the Holles party at the Commons' doors, and after a debate lasting until midnight the moderates, by a majority of 105 votes to 57, carried a resolution to prohibit preaching or expounding Scripture by laymen.[68]

During the previous three years, when the moderates could more accurately be described as the "opposition" rather than the "government," they had consistently upheld the monarchy and more than once put themselves forward as the group favoring a peace settlement with Charles on reasonable terms. Since September 1646, however, they had tended to take a tougher line, and by late December, as they felt themselves to be at the head of affairs, they suddenly became much more aggressive both in religion and politics. A number of factors prompted such an attitude. If good relations were to be maintained with Argyle and the Kirk, and their own internal unity preserved, an anti-Charles policy in politics and a Presbyterian stance in religion were prerequisites. There was also the lurking fear that Charles was negotiating with the radicals who, as their control of the Commons slipped away, were leaning toward a settlement that would make them, rather than Parliament, supreme in England. Charles, moreover, by choosing this moment to attempt to spirit the Duke of York out of the hands of Parliament, cast considerable doubt on his own professions of eagerness to come to London. The moderates were also greatly dis-

66. *CJ*, V, 15; Whitaker, "Diary," BM, Add. MS. 31,116, fol. 293a, b; M*C*, I, 372; newsletter, London, Clar.SPB 29, fol. 67b.

67. Whitelocke, "Annals," BM, Add. MS. 37,344, fol. 76a.

68. Whitaker, "Diary," BM, Add. MS. 31,116, fol. 295b; Whitelocke, "Annals," BM, Add. MS. 37,344, fol. 74b; *CJ*, V, 34–35. Sir Walter Erle and Sir Anthony Irby were tellers for the majority; Haselrig and Cromwell for the minority. (*CJ*, V, 34–35.)

appointed in the King's belated message of December 20. They had hoped for something concrete; they received instead a simple request that the King be permitted to come to London. More fundamental perhaps than all these factors was the growing disquiet at Westminster in the face of the rapidly developing sentiment in favor of the King, which was strongest in London and the adjoining counties. Would the party that brought about a restoration be swept aside in a general royalist reaction?

The King's reply received a cold reception in both Houses. The Lords declared against any treaty on the propositions, and the Commons concurred. On the same day, under the leadership of Holles and Sir William Lewis, the Commons called for the King's consent to the sale of the bishops' lands and to the abolition of the Court of Wards, rejecting a suggestion of the Lords that the King be permitted a grant of £100,000 in lieu of his income from the unpopular court.[69]

The debates in the Commons on the question of the disposition of the King's person in England after the departure of the Scots indicated both a distrust of some counties and a none too friendly disposition toward Charles himself. The suggestion from the Lords that he be taken to Newmarket in Cambridgeshire (a county described by Bellièvre as "assured to the King") was rejected by the Commons on the grounds that this was too close to the Eastern Association. Holmby, in the center of England and from which escape would be difficult, was finally settled upon. The Commons again disagreed with the Lords that Charles be brought to Holmby "with respect had to the safety and preservation of his person . . . " Since the King had broken the peace, why, asked Henry Marten, should Parliament guarantee his safety? Some members demanded that Charles be forever excluded from the government, and even the more moderate-minded were said to have favored his imprisonment.[70] The clause was only agreed to after the moderates had added the rider, "according to the Covenant," and it passed the House by a vote of 133 to 91.[71]

On the following day, however, the matter was again brought up, and the House voted to omit the clause completely.[72] Shortly afterward the Commons, still under moderate leadership, resolved ominously that if, after the Scots withdrew, the King should reject the propositions of New-

---

69. *CJ*, V, 31–32.

70. P. Bellièvre to Brienne, London, Dec. 23, 1646, *MC*, I, 368–369; Whitaker, "Diary," BM, Add. MS. 31,116, fol. 294b; *CJ*, V, 28; Burnet, *Memoirs of the Hamiltons*, p. 309.

71. Whitaker, "Diary," BM, Add. MS. 31,116, fol. 294a; *CJ*, V, 28. Stapleton and Irby were tellers for the majority; Sir Peter Wentworth and Sir Gregory Norton for the minority.

72. Whitaker, "Diary," BM, Add. MS. 31,116, fol. 294a.

castle, Parliament would "maintain the union between the Kingdoms."[73]

Most observers agreed that the shift in the parliamentary balance of power was not necessarily to the King's advantage. By early January the moderates were described as being firmer than ever in their determination to see Charles yield to their demands. Bellièvre regarded the gains of the Holles group as profitable to the King, not so much by virtue of any good intentions on their part, but because their parliamentary rivals would now be forced to court the King's favor and thereby could be obliged "to accept conditions compatible with the monarchy."[74]

There were many in both parties, wrote Clarendon, who were willing to come to terms with the King. They included persons who supported the radicals more on the basis of anti-Scottish sentiments than on political or religious grounds. Among the moderates, on the other hand, many supported the Scottish connection for political reasons, because they saw the Scots as supporters of monarchy and order and also because of their mistaken belief that the "Independents" intended to establish an "odious parity." Clarendon regarded as specious the "pretence" of the moderates to be the defenders of monarchy. Their real intention, he thought, was "to be themselves the monarch." Once again he rejected the contention that the radicals would abolish the monarchy, on the grounds that their own position as property owners would be threatened by the erosion of the common law. Their vaunted equalitarianism was, he argued, simply a device to strengthen their party; their leaders were, in truth, "more afraid of the people than ever they pretended to be of tyranny."[75]

Clarendon was aware of the activities of such men as Lilburne, Overton, and Walwyn and of the growing divergence of aims between them and the parliamentary radicals. In June 1646, with the radicals in the ascendancy, Lilburne had been committed to the Tower by the House of Lords with no perceptible protest from his old friends in the Commons. Since that time a steady stream of broadsides and pamphlets had come from the pens of Lilburne and his cohorts, attacking the holders of power and pelf who had usurped the ancient privileges of the "freemen of England." Increasingly bitter against both major groups in Parliament, Lilburne now urged reform of that institution itself, demanding extension of the franchise and annual Parliaments. In early January Overton and Lilburne produced the pamphlet *Regal Tyranny Discovered* which called for the trial and execution of Charles I and the abolition of the House of Lords. Even less palatable to radi-

73. *CJ*, V, 30.
74. Bellièvre to Brienne, York, Jan. 8, 1647, *MC*, I, 393.
75. Hyde to Jermyn, Jersey, Jan. 1, 1647, Clar.SPB 29, fol. 52a, b.

cals and moderates alike was the assertion that the power of the Commons was "merely derivative" and dependent on the people.[76] The reaction of the Parliament led by Holles was swift. Overton himself was in Newgate, but his wife Mary, who was discovered binding copies of the offending tract, was hailed before the Lords and dragged through the streets of London to Bridewell.[77]

The year had not been without its gains for the radicals, the most important being the establishment of a link, which was to develop into something resembling an alliance, with the Scottish faction headed by the Marquis of Argyle. The smooth-talking Campbell had cooperated closely with the Vane-St. John party in blocking the threatened defection to the King of elements in the Scottish army in May and June of 1646, and, as his influence grew, he had been able to render the alliance between the English moderates and their opposite numbers among the Scots more and more innocuous. Following his visit to London in June the Newcastle propositions had passed the Commons almost without a murmur, and through his influence in the Kirk and the Scottish Parliament the Hamiltonian attempt to mobilize support for Charles in Scotland had been effectively snuffed out. Perhaps the most signal service rendered to the radicals by Argyle—or at least by his friends in the Kirk—was the splitting of the parliamentary moderates on the issue of the covenant, following receipt of Murray's message from the King in late October. This weakened the Holles party and made the possibility of an agreement between that group and the King highly doubtful.

The radicals' own attitude toward the King and the monarchy fluctuated wildly during this period. Until the end of August they appear to have considered a number of solutions ranging from the establishment of a republic following the trial and even the execution of the King to the crowning of the young Duke of Gloucester as their puppet ruler. By early September they had at least temporarily abandoned these schemes and were offering to restore Charles as at least a titular monarch and to permit a limited episcopacy in return for control by their own party of the highest offices of state and of the military power of the nation. It was not the first time, nor would it be the last, that this group would make such an offer, and, as their minority status became ever more obvious, the necessity of this policy became more painfully evident. As early as the autumn of 1646 they appear to have been ready to take the most strenuous measures to prevent any settlement

76. Pauline Gregg, *Free-born John: A Biography of John Lilburne* (London, G. G. Harrap, 1961), p. 151.
77. *Ibid.*

that would place them at the mercy of a hostile parliamentary majority. They had already made it clear that they would not see the New Model disappear without a fight; Cromwell had been prominent in the disputes concerning the disbandment of that force. The "regulating" and even the adjournment of Parliament had been considered. Cromwell himself, apparently finding it difficult to adjust once again to the hurly-burly of parliamentary debate, seems to have considered the idea of military government. In mid-November Fairfax was said to have offered to resign his commission because the radical leaders wanted to give the command of the New Model to Cromwell.[78]

Could an arrangement with Charles I give the radicals both the power they wanted and the protection they needed? Or might a restored monarch, even one shorn of all but titular authority, still be capable of outflanking them by an alliance with the very institution—Parliament—on behalf of which they had originally waged war? It was undeniable that the King had already been able to make things awkward for them in conjunction with a Parliament from which royalists had been purged, and the recruitment of which they themselves had arranged and to some extent controlled. On the other hand, now that Lilburne was leading the revolution into a new and unpredictable phase, the republican solution was considerably less attractive than it had been even two years previously when the world still seemed safe for property-minded oligarchs. This fundamental dilemma was to be reflected in the vacillating character of radical policy throughout the crisis of 1647.

The year 1646 had seen moderate policy shift from cooperation with the radicals in January to relatively firm support for Charles against the threatening attitudes of the radicals in the spring and back again to almost outright hostility toward the King when agreement was reached with the Scots at the end of the year. During the first weeks after the King's flight to the Scots, they had pressed for a settlement and had attempted to soften the hard line taken by the radicals on the question of the militia. With the return of Argyle from Ireland, however, they had found themselves suddenly stripped of Scottish support, and their own collapse had been correspondingly swift. They had watched passively while Argyle and the radicals arranged affairs to their liking and had fallen back on a policy of support for the harsh Newcastle propositions in the hope that the King's acceptance of them would create a new situation which would eventually work to the dis-

78. "Time will permit the truth to be seen but will never destroy the ambition as I recognize it to be." (Cheylieu to Brienne, London, Nov. 19, 1646, BM, Harleian MS. 4551, fols. 566b, 567a.) The differences between Fairfax and Cromwell went back at least to April 1646 when they were reported to have disagreed over the question of the reception of the King on the surrender of Oxford. (Sabran to Mazarin [?], Apr. 23, 1646, PRO, 31/3/79, fols. 44–45.)

advantage of the radicals. To this end they became the strongest supporters of the peace terms because the radicals wanted nothing so much
as the King's rejection of them in order to set the stage for his deposition.

Their agreement with the Scots for the King's return was something
of a charade since Argyle had almost certainly concluded a similar
agreement with his friends, the radicals, in the previous June. A more
serious portent for the future was their failure to do more than make
tentative and rather feeble attempts to reduce the effectiveness of the
New Model by sending part of it to Ireland. Not only had they found
themselves checkmated by the radicals led by Cromwell in the Commons, but had also suffered a serious reverse when the House voted to
disband the forces of Massey and to maintain the New Model for a
further six months.

In September 1646 there had been a distinct change in the attitude
of the Holles group toward the King; this was particularly evident
with respect to the control of the militia. By late September they had
moved to a position close to the one they had previously opposed: indefinite parliamentary control. It is worth noting that the change took
place just at the time when the radicals were making secret overtures
to the King. If, as is probable, the moderates got wind of the radical
terms concerning the militia, the sudden toughening of their attitude
is understandable. If the King had agreed to give the radicals control
of the militia, the move could only have been countered by a firm
stand in favor of parliamentary power.

But by early October the moderates were in complete disarray. Essex
was dead, the King was reported ready to agree with the radicals, and
the harder line they had adopted had brought about a cooling of their
relations with the moderate Loudon group among the Scots. By taking
the lead in the move to sell the lands of the bishops they had made
some friends in London, but had also made it easier for the radicals to
portray them to the King as the uncompromising opponents of episcopacy.

The King's message in October by Murray had been the occasion of
a further weakening of the Holles party owing to the defection of a
number of the genuine Presbyterians who protested against the willingness of the party leadership to forgo the covenant and to agree to
a settlement that would have left the door open for a return of the
bishops. Here was a group within the Holles party that truly deserved
the name Presbyterian, and this was one of the few occasions when religion can be said to have been a decisive factor in the politics of the
Long Parliament.

By January 1647 the moderates had asserted their voting power in
the Commons and had taken over the direction of affairs. Yet when

Holles and Stapleton surveyed the scene, they had little cause for optimism. It is true that the withdrawal of the Scots would set the stage for disbanding the New Model, but it would also remove a most useful counterweight to that force. In Scotland itself the Hamilton and Argyle factions contended for power, but neither could be said to be on good terms with the English moderates or to share common interests with them. In England they had now to contend with the growing unpopularity of the Long Parliament, which was finding expression in the extreme conservatism of neoroyalists and the thrusting radicalism of the Levellers in the army and the cities. Their chief concern was, of course, that their rivals in Parliament might come to an agreement with the King that would enable them to rule England with or without a Parliament.

It is undeniable that the radical peace terms were potentially more attractive to the King. In contrast to the demand of the moderates for parliamentary control of the militia and governmental offices, they asked only that they themselves be installed in the key positions. In this respect an interesting change had taken place. In early 1646, when the radicals were still confident that they could control a majority in the Commons, they were ready to demand virtually perpetual parliamentary authority over the militia. The Holles group had later sought to moderate this stand. By the end of the year the positions had been reversed. A year previously the radicals had demanded Ireland as their private domain; now they were at least willing to shelve the issue. The moderates, on the other hand, with their close ties with London, were in no position to be conciliatory on this point. On religion there was less difference between the leaders of both parties than is commonly supposed. Both had been willing to permit the retention of a tamed episcopacy, and although Holles was now to find it expedient to take a tougher line, the essential difference between them was not the settlement of religion but the treatment of the royal prerogative. If the radicals could retain their military position and be given control of the executive, they could well afford to permit the King the nominal exercise of his prerogatives. But many of the radical leaders cared little for the restoration of Charles and even had good reason to believe that old scores would eventually be settled.

Other possibilities were being explored as 1646 drew to a close. As early as the autumn of 1645 the radicals had considered crowning the Prince of Wales; the idea appears to have gained some support from both of the major factions in the spring of 1646. In late 1646, as the Leveller movement became stronger, it was once again taken up, and the possibility of a rapprochement between the old parties based on a change of monarch became real.

VIII] The Reign of the Moderates

Holles faced a formidable challenge in January 1647: to bring peace, order, and good government to the British Isles after five years of bitter civil war and to do so in such a way as to assure himself and his supporters the fruits of victory.

Like most moderates in times of crisis, those in England were cordially disliked by all other factions. To the royalists and to the King himself they were largely responsible for bringing on the Civil War in the first place. They were often called "Presbyterians," and despite the fact that many, perhaps most, of them would have accepted a limited episcopacy, they were identified in the minds of sectaries and Anglicans alike with a rigid and intolerant Puritan church structure. Their links with the Scots, tenuous as they had become, did nothing to enhance their prestige in the minds of Englishmen. Above all, their power was more theoretical than real and was dependent—in an atmosphere long saturated with violence—on a continued respect for Parliament and its procedures. It was, moreover, becoming uncomfortably clear that many of the arguments that they themselves had so vigorously advanced to justify resistance to the King could, with a bit of pruning, be employed quite effectively against Lords and Commons. To the radicals, not to mention the Levellers, Holles and his followers were the party that had hindered the war effort and prevented any clear-cut victory. As such they had no right to the spoils, and, as long as the radicals could maintain their influence over the New Model, they had no intention of fading gracefully from the scene.

But if Holles' projects were almost foredoomed to failure, they were not without a certain element of statesmanship. Almost immediately after taking over control of the Commons, he attempted to work out a policy designed to enlist the support of the more reasonable among the radical leaders without at the same time alienating the Scottish Kirk party. That policy envisaged a restoration of the monarchy in the person of the Prince of Wales rather than his father; the implementation of a Presbyterian religious settlement in order to gain the backing of the Argyle Scots; and the disbandment of the New Model. The dangerous popular resentment against parliamentary rule was to be assuaged by the abolition of the hated county committees, and the Kirk was to be placated by the crowning of the Prince as a covenanted King. The radicals were probably also assured that, once the political exigencies that dictated a temporary enthusiasm for Presbyterianism had disappeared, a sensible and accommodating religious policy would be implemented.

But despite their attempted rapprochement with the radicals, members of the Holles group were to make few friends during their brief tenure. Their hostile, if not threatening, attitude toward Charles embittered those royalists who had hoped for better things from them; their attempt to enforce the covenant only pushed religious radicals in the army and City still further into opposition. They managed to retain the support of London by military and financial concessions, but the rank and file of the army resented what they regarded as high-handed and parsimonious treatment. They were, accordingly, the more open to the inflammatory doctrines of Lilburne who, from his vantage point in the Tower, surveyed the political maneuvering with his usual keen and minatory eye.

The Holles policy failed not so much because of inherent defects but because, by 1647, new elements had entered the political situation that made it difficult, if not impossible, to effect a settlement as the result of a kind of private agreement between parliamentary factions.

By mid-January 1647 a significant change in the political atmosphere at Westminster could be clearly discerned. The moderates, having demonstrated their power in the Commons, were now disposed to be magnanimous. An almost unprecedented distribution of largess from the public treasury took place: approximately £100,000 was handed out to friend and old foe alike. Most of the recipients were well-known Holles supporters like Walter Long, Sir Samuel Luke, and (less reliably) Bulstrode Whitelocke. But there were significant exceptions, not least of whom was Cromwell himself.

On January 7 Glyn was told to bring in a list of those members who had "suffered for their good affections" in 1628. On the same day, it was resolved that St. John, Samuel Browne, and Lisle (long-standing radicals) should bring in an ordinance for settling lands of the Marquis of Winchester on Cromwell. Two days later, Lord Saye and Sele, long a pillar of the radical cause in the Lords, was voted £10,000 in recompense for his recently abolished office in the Court of Wards. Charles Fleetwood, another former official of that court and a rising figure in the New Model, was granted £2,250, while the radical "recruiter" Nathaniel Bacon received £3,000. About a week later the heirs of the violent radical William Strode were granted £5,000 in recompense for his sufferings under Charles, and Samuel Vassal was awarded the substantial sum of £10,445 in recompense for his losses following his refusal to pay tonnage and poundage. On January 19, the day after the first moves had been made toward disbanding the New Model, the Earl of Northumberland, long a supporter of Vane and St. John in the upper house, was voted £10,000 in lieu of his office in the Court of Wards. The grant to Northumberland provoked a division noteworthy for the fact that Sir William Lewis, a leading moderate, was one of the tellers in favor of the motion, which passed in a thin House by a vote of seventy-five to fifty-five.[1] Meanwhile the committee appointed to arrange for the transfer of the lands to Cromwell had reported that Winchester held only life tenancy of the property. As if to assure Cromwell that he had nothing to fear, the Commons promptly resolved that he should have land "of the like value . . . out of lands of some other Papists in arms . . . "[2]

These actions did not pass unnoticed. One observer reported that "the generality of men murmur strangely that the money which they labor for so hard is so liberally and lavishly given away."[3] Another reported that "the liberal gifts of the Parliament to their own members are much spoken of among the people who say surely the Parliament is dying, in that they distribute their legacies so fast."[4]

Some regarded the lull in the customary party strife as distinctly ominous. Although Clarendon doubted that "the Independents" would "sneak off the stage so tamely," he reflected that there was "some mystery in this calm, united proceeding."[5] Bellièvre was predicting a few days later that if the King remained at Holmby House "the two parties will unite to settle the affairs of the kingdom" without him. His opinion was based not on mere rumor, but on conversations during the previous two weeks with the leaders of all parties.[6] It was widely believed that the two parties were close to agreement, but Clarendon remained skeptical: "no indifferency towards religion," he wrote, "will ever reconcile the Presbyterians and Independents to live quietly together."[7] From this it may be inferred that Clarendon had reason to believe that neither party regarded religion as an insuperable

1. *Journals of the House of Commons* [hereafter cited as *CJ*], V, 44–46, 57.
2. *Ibid.*
3. Letter of intelligence, London, Bodleian Library, Clarendon State Papers [hereafter cited as Clar.SPB], 29, fol. 72a.
4. *Ibid.*, fol. 72b; Salvetti to Gondi, Feb. 5, 1647, Salvetti Correspondence, Transcripts from archives at Florence of correspondence of Florentine ambassadors in England, 1616–1679, BM, Add. MS. 27,962L [hereafter cited as SC, BM, Add. MS. 27,962L], fol. 330b.
5. Hyde to Nicholas, Jan. 28, 1647, Clar.SPB 29, fol. 84b.
6. Bellièvre to Brienne, Feb. 4, 1647, *The Diplomatic Correspondence of Jean de Montereul and the Brothers de Bellièvre, French Ambassadors in England and Scotland, 1645–1648*, ed. J. G. Fotheringham, 2 vols. (Edinburgh, 1898–1899) [hereafter cited as *MC*], I, 450.
7. Hyde to Lord Cottington, Feb. 12, 1647, Clar.SPB 29, fol. 103.

obstacle to a political arrangement. This is borne out by the fact that
the party truce coincided with the implementation by the Holles party
of a strong Presbyterian policy. Although Clarendon was right to be
skeptical of the durability of any agreement between the two factions,
it seems highly probable that important elements in both parties arrived at some kind of rapprochement in January 1647. Sir Lewis Dyve,
writing on February 23, asserted that "some offers of accommodation"
had recently been made by the Holles group to the radicals, but he
assured the King that the radicals were suspicious of Holles and were
at that time exhibiting a distinct willingness to treat with the King.[8]
The truth seems to be that, while certain of the leading radicals were
ready to support a "Prince of Wales" policy, others found it politically
advantageous to exploit whatever possibilities lay in a secret understanding with the King.

One such group was a politically mixed coterie of peers under the
unlikely leadership of the Earl of Northumberland, who was now
veering in the conservative direction and, supported by Holland, Warwick, and Manchester, was ready by late January 1647 to regard the
offer the King had made via Murray in October 1646 as a basis for a
settlement. Their terms were as follows: Parliament was to control the
militia for ten years and to manage the war in Ireland; Presbyterianism without the covenant was to be established for three years with
the implication that a moderate episcopacy would be restored at the
end of that time. Since no mention was made of the ultimate disposition of the militia, one may infer that it was to return to the Crown
at the end of ten years. This was in sharp contrast to the Holles position in September 1646, when it was specified that Parliament would
continue to share the authority even after the period of complete
parliamentary control. The French agent Bellièvre in an effort to
counter Holles' policy of backing the Prince of Wales was attempting
to forge an alliance of Lords, City moderates, and even "Independents"
in order to avoid "some of the greatest evils that can happen."[9] This
may be seen as the first signs of the split in the radical ranks, which
was to become more marked in April and May.

Holles appears to have used financial pressure to bring the dissident
peers into line. Apart from the wooing of Northumberland with financial inducements, there were signs by early February of a joint attack
on the upper house by the members of both factions in the Commons.

8. Sir Lewis Dyve to Charles I, London, Feb. 23, 1647, "The Tower of London
Letter-Book of Sir Lewis Dyve, 1646–1647," ed. H. G. Tibbutt, *Publications of the
Bedfordshire Historical Records Society*, XXXVIII (1958), 55–56 [hereafter cited as
Dyve, "TLB"].
9. Bellièvre to Brienne, London, Jan. 29, Feb. 4, 1647, *MC*, I, 430–432, 451.

On February 3 Mr. John (?) Stephens reported from the Commons' committee appointed to investigate the activities of peers in connection with the sequestration of royalist estates that the Lords had "accepted great sums of money out of those compositions . . . to their particular purses . . . "[10]

A number of peers were singled out for special mention, among whom were Northumberland, Kent, Denbigh, and Saye and Sele, whose takings were listed as £10,000, £4,000, £1,500, and £2,000, respectively. In the cases of Northumberland and Saye, this treatment was in sharp contrast to the rewards showered upon them in early January. Holles' purpose may have been to suggest to these and other Lords the wisdom of joining forces with him and backing his plan for a settlement of the kingdom.[11] Eight days later the potential support for the King had virtually evaporated, ostensibly because of some tactless remarks by Charles, but more probably because Northumberland had been won over, or pushed over, to the support of the Holles policy.

It may be remembered that in the previous December Clarendon had been concerned over the possible existence of a "nose of wax" to be molded to the liking of the parliamentarians. Charles had similar fears, and with specific reference to his eldest son. As early as January 2 he had warned the Queen that if the parliamentarians had "the least imagination that the Prince of Wales will grant more than I, I shall not live long after."[12] On February 18 Secretary Edward Nicholas was informed that an agent of Northumberland or a member of the Commons was to go to France to see the Prince and that some thought that "if the Prince hearken to propositions from hence, his father's condition will be the more dangerous."[13]

Holles continued to develop this strategy throughout February and March, during which time the crucial debates over the disbandment of the army were going on in the Commons. By February 25 Bellièvre, after reporting a plan to kidnap the Prince and bring him to London, noted that many Londoners favored his presence, not only as a mediator between his father and Parliament, but as a potential candidate for the throne itself.[14] It was reported in Paris about two weeks later that the parliamentarians were contemplating sending a deputation

10. *CJ*, V, 70–72.
11. *Ibid.*
12. Charles I to Henrietta Maria, Jan. 2, 1647, *Letters of the Kings of England,* ed. J. O. Halliwell, 2 vols. (London, 1848), I, 440.
13. Nicholas Oudart to Secretary Nicholas, Feb. 18, 1647, *The Nicholas Papers: Correspondence of Sir Edward Nicholas Secretary of State,* ed. Sir G. F. Warner, 4 vols. (London, Camden Society, 1886–1920), I, 77.
14. Bellièvre to Brienne, Feb. 25, 1647, *MC,* II, 20.

to Paris to invite the Prince to return to England.[15] As the army crisis loomed, the Commons agreed on March 17 to discuss "the business concerning moving the King to send for the Prince to come home . . ."[16] Bellièvre wrote a week later that a delegation was about to leave for France to encourage the design, which he regarded as "most detrimental to the King of England."[17] In Edinburgh, meanwhile, Argyle had information that the Prince was ready to go to England and was being urged to do so by Northumberland's brother, Sir Henry Percy, and by the Earl of Norwich, father of General Goring who had himself been involved in an earlier intrigue with the radicals concerning the Prince of Wales.[18] Argyle may or may not have been a party to these projects; at this time he was actually dispatching Dunfermline to the King in order to extract from him a major concession on Presbyterianism.[19] But Argyle was quite capable of exploiting Charles's situation in order to gain ground in the area of Scottish religion and politics on the one hand and to negotiate seriously with the Prince on the other.

Certainly the religious policy pursued by the Holles group at this time would indicate that they hoped to enlist the support of Argyle and the Kirk by requiring that the Prince take the covenant as a condition of his gaining the throne. Nor would such a condition have been unrealistic, since it was well known that both the Prince and his mother were willing to make the most sweeping concessions on religion in exchange for the Crown.[20] Political considerations were uppermost in the minds of the moderates, too, as they now pressed for religious uniformity and the covenant with unprecedented vigor. On the eve of the Scots surrender of the King, some eighteen members of the Commons ostentatiously took the oath. On February 8 the Lords voted that those who refused to take the covenant should be barred from both civil and military positions. The future for the bishops also looked rather bleak when the Lords ordered a public sale of mitres, copes, and other vestments lately carted into London from Oxford.[21]

There were some murmurings against the drift of affairs. The mod-

15. Nani to Doge, Mar. 9, 1647, *Calendar of state papers and manuscripts relating to English affairs existing in the archives and collections of Venice and in other libraries of northern Italy*, vols. 10–38 (1603–1675) [London, H. M. Stationery Office, 1900–1940] [hereafter cited as *CSPV*], *1643–1647*, p. 306.

16. *CJ*, V, 115.

17. Bellièvre to Brienne, London, Mar. 25, 1647, *MC*, II, 88.

18. Montereul to Mazarin, Mar. 30, 1647, *ibid.*, 82.

19. *Ibid.*

20. Bellièvre to Brienne, Newcastle, Jan. 2, 1647, *MC*, I, 387.

21. Bulstrode Whitelocke, "Annals," BM, Add. MS. 37,344 [hereafter cited as Whitelocke, "Annals," BM, Add. MS. 37,344], fol. 80b.

erate-minded Whitelocke protested when the Commons forbade the Earl of Chesterfield the use of the *Book of Common Prayer,* pointing out that the order was "contrary to that liberty of conscience we ourselves claimed formerly."[22] Shortly before this, the Commons had approved the printing of Luther's *Discourses,* but, as if to set limits to heterodoxy, set up a parliamentary committee as a watchdog against all lay preaching. On March 29 the Commons voted to exclude all uncovenanted chaplains from access to the King.[23]

A similar burst of enthusiasm for the covenant was noted in London. In sharp contrast to the mood of the previous November, the government of the City was now prepared to demand that the King grant all proposals and sanction the covenant and that, until he had done so, he should be prevented from approaching London. A petition to this effect was presented on March 17, much to the chagrin of persons like Bellièvre and Charles himself who, up to that point, had been hoping for strong support from the City.[24] It seems highly likely that these developments reflected not so much zeal for Presbyterianism as increased interest among leading elements in London in the project of crowning the Prince of Wales. The refusal of Charles to take the covenant signified his determination to retain episcopacy in some form. It should not be assumed, however, that the moderates' insistence on it necessarily implied a corresponding rejection of bishops. They seem rather to have concluded that episcopacy was not worth the divisions it provoked among persons otherwise ready to defend the established social order. If, as seems likely, the Prince of Wales had intimated that he had no intention of permitting theological differences to block political opportunity, there was every reason to suppose that many otherwise disparate elements in the country would gladly unite behind him. As for Charles, the treatment of him by the Parliament led by Holles was an ill omen for his future.

The King had not long been installed at Holmby House before he was made aware of the attitude of the ruling group at Westminster. Stern economies were to be the order of the day. On February 6, 1647, the gold plate of the altar at Whitehall was ordered melted down to make "white plate" for the King's use at Holmby. After a long debate the Commons ordered £3,000 to be allotted to the King's household with the admonition that the committee be frugal in the spending of the funds. The King was also forbidden to speak privately or to write letters except under the parliamentary committee's direct supervision. Former royalists and persons who had refused the covenant were

22. *Ibid.,* fol. 80a.
23. *CJ,* V, 97, 109.
24. Bellièvre to Brienne, London, Mar. 4, 1647, *MC,* II, 44, 74.

barred from approaching Charles.[25] Far from opening new negotiations with the King, Holles and his followers were no longer satisfied even with the radical-inspired Newcastle propositions, but took care to add to them an unpalatable proviso for the confirmation of the sale of episcopal lands.[26]

In March and April the attitude of the leading parliamentarians toward Charles became hostile and even threatening. In Edinburgh, Montereul foresaw him occupying a "closer prison." There were rumors that he might even be brought to trial on a charge of complicity in the death of his father. This rather bizarre project was to be revived by Cromwell about a year later.[27] In the Commons the King was referred to "in very regrettable terms," and some members demanded that he be transferred to Warwick Castle and that his guardians be changed on the grounds that he was being treated with too much respect. Holles and his followers were described as being restrained from more drastic action only by the presence of their rivals in the Commons.[28] By March 25, as the army crisis was coming to a head, it was predicted that he would be transferred to Warwick Castle "and perhaps deposed." A few days later Argyle was telling Montereul in Edinburgh that he hoped to wring concessions from Charles on the covenant because of his constant fear of being poisoned or assassinated. Clarendon was now convinced that the "contrivers and authors of this scornful carriage towards the King do not intend he shall ever have it in his power to punish them."[29] But if Clarendon saw the deposition of the King as a real possibility, he did not hold, as did Bellièvre, that there was any possibility of abolition of the monarchy itself.

It seems reasonable to conclude from the foregoing that in the first months of 1647 Holles and his party attempted a rapprochement with the radicals on the basis of the deposition of Charles and the crowning of his son. It seems probable, too, that in return Holles received some kind of undertaking from certain radicals that the army would disband quietly. A strong policy in favor of the covenant was another ingredi-

25. Whitelocke, "Annals," BM, Add. MS. 37,344, fol. 78b; Lawrence Whitaker, "Diary of Proceedings in the House of Commons," BM, Add. MS. 31,116 [hereafter cited as Whitaker, "Diary," BM, Add. MS. 31,116], fols. 300b, 301a; Clar.SPB 29, fol. 97a; *CJ*, V, 103.

26. *CJ*, V, 103.

27. Montereul to Mazarin, Edinburgh, Mar. 2, 1647, *MC*, II, 42; Letter of intelligence, London, Mar. 2, 1647, Clar.SPB 29, fol. 134b.

28. Bellièvre to Brienne, London, Mar. 4, 11, 1647, *MC*, II, 21, 54–55; Salvetti to Gondi, London, Mar. 19, 1647, SC, BM, Add. MS. 27,962L, fol. 334b.

29. Bellièvre to Brienne, London, Mar. 25, 1647, *MC*, II, 88; Montereul to Mazarin, Edinburgh, Mar. 30, 1647, *ibid.*, 84; Hyde to Nicholas, Apr. 7, 1647, Clar.SPB 29, fol. 183a.

ent in the Holles strategy, designed to win the support of Argyle and perhaps also to convince the Prince of Wales that drastic religious concessions were the price of the Crown.

The fact that a veteran radical supporter like the Earl of Northumberland became a backer of the Prince of Wales indicated that Holles had succeeded in at least dividing and weakening the opposition. The old flirtation of the leading radicals with republicanism had, moreover, long since evaporated in the face of the genuine populism of Lilburne's Levellers. Faced by Holles in command of a hostile majority in the Commons and further weakened by the emergency of a splinter group oriented toward the Levellers and under the leadership of Marten, the radicals found the choices open to them becoming dangerously limited.

If they shrank from pushing the revolution further in the direction of democracy they could either make their peace with Holles on the basis of the deposition of Charles, the crowning of his son, and the disbanding of the New Model, or use their undoubted power in the army to intimidate Holles' parliamentary majority and perhaps negotiate a mutually advantageous arrangement with Charles. Up to about March 25 they appear to have maintained an attitude of relative passivity, if not cooperation with Holles. After that date, while a number of radicals still made overtures to Charles, Cromwell, at least, attempted to link two mutually incompatible policies: cooperation with Lilburne and support of Holles.

Because Cromwell was one of the key figures in the political developments of the period, no interpretation of events can neglect him. In the New Model something close to a struggle for power had long been brewing between Fairfax and himself. During the summer and early autumn of 1646 Cromwell had taken the lead in resisting any move to weaken the army, but by late May 1647 he was prepared to use the army as the basis of a political coup. The key question is whether he changed his mind, at least outwardly, in the intervening period and agreed to cooperate with Holles and Stapleton, perhaps on the basis of negotiations with the Prince of Wales. Insufficient evidence precludes certainty on this matter, but the indications are that some kind of understanding was reached. The steps taken in January to reward Cromwell with extensive lands almost certainly had the approval of Holles and Stapleton, and it is doubtful that they would have been prepared to be so generous if they had not received some earnest of political cooperation. Lilburne certainly did not hide his view of Cromwell's attitude when, in March 1647, after attacking Vane and St. John, he told Cromwell that he had reason to believe that he had opposed the army petition and concluded: "Accursed be the day that ever the House of Commons bribed you with a vote of £2,500 to betray and destroy us."[30]

The day the Commons began the debate on the disbanding of the army (February 7), Cromwell, perhaps rather conveniently, reported sick with a "dangerous impostume in his head."[31] But Cromwell's illness, genuine or otherwise, does not explain his and his friends' protracted absence from the Commons during this critical period. Holles complained that the leading radicals were frequently absent from the committee of both kingdoms.[32] An examination of the attendance records of the Derby House Committee for Irish Affairs reveals a sharp decrease in the attendance of the leading radicals on the committee between mid-February 1647 and late June of the same year when they were restored to power.[33] In the divisions on questions over the disbanding of the army, it is noteworthy that although the radicals, at least to mid-March, were able to muster considerable voting strength in the Commons against the policies of Holles and Stapleton, the House leadership appears to have passed to persons like Haselrig, Evelyn, and Mildmay. With the beginning of the army crisis about March 18, however, a sharp decline in attendance was noticeable, the radicals being no longer able to mount effective resistance to Holles' policies.[34] If, as seems probable, radical leaders like Cromwell, Vane, and St. John had undertaken to cooperate or at least to remain passively on the side lines during Holles' campaign to reduce the army, the disarray of their party is understandable.

Sir John Berkeley, one of the key royalists in the crisis of 1647 and a man in close contact with the leaders of all factions at the time, asserted that Cromwell, in the period just before the attempted disbanding of the army, had been hopeful of gaining the confidence of the Holles group and of persuading them to keep the army in existence and to treat it as their "praetorian band." He stated further that, although Cromwell was greatly chagrined at the decision to order the disbandment, he dared not oppose it in Parliament "because he had many ill-willers in the army," which, he feared, under such influences, would obey Parliament and abandon him. One of the "ill-willers" was, in all probability, Fairfax himself.[35]

30. Lilburne to Cromwell, Mar. 25, 1647, *Jonah's Cry out of the Whale's Belly* (London, 1647), BM, E.400(5).

31. Letter of intelligence, London, Feb. 8, 1647, Clar.SPB 29, fol. 97.

32. W. C. Abbott, *The Writings and Speeches of Oliver Cromwell*, 4 vols. (Cambridge, Mass., Harvard University Press, 1937–1947), I, 435–436.

33. Day Book of the Committee for Irish Affairs, Public Record Office, State Papers Domestic, Interregnum, E.26.

34. *CJ*, V, 90–128.

35. "Memoirs of Sir John Berkley [sic] containing an account of his negotiations with lieutenant-general Cromwell, Commissary-general Ireton, and other officers of

The campaign for the disbanding of the army opened on February 7 with a full-scale but inconclusive debate. When the subject was considered again both factions had mustered all available supporters for a crucial trial of strength. In the face of determined resistance from the radicals, the House voted to disband the foot soldiers in England and to maintain a force of only 5,400 horse and 1,000 dragoons. But the balance was remarkably even at this point. In two divisions on successive days the moderates had a margin of only two votes in the first and ten in the second.[36] When, on March 5, Holles, for unexplained reasons, attempted to oust Fairfax from the post of commander in chief, he found that he had overplayed his hand and was defeated by a margin of 159 votes to 147.[37]

Fairfax was widely recognized as a person of moderate opinions, and it is therefore not surprising that he found solid support in the Commons. Cromwell was a somewhat different case. On March 5 in a move clearly aimed at him the House debated whether any officer under Fairfax should be over the rank of colonel and whether any member of the Commons should have a command. Three days later the moderates succeeded in passing resolutions embodying these ideas. They were more successful, too, on the issue of religious conformity in the army and mustered 136 votes as against 108 for the radicals in favor of requiring all army officers to conform to the church government approved by Parliament.[38] But at least one observer refused to take such victories too seriously. "I never thought the Independents low," wrote Clarendon, "nor will they give over their designs upon any disadvantage in the House . . . "[39]

---

the army for restoring King Charles I to the exercise of the government of England," printed in *Harleian Miscellany: or a collection of scarce, curious, and entertaining tracts . . . found in the late Earl of Oxford's library*, ed. T. Park, 10 vols. (London, 1808–1813) [hereafter cited Berkeley, "Memoirs," *Harl. Misc.*], IX, 471–472. Edward Wogan, at this time captain of dragoons in the New Model and who later broke with Cromwell, recalled with respect to Holles' plans for the army that "Cromwell seemed to be as forward for this as any in the House." ("Colonel Wogan's Narrative," *Selections from the papers of William Clarke, secretary to the council of the army 1647–9 and to General Monck and the commanders of the army in Scotland 1651–60*, ed. C. H. Firth, 4 vols. [Westminster, 1891–1901] [hereafter cited as *Clarke Papers*], I, 425.)

36. Whitaker, "Diary," BM, Add. MS. 31,116, fol. 302b; Whitelocke, "Annals," BM, Add. MS. 37,344, fol. 79b; *CJ*, V, 90, 91; *MC*, II, 18.

37. Whitaker, "Diary," BM, Add. MS. 31,116, fols. 303b, 304a; *CJ*, V, 106, 107. Sir William Armine and Evelyn of Wilts. were tellers for the majority; Erle and Sir W. Lewis for the minority. (*CJ*, V, 106–107.)

38. Whitaker, "Diary," BM, Add. MS. 31,116, fol. 304a. Holles and Stapleton were tellers for the majority; Haselrig and Evelyn of Wilts. for the minority. (*CJ*, V, 107–108.)

39. Hyde to Nicholas, Mar. 7, 1647, Clar.SPB 29, fol. 142b; Robert Monteith, *The history of the troubles of Great Britain, containing a particular account of the*

The moderates had arranged that their moves against the New Model would be accompanied by a chorus of petitions from the associated counties demanding the very changes that they proposed to carry out.[40] A group from Essex expressed fears on March 11 that the army intended to have "an awing influence" on Parliament and that some persons in the army would attempt to block both the disbanding of the force and the establishment of national church government.[41] Six days later the Commons betrayed their nervousness by protesting to Fairfax against the presence of some units of the army "much nearer" to London than the twenty-five miles that Fairfax had himself ordered. By March 19 serious disturbances were reported in the army including violent demonstrations against the plan to dispatch the New Model infantry to Ireland.[42]

A significant petition was presented to the House on March 22 from a group of officers headed by none other than Sir Thomas Fairfax. They were concerned not only with army matters but with public affairs as well. They requested that Parliament hasten the establishment of church government and abolish the hated county committees. Both requests had a Presbyterian ring since it was well known that the county committees tended to be dominated by the radicals.

A parliamentary committee had, meanwhile, encountered an ominous disposition among the officers at Saffron Walden to attach conditions to any agreement for future service. Sir John Clotworthy, who with Waller was one of the leading spirits in this committee, reported on March 27 that a rebellious petition was being circulated in the army that imposed "unfitting" conditions on any service in Ireland. Two days later it was reported in the House that Colonel Pride (of the famous purge) had forced some 1,100 men of his regiment to subscribe.[43] Ireton was absent from the House when Waller made his report, but on his return he denied that any such petition existed. The House was impressed by Ireton's confidence, at least, that is, until the unexpected arrival of a letter from a major in Lincolnshire to the effect that a petition had been sent from army headquarters to be subscribed to by the regiment and returned to "Commissary General Ireton and others."[44] Amid the general uproar that followed, the embarrassed Ireton rose and, after admitting that the petition existed, protested that he

most remarkable passages in Scotland, from the years 1633 to 1650 (London, 1735), p. 258; Salvetti to the Secretary, Mar. 12, 1647, SC, BM, Add. MS. 27,962L, fol. 332a.

40. Oudart to Nicholas, Feb. 18, 1647, *Nicholas Papers*, I, 74–75.
41. *Journals of the House of Lords* [hereafter cited as *LJ*], IX, 72.
42. *CJ*, V, 115; Whitelocke, "Annals," BM, Add. MS. 37,344, fol. 81b.
43. Whitaker, "Diary," BM, Add. MS. 31,116, fol. 306a, b.
44. Sir William Waller, *Vindication of the character and conduct of Sir William Waller* (London, 1793), pp. 56–62.

and other officers had been forced to accept it in order to avoid one that would have been still more extreme. There was "a great inflammation" in the army, he warned, and great caution was called for in the handling of it.[45]

Waller, on the other hand, claimed that the leading officers, far from merely yielding to the petition, had not only "framed and minted" it, but had applied strong pressure on dissident spirits among them to agree to it. "The whole design," he declared flatly, "was carried on by Lieutenant General Hammond, Commissary General Ireton, Colonel Lilburn, Lieutenant Colonel Pride and some others."[46]

The moderates reacted by passing a resolution calling for the immediate disbanding of all foot in England and Wales other than those who were to serve in Ireland or in English garrisons. After summoning some of the leading officers to appear before the House, Holles drew up a declaration that condemned the army petitioners, going so far as to term the instigators "enemies of the state."[47] Colonel Pride was brought to the bar of the House and charged with reading the petition at the head of his regiment and intimidating reluctant subscribers. Pride coolly denied the charge, on the interesting grounds that the petition was read not at the head of the regiment but company by company. On the following day the enraged Holles became involved in a near duel with Ireton over the issue of the complicity of the officers.[48]

To Holles and his cohorts, the project of the disbanding of the army now appeared more urgent than ever. Stapleton was described as declaring that either their party or the army must go under.[49] But there could be no disbanding without a substantial outlay for the soldiers' arrears of pay, and for this the assistance of the London interests would be needed. There were few worries on this score; so anxious were the leading Londoners to be rid of the army that they were more than willing to loose the purse strings.

But if conservative elements were powerful in the Court of Aldermen and the Common Council, Lilburne and his followers were becoming increasingly vociferous. Moreover, the manner in which political agitation in the army and the demands of the Levellers in the City

45. *Ibid.*
46. *Ibid.*, pp. 55–62.
47. *CJ*, V, 129; A. Warren, *A Just Vindication of the Army* (London, 1647), BM, E.410(18), p. 41.
48. *Memoirs of Denzil, Lord Holles* (London, 1699) [hereafter cited as Holles, *Memoirs*], p. 80; Letter of intelligence, London, Clar.SPB 29, fol. 165b; John Harrington, Parliamentary Diary, 1646–1647, BM, Add. MS. 10,114, fol. 22b; *CJ*, V, 133; Salvetti to the Secretary, SC, BM, Add. MS. 27,962L, fol. 342.
49. A. Warren, *A Just Vindication of the Army* (London, 1647), BM, E.410(18), pp. 5–6.

appeared to reinforce one another was, in conservative eyes, a decidedly ominous development. Parliament itself was becoming a popular target of abuse. The London populace had never become reconciled to Pym's excise tax, and they were increasingly critical, if not scornful, of the manner in which public moneys found their way into the pockets of members of both Houses. All the pent-up animosity against Parliament, as well as the determination of Lilburne and his followers to convert the revolution into a movement for social justice and relative democracy, was embodied in the famous "Large Petition" of the Levellers, the circulation of which coincided with the rising tide of agitation in the New Model. The panic-stricken Londoners now demanded that Parliament suppress the petition, disband the army, and give London the control of its own militia. The Commons cooperated to the extent of arresting two of the Leveller ringleaders, only to find themselves besieged by a mob of shouting Londoners demanding their release.

Although the majority of the Commons, including adherents of both major parties, was strongly opposed to the Levellers, Lilburne now received significant support from the splinter group of extreme radicals led by Marten. A wedge was thus driven into the old radical formation, making the prospect of their regaining control of the Commons even more remote. Marten was still his old, irrepressible self and was finding the political climate of 1647 much more congenial to his views on Charles and related topics than was that of 1643, when he had lost his seat for his excessively free expression of them. Only two days before the appearance of the Leveller mob, during a debate on the King's request for chaplains, Marten had suggested that they should be provided in order that they might "prepare him for heaven."[50] A short time later, when the Commons considered whether the common people should continue to be permitted to approach the King seeking a cure for scrofula by being "touched for the King's evil," Marten had observed that an acceptable substitute for the laying on of the royal hands might be the application of the parliamentary great seal to the affected parts. A skeptical republican of a secularist cast of mind, Marten was a forerunner of a type that was to become more familiar in the eighteenth century. With his formidable assistance in the Commons, the intensifying agitation of the Levellers grew in counterpoint to the work of the agitators and dissident officers in the New Model, until the climax was reached in June with the army coup at Holmby.

Throughout the spring of 1647 there were strong indications that the understanding arrived at between the leading radicals and the

50. Letter of intelligence, London, Mar. 18, 1647, Clar. SPB 29, fol. 158a.

followers of Holles in January was still in effect. Radical estrangement from the Levellers, meanwhile, continued to deepen, and the appearance of the Marten group in the Commons as a separate entity was the measure of that division.

The split had been deepened by Lilburne himself when he appeared before a parliamentary committee in early February and proceeded to launch a blistering attack on the Long Parliament and all its works and pomps, including Pym's policy in 1640 and 1641. The Parliament, he said, had practiced a far worse tyranny than that of Charles and "destroys us with unknown, unlimited and arbitrary privileges, more than all the prerogatives of any King of England . . . and do not only act the Parliamentary power, but also the regal power." Not only had he a number of good things to say about Charles, but he singled out Pym and his policies for particular attack. The Pym party had moved against Strafford, he said, because he had been the main obstacle in preventing their getting "mighty places of honour and profit that it is now too much apparent they then aspired unto."[51] In the gathering of evidence against Strafford he declared: "it was screwed to the highest pin, if it were not higher than in honesty and justice it should . . . " This indirect attack on St. John was accompanied by a more direct assault on Sir Henry Vane, Sr., whom he blamed for the breakup of the Short Parliament and the consequent "blowing of coals to the fomenting and increasing of divisions between the King and his people."[52] One can almost envisage the jaws of the parliamentary committee men dropping as they listened to these words of Lilburne. Here was the firebrand himself, whose ideas they piously rejected as altogether too radical, daring to defend Charles. The more astute among them may well have seen in Lilburne's words the possibility of a kind of seventeenth-century version of "Tory democracy" and found it a profoundly disturbing prospect.

Sir Lewis Dyve may have been referring to his newfound friend Lilburne when he told Charles in late February that the party who up to that time had been most opposed to him had now swung around in his favor and that "some of the greatest repute amongst them" were ready, if they could enjoy freedom of conscience under his protection, to risk their lives for him. They took this position, Dyve said, because they knew that their enemies aimed at their utter ruin.[53]

The leading radicals in the Commons were cool, if not actually hostile, toward the "Large Petition" of the Levellers. Walwyn stated that

51. John Lilburne, *The Resolved Man's Resolution* (London, 1647), BM, E.387(4), pp. 13, 20.
52. *Ibid.*, pp. 14, 15.
53. Dyve to Charles I, Feb. 23, 1647, "TLB," p. 55.

"most of the upper-most Independents stood aloof, and look't on" when he and his friends were enlisting support for the petition.[54] The volatile Lilburne was furious, and in a letter of March 25 he castigated Cromwell's friends as "silken Independents," contemptuously dismissing Vane and St. John as "covetous earth-worms." He further accused Cromwell of having opposed a petition of the common soldiers that he described as "the hopes of our outward preservation."[55]

Cromwell appears to have been increasingly restive in the face of the moves against the army, which, whatever understanding he may have reached with Holles, meant the virtual extinction of his own influence over the course of events. There were those, he had complained to Fairfax, who had "so much malice against the army as besots them."[56] He knew, on the other hand, that an alliance with his old friend Lilburne was filled with danger and was made doubly so now that Lilburne was combining his populism with a newfound sympathy for the Crown.

There were other difficulties in the way of an alliance between the "old" parliamentary radicals and the Levellers, not least of which was the Leveller program itself. The Large Petition could have little appeal for leading parliamentarians. It called for, among other things, the dissolution of "that oppressive company of Merchant Adventurers" and the prevention of "all such others by great penalties forever." Such ideas were, of course, no more than an extension of the antimonopoly agitation that had once been the stock-in-trade of the parliamentary opposition. By 1647, however, they were distinctly unpalatable to the moderates, for whom London money was a *sine qua non*, and were no less distasteful to the radicals who, since 1644, had been careful to protect the interests of the Merchant Adventurers and the other great London companies against the demands of "the meaner sort."[57] The seventh article of the petition, which called for a reform of the legal profession, including the limitation of their fees "under strict penalties," could not have been attractive to a party that had as one of its leaders Mr. Solicitor St. John and in whose ranks the legal profession was well represented.[58]

Lilburne's suspicion that Vane and St. John had made some arrange-

54. "Walwyn's Just Defense against the Aspersions Cast upon him," in *The Leveller Tracts, 1647–1653*, ed. W. Haller and G. Davies (New York, Columbia University Press, 1944), p. 4.

55. Lilburne to Cromwell, Mar. 25, 1647, in *Jonah's Cry out of the Whale's Belly* (London, 1647), BM, E.400(5), p. 4.

56. Cromwell to Fairfax, c. Mar. 11, 1647, Abbott, *Writings and Speeches*, I, 430.

57. Margaret James, *Social Problems and Policy during the Puritan Revolution* (London, Routledge & Sons, 1930), pp. 144–158.

58. D. Brunton and D. H. Pennington, *Members of the Long Parliament* (London, Allen & Unwin, 1954), pp. 5, 26, 46, 132.

ment with Holles is indicated by his attacks on Vane, in particular, whom he accused in April 1647 of "some subtle, cunning but mischievous late underhand dealings . . . " and declared that he would soon be revealed as one who was determined "to keep the people in silence, from acting and stirring to deliver themselves from bondage."[59]

The moves Holles had made in March concerning the future composition of the army in England had a distinctly anti-Cromwellian flavor and had in fact excluded Cromwell from any command. On April 8, however, the Commons resolved without a division that Cromwell's cavalry regiment under the command of Major Robert Huntingdon (still, at this time, a close friend of Cromwell) should be retained. The move can only be interpreted as an extension of the olive branch by Holles who only a few days before had challenged Cromwell's son-in-law to a duel, and it marks the beginning of a period of cooperation between the two men that was to last until mid-May.

Two days later Lilburne wrote to Cromwell expressing his disgust with him and his "wise friends that are not able to trust God with three half pence . . . " The fact that they sat in the House in silence in the face of "the base things that are continually acted . . . , " he charged, made them, in effect, approvers of them and "treacherous betrayers of your friends and country . . . "[60]

During April 1647 the Leveller influence spread rapidly throughout the army. It was soon clear that back pay was the least of the soldiers' demands. Nothing less than a new revolution was brewing, aimed now, not so much at Charles, toward whom Lilburne himself was actually veering, but at the parliamentary oligarchs and in particular at the Holles-led majority. It became increasingly evident, too, that Holles' intention to disband the army was being counterbalanced by an equal and opposite determination on the part of that body to purge Parliament of its enemies.

The first hint of a parliamentary purge came on March 25 when the Commons ordered the arrest of the publishers of a pamphlet that warned of a plot by the majority of the Commons "to expell the most faithful."[61] It soon became evident, however, that such intentions were much more in the minds of the accusers than the accused. In a document entitled "The Soldiers' Queries," drawn up after Parliament's condemnation of the army petition, the authors first questioned the legality of the parliamentary declaration and then asked whether the

59. Lilburne, *The Resolved Man's Resolution* (London, 1647), BM, E.387(4), p. 16.

60. Lilburne, "A Second Letter to Lieut. General Cromwell," in *Jonah's Cry out of the Whale's Belly* (London, 1647), BM, E.400(5), pp. 6–7.

61. *CJ*, V, 123–124.

army might not now be entitled to use "the best means" to know who the persons were who "hand over head, were so nimble to incense the whole kingdom against us?" The soldiers questioned the legality of the election of certain members of the Holles party and asked whether such men "have not sat long enough in Parliament." An alliance between the extreme parliamentary radicals and the authors of the manifesto was indicated by the question as to whether, if there existed "a Party in the House not able to propagate righteousness, the several Counties ought not to assist them in such occasions?" The final query was nothing if not explicit: "whether these men, having no legal election, who for the most part have acted things so destructive, have not sat long enough in Parliament."[62] By April 26 the soldiers were described as insisting that they must see the kingdom settled before they would disband, and furthermore that they, as true representatives of the people, were the proper persons to regulate Parliament.[63]

By May 4 a detailed list of instructions had been drawn up at Saffron Walden that distinctly foreshadowed the coup at Holmby a month later. The document called for the disarming of "projecting parties, namely Presbyterians," as well as measures to be taken to prevent the seizure of the King. The soldiers demanded that justice be done on "all offenders whomsoever," and the general officers would be enjoined "not to depart from the Army until these storms be overblown, the subject's liberty confirmed, the kingdom settled, delinquents detected and punished, the soldiers and sufferers satisfied and rewarded."[64] It is noteworthy that the question of soldiers' pay is placed last on the list. Another army declaration of May 1647 envisaged not only the expulsion of offending members of Parliament, but their "condigne punishment" which would be extended to all "obstructors of the Army and Kingdom."[65] Money alone could scarcely satisfy an army that refused to disband until the "real freedom of the kingdom" was established.[66]

Cromwell found himself in an extremely difficult position. By mid-April, if he had made any firm commitment, it was to Holles rather than to Lilburne. On the other hand, it seems clear that, despite his lack of enthusiasm for Lilburne's political aims, which by November 1647 was to be converted into outright hostility, he was not above giving aid and comfort to the turbulent soldiers even as he put himself forward to Holles as the one man capable of handling the situation. Like a man in a log-filled river, jumping from one whirling cylinder

62. "The Soldiers' Queries," Clar.SPB 29, fols. 232–233.
63. Letter of intelligence, London, Apr. 26, 1647, Clar.SPB 29, fol. 195b.
64. "Advertisements for the Managers of the Counsels of the Army," printed in *Puritanism and Liberty,* ed. A. S. P. Woodhouse (London, Dent, 1951), pp. 398–399.
65. "The Resolution of the Army," May 1647, Clar.SPB 29, fol. 231a.
66. *Ibid.*

to another, Cromwell was searching desperately for some combination of forces that would guarantee his personal position without at the same time permitting the country to slide into anarchy.

Robert Huntingdon, a major in Cromwell's regiment, and Captain Wogan both stated emphatically that Cromwell and Ireton actively promoted the rebellious spirit in the army and that Ireton was not only the author of a number of papers sent to Parliament by the discontented soldiers, but had encouraged them to send representatives to army headquarters. Huntingdon quoted Cromwell as explicitly instructing the troops not to confine their demands to the issue of back pay, telling them that they were "in a double capacity as soldiers and commoners" and that even if they received their pay they had "something else to stand upon as commoners."[67] Wogan provided an interesting picture of Cromwell's method of controlling the agitators through his close friend Captain John Reynolds, whom they elected their chairman.[68] Even the soldiers' threat to purge the Commons of the enemies of the army appears to have been given considerable moral support by Cromwell and Ireton. Sir Harbottle Grimston recalled years later that two officers had accused Cromwell, in the Commons itself, of having suggested just such a course of action to the council of officers.[69] That Cromwell and Ireton had considered such a step but had thought better of it is indicated by John Wildman's statement that they had "professed themselves pained to the very hearts, because their way was not clear to purge the House from these unworthy men."[70]

Cromwell was also aware that the New Model contained a strong conservative element. Thousands of its soldiers were described as still using the *Book of Common Prayer,* and many had fought for the King.[71] A substantial minority of its officers were, moreover, strongly opposed to the policies of Cromwell and Ireton.[72] An agreement between the army and the King might break the power of the Holles party, put out the Leveller fire, and heal at least some of the divisions among the parliamentary radicals and in the New Model itself. At any rate, sometime before April 21 an unidentified group of officers proposed to restore the King if he would come under the army's protection. Charles rejected the offer on the grounds that its acceptance

67. Narrative of Major Robert Huntingdon, *LJ*, X, 409.
68. "Colonel Wogan's Narrative, *Clarke Papers,* I, 426–427.
69. Burnet, *History*, I, 25, quoted in Abbott, *Writings and Speeches,* I, 462.
70. "Putney Projects," p. 45, quoted in S. R. Gardiner, *History of the Great Civil War, 1642–1649,* 4 vols. (London, 1893) [hereafter cited as Gardiner, *GCW*], III, 283, n. 1.
71. Letter of intelligence, London, June 4, 1647, Clar.SPB 29, fol. 235a.
72. *A Vindication of a hundred and sixty seven Officers that are come off from the army* (London, 1647), BM, E.394(3); see also *Clarke Papers,* I, 33–82.

would provoke renewed civil war, but promised to remember the soldiers' good offices.[73]

Dyve described the overture as having originated from military persons of "very considerable power," while Bellièvre wrote that negotiations on behalf of the King had been carried on with "the most important" and influential persons in the army.[74] That Cromwell was directly involved is highly unlikely, but there is reason to believe that Ireton was connected with the overture.[75]

When news of the offer leaked out there were bitter words. Marten declared that the King ought to be brought to the bar of the House rather than negotiated with.[76] Some of the soldiers took the opportunity during Cromwell's visit to the New Model after April 30 to tell him rather pointedly that they thought it a "great scandal" that anyone should say that the army would ask the King to come to them and that "they would set the Crown on his head."[77]

It was soon clear that the proposals had deepened the divisions in both the parliamentary and military wings of the radical group. In the army there was danger of a disastrous cleavage as some regiments supported the offer while others as violently opposed it. The idea was dropped, but not forgotten.[78]

The question of the identity of the group involved in this negotiation remains a difficult one. Relations between Fairfax and Cromwell had not been such as to make cooperation between them likely, and, if one can judge from the anger exhibited by Fairfax at the time of the seizure of the King at Holmby, it is improbable that he would have approved of a scheme that implied a similar move at an earlier date. Moreover, he left the army on April 19 and went to London, ostensibly for reasons of health, but more probably because he opposed the offer that was about to be made to the King. Although Cromwell's position at this time was still one of opposition to Charles, he may have been considering the possibility of a change. Only a month later Dyve was describing him to Charles as being fearful of the King's restoration on the grounds that he would never be able to forget Crom-

73. Letter of intelligence, London, Clar.SPB 29, fol. 197; Bodleian Library, Carte MS. 20, fol. 630, quoted in Gardiner, *GCW*, III, 239; Salvetti to Gondi, Apr. 30, 1647, SC, BM, Add. MS. 27,962L, fol. 357a.
74. Dyve, "TLB," p. 56; Bellièvre to Brienne, London, May 17, 1647, *MC*, II, 144–145.
75. See Gardiner, *GCW*, III, 239–240.
76. Letter of intelligence, London, Apr. 26, 1647, Clar.SPB 29, fol. 195b.
77. John Rushworth, *Historical Collections*, 7 vols. (London, 1654–1701) [hereafter cited as Rushworth, *Hist. Coll.*], I, pt. iv, 480.
78. Dyve to Charles I, May 22, 1647, "TLB," p. 56.

well's past hostility. Should the King be able to rid him of the fear of royal revenge, Dyve suggested, "he may yet happily prove an instrument of great service to you in the army."[79]

Holles knew that Cromwell was not yet prepared to entrust his future either to Charles or to Lilburne and that he stood to gain his support if he could provide him with a third possibility. By mid-April the parliamentary radicals were in complete disarray and were described as divided over policy into three groups: those who favored dealing with the King; those who mistrusted him; and those who were "heartless."[80] Lord Saye was probably the leader of the first group while Marten was the most vocal member of the last. Cromwell, perhaps a member of the second group, was aware of the growing impotence of his party in Parliament and of the deterioration of his own position in the army. "Cromwell and all the Independent party are exceedingly sunk in spirit," ran a report from London of April 15. The party was virtually leaderless in the House at this time, with Cromwell and Vane remaining studiously in the background.[81]

There are indications that Holles, in an attempt to win the support at least of some of the radicals, now considered more extreme solutions to England's problems than the relatively mild one of deposing Charles and crowning his son.

The Prince of Wales project, although it was to be revived shortly, seems by mid-April to have gone sour. Northumberland, who had supported the policy in February, informed Argyle in early April that "the English" had no intention of placing any member of the royal family on the throne, because this would link their cause, which was "that of the public," too closely with a single individual.[82]

Northumberland may or may not have been speaking for Holles, but it is significant that negotiations with the Prince, so often talked of in March, were scarcely mentioned by observers after early April, when the army crisis became acute. At the same time the attitude of Holles toward the King hardened perceptibly. The Newcastle propositions were insisted upon, and it was widely believed that drastic action would be taken against Charles on his anticipated refusal.[83] On April 8 the "Presbyterians" (moderates) were described as declaring that "they no longer require a King."[84] As for the future government

79. Dyve to Charles I, May 24, 1647, *ibid.*, p. 57.
80. Bellièvre to Brienne, London, Apr. 8, 1647, *MC*, II, 147.
81. Letter of intelligence, London, Apr. 15, 1647, Clar.SPB 29, fols. 193, 195, 203.
82. Montereul to Mazarin, Edinburgh, Apr. 6, 1647, *MC*, II, 95.
83. Letter of intelligence, London, Clar.SPB 29, fol. 193.
84. Bellièvre to Brienne, London, *MC*, II, 109.

of England, there was talk that Holles and his followers intended to "make a Committee of State and a new model of government."[85]

Did Holles offer Cromwell a prominent position on a future Council of State in return for his support in the army crisis? Dogmatism on the point is precluded by insufficiency of evidence, but it is clear that among the groups bidding for Cromwell's support at this time the Holles faction had a prominent place. It seems equally clear that Cromwell was ready to talk business. Fearing that the dissension between army and Parliament might bring about a restoration of Charles, he "subtly endeavoured" to disband the army "by drawing most of the principal officers of the army with large promises of reward from the parliament, to be guided by his sole directions, tending to the destruction of his own party." This, Dyve says, was done in conjunction with "the Presbyterian party" and would, if successful, have ended in the disbandment of the army and the destruction of the King.[86]

Holles and Cromwell probably reached an agreement sometime between the King's rejection of the army overture on April 21 and April 30, when, with Fleetwood, Ireton, and Skippon he was commissioned by Parliament to go to Saffron Walden to bring the soldiers under control. His condemnation of the letters presented to the House by the three agitators, Edward Sexby, Thomas Sheppard, and William Allen, had rendered him suspect to the Lilburne elements in the New Model. It was, therefore, in his interest to see their wings clipped. Holles took care to give rewards for services rendered—or hoped for. On April 29 Skippon was voted £1,000; on May 6 an ordinance was brought in granting "diverse manors, advowsons, lands and tenements" of the Earl of Worcester to Cromwell. Fairfax was rewarded with lands valued at £5,000.[87]

Many of the soldiers felt a sense of betrayal at the news of the grants to the generals. One of the army's correspondents in London lamented: "Alas poor England!" "When will be a remedy for thy maladies? or when will thy Egyptian bondage end? . . . for there is no peace to be expected among the sons of men . . . "[88]

Holles now took steps to cement relations with London and to use the City as a financial and military counterweight to the New Model. If the army was to be disbanded, Parliament needed money, and Holles' friends in the City were more than willing to advance large sums for the purpose if, at the same time, they could rid themselves of the

---

85. Letter of intelligence, London, Apr. 15, 1647, Clar.SPB 29, fol. 193; Salvetti to Gondi, Apr. 16, 1647, SC, BM, Add. MS. 27,962L, fol. 348a.
86. Dyve to Charles I, May 24, 1647, "TLB," p. 57.
87. *CJ*, V, 162.
88. Letter of intelligence to the army, London, May 6, 1647, *Clarke Papers*, I, 26.

radical-dominated London militia committee. Accordingly, a week after an ordinance had been introduced in the Commons to transfer the authority over the militia from the committee to the Common Council, a parliamentary committee went to the City to negotiate a loan for £200,000.[89]

The ordinance for the City militia did not pass without vigorous clashes on the floor of the House between Alderman Pennington, who led the fight for the old militia committee and London Recorder John Glyn, who was the chief Holles spokesman. On April 15 the measure passed by a vote of eighty-one to sixty-one, and twelve days later the old committee, dominated by radical stalwarts like Pennington, Fowke, and John Warner, was ordered dissolved. The military resources of London were now at the disposal of Holles, and there was at least the possibility of a confrontation between the trained bands and the New Model.[90]

The Londoners drove a hard bargain in their negotiations with Holles over the £200,000 loan. The closely pressed moderates had already offered the lands of bishops, "Papists," and delinquents as security, but the Londoners demanded not only the additional security of royalist compositions at Goldsmiths' Hall but the authority to disburse the funds to the army.[91]

By early May the more extreme radicals in the Commons were ready to back, and perhaps to inspire, petitions of a Leveller character. Pressure on the Holles party from the "meaner sort" took the form of petitions to the Commons on May 4 and May 20, and in both cases they received an important measure of radical support. Whitaker described the first as coming from "Londoners of an inferior rank" and said that they desired "such a kind of liberty as the . . . [House] disliked."[92] The petition, described by Harrington as coming from the "Independent Londoners," provoked a long debate in the House, but was finally rejected by a vote of eighty to fifty-four.[93] The Levellers returned to the attack on May 20, at which time they were supported by a much larger group of radicals. The moderates, after moving that

89. *CJ*, V, 134.
90. Whitaker, "Diary," BM, Add. MS. 31,116, fol. 306b; Whitelocke, "Annals," BM, Add. MS. 37,344, fol. 85b; John Harrington, Parliamentary Diary, 1646–1647, BM, Add. MS. 10,114, fol. 24a. In the division over the militia committee, Stapleton and Glyn were tellers for the majority; Sir John Danvers and Haselrig for the minority. (*CJ*, V, 143.) On May 4 Pennington received some balm for his wounds in the form of £3,000 for "losses and damages." (*CJ*, V, 161.)
91. Letter of intelligence, London, Apr. 19, 1647, Clar.SPB 29, fol. 195a; Rushworth, *Hist. Coll.*, I, pt. iv, 476.
92. Whitaker, "Diary," BM, Add. MS. 31,116, fol. 309a.
93. *CJ*, V, 162. Holles and Stapleton were tellers for the majority; Evelyn of Wilts. and Haselrig for the minority. (*Ibid.*)

this petition together with the "Large Petition" of the Levellers should be burned by the common hangman, carried their point only by the relatively narrow margin of ninety-four votes to eighty-six in the first division and ninety-six to seventy-eight in the second.[94]

Throughout this period the attitude of the Holles group toward Charles I was consistently hostile; a change seems to have been considered only when it became clear that the army would rebel and might even seize the King. In mid-April when Holles and his supporters were reputed to be contemplating revolutionary changes in the government, the King was a closely guarded prisoner. Charles was ready to make substantial concessions to Parliament, but saw no evidence that any communication from him would be well received in London.[95] He was prepared to consent to Presbyterianism for three years provided that he and his household were accorded freedom of religion, to permit the assembly of divines, together with twenty clerics of his own choosing, to determine the religious settlement, and to grant the militia to Parliament for ten years provided that at the end of that time it be returned to the Crown. If these terms were accepted, he was ready to give satisfaction concerning Ireland.

Colonel Joseph Bamfield, Charles's agent in London, conveyed the offer to "some of the chiefs of both houses who I had gained into the King's interest," and they in turn had consulted "such of their friends as they could trust."[96] Presumably Holles and Stapleton were among those consulted, but little was to be expected from them at this juncture. Bamfield probably placed higher hopes in the group in the Lords centered around the Earl of Holland. Those whom Bamfield contacted demanded further concessions from the King, the nature of which can only be surmised from the context of the King's next letter of April 27. Charles rejected the demand that he omit two clauses (probably those limiting parliamentary authority over the militia to ten years and Presbyterianism to three) and declared that he thought it folly to believe that the parliamentarians "care not to conserve, what they desire with so much earnestness . . . "[97]

Holles and his supporters evinced little interest in the King's proposals and contented themselves with assuring Bamfield that once the army had been disbanded negotiations could go ahead with the King

94. *Ibid.,* 179. In the first division, Holles and Sir W. Erle were tellers for the majority; Mr. Pierrepont and Evelyn of Wilts. for the minority. In the second, Holles, Sir E. Massey, Sir W. Armine, and Evelyn of Wilts. were tellers for the majority and the minority, respectively. (*Ibid.*)

95. Charles I to Colonel Bamfield, Apr. 15, 1647, *Colonel Joseph Bamfield's Apologie written by himself and printed at his desire* (The Hague? 1685) [hereafter cited as Bamfield, *Apologie*], pp. 20–22.

96. *Ibid.*

97. *Ibid.*

"in greater liberty and security." Bamfield suspected, however, that the disappearance of the army would weaken rather than strengthen the King's position and urged Charles to send an official proposal to Parliament while there was yet time.[98] Charles replied that he would favor the disbanding of the army if he were assured that he would then be treated "sincerely and moderately," but the "very ill usage" he had received up to this point made him skeptical. He then suggested that Bamfield point out to the parliamentary leaders that his own attitude was more reasonable than was that of the fomenters of the army disorders and that only by an agreement with the King could Parliament regain control of the situation.[99]

Bamfield was aware that Cromwell and Fairfax had both received handsome rewards from Parliament, and in his reply he probably warned the King that Cromwell was now ready to back Holles in the disbanding program and that these developments boded no good for Charles. Bamfield tantalizes us by stating that the contents of his own letter may be "guessed at" from the King's reply of May 16. The King's willingness to deal with the radicals to counterbalance Holles was now made clear. Since, he declared, those parliamentarians "who pretend to be my friends" had virtually ignored what Bamfield had offered in his name, he had come to the conclusion that he could "expect nothing from them but extreme rigour when they have no competitors; for in the incertainty of their affairs; they may judge me necessary, but then useless."[100] The King's words reflected his chagrin at the cold reception accorded his formal message to Parliament on May 12, setting forth his position on a peace settlement and publicly offering the terms on religion, the militia, and Ireland that he had privately communicated on April 15.

The effect of the King's message was to alienate the radicals without attracting any firm support from the moderates. Holles was in a dilemma. His agreement with Cromwell appears to have been predicated on a policy hostile to Charles, and it was only with Cromwell's support that he could hope to disband the army. Any sign of agreement between Holles and the King would tend to force Cromwell back to the army which, in turn, might seize the King's person in order to prevent a settlement between him and the moderates. On the other hand, if Holles lost the support of Cromwell without gaining that of the King, he would be left with nothing and would, in effect, have paved the way for an agreement between an aggrieved Charles and the

98. *Ibid.*
99. Charles I to Colonel Bamfield, May 8, 1647, Bamfield, *Apologie,* pp. 23–24; Salvetti to the Secretary, May 14, 1647, SC, BM, Add. MS. 27,962L, fol. 362b.
100. Charles I to Colonel Bamfield, May 16, 1647, Bamfield, *Apologie,* pp. 23–24.

leaders of the army. He chose to keep his distance from the King, and only after it was clear that Cromwell was swinging back to the army did Holles begin seriously to consider projects such as a military alliance with the Scots and an attempt to forestall the army by inviting the King to London. The change in policy took place sometime between May 16, when the King still looked in vain for some sign of favor from Holles, and May 23, when discussions were carried on among Holles, Lauderdale, and Bellièvre, with a view to military aid from the Scots.

The day before the King's message was read, on May 18, Bellièvre felt that "the Presbyterians evidently dare not and cannot declare themselves for him." At this stage Bellièvre quite clearly looked on the army rather than on the Holles group as a source of potential support for the King and explicitly regretted the King's message of May 12 which seemed to pit him against the Independents "and consequently against those who have influence in the army, with the most important of whom I was beginning to have matters arranged in a very good condition."[101] Royalist observers in London agreed with Bellièvre. One of them, after characterizing some unspecified propositions the Holles group was said to have made to Charles via the Queen as designed to ruin the King, predicted confidently that the moderates would soon be ousted, in which case royalist exiles would be able to return to England, and "they [the Holles group] will be contented to recreate themselves in France."[102]

On May 20 the moderates in the Lords voted to invite the King to Oatlands, but on the following day the Commons refused to agree. As late as May 27 Bellièvre reported that those who had "the most intention to serve the King" were afraid to take any action.[103]

One of the most crucial questions in the shifts and countershifts of the main protagonists relates to the timing of Cromwell's decision to abandon Holles and to cast in his lot with the army. S. R. Gardiner holds that he took this step only after May 25. It was, he claims, the Commons' vote on that date calling for the disbandment of the army that provoked his decision because it had "flung his [Cromwell's] mediation to the winds." In this view, Cromwell is seen almost as the impartial arbiter, pushed against his will into opting for military force as the only alternative to injustice.[104]

Cromwell knew that if he permitted the army to crush Parliament he would make a mockery of the cause for which he had fought. On

101. Bellièvre to Brienne, London, May 17, 1647, *MC*, II, 144.
102. Letter of intelligence, London, May 19, 1647, Clar.SPB 29, fol. 221a, b; "A Continuation of certain special and remarkable passages . . ." July 2–9, 1647, BM, E.397(13).
103. Bellièvre to Brienne, May 27, 1647, *MC*, II, 153–154.
104. Gardiner, *GCW*, III, 265.

the other hand, his personal situation by early May was extremely precarious, and, as he became more and more suspect, the necessity for a
choice between Westminster and Saffron Walden became more and
more pressing. The agonizing nature of this choice is apparent from
the contrast between his words and his actions. On May 16 he reminded
the officers of the New Model of their duty to preserve in their soldiers
a respect for "that authority that is over both us and them." "If that
authority falls to nothing," he warned, "nothing can follow but confusion."[105] It did not follow, however, that he was telling his listeners
to obey the orders of Holles. His actions and those of officers close to
him indicated, indeed, that he now aimed at strengthening his hand
in the army with the object of destroying the Holles party without at
the same time irreparably damaging the prestige of Parliament.

In this connection, the genesis of the declaration of the army, drawn
up by the officers on May 16, is of considerable interest. The declaration placed the officers firmly on the side of the rank and file of the
army and contained, besides a demand for a more satisfactory offer regarding back pay, an attack on Parliament for its toleration of calumnies against the soldiers. Ireton suggested that such a document be
drawn up, and, according to Major Huntingdon, he not only drafted
it, but advised the soldiers that they were under no obligation to disband until their grievances were redressed.[106]

In the interval between May 16 and the presentation of the declaration by Cromwell to Parliament on May 21, the officers, far from encouraging the soldiers to obey Parliament, were afraid that Parliament
might make an offer that would satisfy them. If that happened, they
foresaw their own isolation and destruction. On May 18, a high-ranking officer wrote a letter from London in which he warned his fellow
officers of just such an eventuality. Parliament, he wrote, intended to
pay the soldiers all their arrears "and so to divide the soldiers from
their officers." To forestall such a move, the officers should contact the
soldiers in order "to set them right in this business, and to try them,
whether they will stick to their officers, though they should be paid
their arrears . . . "[107] On the following day the agitators wrote a letter
to the regiments warning them that if they accepted their arrears and
disbanded they would find themselves either forced to fight in Ireland
or else "hanged in England . . . " "Stand with your officers . . . , " they
urged, "and resolve neither to take money, nor march from one another, but let all your actions be joined."[108] It is evident that, at this

105. *Clarke Papers,* I, 72–73.
106. *Ibid.,* 77; Gardiner, *GCW,* III, 249.
107. *Clarke Papers,* I, 84.
108. *Ibid.,* 87.

juncture, parliamentary generosity was the last thing desired by those who controlled the New Model.

On May 21 Cromwell made his position clear by defending the stand taken by the officers in the declaration. His words, which must have grated on Holles's ears, created the impression of complete solidarity between officers and men: "the officers," he said, "thus joining with the soldiers again in a regular way to make known and give vent to their grievances hath contributed much to allay precedent distempers . . . "[109] Three days later Dyve was describing Cromwell as having made up his mind to support the army against Parliament. He attributed the decision to Cromwell's realization that he was deeply suspect "both in the Army and in the House" and that he had been "at last enforced to forsake the House and to adhere to the interest of the Army for his own preservation."[110]

Holles was bitter about Cromwell's role in the crisis. Instead of separating the regiments and attempting to quiet them, he recalled, Cromwell and the other parliamentary commissioners had drawn the officers together and "by asking what they will have, further enflamed them." This, he said, was "a strange way of quieting an Army that was in a way to Rebellion."[111]

Cromwell's decision to abandon Holles in favor of the army was probably taken sometime between May 6 and May 15, when the officers began their meetings in the church at Saffron Walden that were to produce Ireton's antiparliamentary declaration.

William Walwyn, who was a kind of *éminence grise* of the Leveller movement, provides some important evidence relating to Cromwell's change of heart. He himself, he later recalled, had persuaded Cromwell to make common cause with the Levellers after warning him that if he did not "it would be his ruin," but that if he moved in time, he would not only preserve himself and his friends, but would do so without spilling one drop of blood. According to Walwyn, Cromwell accepted the proposal, and from that point on relations between the radicals and the Leveller leader were excellent: "all the time the army disputed with the Parliament . . . they would . . . come to my house day by day, and sit and discourse friendly and cheerfully . . . and refresh themselves in my Garden . . . that I would often say within myself . . . the falling out of lovers is the renewing of love."[112] One of the

109. Abbott, *Writings and Speeches*, I, 450; Salvetti to the Grand Duke, May 21, 1647, SC, BM, Add. MS. 27,962L fol. 364b.

110. Dyve, "TLB," p. 57.

111. Holles, *Memoirs*, pp. 91–92.

112. "Walwyn's Just Defense," printed in *Leveller Tracts*, ed. Haller and Davies, p. 358.

results of this rapprochement was Cromwell's advice to the radicals in Parliament to support the Leveller petition of May 20.

It is paradoxical that Cromwell's association with the Levellers appears to have been an important factor in encouraging him to deal with Charles. As we have seen, Lilburne's hostility to the Long Parliament—combined perhaps with the influence of Dyve in the Tower—had brought about a distinct change in the Leveller's orientation, and within weeks he was to be explicitly urging Cromwell to come to terms with the King. As late as May 24, however, Cromwell was still reluctant to deal with Charles on the grounds that he would eventually suffer at the King's hands for his past record. Dyve felt that if Cromwell's fears on that score could be allayed, he might yet prove helpful to the King.[113]

Since Holles was far from any agreement with the King when Cromwell presented his report on May 21, his sense of outrage at what he regarded as Cromwell's treachery is understandable. Holles now felt himself obliged to turn to the Scots, an increasingly dubious alternative. The ascendancy of his own party had been paralleled by Argyle's success in winning virtual supremacy in Scotland. But since in the past Argyle's associations had been mainly with Holles's enemies, and since the Hamiltonian party had alienated Holles by their opposition to the handing over of the King, it is not surprising that, after February, there had been little cooperation between the two countries.

Argyle's position had recently been enormously strengthened by the "new modelling" of the Scottish army. A large part of the army had been disbanded, leaving a force of 6,000 foot and 1,200 horse, most, if not all of whom, were regarded as in Argyle's camp. The Kirk had cooperated enthusiastically in the task of purging the army of Argyle's opponents, with the result that by June 1647 his ascendancy over Hamilton was assured.[114]

We have no information on the relations between Argyle and the English radicals at this time, but by September 1647, at least, he was once again working closely with them. As his shrewd eyes surveyed the English scene in May 1647 he appeared to have been more concerned to "await the issue," as Carlyle put it, than to make any irrevocable commitments in either direction. When Cromwell later emerged as the English strong man, there were no barriers standing in the way of cooperation between the two men.

There is, however, evidence pointing to a degree of cooperation between Holles and Argyle. The strongly procovenant policy pushed by

113. Dyve, "TLB," p. 57.
114. *Memoirs of Henry Guthry, Bishop of Dunkeld*, ed. George Crawford (Glasgow, 1748), pp. 240–241.

Holles in February and March was almost certainly carried out with an eye to northern predilections, and Argyle was probably party to a plan to install the Prince of Wales on the throne. By April 6, however, he was assuring Bellièvre that there was no such possibility and appeared to be much more keenly interested in reviving James I's pet project of a political union of the two kingdoms based on a common system of religious uniformity.[115] On April 22 Lauderdale and Dunfermline arrived in London to look after Scottish interests, but as late as April 20 Montereul had reported from Edinburgh that there was "little concerted" between the Scots and the English Parliament, adding that "London does not pay much attention to Edinburgh."[116]

By late May Holles was in an extremely difficult position. His treatment of Charles I had been throughout the previous five months consistently hostile. If this had been the price of Cromwell's support, it was now clear that the price was too high. His range of choice had become dangerously narrow. Could he now make common cause with that group of Lords who had supported a settlement with the King since the previous January, or had he burned his bridges as far as any agreement with Charles was concerned? One thing was clear: he could get nowhere against the New Model without the support of the Scots. But they were dominated by Argyle who was a very doubtful ally. Argyle was, moreover, no friend of Charles and could not be expected to support any policy based on a settlement with the King. The Prince of Wales was perhaps a different matter.

Holles opened serious discussions with Lauderdale and Bellièvre on May 23 with a view to rescuing something from the wreckage of his policy. He now took for granted that the army would not disband and would probably seize the King, and various schemes for forestalling the New Model were discussed without conclusion. The idea of bringing the Scottish army back into England was broached, but no decision was reached.[117] Holles may well have been hesitant to earn the opprobrium of inviting Scots to fight Englishmen once again. Finally, the fact that Argyle ruled Scotland raised the disquieting possibility that he might be playing into the hands of his enemies.

Regretting too late that they had not come to an agreement with the King, the moderate leaders told Bamfield that they would invite Charles to London, but feared that the army would seize him before he could come. On June 1 Bamfield, at their suggestion, wrote to the King to warn him of the danger from the army and to suggest that

115. Montereul to Mazarin, Apr. 6, 1647, Edinburgh, *MC*, II, 95.
116. Montereul to Mazarin, Apr. 20, 1647, Edinburgh, *ibid.*, 117.
117. Joachimi to the States General, May 23, 1647, quoted in Gardiner, *GCW*, III, 259.

he escape in disguise, assuring him that if he did so he could expect to come to "a reasonable accord" with Parliament.[118] The King replied on the following day that he could see no way of preventing himself from falling into the hands of the army. The next morning Bamfield heard of the coup of Cornet Joyce.[119]

It seems clear that at no time before the King's seizure by the army was there any definite agreement between Charles, on the one hand, and the Holles group and the Scots, on the other.[120] The truth appears to be, rather, that the dilemma in which the moderates found themselves produced a kind of paralysis. As late as June 3, the date of Joyce's appearance at Holmby House, the disgusted Bellièvre was writing to Brienne that, although a dozen schemes had been broached, it had been impossible "to engage those members of Parliament . . . to carry any one into execution."[121]

With the King in the hands of the army, the radicals were once again in control of affairs. Bellièvre wondered whether their resumption of power would cause them to "revert to their old maxims destructive of all monarchy," which they seemed to have abandoned during the preceding months. He believed that the King's best hope lay now in supporting the Holles group so that the radicals would be forced to turn to the King and to the royalists.[122]

Holles had, however, lost all chance to assume the direction of policy and to give to the divided country a solution that might have prevented a second civil war. His position had been difficult from the outset, and only a leader of consummate skill could have offset the trump card held by the radicals in the New Model. Neither Holles nor Stapleton possessed the necessary qualities of patience, tact, and diplomacy the situation called for. There was little of the sinuous negotiator about Holles; his challenging Ireton to a duel was characteristic, demonstrating that he was still the same man who had grappled with the Speaker in the Parliament of 1629. Stapleton was a person of much the same stamp, and the remark attributed to him that "either the Army must down or they [the moderates]" was typical.

The decision to carry out a frontal assault on their opponents' citadel, the New Model, was neither necessary nor wise. The army was anything but a monolithic body: there were many divisions within it,

118. Bamfield, *Apologie*, pp. 24–25.

119. Charles I to Colonel Bamfield, June 2, 1647, *ibid.*, pp. 25–26.

120. Gardiner's statement that the King's proposal read on May 18 was "at once accepted not only by the English Presbyterians but even by the Scottish Commissioners as a fitting basis of accommodation" is not supported by the available evidence. (See Gardiner, *GCW*, III, 253.)

121. Bellièvre to Brienne, London, June 2, 1647, *MC*, II, 160.

122. *Ibid.*

both real and potential. Far from exploiting these differences, Holles helped to promote an artificial unity by adopting policies that could too easily be portrayed as high-handed and parsimonious.

There were elements of statesmanship in his promotion of the project of offering the crown to the Prince of Wales, and if the King could have been persuaded to abdicate, his son might have gained the support of many otherwise disparate elements. But the royalists appear to have been alienated by the harsh treatment of Charles and by Holles's adoption of a rigorous and artificial Presbyterian stance. He won the backing of at least a portion of the radicals for his policy concerning the Prince of Wales; if the disbandment of the army had been postponed, fear of the Levellers might well have prompted the kind of parliamentary realignment that actually took place in the autumn of 1647. But the premature attempt to disband the army provoked the expected reaction and ended the possibility of a settlement based on any consensus of parliamentary opinion. By June 3 the moderates had lost whatever opportunity they had ever had to shape the course of the Puritan Revolution. This was now to pass into more determined and more violent hands.

IX] The King in the Balance of Power

The Holmby House coup marked the emergence of the army as a formidable political power. Cromwell was the man of the hour, and, until his death in 1658, he was to dominate English affairs. Yet at this point "dominate" is much too strong a word. Indeed much of the interest of a study of this period lies in a consideration of the extreme difficulty of his situation and of the various stratagems to which he was driven in order to maintain a precarious equilibrium. It may be true, as some contemporaries thought, that Cromwell was a man of overmastering ambition, but it is not necessary to assume this in order to account for most of his actions.

Fundamental to the situation was the fragmentation of parties and groups; no longer could one man, or one group of men, hope to control events in a "parliamentary way." Cromwell's influence in the Commons was at a low ebb. His dealings with Holles appear to have alienated many of his old friends; this may, in fact, have been the origin of his break with Vane, which was to come in December 1647. Nor was there any noticeable enthusiasm among the "old radicals" for the course upon which Cromwell and Ireton now embarked, and which was to be finally embodied in the Heads of the Proposals. As for the Levellers, Cromwell's own attitude was distinctly ambivalent, while their feelings towards him were characterized by deep suspicion.

The policy he now adopted was the greatest gamble of his career. It envisaged what amounted to a personal agreement between Cromwell and the King that might well have made him virtual Protector of England under a titular monarch. There were great dangers in any such arrangement. It could be effected only with the support of the army, yet Cromwell's hold on the New Model could not remain firm or even secure without the support of the Levellers. Although Lilburne favored negotiations with the King, he was hostile to any settlement that would restore the monarchy only in order to place the "grandees" of the army in a position to overawe Parliament and the freeborn people of England. Even old parliamentary cohorts like Vane and St. John could be expected to be cool toward a policy that would not only restore Charles I, but that might install military rather than parliamentary leaders in the key positions of power. Given the strong popular reaction against the Long Parliament (or the remnant thereof), there was every likelihood that a new Parliament—even one excluding royalists—would have a strong conservative majority. In that event the radical leaders would find themselves dependent on the executive for protection against a hostile legislature. Cromwell's position would be reasonably secure, but what of his old friends? " 'Ware the halter [hangman's noose], friend!" was a favorite admonition of royalist pamphleteers, and the possibility of ending their days at Tyburn was one that certain radicals could not dismiss lightly. Cromwell, on the other hand, could expect the King's restoration to be greeted with a substantial measure of public enthusiasm and could himself expect to be a beneficiary of such a reaction.

It was well known, after all, that from the death of Pym in December 1643 to the recruiting of the Commons two years later, only about 200 of the 524 original members of the Long Parliament could ever be persuaded, at any one time, to attend the House. Of these, at least half were usually ranged against the radicals. The average attendance was indeed closer to 120, of which the radicals could rely only on a well-disciplined core of about sixty-five members. The awkward fact was that the vast majority of the members elected in 1640 proved to be either lukewarm to the parliamentary cause or actively royalist. Even the New Model itself included a substantial number of soldiers who were to become outspoken in their support of the King's restoration.

There were, then, grave risks for Cromwell in such a policy. In order to make his own position secure, the prerogatives of the executive branch of the government would have to be strengthened and a standing army maintained for years to come. Even then, he could perhaps be easily overthrown by a combination of former royalists and those who might regard him as a traitor to the parliamentary cause. He might have been considered a traitor, not so much because he restored the King, but because he would have effectively prevented Parliament from gaining the objective for which many thought the war had been fought: supremacy.

Viewed in this light, Cromwell's move to restore Charles can be seen as a calculated risk for the highest stakes. The gamble failed, and Cromwell's prestige was dealt an almost fatal blow. The reasons for the failure are complex. If, as S. R. Gardiner constantly reiterates, Charles could not be trusted, neither could any of the other protagonists in the tense and tricky atmosphere of 1647. The policy embodied in the Heads of the Proposals failed not so much because of the character of Charles—although that was a factor—but because by December 1647 Cromwell's position had become virtually untenable. He

had both lost the support of the Levellers and failed to gain the confidence of the more moderate elements in the army, even coming to
fear that this group, both in army and Parliament, would be so
strengthened by a peace settlement as to threaten his own position.

Cromwell's relations with Fairfax are instructive. The two men had
not been on the best of terms, and the Holmby coup did nothing to
mend matters. It was carried out against the wishes of the army commander who, nevertheless, soon discovered that Cromwell had the
King's ear and that his own offers of assistance to Charles were distinctly unwelcome. The King, in what was even for him an unusual
display of political myopia, rebuffed Fairfax with the words: "Sir, I
have as good interest in the army as you." Fairfax later characterized
this answer as more shocking and as causing him more grief and vexa-
tion than all the trouble and fatigues he had met in the whole war.[1]
He perceived, he recalled, what a "broken reed" the King was relying
on, but the weakness of his own position was revealed when he attempted to have Joyce court-martialed for his action: "the officers
whether for fear of the distempered soldiers or rather (as I suspected)
a secret allowance for what was done, made all my endeavours in this
ineffectual."[2] Charles had once again effectively eliminated an important source of potential support. Not until the autumn of 1648 did
Fairfax reemerge as a significant factor in the political scene; as before,
he was in opposition to Cromwell, and with no better success.

Although the seizure of the King was, in its implications, a fatal
blow to the Holles party in the Commons, they clung to the shreds
of authority until June 26 when the army forced the eleven members
to withdraw from the House.

The reemergence of Vane and St. John in early June was a straw
in the wind. But Holles was not disposed to give up without a fight,
and he now turned to the veterans of the armies of Essex, Waller, and
Massey (all of whom had been disbanded by the radicals) to counterbalance the pressure of the New Model. Massey rode through the
streets of London attempting to enlist support, declaring that Cromwell "had betrayed them all, and was fled from London without
license or order . . ."[3] The strategy achieved only a limited success,
and, although the "reformadoes" did their best to intimidate the Com-

---

1. Laurence Eachard, *A History of England* (London, 1718), p. 634; Sir William
Dugdale, *Memoirs of the Two Last Years of the Reign of King Charles I* (London,
1702), pp. 151–152.

2. Sir Thomas Fairfax, *Short Memorials*, in *Select Tracts Relating to the Civil
Wars*, ed. Francis Maseres, 2 vols. (London, 1815), II, 448.

3. Letter of intelligence, London, June 7, 1647, Bodleian Library, Clarendon State
Papers [hereafter cited as Clar.SPB], 29, fol. 236a.

mons radicals, their activities only postponed the evil day for the Holles faction.

Two elements in the City could be counted upon to support their respective friends in Parliament: the former soldiers, on whom the Holles party depended, and the apprentices, many of whom were followers of Lilburne. On June 7 the reformadoes appeared at the door of the House in large and threatening numbers[4] and left only after the House voted to distribute £10,000 in back pay among them. On the same day the London militia committee was asked to provide a guard for the House.

Holles now attempted to shore up his position by offering the New Model a more comprehensive ordinance for indemnity and back pay. The balance of power was, however, swinging inexorably against him,[5] and although he openly accused Cromwell, Fleetwood, and Haselrig of being privy to the seizure of the King, he lacked the strength to force the issue and was actually defeated on the same day by a vote of 119 to 86 over a resolution to concur with the Lords in their vote for removing the King to Oatlands. His weakness was further emphasized by the fact that three of the four commissioners named to negotiate with the army were radicals.[6]

If Holles hoped for great things from London he was soon disappointed. Cromwell effectively countered his attempt to mobilize support in the City by the simple expedient of hinting that the New Model might sack the capital. It was soon apparent that Sir John Gayer either would not or could not carry the aldermen and Common Councillors with him in support of a policy that meant a collision with the army.

On June 14, when the trained bands were mustered, supposedly in preparation for the coming struggle, they simply refused to fight.[7] The defection of this force was the signal for an all-out assault on the lord mayor, led by the radicals' old ally, John Fowke. With four aldermen and eight Common Councillors, Fowke went to army headquarters where he assured the officers of the City's undying friendship.[8] Crom-

4. John Harrington, Parliamentary Diary, 1646–1647, BM, Add. MS. 10,114, fol. 25a.

5. *Ibid.*

6. Lawrence Whitaker, "Diary of Proceedings in the House of Commons," BM, Add. MS. 31,116 [hereafter cited as Whitaker, "Diary," BM, Add. MS. 31,116], fol. 312b; *Journals of the House of Commons* [hereafter cited as *CJ*], V, 203. The commissioners named were Philip Skippon, Sir Henry Vane, Jr., Mr. Ashurst, and William Jephson. (*CJ*, V, 201.)

7. Denton to Verney, London, June 14, 1647, Sir H. Verney Manuscripts, BM, microfilm 636/7 [hereafter cited as Verney MSS, BM, M,636/7].

8. Rushworth to Lord Fairfax, St. Albans, June 15, 1647, *Memorials of the Civil War; correspondence of the Fairfax family*, ed. R. Bell, 2 vols. (London, 1849)

well now wasted no time in bringing charges against Holles and ten of his closest supporters.

As for the relations between Holles and the Scots, one should ask whether there was the possibility of a new Scottish invasion in support of Holles and the parliamentary moderates. S. R. Gardiner thinks there was and tends to justify Cromwell's actions in the light of this supposed threat. In dealing with this problem it is necessary to distinguish between the hopes and plans of Holles and some of the Scots on the one hand and the probability of their fulfillment on the other.

On June 1 Dunfermline was reported to be going to France with instructions from the Scots "and the English Presbyterians." He was to persuade Henrietta Maria to send the Prince of Wales into Scotland "in order to come with all the forces of that Kingdom into England and join the Presbyterians."[9] Bellièvre added that the "principal" members of the Presbyterians would declare for the King. There is, of course, a contradiction that must be explained. If, as seems likely, the Dunfermline mission was the result of an agreement between Holles and the Scots, it probably represented not so much a change of heart with respect to the King as a continuation of the policy of support for the Prince of Wales. On the Scottish side, it was in Argyle's interest, whatever his relations with Holles, to gain control of the person of the Prince of Wales. Bellièvre's comments are worth noting. He doubted that the Queen would risk the loss of the Prince and was skeptical about Dunfermline himself, whom he described as depending "absolutely on . . . Argyle, who is one of the subjects of this island that has done most harm to his King."[10] Another observer appears also to have doubted Dunfermline's motives, or at least his wisdom, when he reported that another envoy had gone to the Queen in Paris to acquaint her "with the right state of affairs and visible declination of the Presbyterian party."[11]

Argyle, on the other hand, could not be indifferent to the implications of the Holmby House coup. If Cromwell's decision to back Charles had been an effective counterbalance to the support of his son by the parliamentary moderates, it had also represented a distinct

---

[hereafter cited as *Fairfax Correspondence*], I, 355; Whitaker, "Diary," BM, Add. MS. 31,116, fol. 313b; Salvetti to Gondi, June 18, 1647, Salvetti Correspondence, Transcripts from archives at Florence of correspondence of Florentine ambassadors in England, 1616–1679, BM, Add. MS. 27,962L [hereafter cited as SC, BM, Add. MS. 27,962L], fol. 387b.

9. Bellièvre to Brienne, London, June 7, 1647, *The Diplomatic Correspondence of Jean de Montereul and the Brothers de Bellièvre, French Ambassadors in England and Scotland, 1645–1648*, ed. J. G. Fotheringham, 2 vols. (Edinburgh, 1898–1899) [hereafter cited as *MC*], II, 163.

10. Bellièvre to Brienne, London, June 7, 1647, *ibid.*, 164.

11. Letter of intelligence, London, June 10, 1647, Clar.SPB 29, fol. 240a.

reverse for Argyle. Such an alliance, if it held, would almost certainly have meant his ruin. For the moment it was in his interests to make all possible use of the deep reservoirs of ill will felt by many Kirk members for the English Independents; to curry favor with the Prince of Wales; and to recruit the Scottish army as insurance against all eventualities. He was careful, however, to avoid any action that would preclude a rapprochement with Cromwell in the event of a switch in policy. Neither man seems to have regarded theological differences as a bar to a political entente. For the time being, however, the army's link with Charles gave Argyle no choice but to take defensive measures.

The Hamiltonian Scots were in a difficult position. They had not been on good terms with Holles and were aware of his hostility to Charles, whom they tended to support. In contrast to Argyle, Hamilton had some claim on Charles's friendship. Accordingly, Cromwell's support of the King opened up new possibilities for him, and he was understandably reluctant to campaign for the return of the King to the custody of Parliament. The Scottish army was, moreover, controlled by the Argyle faction and any increase in its strength could only make the position of the Marquis even more powerful.

Thus it was that Lauderdale's rather hasty offers of assistance were not only greeted coldly by the English moderates, but disowned in Edinburgh itself. When Hamilton argued in late June against intervention, he pointed out that it was not apparent that the English Presbyterians "invited them to take up arms, or that their King asked assisance from them."[12] Hamilton had already been informed by Sir Robert Moray that the King was "not badly satisfied with the Independents" and that "he does not wish at all that they should raise forces here to go into England."[13] About a week earlier Montereul had observed that the Holles party had "neither asked for any assistance here [Scotland], nor even thanked . . . Lauderdale for what he was in haste to offer to them in London . . ."[14] So tenuous was the relationship between the Scots and the English moderates that the Scots actually hesitated to take military measures for fear of an agreement between the two English factions.[15]

The truth seems to be that the only substantial group in Scotland eager for a trial of strength with the New Model was the General Assembly of the Scottish Kirk. In early July that body issued what

12. Montereul to Mazarin, Edinburgh, July 6, 1647, *MC*, II, 188.
13. Montereul to Brienne, July 3, 1647, Bodleian Library, Carte MS. 83, fols. 187a, 188a.
14. Montereul to Mazarin, Edinburgh, June 29, 1647, *MC*, II, 182.
15. *Ibid.*, 175; Salvetti to the Secretary, London, June 25, 1647, SC, BM, Add. MS. 27,962L, fol. 394a.

amounted to a call to arms against the hated Independents. Despite the fact that, according to Montereul, Charles had "no wish whatever that an army be raised here to pass into England," they presented themselves to the people in the rather unfamiliar role of supporters of the rights and liberties of the King. "They . . . pressed the people to take arms to free him," wrote the skeptical Frenchman, "whom they held prisoner so long and whom they have freed in order to deliver him to his enemies."[16] Whatever the sincerity of the ministers, one may assume that Argyle was not yet prepared to lead the Scottish hosts to the rescue of Charles I. Whether or not he was in actual communication with Cromwell at this time is uncertain, but it is interesting to note that George Gillespie, one of his closest friends in the Kirk, was suspected of corresponding secretly with the "sectaries."[17]

It is not known what Cromwell thought about the Scots at this time, but he was probably not unduly worried. His support of the King could be expected to appeal to a large percentage of the people of England. If, under the aegis of the Kirk, the Argyle Scots invaded England with the supposed aim of rescuing Charles from the army, they would be faced by a virtually united people. But the possibility was never a real one. Argyle was much too shrewd to embark on such a harebrained crusade.

In London, meanwhile, the army's arrogant demand that the Commons surrender the eleven members acted as a catalyst and effected a partial and temporary realignment of parliamentary forces. Whatever their political inclinations, the members at Westminster were aware that their yielding to such demands could set a dangerous precedent. If Holles and his friends could be purged today, who tomorrow? The parliamentarians were uncomfortably aware that the Levellers, in their general hostility toward Parliament, made no very fine distinctions between either of the old parties and that Cromwell and Ireton were having difficulty controlling them. Vane and St. John must also have noted that since the Holmby coup their two military friends had emerged as the true holders of the political initiative in the kingdom. They appear to have neither relished the new situation nor to have been at all enthusiastic over Cromwellian compromises with Lilburne on the one hand and with the King on the other.

Parliament was notably slow in bowing to the demands of the army. As early as June 14 Bellièvre reported that the Londoners and the

16. Montereul to Brienne, July 3, 1647, Bodleian Library, Carte MS. 83, fols. 187b, 188a.
17. Gilbert Burnet, *Memoirs of the lives and actions of James and William, Dukes of Hamilton* (London, 1677) [hereafter cited as Burnet, *Memoirs of the Hamiltons*], p. 319.

parliamentary moderates were so afraid of the army that there was danger that this fear might "make the two parties agree without the King . . . towards which those who have engaged to ruin him continue to use all the effort in their power." Three days later the French envoy reported that the collapse of London had encouraged those who were "trying to bring the two parties to an agreement against the King."[18]

If parliamentarians of all shades of opinion were beginning to fear that the ground was being cut from beneath them by a private under-standing between the army leaders and Charles, they had good reason for concern. The Heads of the Proposals, which Ireton was to produce in July, were foreshadowed by a series of liberal propositions allegedly drawn up by the army on June 19. The King was to be restored to his "crown and dignity," the Queen permitted to return, and episcopacy reinstated. Charles was also asked to call the New Model "his army," to act as "umpire" in its dispute with Parliament, and to consent to a general amnesty. Parliament was to be dissolved by August 1, 1647, and new elections were to be called.[19] Such terms were distinctly un-palatable to either party at Westminster as was the "Declaration" of the army of June 14, which called for a purge of unfit members, a time limit for the Long Parliament, and the redistribution of electoral seats.[20] Cromwell and Ireton were soon assuring the King that "many things therein were proposed only to give satisfaction to others who were our friends."[21] They must also have felt the need to soothe the members at Westminster, among whom "even such as favoured the army were offended at this conduct."[22] The army proposals were said to have caused "extreme perplexity and confusion" in Parliament, particularly that for the "reinstatement of the Royal person."[23] "The Army's adherents in both Houses," recalled Bamfield, " . . . continually clamoured in Parliament at the seeming liberty which the King had,

18. Bellièvre to Brienne, London, June 14, 21, 1647, *MC*, II, 165, 170.

19. Clar.SPB 29, fol. 242a; see also Bodleian Library, Rawlinson MSS., d.399/33, quoted in S. R. Gardiner, *History of the Great Civil War, 1642–1649*, 4 vols. (London, 1893) [hereafter cited as Gardiner, *GCW*], III, 300–301.

20. *Puritanism and Liberty*, ed. A. S. P. Woodhouse (London, Dent, 1951), pp. 407–408.

21. Robert Huntingdon, "Sundry Reasons inducing Major Robert Huntingdon to lay down his Commission," *Journals of the House of Lords* [hereafter cited as *LJ*], X, 409.

22. Robert Monteith, *The history of the troubles of Great Britain, containing a particular account of the most remarkable passages in Scotland, from the years 1633 to 1650* (London, 1735), p. 285.

23. Advices from London, June 24, 1647, *Calendar of state papers and manu-scripts relating to English affairs existing in the archives and collections of Venice and in other libraries of northern Italy*, vol. 10–38 (1603–1675) [London, H. M. Stationery Office, 1900–1940] [hereafter cited as *CSPV*], *1647–1652*, pp. 3–4.

often alleging that he should be more restrained, and that the chief delinquents . . . ought to be brought to condigne punishment."[24]

A new and dangerously eccentric factor had in fact been added to the political equation: Lilburne's support of an agreement between the army and the King. As far back as February 1647 Lilburne had exhibited disquieting symptoms of a leaning toward the Crown and even toward the King himself. A coalition of Levellers and royalists backed by the New Model was, for the Parliament men, a prospect too horrible to contemplate; it must have made their past differences seem insignificant compared to the threat of the future.

The danger was a real, if temporary one. On June 22, Lilburne urged Cromwell and his associates to "endeavour to understand the King, and let him understand you, and deal with him as becomes honest men that play above board . . . " An agreement with the King was vitally necessary, Lilburne went on, "without which the peace of the Kingdom can never be settled . . . the Parliament having so tyrannized that they are grown as hateful to just men as the Devil." Lilburne believed that the King, on the other hand, would "grant anything that is rational that you or the Kingdom can desire at his hands."[25] In the same letter Lilburne once again attacked Vane and St. John. After promising Cromwell his strongest support he added: "But never was I so afraid of mine enemies, as of divers of those great ones I have looked upon as your chief counsellors."[26] The Leveller concluded with an exhortation to Cromwell to march on London in order to effect the expulsion of the eleven members.

A mixture of fear and resentment in the face of such demands probably prompted the radicals in the Commons to join in a general resistance to the army pressure for the expulsion of the moderate leaders. On June 21 both houses were described as ready to protect their members until "a more particular charge" should be brought against them.[27] Two days later the startled Commons debated the unwelcome army demand that a date be set for the termination of Parliament. After an inconclusive discussion, the distasteful matter was referred to a committee of the whole. On June 25, while the New Model threatened to march on London, the Commons stubbornly voted that the actions of the eleven members had not been such as would justify their suspension. They were then permitted to withdraw voluntarily.

24. *Colonel Joseph Bamfield's Apologie written by himself and printed at his desire* (The Hague? 1685) [hereafter cited as Bamfield *Apologie*], p. 27.
25. Lilburne to Cromwell, June 22, 1647, *Jonah's Cry out of the Whale's Belly* (London, 1647), BM, E.400(5), p. 8.
26. *Ibid.*
27. Clar.SPB 29, fol. 246a.

Three days later it was still believed that an agreement between the two parties was being worked out. Messrs. Philip Nye and Stephen Marshall were said to have been delegated "to temper the expedients about religion." An indication that Cromwell had been prevailed upon to pull in his horns was provided by a letter from the army agreeing to postpone more specific charges against the eleven members.[28]

It was probably about this time that Holles adopted a more conciliatory attitude in the face of what must have appeared an invincible combination. Through a royalist agent (Bamfield) he encouraged the King to insist that the military leaders clarify their terms. He accepted the policy of general religious toleration at which they aimed, but rejected the idea that control of the militia could reside "in the officers of the army." But if the army leaders, the King, and the parliamentary radicals were agreed, the moderates told Bamfield, "there could be no insurmountable difficulty in the business; nor any opposition, except for the Scottish ministers . . . "[29] It would seem that Holles was attempting to make political capital out of the developing split between Cromwell and Lilburne on the one hand and the Vane-St. John faction on the other.

But this alignment of forces was short lived. By the end of June Cromwell had virtually deserted Lilburne and was once again on good terms with the radical leaders who only a short time before had found it necessary to warn him not "to do the King's business so fast."[30] By June 28 the commanders were assuring Parliament that they were so conscious of its privileges that they would not even press for the suspension of the eleven members.[31] The Commons resolved on the same day that they regarded the New Model as their army and would maintain it. Bellièvre, noting the change, concluded that the radicals and the soldiers were "all powerful in the Kingdom."[32]

Lilburne, still in the Tower, reacted by bluntly accusing Cromwell of treason to the cause and concluded a letter to him by saying that he was now obliged to withdraw his "good thoughts wholly" from him and his associates.[33] As for the parliamentary radicals, Lilburne declared that he would "rather cut Sir Harry Vane's throat than Holles's."[34]

28. *CJ*, V, 223; Letter of intelligence, London, June 28, 1647, Clar.SPB 29, fol. 249a.

29. Bamfield, *Apologie*, pp. 28–29.

30. Letter of intelligence, London, July 5, 1647, Clar.SPB 29, fol. 263b.

31. Bulstrode Whitelocke, "Annals," BM, Add. MS. 37,344 [hereafter cited as Whitelocke, "Annals," BM, Add. MS. 37,344], fol. 95b; Sir William Waller, *Vindication of the character and conduct of Sir William Waller* (London, 1793), p. 172.

32. Bellièvre to Brienne, London, June 28, 1647, *MC*, II, 179.

33. Lilburne to Cromwell, July 1, 1647, BM, E.400(5), p. 10.

34. Newsletter from London, *Selections from the papers of William Clarke, secretary to the council of the army 1647–9 and to General Monck and the command-*

Lilburne's fury at Cromwell was considerably intensified by the latter's maneuver of using the council of war (from which the soldiers' representatives were excluded) as the main policy-making body. Such behavior, wrote Lilburne, "merits a kicking (if not worse) out of the Army."[35] In that body, meanwhile, Colonel Rainsborough was preparing to exploit the situation and even to challenge Cromwell's ascendancy. The struggle between the two men was to be one of the key elements in the army crisis of November 1647. It was clear, too, that the increasingly vociferous demand of the Levellers for a thoroughgoing purge of Parliament, with little respect to persons or parties, was a threat to all but Marten's faction.

On July 5 it was reported that the New Model was "not of a just temper for the chief of the Independents" and that the result might even be an alliance between the "Independents" and the City of London.[36]

Cromwell was aware, however, that he must retain control of the army at all costs, and, reversing the stand of June 28, he assigned Ireton the task of drawing up specific charges against the eleven members. Waller, one of the accused, contended that Ireton hurriedly dictated most of the charges, and when some of the bystanders questioned the validity of the accusations, the reply was that "it was in this business, as in a Chancery Bill, wherein, though there were never so many falsities, yet any one truth would be enough to make it hold . . . "[37] On July 6 Colonel Adrian Scroop duly arrived at the Commons to impeach the Eleven Members of "high crimes and misdemeanors";[38] at the same time the old Saville charges were revived against Holles.[39] By July 8 the remnants of the moderates were scattered, and one observer noted that "House or city will not hardly yield you a professed presbyterian."[40]

The extremists in the army made it unmistakably clear that they aimed at a much more vigorous purge. They demanded that all who had either assisted the King, accepted pardons from him, or executed his commissions of array for the mobilization of royalists should be expelled.[41] John Rushworth, who was acting as secretary to Fairfax at

---

ers of the army in Scotland 1651–60, ed. C. H. Firth, 4 vols. (Westminster, 1891–1901) [hereafter cited as Clarke Papers], I, 158.

35. Lilburne, Jonah's Cry out of the Whale's Belly (London, 1647), BM, E.400(5), p. 14.

36. Letter of intelligence, London, Clar.SPB 29, fol. 263b.

37. Waller, Vindication, pp. 174–176.

38. CJ, V, 236.

39. Whitelocke, "Annals," BM, Add. MS. 37,344, fol. 97a.

40. Letter of intelligence, Hatfield, July 8, 1647, Clar.SPB 29, fol. 265b.

41. Whitaker, "Diary," BM, Add. MS. 31,116, fol. 316b.

this time, strongly favored this policy and calculated that it would rid the House of over thirty moderate supporters.[42]

It was only with considerable difficulty that Cromwell and Ireton deflected the Leveller demands for a march on London and a massive expulsion of Parliament men. In a debate with the agitators on July 16 Cromwell admitted that he himself had entertained such thoughts, but he reminded the Levellers that "there is a party there that has been faithful from the sitting of the parliament to this very day . . . "[43] That party was gaining strength, he declared, adding that the steps that the army was taking would "make them gain more."[44] The agitator Allen bluntly disagreed. Their friends in Parliament were losing ground, he declared, and he repeated the demand for a march on London. Ireton, in support of Cromwell, pointed out that many of their enemies were leaving the House and urged that the army "have some love" for the group in Parliament "that are friends to our interest."[45] Both men were uncomfortably aware that the agitators had no more "love" for many of Cromwell's friends in the Commons than they did for the moderates, and the type of purge they envisaged would have rid the House of all but members of the Marten and Mildmay type. That the dispute was one between two factions among the officers, as well as between officers and agitators, was indicated by a report of July 19, stating that on the previous day the officers were "much discomposed" for fear that "some misunderstanding might have risen among themselves."[46]

During a discussion with the army officers about July 12 Sir John Berkeley asked what they would do in case Parliament did not agree to the settlement that they might make with the King. Most were hesitant about replying. Rainsborough, however, exemplified the aggressive attitude of the Levellers toward Parliament by blurting out: "if they will not agree, we will make them." About July 28, when the Heads of the Proposals were formally presented, Charles, in an almost incredible display of political ineptitude, chose to embarrass Cromwell and Ireton before their fellow officers by telling them that they would "fall to ruin" if he did not sustain them. Rainsborough, despite his threats to force the settlement on Parliament, "of all the army seemed the least to wish the accord." He left the conference and went to the army where, according to Berkeley, he "inflamed" the soldiers against

42. Rushworth to Lord Fairfax, July 13, 1647, *Fairfax Correspondence*, I, 367–368; *LJ*, IX, 320.
43. Speech of Cromwell to the army council, July 16, 1647, *Clarke Papers*, I, 192–193.
44. *Ibid.*
45. *Clarke Papers*, I, 195.
46. Letter of intelligence, London, July 19, 1647, Clar.SPB 30, fol. 7a.

the King. It is highly likely that he also made use of the incident to attempt to discredit the whole policy of Cromwell and Ireton.[47] On July 21 Sir Edward Ford, Ireton's brother-in-law, reported that fear of the agitators and apprehension "for their own safety" had prompted both army and Parliament "grandees" to agree to support the King.[48]

The question of the objectives and motives of Cromwell and the leading radicals at this time is at once a difficult and insistent one. The evidence will not sustain dogmatic judgments, and it is probable that, at times, the protagonists themselves were unsure of their motives. It may be useful, however, to summarize what contemporary observers felt about the underlying aims of the contending groups.

Clarendon was not an eyewitness, but he was the recipient of a constant stream of information from London; he was a former member of Parliament and was personally acquainted with many of the leading figures. The seizure of the King by the radicals, he thought, was prompted by motives of self-interest, not to say self-preservation. If the moderates had successfully disbanded the army, he wrote, the leading radicals would have been prosecuted "as the highest delinquents." He characterized the offers made by Cromwell and Ireton to the King as sincere though based on self-interest. Charles's safety ultimately depended, he thought, on the maintenance of a balance of power between the two parties in Parliament. If the moderates disappeared, the radicals would "use him [Charles] no better than they intended to."[49]

Many other hardheaded observers believed that Fairfax, Cromwell, and Ireton were honestly ready to support the King. Fairfax declared that he wished himself "much confusion" if he did not "intend really to the King,"[50] and a few days later some of the leading officers of the New Model claimed that it was "the resolution of the whole army" to restore the King "in his authority and power with honor."[51]

The policy of indiscriminate recruiting of former members of the royal armies appears to have resulted in the formation of a group of royalist sympathizers within the New Model itself. This element was well represented among the agitators, some of whom went so far as to advise Berkeley that, if Cromwell did not seem to be sincere in his

47. "Memoirs of Sir John Berkley [sic] containing an account of his negotiations with lieutenant-general Cromwell, Commissary-general Ireton, and other officers of the army for restoring King Charles I to the exercise of the government of England," printed in *Harleian Miscellany: or a collection of scarce, curious, and entertaining tracts . . . found in the late Earl of Oxford's library,* ed. T. Park, 10 vols. (London, 1808–1813) [hereafter cited Berkeley, "Memoirs," *Harl. Misc.*], IX, 475–477.
48. Sir E. Ford to Lord Hopton, London, July 21, 1647, Clar.SPB 30, fol. 11a.
49. Hyde to Nicholas, July 29, 1647, Clar.SPB 29, fol. 250a.
50. Letter of intelligence, London, June 28, 1647, Clar.SPB 29, fol. 249a.
51. Letter of intelligence, London, July 1, 1647, Clar.SPB 29, fol. 256a, b.

dealings with the King, they would "set him right either with or against his will."[52] Berkeley, a witness of impressive authority, believed that both Cromwell and Ireton were honest in their dealings with the King at this time. The King himself tended to regard their actions as being prompted solely by motives of self-interest, although he described the army offers as "much more frank and satisfactory . . . than ever was offered me by the presbyterians."[53] The day after he wrote these words, however, Charles told Berkeley that he distrusted the whole army with the single exception of Major Huntingdon; he was doubtless encouraged in this attitude by Lauderdale and the moderates who shuddered at the prospect of agreement between Charles and the Cromwellian radicals.

Ireton's record in 1647 attests to his sincerity. His declaration that "rather than His Majesty should continue thus enslaved by that vile party [the moderates], if but five men would join with him, he would adventure his life in order to his redemption,"[54] was characteristic, and apparently honest. Berkeley spent an entire night discussing the army proposals with him and was impressed by the coherence and frankness of Ireton's position. The army could not be depended upon, he told Berkeley, and therefore it was imperative that an agreement be made quickly. Because their "many malicious enemies both in the parliament and army" would accuse Cromwell and himself of "betraying their party," it was necessary that a certain number of royalists should be excluded from pardon.[55] When Berkeley proposed, however, that royalists be admitted to the next Parliament, Ireton objected and, indirectly admitting the minority status of his party, told Berkeley that he would be afraid of "a parliament wherein the King's party should have the major vote."[56]

Other observers took a more jaundiced view of the intentions of the Cromwellians. The Venetian representative thought that the army officers would "bargain for their own interests at the expense of the King."[57] One royalist felt that the radical leaders still planned to revolutionize the government and had been forced to change their tactics only because of the "general temper of the people."[58] Rushworth, a firm radical, pointed out that if the royalists thought that the army

52. Berkeley, "Memoirs," *Harl. Misc.*, IX, 473–476.
53. Charles I to Earl of Lanark, July 12, 1647, Burnet, *Memoirs of the Hamiltons*, p. 316.
54. Sir William Dugdale, *The Life, diary [1643–86] and correspondence [1635–86]*, ed. W. Hamper (London, 1827) [hereafter cited as Dugdale, *Life*], pp. 153–154.
55. Berkeley, "Memoirs," *Harl. Misc.*, IX, 473–474.
56. *Ibid.*
57. Advices from London, *CSPV, 1647–1652*, p. 4; see also Salvetti to the Secretary, July 23, SC, BM, Add. MS. 27,962L, fol. 405a.
58. Letter of intelligence, London, July 5, 1647, Clar.SPB 29, fol. 263.

"acts their game," they were mistaken. Concessions for the sake of peace might be granted, but there were certainly no intentions "to set them up in their authority again . . . for certainly the army will never desert the interest of the Parliament . . . "[59] Although Bellièvre regarded the army proposals as "ruinous" to the King and his posterity, he felt, nevertheless, that Charles would have a better chance to regain his authority in a settlement influenced by Independent ideas on church government.[60] He continued to feel, however, that the King was lost if the radicals gained complete power or if the moderates and radicals came to an agreement, which he regarded as a real possibility.[61] By July 22 he described the radicals as doing their utmost "to ruin him [Charles]."[62]

The ambiguity of radical intentions was underlined by a report that a group of members of Parliament, described as "the king's most mortal enemies," had about this time gone through Secretary Sir Francis Windebank's papers, seeking evidence out of which a charge against the King might be constructed. The well-known ministers Stephen Marshall and Phillip Nye, on their return from the army, reportedly declared that "the King should never have any power more, the army would look to that." He and his family would have liberty of conscience, they said, but he would have nothing to do with government.[63]

If the historian could decide issues by a kind of box score of witnesses, the weight of opinion, at this juncture at least, would be in favor of the sincerity of Cromwell and Ireton. Much more cogent, however, is the argument arising from the political situation itself and from the character of the army proposals. Cromwell and Ireton had much to gain but also much to lose by a policy of support for Charles. Ireton was fully aware of the dangers, and he made this clear to Berkeley. It is, accordingly, difficult to see why they would risk their position in the army simply in order to dupe the King. The proposals themselves had, moreover, an inherent credibility; their terms accorded well with the real interests of the army commanders.

59. Rushworth to Lord Fairfax, July 6, 1647, *Fairfax Correspondence*, I, 365.
60. Bellièvre to Brienne, London, July 15, 1647, *MC*, II, 196.
61. Bellièvre to Brienne, London, July 19, 1647, *ibid.*, 198.
62. Bellièvre to Brienne, London, July 22, 1647, *ibid.*, 204.
63. *Some Queries propounded to the Common Council and Citizens of London concerning the Army's Demand of having the Militia of London of the 4th of May changed. Wherein the unreasonableness and danger of that proposal and the justifiableness of the City's refusal are fully demonstrated* (London, 1647), BM, E.400-(26), pp. 3–4; *A true Alarum to England, but more especially to London, and a relation of the treacherous combination between Errorists and Malignants. Also the horrid design which the Army drive on to enslave the Kingdom* (London, 1647), BM, E.400(20), p. 5.

At this point of his career Cromwell should be thought of not as maker or breaker of kings, but as an increasingly isolated figure in serious danger of being destroyed by the revolution he had himself helped to make. To assume that he was oblivious to the more attractive possibilities of the situation would be to underestimate the man, but the future dictator of England must at this point have been concerned, not so much with dreams of supreme power, as with considerations of political—and even personal—survival.

His old friends Vane and St. John were at best hesitant about the direction of his policies since the coup at Holmby. Their control of the Commons was more than ever dependent on the support of the army, which was itself highly dubious. Cromwell's alliance with Lilburne had been a tentative step in the direction of following the popular wave wherever it led, and although he had appeared momentarily ready to travel that classic route to supreme power, he had abruptly drawn back. He thus presented to his enemies a golden opportunity to exploit the resentment of the Levellers; Rainsborough quickly seized this opportunity.

Cromwell's predicament, from which he was never to extricate himself, was that he had already gone too far on the revolutionary road to retain the support of the average middle-class English parliamentarian and, indeed, of many of the conservative-minded of the "meaner sort." He was, on the other hand, constitutionally incapable of becoming a tribune of the plebs. The Heads of the Proposals reflect that dilemma all too clearly.

Historians have usually regarded the proposals as the ingredients of an enlightened plan, far ahead of its time, which failed to bring about a general settlement only because of the unrealistic obstinacy of Charles I. Gardiner contrasts them with the Newcastle propositions, which he treats as a brainchild of the "Presbyterians," and hold that the army proposals were more democratic: "The Independent idea was to bring Parliament itself under popular control."[64] Contemporaries would hardly have agreed with this judgment; indeed, they regarded the spirit of the proposals as inimical to the idea of parliamentary supremacy.

Ireton, in drafting the document, had been careful to include items calculated to please the Levellers. Thus there was to be a reform of the constituencies giving greater equality of representation, as well as biennial Parliaments. The hated excise tax was to be removed from the necessities of life and eventually abolished; "all monopolies" would be done away with; "some remedy" was to be applied to tithes; and legal abuses were to be curbed. The religious settlement envisaged was

64. Gardiner, *GCW*, III, 330.

genuinely enlightened and reflected the convictions of Cromwell and Ireton: a tamed episcopacy was to be permitted, with wide toleration of dissent and abolition of civil penalties for ecclesiastical offenses. The key articles were those dealing with the Council of State, especially with its composition. No mention was made of a parliamentary voice in the naming of the council's members, an omission that could hardly have been accidental. It was to be placed in the hands of "trusty and able persons now to be agreed upon." Gardiner notes that since no mention was made of the manner of appointing the successors of the first appointees, they would presumably be named by the King, and tends to glide over the much more important question of the naming of the first councillors. It seems clear that an essential feature of the settlement was to be that the King agree to grant Cromwell, Ireton, and their friends control of the Council of State and, through it, of the executive branch of the government. In this connection it is important to note that this new body was to inherit many of the privileges of the old Privy Council vis-à-vis Parliament, while acquiring a new and significant measure of control over the King himself.

There was nothing particularly new in this attempt by the radicals to gain control of the executive. As early as the spring of 1645 they had realized that their minority status necessitated this approach. In their negotiations with Digby they had wanted assurance that "the persons who treated would have the power to dispose of all places." On that occasion, and again in the autumn of that year, they had proposed to use the power of the army to force this type of settlement on Parliament. A year later they were again offering to restore Charles, provided that he gave them control of the militia and the great offices of the kingdom. It was one of history's more finely contrived ironies that the leaders of this party, which had so vigorously opposed the prerogative, should now find themselves obliged to use those very powers to protect themselves against the great uncomprehending majority.

While the King and the army negotiated, the parliamentary radicals were quietly consolidating their position. On July 17, by a vote of seventy-six to thirty-nine, they succeeded in appointing Sir Thomas Fairfax as supreme commander of all land forces in England and Wales, and thereby placed those forces in the north and west and in Wales, which were regarded as areas supporting the moderates, under more trustworthy control.[65] Many garrisons were ordered disbanded, and on July 20 the army demanded that the militia of London be placed in radical hands once again.

The Holles group sprang to the defense of their allies in London and demanded that the House reject the army directive until the army

65. *CJ*, V, 248.

had informed them about "all other proposals," but they were defeated in a division by eighty votes to sixty-eight.[66] The eleven members, who up to this point had perhaps been hoping for some kind of
rapprochement with the radicals, now conceded defeat and on July
20 obtained permission to leave the country.[67]

But the Londoners were determined to fight, and on July 22 approximately 3,000 reformadoes met in St. James's field and demanded that
the King be brought to London.[68] Thus began the mob violence that
culminated in the invasion of the floor of the House on July 26. The
boisterous apprentices seem to have given Speaker Lenthall a particularly rough time. They demanded to know if he was a good servant of
the King. Unsatisfied with his murmured reply, they instructed him to
shout "God save the King: being intimidated he did this in a very
low voice, whereupon they made him raise it so that everyone there
should hear."[69] Before the mob retired, they had forced the Commons
to unseat the newly appointed and radical-dominated militia committee of London and to pass a resolution in favor of inviting the King to
the City.

Holles later categorically denied any responsibility for the mob violence, or even prior knowledge of the apprentice's intentions. He and
the other moderate leaders, he said, had decided to withdraw completely from the scene and were to meet at the Bell Tavern in King
Street to settle accounts before leaving London for the country or for
the Continent. When details of the mob scene in the Commons reached
them, they interrupted their dinner and left the area. But when the
radicals later heard of the meeting they accused Holles and his friends
of using the tavern as a kind of command post from which to direct
operations in Westminster Hall, "when," asserted Holles indignantly,
"we were as innocent of it as any of those who cry out against us . . . "[70]

Holles may indeed have been innocent of any complicity in the apprentices' invasion of the Commons, but he was not slow to take advantage of the resulting change in the balance of power. He and his
friends were soon reoccupying the seats of the mighty. Massey and
Waller emerged as the military commanders of the City's forces, and a
trial of strength between London and the New Model seemed immi-

66. *Ibid.*, 253. Haselrig and Evelyn of Wilts. and Sir Anthony Irby and Tate
were tellers for the majority and the minority, respectively. (*Ibid.*)

67. *CJ*, V, 251.

68. Sir Edward Ford to Lord Hopton, July 22, 1647, Clar.SPB 30, fol. 12a.

69. Advices from London, July 30, 1647, *CSPV, 1647–1652*, p. 10.

70. *Memoirs of Denzil, Lord Holles* (London, 1699) [hereafter cited as Holles,
Memoirs], pp. 153–154; Salvetti thought that the "contrary faction" would "sooner
take up the sword" than submit to the "Independents." (Salvetti to the Secretary,
July 23, 1647, SC, BM, Add. MS. 27,962L, fol. 406b.)

nent. In such a situation the position of Vane, St. John, and their followers became extremely delicate. On July 30 fifty-seven of them, together with eight peers, fled to the army. Their departure made a thin
House even thinner; but much more serious in its implications was
the fact that they had managed to persuade the Speakers of both
Houses to accompany them.

Despite the indignities forced on him by the mob, Lenthall had
originally no intention of leaving and had declared on July 28 that
the reports that he intended to desert the Commons were false and
scandalous, and "that he would rather die in the chair, than basely
desert the office, with which he had been honored."[71] Cromwell and
St. John had rather different plans and were prepared to bring strong
pressure on the Speaker to leave the House. Lenthall appears to have
been vulnerable to charges of peculation and of correspondence with
the King. Lilburne had so accused him two years before and had been
shut in the Tower for his pains. Cromwell may, as Monteith and others
assert, have threatened Lenthall with exposure to bring him into line.
According to Holles, a letter, partly in Rushworth's hand but "no
doubt . . . from Sir Thomas Fairfax and Mr. Cromwell," was sent to
the Speaker, advising him against appearing in the House and urging
him to follow St. John's directions, adding that he could be assured of
the protection of the army.[72] Ludlow recalled that Haselrig had led
the way in persuading Lenthall to desert the chair, "to which he consented with some difficulty."[73] Lenthall claimed at the time that he
had fled the House in fear of his life, but shortly before his death he
gave a different explanation: "Cromwell and his agents deceived a
wiser man than myself; that excellent King, and then might deceive
me also; and so they did. I knew the Presbyterians would never restore
the King to his just rights; those men swore they would."[74]

Holles was understandably reluctant to admit that the flight of a
number of members, even including the Speaker, to a rebellious army
could render his position "unconstitutional." Two new Speakers were
hastily appointed: the Lords installed that old target of the radicals,
Lord Willoughby of Parham, while in the Commons, a veteran parliamentarian and member for Grantham, Henry Pelham, was chosen. But
if the moderates once again ruled the House, they controlled little else.

71. Monteith, *History of the troubles*, p. 298.

72. Holles, *Memoirs*, p. 147; *A Brief Narration of the Mysteries of State carried
on by the Spanish Faction in England since the reign of Queen Elizabeth, especially declaring how Cromwell and his party were confederate with the Spanish
faction* (The Hague, 1651), BM, E.637(2), pp. 39–40.

73. *Memoirs of Edmund Ludlow*, ed. C. H. Firth, 2 vols. (Oxford, 1894) [here-
after cited as Ludlow, *Memoirs*], I, 207.

74. Dugdale, *Life*, pp. 300–303; see also *Clarke Papers*, I, 219, n. (a).

Outside of London the New Model was unchallenged, and the factions within that body were beginning to take on even more importance than the divisions within the Commons. Until August 6, when the army marched through a sullen London, Holles and Stapleton contented themselves with resolutions calling for the King's return to the City and for negotiations with him by representatives of both kingdoms. They were not completely unopposed. In divisions on July 31 and August 2 the opposition mustered twenty-two and thirty-two votes, respectively.[75]

The period between the flight of the radicals to the army on July 30 and the march on London seven days later was an extremely critical one for the three people at the center of the stage: Charles I, Cromwell, and Ireton. Cromwell and Ireton were attempting to gain the King's consent to the Heads of the Proposals, but Charles seems to have been convinced both that time was on his side, and that he could improve upon the offer. Cromwell and Ireton were acutely conscious of the army's volatile state and were anxious to obtain an agreement with the King while the external danger from the trained bands of London kept the army still reasonably united. The King, on the other hand, was aware of Cromwell's relative isolation and of his increasing dependence on the Crown. He was conscious, too, of the growing support throughout the country for his own position. It was easy for him to conclude that Cromwell needed him much more than he needed Cromwell. In doing so he underestimated both the difficulty of making potential support actual and Cromwell's cat-like facility for landing on his feet.

The extent to which Cromwell was aware of danger from the Levellers at this time is underlined by his reluctance to support the privileges of the Lords. When the radical members who had fled Westminster met the army officers, it was decided to draw up a kind of manifesto or declaration of policy. A draft was prepared, which was found to have omitted any section in which the privileges of the upper house were guaranteed or the peerage itself upheld. A clause was thereupon inserted to supply the defect, and Cromwell, Ireton, and Haselrig were asked to consent to it. Cromwell "made answer with some hesitation, that it was a matter of great concernement, and he desired further time to deliberate."[76] Ireton's ready agreement, on the other hand, prefigured his staunch defense of the constitution during the Putney debates. Haselrig was noncommittal. The next day, however, Cromwell indicated his agreement with Ireton, declaring that since the peers had risked their lives in the cause he would engage his service and life to

75. *CJ*, V, 262.
76. Waller, *Vindication*, pp. 191–197.

uphold them. Nevertheless, when the joint statement of army officers and radical parliamentarians was published, the clause was omitted.[77]

Twenty-four hours before it was generally known in the army that the Londoners would surrender, the City had sent word to the headquarters that they would not resist. Equipped with this information, Cromwell and Ireton suggested to the King that he write them a "kind letter." It was probably in reply to this message that Charles dispatched Major Huntingdon with a verbal statement to Cromwell and Ireton, assuring them that they would be trusted by Charles "for a settlement of the kingdom." Ireton, highly enthusiastic about the receipt of this message, told Huntingdon that by not declaring against the army the King had given them a great advantage over their opponents and that if they did not now make good their promises to him they would be "the veriest Knaves that ever lived."[78] If Waller can be believed, Ireton had good reason to be grateful. He regarded the London forces as a formidable body of fighting men, well equipped, and many of them veterans of campaigns under the Earl of Essex.[79]

Berkeley was desperately anxious for a firm agreement with the army leaders before it was too late. But, despite his best efforts, there was a delay of twenty-four hours before Charles signed the letter, and it was delivered to army headquarters only after the London surrender had been received.[80] The royalist delegation that bore the King's answer was soon made aware of the significance of London's collapse. Neither Cromwell nor Ireton would speak with them, but informed them through Colonel Richard Deane that they feared "the army would now be of another temper, there being then many other considerable men added to their councils, who perhaps might scruple the good they intended the King."[81] After the army's march on London, the change in Cromwell and Ireton was even more marked. In a conversation with John Ashburnham they accused the King not only of negotiating with the Scots behind their backs, but of ordering his followers to make common cause with Holles and the Londoners. These revelations, they said, "were great allays to their thoughts of serving him."[82]

Since the Scots had long since been regarded by all parties as an ac-

77. *Ibid.*

78. "Sundry Reasons inducing Major Robert Huntington to lay down his Commission," *LJ*, X, 410.

79. Waller, *Vindication*, p. 189.

80. Berkeley, "Memoirs," *Harl. Misc.*, IX, 477.

81. John Ashburnham, *A narrative by John Ashburnham of his attendance on King Charles the First*, 2 vols. (London, 1830), II, 92–93.

82. *Ibid.*

cepted factor in the struggle for power, Cromwell's air of shocked surprise that the King should be negotiating with them appears somewhat disingenuous. As for the Holles group, it seems clear that Charles had refused to give them any understanding that would commit him against the army. His attitude toward them was, indeed, one of distinct hostility. When Bamfield told the King of the possibility of their support, Charles was unmoved: "Most of those with whom you treat," he told Bamfield, "play now their own after game; they began these troubles, which have brought me to this estate, and having by their own improvidence through their rigid dealing, when they had the power to have agreed with me, lost the dignity, and authority of Parliament, would now recover themselves at my hazard; wherefore I shall go as far along with them, as I find consistent with the public and my own interest . . ."[83]

As early as August 5 Bellièvre had concluded regretfully that the King had lost the opportunity of regaining his throne. If he had allied with either London or the army, he might have accomplished this end, but Charles did neither.[84]

Whether, if the King had enthusiastically and promptly accepted the support offered him by Cromwell and Ireton, they would, in turn, have been willing to stand by the agreement at all costs is a question that given Cromwell's strong instincts for survival, cannot be answered with any degree of certainty. In any case, the King's reluctance to give effective control of the executive to a relatively small faction in the face of strong evidence that the nation as a whole would be distinctly hostile to such a move is understandable. But so too, in such a situation, was Cromwell's reluctance to risk all for Charles.

On August 7 the army marched through London to the accompaniment of obsequious bows from aldermen and Common Councillors assembled for the occasion at Hyde Park and Charing Cross. By all the rules of realpolitik, Holles should have accepted the inevitable. But he was still determined to defend the dignity of Parliament and to dare Cromwell to use force against it. Within a week he was crushing the radicals by an overwhelming majority of votes.

On the very day of the army's arrival, the Holles party defeated a motion to give Fairfax a free hand in the Tower by eighty to fifty-nine votes.[85] On the same day a motion to nullify the acts of Parliament that had been passed during the Speaker's absence was defeated without a division. Radical reinforcements poured into the House, and by

83. Bamfield, *Apologie*, p. 32.
84. Bellièvre to Brienne, London, Aug. 5, 1647, *MC*, II, 221.
85. *CJ*, V, 269. Sir W. Erle and John Ashe and Haselrig and Sir William Constable were tellers for the majority and the minority, respectively. (*Ibid.*)

August 9, confident that they controlled enough votes to crush Holles, they pressed for a similar resolution designed to convict Holles of unconstitutional action. In a voice vote on the question the radicals appeared to be in an overwhelming majority. Hoping, apparently, to drive home their victory and to acquire an accurate list of their enemies, the radicals called for a division. They were disturbed to find that out of 189 members voting they had but a majority of 1. Even this slim victory was converted into a defeat, when three members, Sir Samuel Rolle, Sir Anthony Irby, and William Ashurst, who had drifted into a committee room to avoid voting, recorded their votes with Holles.[86]

For a time the moderate strength actually increased in the House. On August 10 they mustered 120 votes against 70 for the radicals, and on the following day by 110 votes to 76 they defeated a radical attempt to nullify the acts of the Houses during their absence.[87] Such victories were "hardly credible" to one royalist observer. The moderate majority, he thought, was the only thing that prevented the leaders of that party "from being questioned for their lives." St. John was said to have been so furious at being frustrated on the floor of the Commons that he declared that "the longest sword" should carry the day.[88]

Cromwell began now to enlist the support of Lilburne and his followers, with whom relations had been difficult since early July. Lilburne had confidently expected that the army's march on London would mean his own release from the Tower and was enraged to find himself still within those ancient walls even after the army's triumphal progress through the City on August 7.[89] The lieutenant general was his main target, and in a letter to him on August 13 Lilburne demanded his release, threatening to publish an attack on Cromwell if it were not granted. Cromwell's reply has not survived, but on the following day the Levellers demanded that the army purge the House, a step which, if not requested by Cromwell, was certainly in his inter-

---

86. *CJ*, V, 270; Denton to Verney, Aug. 12, 1647, Verney MSS, BM, M,636/7; John Harrington, Parliamentary Diary, 1646–1647, BM, Add. MS. 10,114, fol. 25b. Sir Ralph Assheton and Thomas Gewen and Haselrig and Evelyn of Wilts. were tellers for the majority and the minority, respectively. (*CJ*, V, 270.)

87. John Harrington, Parliamentary Diary, 1646–1647, BM, Add. MS. 10,114, fol. 25b; *CJ*, V, 271. In the division of Aug. 11, Edward Baynton and John Swinfen and Haselrig and Evelyn of Wilts. were tellers for the majority and the minority, respectively. (*CJ*, V, 271.)

88. Letter of intelligence from Sir E. Ford, London, Aug. 12, 1647, Clar.SPB 30, fol. 36a, b; Marchamont Needham, *A Plea for the King and Kingdom by way of Answer to the late Remonstrance of the Army presented to the House of Commons on 20 Nov.* (London, 1648), BM, E.474(2), p. 1.

89. "Sundry Reasons inducing Major Robert Huntington to lay down his Commission," *LJ*, X, 410.

est.[90] The petitioners insisted that the members who had sat after the flight of the radicals to the army should be expelled. In doing this, they implicitly abandoned their tendency to lump together all groups in the Commons except Marten and his followers as equally deserving condemnation. It was this attitude that Cromwell and Ireton had attacked during the Reading debates in mid-July.

Holles and the other moderate leaders apparently interpreted the Leveller petition as advance notice of Cromwell's intention, and on August 16 five of them—Stapleton, Lewis, Waller, Clotworthy, and Long—fled the country. Holles himself followed a few days later. It was Stapleton's last journey; a few days after his arrival in Calais he fell ill and died.

By August 18 Cromwell had obtained an order from the army council for a march to Westminster. Two days later, after overriding Fairfax's weak opposition, he had placed a regiment of cavalry in Hyde Park. On that day the radicals finally won a division nullifying the acts during the Speaker's absence by 112 votes to 83.[91] By August 21, the victory of the radicals was complete and large numbers of the moderates had retired to the country.[92]

It is significant that Cromwell stopped short of carrying out the demands of the Levellers, that is, directly purging the House of all members who had sat during the Speaker's absence. The eleven members had silently slipped away, but the privileges of Parliament were still, at least technically, intact, and large numbers of Holles' followers remained in their seats.

This situation, if not to Cromwell's liking, was certainly in his interest. If, as seems probable, his concern for an agreement with Charles had now almost evaporated, it was all the more important that he be able to balance Rainsborough, Lilburne, and the Levellers by the legal and constitutional prestige of Parliament.

90. Pauline Gregg, *Free-born John: A Biography of John Lilburne* (London, G. G. Harrap, 1961), pp. 190–191.
91. *CJ*, V, 280. Haselrig and Evelyn of Wilts. and Sir W. Erle and Peter Brooke were tellers for the majority and the minority, respectively. (*Ibid.*)
92. John Harrington, Parliamentary Diary, 1646–1647, BM, Add. MS. 10,114, fol. 26a.

X] The Crisis of the Revolution

Before plunging into the complexities of the period between the flight of the moderate leaders in mid-August 1647 and Cromwell's final break with the King in January 1648, it may be helpful to summarize its main features and to indicate some of the problems to be explored.

Outwardly at least, until about September 25, Cromwell continued to stand by the Heads of the Proposals. At the same time, however, Parliament revived the Newcastle propositions, a move that aroused deep royalist suspicions. Charles, following Cromwell's advice and confident that he was in firm control of events, rejected the parliamentary propositions in favor of the army's terms. Cromwell, on the other hand, faced by the enmity of Lilburne, Marten, and Rainsborough, found his ascendancy threatened both in army and Parliament and by late September had conceded defeat for the policy embodied in the Heads of the Proposals. He then emerged as the builder of a coalition of radicals and moderates in the Commons, held together largely by fear of the Levellers but pursuing policies inimical to a restoration of Charles I.

During the subsequent Putney debates, Cromwell's destruction at the hands of his enemy Rainsborough appeared imminent. But Cromwell rather mysteriously regained control and further stabilized his position by permitting the King to escape from Hampton Court after which he succeeded—perhaps with Lilburne's help—in crushing a mutiny of the Rainsborough elements in the army. Cromwell then executed an about-face: concluded an agreement with Rainsborough on terms extremely hostile to the King; frightened the moderates out of the Commons; and embarked on the policy that produced the "vote of no addresses" in January 1648.

The questions that occur to the historian of this most interesting and truly dramatic period of the revolution are almost endless and are much easier to ask than to answer. Most center around Cromwell and his motives. The impression of the man that some historians have tended to create—the plain, blunt soldier, at home on the battlefield but somewhat at sea in the problems of politics—is surely far from the truth. It would be nearer the mark to stress the subtlety and complexity of a personality who was both better and worse than he has often been portrayed.

The comments of Waller, who was first his friend and later his enemy, are worth recording: "I cannot but mention the wonder which I have oft times had to see this eagle in his eirey. He at that time [early 1643] had never shown extraordinary parts, nor do I think that he did himself believe that he had them, for although he was blunt, he did not bear himself with pride, or disdain. As an officer he was obedient, and did never dispute my orders . . . He did, indeed, seem to have great cunning, and whilst he was cautious of his own words . . . he made others talk, until he had, as it were, sifted them, and known their inmost designs . . . "[1] Cromwell was forced to draw upon all his craft, tactical genius, and generous measure of ruthlessness to emerge unscathed from the maelstrom of 1647; these qualities were particularly demanded in the period outlined above.

To what extent, one may ask, was he behaving honestly when he advised Charles to reject the parliamentary propositions? Did he connive at Parliament's rejection of the King's answer in late September? His relationship with Lilburne is another conundrum. Did Lilburne agree to support Cromwell against Rainsborough only to find himself discarded in favor of the same Rainsborough a few weeks later? Had Cromwell by December 1647 decided to cut the Gordian knot by bringing the King to trial and perhaps executing him? Finally, the most interesting and most unanswerable question of all: to what extent did Cromwell do violence to his own conscience by his treatment of Charles on the one hand and Lilburne on the other?

Parliamentary politics in the period was characterized by a realignment of parties. The moderates, greatly weakened and largely without a leader, after linking up briefly with the Marten group to block Cromwell, were then ready to combine with him in an anti-Leveller alliance. This lasted until early December, at which time Cromwell's agreement with Rainsborough came into play, and they found themselves once again in political limbo.

The flight of the moderate leaders in August 1647 by no means solved the problems facing Cromwell and Ireton. They had made a public demonstration of their willingness to support the King and to effect a settlement which, although it contained many liberal and enlightened elements, tended to alienate both moderates and extreme radicals. Had the Civil War been fought, they asked themselves, in order to place the army "grandees" in the seats of power? Moderates, Levellers, and at least some "old" radicals were enraged at the

1. Sir William Waller, *Vindication of the character and conduct of Sir William Waller* (London, 1793), pp. 124–126.

thought. They had failed, moreover, to gain the unequivocal support of the King, and their ambiguous attitude toward him tended to dishearten and alienate royalists who otherwise might be expected to give them strong support. By forcing the eleven moderate leaders to flee the country they had lessened their chances of organizing a kind of united front against the Levellers. In the Commons, Marten led a sizable group of irreconcilables who regarded Cromwell as a traitor to the cause. As a result, Cromwell could count on the genuine support of only a small number of Commons members. A combination of moderates and extreme radicals could, and at crucial times did, make control of the Commons impossible.

But in spite of their moves against the leading moderates, which were intensified in early September, the Cromwell-Vane group seems to have been anxious to conciliate the rank and file of that party. Thus on August 20, after the radicals, backed by Cromwell's troopers, had imposed their will on the Commons, the House voted that only the most active persons involved in the moderate coup of July 26 should be prosecuted.[2] Ten days later the radicals were said to be negotiating with the "Presbyterians."[3] On September 6 a royalist observer regarded the presentation of the parliamentary propositions to the King as a sign that "the army will join with the moderate Presbyters."[4] Lord Willoughby of Parham, long a favorite target of the radicals, was one of the seven Lords impeached in early September. He was, however, in no great danger, if we may judge by the fact that Sir Henry Vane, Jr., advised Whitelocke that Parham, Whitelocke's brother-in-law, should lie low until the storm passed.[5] Whitelocke himself was typically anxious to assure the radicals that he had not deserted them, and his characteristically smug note that he was "much courted" by St. John and his party may be taken as a further indication of that group's anxiety to make as many friends as possible.

Lilburne angrily accused Cromwell and his friends of aiming at an alliance with the Presbyterians, citing as evidence the passage of a recent ordinance for the provision of tithes. The radicals, he declared, hoped to wean that party away from the Scots and because of this had not purged the House. Cromwell intended, he charged, "to hold a

2. *Journals of the House of Commons* [hereafter cited as *CJ*], V, 280.

3. Bellièvre to Brienne, London, Aug. 30, 1647, *The Diplomatic Correspondence of Jean de Montereul and the Brothers de Bellièvre, French Ambassadors in England and Scotland, 1645–1648*, ed. J. G. Fotheringham, 2 vols. (Edinburgh, 1898–1899) [hereafter cited as *MC*], II, 43–44.

4. Anthony Jackson to Nicholas, Hampton Court, Sept. 6, 1647, *The Nicholas Papers: Correspondence of Sir Edward Nicholas Secretary of State*, ed. Sir G. F. Warner, 4 vols. (London, Camden Society, 1886–1920), I, 88.

5. Bulstrode Whitelocke, "Annals," BM, Add. MS. 37,344 [hereafter cited as Whitelocke, "Annals," BM, Add. MS. 37,344], fol. 110a.

whip over those guilty and wicked knaves . . . that sat in the late juncto . . ."[6] They had been kept in the House by Cromwell and Vane "to make them serve their ends," affirmed Marchamont Needham in his scurrilous and entertaining journal *Mercurius Pragmaticus*.[7]

The decision of September 18 that the House should be "called"— that all members would be required to be present— was an indication that the radicals now looked upon a full Commons with a much friendlier eye than they had one year before. Their mood of deepening conservatism was also exemplified by the passage of an ordinance for more stringent control of the press. By the end of September, if not before, the alliance between the Cromwellian radicals and the moderates had become a real, if temporary, factor in the political calculations of the time.

The threat from the Levellers and other more conservative groups in the army made it imperative that Cromwell acquire a firmer base in Parliament. Movements against him had rapidly gained momentum after the march on London in early August. A split among the officers had been reported on August 13, and a personal enmity toward the King among some of them was one of the factors in retarding a settlement.[8]

Cromwell and Ireton were, at this stage, in more danger than was the King. According to Dyve, who was in a position to know, the agitators intended to seize "eleven of their principal officers whom they held most suspected in this business and to proceed with them by way of fact as betrayers of the army."[9] In the Commons, a few days later, Marten launched a vicious attack on the Cromwellian radicals, declaring that if their object was to "enslave the people, they should be Jews, Turks to him . . ."[10] Despite the presence of Cromwell's horsemen in Westminister, Marten's star continued to rise, and on August 26 he was named chairman of a committee to which a Leveller petition in favor of Lilburne's release was referred. Cromwell—with some reason—felt his life to be in danger and confessed to Berkeley about this time that he was "afraid to lie in his own quarters."[11]

6. Lilburne to Marten, Sept. 15, 1647, BM, E.407(41), pp. 4–6.
7. *Mercurius Pragmaticus* [hereafter cited as *Merc. Prag.*], Sept. 28–Oct. 6, 1647, BM, Burney Collection, 14.
8. "The Tower of London Letter-Book of Sir Lewis Dyve, 1646–1647," ed. H. G. Tibbutt, *Publications of the Bedfordshire Historical Records Society*, XXXVIII (1958) [hereafter cited as Dyve, "TLB"] p. 78.
9. Dyve to Charles I, Aug. 13, 1647, *ibid.*
10. John Harrington, Parliamentary Diary, 1646–1647, BM, Add. MS. 10,114, fol. 26a.
11. "Memoirs of Sir John Berkley [*sic*] containing an account of his negotiations with lieutenant-general Cromwell, Commissary-general Ireton, and other officers of the army for restoring King Charles I to the exercise of the government of England," printed in *Harleian Miscellany: or a collection of scarce, curious, and enter-*

The threat was not only from the Levellers; there was still a strong conservative group of officers and men in the New Model, and the possibility that this group might effect an anti-Cromwell coup may have accounted for the stubbornness with which the Commons' moderates clung to their seats, even after the army's march on London.[12] The flight of the eleven members relieved some of the pressure, but, despite his use of force to intimidate the moderate leaders, Cromwell apparently recognized that he could not hope to cope with the situation without strong parliamentary support. Accordingly, having destroyed the leadership of the moderate party, he set about to conciliate the main body.

Could he gain their support without sacrificing the Heads of the Proposals? A categorical answer is impossible, but certain observations may be made. As we have seen, the moderate leaders had earlier been willing to give qualified support to the ideas embodied in the Proposals and had felt reasonably confident that they could produce an essentially parliamentary settlement, particularly on the key point: control of the militia. Since then the probable composition and projected role of the Council of State had become clearer, and Cromwell's use of the army against Parliament had provided a concrete example of what might be expected. It seems, therefore, highly probable that the price the moderates, and also some radicals, exacted for their support was the reaffirmation by Cromwell of a parliamentary settlement, rather than the essentially personal one implied by the Heads of the Proposals.

Moreover, according to reports, Cromwell and the King were far from agreement on some key aspects of the proposals, over which "a big quarrel" was said to have taken place between them. Cromwell had now made the implications of the original proposals explicit: the army commanders would continue to play a key role in affairs after the restoration of the King and would share with Parliament the control of the executive and the militia, with power "to declare war or peace . . . within the State or outside the State." The King was described as "very much against this point."[13]

It is in this context that the behavior of Cromwell and Ireton in relation to the revival by Parliament on August 26 of the Newcastle propositions must be examined. Since they were still actively seeking Charles's consent to the army proposals, they might have been ex-

---

taining tracts . . . found in the late Earl of Oxford's library, ed. T. Park, 10 vols. (London, 1808–1813) [hereafter cited as Berkeley, "Memoirs," *Harl. Misc.*], IX, 478.

12. Dyve, "TLB," p. 78.

13. Roman transcripts, Aug. 27, 1647, PRO, 31/9/46 [hereafter cited as RT], fols. 78–79.

pected to have opposed—and indeed prevented—any revival by Parliament of the terms that had never been designed for acceptance and were known to be anathema to the King. Instead, they actually supported the motion to revive the Newcastle propositions and to send them to Charles for his consent.

The day before this, Ireton had sent Major Huntingdon to reassure the King that the hated propositions were being sent to him only to please the Scots and that the King was neither expected nor desired to sign them, or even to consider them, and that no moves would be made against him if he refused to do so.[14]

Gardiner, in his interpretation of this incident, accepted Ireton's statement almost at face value and thought that the real purpose of the move was to frighten Charles into a more conciliatory attitude toward the army proposals. Although this may have been the effect, it was not necessarily its purpose. Gardiner also gives the impression that, at this point, Cromwell and Ireton were still single-mindedly seeking agreement with the King and ignores John Ashburnham's statement that even before the army's march on London their attitude had changed drastically.[15]

The day after the Commons voted to send the propositions, Cromwell asked Huntingdon whether the King was surprised at this development. He answered that because of Ireton's message assuring him that the votes were mere matters of form he had not been alarmed. Cromwell then declared "that really it was the truth; and that we (speaking of the parliament) intended nothing else by it but to satisfy the Scot, which otherwise might be troublesome." But when the King heard that Ireton and Cromwell had supported the motion to send the propositions, he became distinctly suspicious. Huntingdon once again relayed the King's thoughts to the two officers, and this time was given the rather unconvincing explanation that they had so acted in order that Parliament's "unreasonableness might the better appear to the kingdom." Both then made positive declarations of their continued support of the King, Ireton affirming that they would "purge and purge, and never leave purging the Houses, till they had made them of such a temper as should do His Majesty's business; and rather than they would fall short of what was promised they would join with French, Spaniard, cavalier, or any that would join with them, to force them to it." On receipt of this message the King dryly remarked that "if they do, they would do more than he durst do." But Cromwell was

14. "Sundry Reasons inducing Major Robert Huntington to lay down his Commission," *Journals of the House of Lords* [hereafter cited as *LJ*], X, 410.
15. S. R. Gardiner, *History of the Great Civil War, 1642–1649,* 4 vols. (London, 1893) [hereafter cited as Gardiner, *GCW*], III, 355–356; *ibid.,* 354.

certainly willing to entertain the possibility that he might not be able to live up to his promises. When Huntingdon asked him to give warning to the King in case anything should happen "which might hinder the accomplishment of this his fair intention," in order that the King might "avoid the danger," Cromwell agreed to do so.[16] The King then prepared his answer to the parliamentary propositions and forwarded it to Cromwell and Ireton for revision. This having been done, the final version was sent to Parliament on September 9. Two weeks passed before it was formally debated in the Commons.

Were Cromwell and Ireton intentionally placing the King in a false position with a view to siding with Parliament when the time was right? In spite of Huntingdon's assertion that the whole episode was but another example of Cromwell's "perfidiousness," the question remains open. Bellièvre observed that the sending of the propositions was done only "in order to amuse the simple" and described the leading radicals as reluctant to take any important steps "until they see their affairs perfectly established." But he thought Charles mistaken in his idea that the self-interest of the army leaders must force them to support him. If, he wrote, the army could settle its affairs without the King, "upon which it is engaged and is succeeding," it would ruin him by degrees if not "all at once." The radical leaders, he said, were negotiating with all their potential enemies—Scots, Presbyterians, and Catholics—and he felt that the King was risking much if he allowed himself to be guided by "promises he imagines he has from his enemies . . ."[17] Despite the assurances of the army leaders that the sending of the propositions was only a matter of form, the royalists regarded their very presentation as being against the King's interest, and they tried to prevent it.[18]

It is not necessary to go as far as Huntingdon to recognize that Ireton's assurance to the King that the propositions had been revived because of Scottish pressure was, to say the least, disingenuous. Parliament ignored, in fact, the wishes of the Scots both in the form of the propositions and the timing of their presentation. The "Hamiltonian" Scots favored negotiation with Charles on the basis of his offer of May 12, and commissioners were then on the way from Scotland with this in mind. On September 3 the Scottish commissioners in London had actually been obliged to deny that they were delaying the sending of the propositions, and while they reluctantly agreed to their delivery,

16. Sir William Dugdale, *The Life, diary [1643–86] and correspondence* [1635–86], ed. W. Hamper (London, 1827), pp. 157–158.

17. Bellièvre to Brienne, London, Aug. 30, 1647, *MC*, II, 243–244; Bellièvre to Brienne, London, Sept. 6, 1647, *ibid.*, 249–250.

18. John Ashburnham, *A narrative by John Ashburnham of his attendance on King Charles the First*, 2 vols. (London, 1830), II, 96–97.

they protested strongly against Parliament's action "of so short a day peremptorily appointed by your lordships without our knowledge or consent."[19] On the following day Lanark wrote to Charles assuring him that they were instructing the commissioners in London "to delay their concurrence in sending the propositions of peace to your Majesty till the Chancellor's coming . . ."[20]

If there was a party in Scotland that would be pleased at the revival of the Newcastle propositions, it was that of the Marquis of Argyle. On August 9 Argyle had served notice that, far from being willing to lead an expedition into England to rescue the King, he was opposed to any action that might lead to a rupture between the two countries. Argyle appears to have been in close touch with the English radicals, and it was owing to his influence that instructions to the Scottish commissioners were framed so as to prevent their doing anything that might produce "any alteration in the good understanding between the two kingdoms." He ws also responsible for amendments implying that the Scots would not be obliged "to restore their King into a better condition." The Earl of Manchester, once again on good terms with Cromwell, had written to Argyle urging him to be "a good instrument to prevent the raising of an army in Scotland." "One of the most important persons of the English army" had also written to Lauderdale assuring him that if Scotland would "agree with the Independents on the single point of abandoning their King they would both easily remain agreed on all the rest."[21] In the context of English politics, meanwhile, Cromwell was being described as increasingly conscious of the risks involved in an agreement with the King. Such an undertaking might well be disavowed either by the King on grounds of duress or, worse still, by a subsequently elected Parliament which could be expected to be hostile to Cromwell and his friends.[22] Such thoughts were not novel: "Oh for a new chosen Parliament to find out that almost unfathomable knavery that is amongst divers of this Parliament . . . ," Lilburne had written in the previous April.[23]

19. Scottish commissioners to Parliament, Sept. 3, 1647, Bodleian Library, Tanner Manuscripts, 58, (2), fol. 504b.
20. Gilbert Burnet, *Memoirs of the lives and actions of James and William, Dukes of Hamilton* (London, 1677) [hereafter cited as Burnet, *Memoirs of the Hamiltons*], p. 322.
21. Montereul to Mazarin, Edinburgh, Aug. 24, 31, Sept. 7, 1647, *MC*, II, 242, 247–248, 254.
22. RT, Sept. 3, 1647, PRO, 31/9/46, fols. 81–82; Salvetti to Gondi, Sept. 3, 1647, Salvetti Correspondence, Transcripts from archives at Florence of correspondence of Florentine ambassadors in England, 1616–1679, BM, Add. MS. 27,962L [hereafter cited as SC, BM, Add. MS. 27,962L], fol. 432a.
23. Lilburne, *The Resolved Man's Resolution* (London, 1647), BM, E.387(4), pp. 21–22.

In order to stabilize the situation, it was imperative that the Levellers be placated. Accordingly, on September 5, Cromwell visited Lilburne in the Tower and attempted to persuade him to refrain from further attacks on the Parliament which, he asserted, would soon effect a settlement in the kingdom that would be "much to his [Lilburne's] satisfaction."[24] Lilburne's disconcerting reply was that, compared to the record of the Long Parliament, the greatest crimes of which the King was accused, were "both glorious and righteous." Lilburne went further and bluntly informed Cromwell that he would do everything in his power to "destroy" those people who would be so tyrannical as to prolong his imprisonment. When Cromwell asked if he would remain silent in return for his freedom, Lilburne would give him no guarantees whatsoever. In response to an offer of honorable employment in the army, Lilburne declared that he would not be engaged either "in the Parliament's nor in the army service for all the gold in the world." Cromwell, with what must have been a herculean effort at self-control, remained at least outwardly affable and left Lilburne with the promise to do all in his power to effect his release "in a very short time."[25] On the following day, however, when Marten wanted the House to consider Lilburne's case, the matter was put off despite (or because of) Cromwell's presence in the House.[26]

The extreme radicals maintained the pressure. Marten now demanded that the King's name be omitted from the indictment then being drawn up against seven of the moderate Lords. In the army the agitators had been calling for the release of persons imprisoned for statements against the King, and Fairfax went so far as to write to Parliament in their support. The Commons, anxious to oblige, ordered the release of James Symball, who had been charged with speaking against the King.[27]

Cromwell appears now to have turned against Lilburne. On September 14 he supported a motion permitting the Lords to search for precedents relating to their jurisdiction in such cases as Lilburne's. Lilburne regarded this as dishonest behavior and redoubled his activities against Cromwell, whom he described as being "closely glued . . . to those four sons of Machievel . . . the Lord Saye . . . Wharton, the younger Sir Henry Vane and Solicitor St. John"[28] and urged Marten to work hard for a purge of Parliament. The House re-

---

24. Dyve to Charles I, "TLB," p. 85.
25. *Ibid.*
26. Pauline Gregg, *Free-born John: A Biography of John Lilburne* (London, G. G. Harrap, 1961), p. 195.
27. Whitelocke, "Annals," BM, Add. MS. 37,344, fol. 111a; *CJ*, V, 301.
28. Lilburne to Marten, Sept. 15, 1647, BM, E.407(41), pp. 4–6.

jected a Leveller petition demanding such a purge, but on the next day weakened and permitted it to be read.[29]

Cromwell's problems were further complicated by an ominous quarrel with Rainsborough that had erupted over the filling of the post of vice-admiral. Rainsborough discovered that Cromwell had been secretly working against his candidature because he feared that his rival might thereby obtain backing in the navy to supplement his already powerful position in the army.[30] Cromwell had now to contend not only with the hostility of Lilburne in the Tower but also with the open enmity of Rainsborough in the army and of Marten in the Commons. All three were prepared to go to almost any lengths in order to block what they considered to be the nefarious aims of Cromwell.

All contending groups had their own opinions concerning the terms upon which the monarchy should be restored—if at all—but even those who saw merit in some aspects of the Heads of the Proposals could unite with the rest in determined opposition to the prospect of Cromwell and Ireton becoming the power behind the throne. By mid-September Cromwell's position had become nearly untenable. He could no longer trust the army, and a combination of his parliamentary opponents could frustrate any of his plans. His attempt to combine a relatively enlightened settlement with guarantees for his own position in any future government had been interpreted, rightly or wrongly, as a shameless lunge after supreme power. If as early as mid-August he was having second thoughts with respect to an agreement with the King, by mid-September he seems to have been actively looking for a way out. Did Cromwell deliberately allow himself to be defeated and the Heads of the Proposals rejected by Parliament in order to extricate himself from what had become an impossible position? Questions such as this are more easily asked than answered but the available evidence is worth examining.

The day before the King's reply was to be read, which, in obedience to Cromwell's instructions, rejected the parliamentary propositions, there was still no clear indication of the reaction to be expected in the Commons. Bellièvre, who knew that the King had requested that negotiations proceed on the basis of the Heads of the Proposals, feared that Charles was now more than ever at the mercy of the army leaders, who might still use their power "in order to destroy the King and not . . . to restore him as he continues to persuade himself."[31]

29. Letter of intelligence from Sir E. Ford, London, Sept. 16, 1647, Bodleian Library, Clarendon State Papers [hereafter cited as Clar.SPB], 30, fol. 65a.
30. Dyve to Charles I, Sept. 5, 1647, "TLB," pp. 84, 85.
31. Bellièvre to Brienne, London, Sept. 13, 1647, MC, II, 256.

The House heard the King's answer on September 14, and its re-action indicated either that Cromwell's supporters were not in complete control or that the way was being paved for a change of policy. Debate was delayed until the following Friday (September 17), and it was reported that the Commons had considered the reply "no positive answer."[32] One very cogent reason for putting off debate in the House was the fact that Cromwell had by no means established his position in the army. He found himself under pressure on the one hand from 4,000 officers and soldiers petitioning for a reconciliation with the King[33] and on the other from Rainsborough and his supporters who strongly opposed the policy embodied in the Heads of the Proposals. Cromwell's attempt to win the support of the army council on September 16 provoked an open clash with Rainsborough over the whole question of further negotiation with Charles, and, specifically, whether the army would continue to stand by the proposals, which the King was now willing to regard as a basis for negotiation. During the debate, if it can be called that, Rainsborough completely lost control of himself and shouted at Cromwell that "one of them must not live."[34]

Vane had told the Commons on the previous day that the parliamentary commissioners had discussed the Heads of the Proposals with the army and that they would be presented to the houses.[35] Some royalists were hopeful that Parliament would accept the King's answer and proceed on the basis indicated by Vane. Others were less sanguine, one observer noting that the various parliamentary parties were "at a non plus and know not what to do."[36] But Lord Saye and some of the army officers were quoted as asking why, if the country was to be ruled by a King, it might not be "this man [Charles] rather than another."[37] Against this must be put Bellièvre's report on the same day, that the radicals were continuing to negotiate with the Scots with the object of coming to terms with them "without the King."[38]

A split between Parliament and the army over adherence to the Heads of the Proposals was rumored by September 20.[39] Parliament was reportedly dissatisfied with the King's answer, and it was expected that debate would be still further postponed. These disagreements may have reflected a split within the radical party itself, and by Sep-

32. Letter of intelligence, London, Sept. 16, 1647, Clar.SPB 30, fol. 65a.
33. Bellièvre to Brienne, London, Sept. 16, 1647, MC, II, 262; Gardiner, GCW, III, 365.
34. Letter of intelligence from Ford, London, Sept. 20, 1647, Clar.SPB 30, fol. 67b.
35. CJ, V, 302.
36. W. Dickenson to Hyde, London, Sept. 15, 1647, Clar.SPB 30, fol. 59a; E. Upton to Mr. Edwards, Sept. 15, 1647, Clar.SPB 30, fol. 60a.
37. Clar.SPB 30, fol. 60a.
38. Bellièvre to Brienne, Sept. 16, 1647, MC, II, 262.
39. Letter of intelligence from Ford, London, Sept. 20, 1647, Clar.SPB 30, fol. 67b.

tember 24, when the Commons resolved without a division that the King's answer was a refusal of the parliamentary propositions, it was becoming increasingly clear either that the opponents of the army proposals in the Commons were gaining the upper hand or that the Vane-St. John group were preparing to abandon the proposals.

The debate on the King's answer of September 22 and 23 must be regarded as one of the most crucial of the Revolution, but its exact character remains obscure. According to Berkeley and other royalist sources, Cromwell, Ireton, Vane, "and all their friends,"[40] which included St. John, Nathaniel Fiennes, and Lord Saye, supported Charles's request for a personal treaty on the army proposals,[41] but found themselevs outnumbered and temporarily deserted by many of their old supporters.[42] It was probably during this debate that Thomas Scott, a Leveller sympathizer, accused Cromwell and other officers in the army of underhand dealings with the King. The embattled Cromwell countered with a characteristic blast at the Levellers.[43]

In addition to the defections from their own ranks, the radical leaders were faced by an unholy alliance of the moderates and extreme radicals who worked against them both in Parliament and in the army.[44] Marten called for a declaration against any further dealings with the King, and but for the opposition of Cromwell and Ireton a resolution to that effect might have been carried. Yet by taking the notably equivocal ground that the time was not ripe for such a move because the King's supporters in the army were still too strong, Cromwell demonstrated that he had moved some considerable distance from the position he had taken in his forthright declarations to Major Huntingdon three weeks before.[45]

At least one royalist observer found the support of Cromwell and Ireton for the King somewhat ambiguous and wrote that "the reality of their intentions [is] not clearly discerned."[46] The members themselves, he said, were hard put to predict how affairs would turn out. Most of them regarded the King as "in greater danger than ever." Bellièvre, unmoved by the turn of events, continued to regard the debates as mere outward show: "all is directed by the same council . . . what is

40. Berkeley, "Memoirs," Harl. Misc., IX, 478.
41. Letter of intelligence from Ford, London, Sept. 28, 1647, Clar.SPB 30, fol. 76a.
42. Berkeley, "Memoirs," Harl. Misc., IX, 478.
43. William Smith to Sir R. Leveson, London, Sept. 27, 1647, Manuscripts of the Duke of Sutherland, Fifth Report of the Royal Commission on Historical Manuscripts, Part I, Report and Appendix (London, H. M. Stationery Office, 1876), p. 173.
44. John Rushworth, Historical Collections, 7 vols. (London, 1654–1701) [hereafter cited as Rushworth, Hist. Coll.], II, pt. iv, 18.
45. Ford to Hopton, London, Sept. 28, 1647, Clar.SPB 30, fol. 76a.
46. Letter of intelligence, London, Sept. 27, 1647, Clar.SPB 30, fols. 73b, 74a.

done for appearance sake is but in order to satisfy a different interest . . . "[47] He doubted that Cromwell had really lost control of Parliament and found it difficult to believe that the army could not force the
houses to do its bidding. Parliament, he reflected, now existed only by
the protection of the army, which had already "driven out whom they
pleased." Radical leaders, he insisted gloomily, would ruin the King
"as soon as it be possible for them to do so . . . "[48]

Cromwell and Vane had indeed found themselves outnumbered in
these debates, but it is by no means clear that they had lost control of
the Commons. On September 21, after the houses had voted that the
King had rejected the propositions, it was Evelyn—ever the willing
worker in the radical cause—who took the vote to the Lords. If Evelyn
was rebelling against Cromwell and the other radical leaders it is odd
that he should be a teller with Cromwell on the following day, when
the Commons voted eighty-four to thirty-four in favor of going into
Committee of the Whole to discuss policy with respect to the King.
Rainsborough and Wentworth were tellers for the opposition, and the
fact that they could muster only thirty-four votes indicated that there
was no important defection from the radical ranks.[49]

The proceedings of the Commons on September 23, 1647, were
among the most momentous of the Revolution. But since Cromwell
was mostly absent, it is difficult to judge his attitude toward the events
of that day. We may surmise, however, that he was neither surprised
nor shocked by what had happened during his absence. The worst
fears of the royalists had been realized. The Commons, by their votes
to transform the more significant of the propositions into bills and to
rule out any further approaches to the King, had not only thrown out
the Heads of the Proposals, but had, in effect, closed the door to any
accommodation with Charles. It should be noted that the usual radical tellers, Haselrig (one of Cromwell's strongest supporters) and Evelyn, were with the majority against Wentworth and Marten for the
minority and won the division by seventy votes to twenty-three.[50] There
is no reason to suppose that this vote, itself a prelude to the abandonment of the idea of a treaty with the King, was against the wishes of
the radical leaders. The truth seems to be that on September 22 and
23, if not before, Cromwell and his friends decided to abandon the
policy represented by the Heads of the Proposals in favor of a further
rapprochement with the moderates and the Presbyterians. If, as G. M.
Young has asserted, the Commons had, in effect, passed a vote of no

47. Bellièvre to Brienne, London, Sept. 23, 1647, *MC*, II, 268.
48. *Ibid.;* Bellièvre to Brienne, London, Sept. 23, 1647, *MC*, II, 270; Salvetti to
the Secretary, London, Sept. 24, 1647, SC, BM, Add. MS. 27,962L, fol. 443b.
49. *CJ*, V, 311. This was Sir John Evelyn of Wilts.
50. *Ibid.*, 314.

confidence in Cromwell,[51] the fact that he emerged in the ensuing weeks as more than ever the leader of the House defies explanation.

The Vane-St. John group now moved swiftly to stabilize the situation. They strengthened their grip on London by the impeachment of the mayor and five aldermen and by the election of the strong radical, Warner, as lord mayor. The threat from Rainsborough in the army was at least temporarily appeased by his appointment as vice-admiral of the navy and by a vote of the Commons to grant him £1,000. By late September the divisions among the army officers were regarded as slight,[52] and it was reported in London that unless the King agreed to the new propositions to be sent in the form of bills, the army would join with Parliament to settle the affairs of the kingdom.

One of the propositions that became a bill was that to abolish episcopacy, and by September 27 at least two members, Francis Allen and Robert Reynolds, demonstrated their confidence in its eventual implementation by the purchase of episcopal lands.[53] This was the beginning of a considerable acquisition of such property among the radicals in the autumn of 1647. Nor were Irish lands forgotten. The claims of the Irish "lobby" were taken care of by a resolution requiring the King to invalidate the Irish Cessation. By the end of September confidence in the intentions of Cromwell and Ireton was rapidly waning among royalists like Sir Edward Ford, who still regarded Fairfax as sincere, but doubted whether the other officers were "sound at heart."[54]

The army leaders were reportedly ready to abandon their old proposals on the grounds that if such liberal conditions were given the King "they and the Kingdom will be undone." By October 4 supporters of the King in London had become decidedly pessimistic.[55] One noted nervously that the army appeared to tolerate suggestions for imprisoning the King in the Tower and "disposing" of his person.[56] By October 7 the officers were described as divided not so much over the King's restoration but as to whether or not they should "consent to his destruction." Pessimism was spreading. "Time," wrote one morose royalist, "will change our hopes into slavery . . . miracles being

51. G. M. Young, *Charles I and Cromwell* (London, Rupert Hart-Davis, 1935), pp. 67–69.

52. Bellièvre to Brienne, London, Sept. 27, 1647, *MC*, II, 271.

53. List of purchasers of bishops' lands, Bodleian Library, Rawlinson Manuscripts, B.238, fol. 1.

54. Letter of intelligence from Ford, London, Sept. 30, 1647, Clar.SPB 30, fol. 77a.

55. Letter of intelligence from London, Oct. 4, 1647, Clar.SPB 30, fol. 116.

56. Advices from London, Oct. 7, 1647, *Calendar of state papers and manuscripts relating to English affairs existing in the archives and collections of Venice and in other libraries of northern Italy*, vols. 10–38 (1603–1675) [London, H. M. Stationery Office, 1900–1940] [hereafter cited as *CSPV*], *1647–1652*, p. 24.

ceased, and the power of an army so well known to those that manage it."[57]

Ireton, however, seems to have been outraged by Cromwell's change of policy, and a significant quarrel between them materialized, apparently over Parliament's vote of September 23. Ireton was said to have assured some royalists that it would be rejected at army headquarters.[58] When he realized that the army proposals were in fact a dead letter, "Like an honest man" he offered to resign his commission.[59]

Cromwell was now intent on an understanding with the parliamentary moderates, a move made all the more necessary by the emergence of a new and more extreme group of Levellers in the army. The extent to which the Levellers were equalitarians may be a matter of debate, but there is no doubt about the fears of the more substantial parliamentarians with respect to their program. The "spirit of parity," wrote one observer, "affrights the rich man sorely."[60] By early October the situation in the army was again deteriorating with the ousting of the moderate-minded agitators in five regiments and their replacement by men well to the left of Lilburne who was himself actually making overtures to the King.[61] The impeachment of Fairfax, Cromwell, and their leading supporters, the abolition of the monarchy, and the establishment of a republic were now believed to be cardinal points in the program of this group.[62]

The decision to "call" the House was seen as a move to gather "as great a number as they can to countenance the sweet stuff that is now abrewing."[63] Even old leaders of the moderates like Waller, Massey, and Long, it was predicted, would be permitted to sit again "now that the sting of that faction is taken out . . . "[64] On October 9, 159 absent members were fined £20 each. By October 12, however, many of the absentees had returned and were forgiven.[65]

Though the influx of members greatly strengthened the moderates, they gave no sign of any determination to follow a policy of their own making. One royalist commentator characterized the old parties as having been "resolved out of their own principles into one single faction," and he compared them rather unkindly with the animals in the ark,

57. Letter of intelligence, London, Oct. 7, 1647, Clar.SPB 30, fols. 124a, 139b.
58. Newsletter, RT, PRO, 31/9/46, fol. 99a.
59. Letter of intelligence, London, Oct. 11, 1647, Clar.SPB 30, fol. 135a.
60. Letter of intelligence, London, Oct. 5, 1647, Clar.SPB 30, fol. 124a.
61. Dyve, "TLB," p. 92; Gregg, *Free-born John*, pp. 195–200; H. N. Brailsford, *The Levellers and the English Revolution* (London, Cresset Press, 1961), p. 256.
62. Letter of intelligence, London, Oct. 7, 1647, Clar.SPB 30, fol. 124a; Gardiner, *GCW*, III, 378.
63. *Merc. Prag.*, Oct. 5–12, 1647, BM, Burney Collection, 14.
64. *Ibid.*
65. *The Kingdom's Weekly Intelligencer*, Oct. 12, 1647, BM, E.411(11), p. 694.

who forgot their natural enmity in the face of a common danger. He had seen, he wrote, "a grand Presbyter . . . lead a whole committee of Independents by the nose . . . and the like to be done by a grand Independent among a pack of Presbyters."[66]

The policy of accommodating almost all shades of opinion, except Anglicanism and Catholicism, was particularly apparent in the religious sphere. The Commons voted that the King must accept the abolition of the *Book of Common Prayer* and the establishment of Presbyterianism. The setting up of Presbyterianism by a Parliament dominated by "Independents" was regarded as evidence that the religious issue had never been a serious one; the "princes of Independency," one royalist declared, could "endure a Presbytery as well as any government else, so it be of their own setting up . . . "[67] This was probably a fairly accurate summary of Cromwell's own thinking. He was notably active at this point, and although he showed his concern for the sectaries by personally thanking some petitioners who favored lay preaching, he appears to have been quite ready to accept Presbyterianism at least for a trial period of three years.

The determination of what must now be called the "Cromwellian radicals" to please most Puritans can be seen in the generous degree of toleration granted to dissenters. Such persons were to be absolved from attendance at regular church services, provided they attended some other public worship. But no such privileges were to be accorded supporters of the *Book of Common Prayer,* and the King himself was not to be permitted the exercise of his religion.[68] It can be assumed that Cromwell approved of these measures.

Not all witnesses agreed that the Commons unanimously favored abandoning the King. The calling of the House had resulted in added strength among the moderates, and although they were without effective leadership and seemed to have had no intention of opposing the radicals frontally, they exerted a certain irenic influence. Despite the draconic measures with respect to religion and the increasingly brisk sale of bishops' lands, it was thought that, if a treaty were arranged, Parliament might still make important concessions to the King. Even among the Independents it was reported that there were many "moderates" who favored monarchy and were "not ill affected to the King's person."[69]

Despite a lurking fear among members of both parties that the restoration of the King might unleash a royalist reaction of disastrous

66. *Merc. Prag.,* Oct. 12–20, 1647, BM, Burney Collection, 14; Salvetti to the Secretary, London, Oct. 15, 1647, SC, BM, Add. MS. 27,962L, fol. 455a.

67. *Merc. Prag.,* Oct. 12–20, 1647, BM, Burney Collection, 14.

68. *CJ,* V, 333.

69. Letter of intelligence, London, Oct. 18, 1647, Clar.SPB 30, fol. 144b.

proportions, the climate of opinion at Westminster in the days leading up to the famous Putney debates at the end of October was conciliatory. "The generality of the Houses" was described as favoring concessions to the King on points relating to his family, his Church, and his friends.[70] The Lords were said to be ready to send a committee with the propositions; though the committee would be powerless to negotiate, it would inform the King verbally of the basis on which Parliament would moderate its stand.[71] Another report had it that the King was to be told that the houses intended to "double their number" and to have a personal treaty with him.[72]

But if many in the Commons favored negotiations, the direction of affairs at Westminster still lay in the hands of Cromwell and his friends, and it is difficult to interpret their policy as anything but inimical to the interests of the King. Cromwell seems to have abandoned the type of settlement embodied in the Heads of the Proposals and to have assumed a position reminiscent of that of Holles in which he was shielded by the aura of constitutionalism that still clung, however faintly, to Parliament at Westminster. But just as the hostility that Holles had displayed toward the King in the first six months of 1647 had given Cromwell his opportunity, so now Lilburne was attempting to counter Cromwell's influence in Parliament by his own overtures to Charles. Lilburne had viciously attacked Cromwell for the character of his dealings with the King in July and August; he was even more fiercely opposed to his rapprochement with the parliamentary moderates, interpreting Cromwell's "Presbyterian" policy as an attempt to gain the military support of the Scots in order to crush his democratic opponents in England.

By late September Lilburne, doubly embittered by Cromwell's policies and by his refusal to free him from the Tower, had been ready to appeal to the "hob-nails and the clouted shoes" in order to bring him down.[73] But Lilburne's intention was not to appeal to republican extremists against Cromwell's "royalism"; it was, rather, to persuade the anti-Cromwellian elements in the army to support him in a program that envisaged a new mutiny against the army "grandees" followed by the restoration of a monarch committed to the implementation of the Leveller program. To this end Lilburne was instrumental in bringing about a kind of minor revolution in five regiments, which resulted in the election of new agitators of an anti-Cromwellian stripe.[74] But there were difficulties in the way of such a policy, not the least of which was

---

70. Letter of intelligence, London, Oct. 20, 1647, Clar.SPB 30, fol. 145a.
71. Grignon to Mazarin, London, Oct. 25, 1647, PRO, 38/3/85, fol. 150b.
72. Clar.SPB 30, fol. 145a.
73. Lilburne to Marten, Sept. 15, 1647, quoted in Gregg, *Free-born John*, p. 195.
74. *Ibid.*

the fact that up to 1647 the main thrust of Leveller thinking had been of a republican character, or at the very least, extremely hostile to Charles. Moreover, much of the anti-Cromwellian feeling derived from resentment at those very dealings with the King which Lilburne himself had recommended. Lilburne's newfound sympathy for the Crown, in part the result of the influence of men like Sir Lewis Dyve and Judge David Jenkins who shared his life in the Tower, did not sit too well with many of his old friends and rendered him vulnerable to charges—which Cromwell and Ireton are said to have brought against him—of "driv[ing] on the King's design."[75]

In the minds of the solid citizenry of London, however, Lilburne was the dangerous leader of a conspiracy against the constitution and the rights of property. The task of creating a united front behind the Leveller program called for diplomatic abilities of a high order, qualities which, for all his virtues, Lilburne notably lacked. Lilburne's friendship with the moderate parliamentarian Sir John Maynard, recently imprisoned in the Tower, did result in a significant link with the moderates, which was to be a political factor of some importance down to Pride's Purge itself, but for most Parliament men it seems never to have been more than a marriage of convenience. One looks in vain for any sign of a public espousal of the Leveller program.

In late October 1647 fear of the Levellers was the operative factor. A new war was dreaded by "all men of estates," not least because of the possibility that "the popular party in the Houses and army should prevail."[76] Cromwell and his followers were described as having abandoned their attacks on the moderates in the Commons, "lest they should give an example to the Agitators to practice the same upon themselves."[77] The Levellers, it was said, intended to impeach both Cromwell and Ireton, "by the Houses and by the Army."[78] By October 28 it was rumored that Fairfax was also to come under attack and that both he and Cromwell were to be accused of having accepted bribes from the City of London "to save it from being plundered."[79] In some quarters the fall of Cromwell was imminently and cheerfully expected.[80]

Although Cromwell's influence in Parliament was still strong, his prestige in the army was slipping fast. Rainsborough was very much

75. William Walwyn, *Englands weeping Spectacle; or the sad condition of Lieutenant Colonel John Lilburne crying to all who have any conscience for assistance and deliverance from his unjust sufferings* (London, 1647), BM, E.450(7), p. 9.
76. Letter of intelligence, London, Oct. 20, 1647, Clar.SPB 30, fol. 145a.
77. *Merc. Prag.*, Oct. 19–26, 1647, BM, Burney Collection, 14.
78. Letter of intelligence, London, Oct. 18, 1647, Clar.SPB 30, fol. 144a.
79. Letter of intelligence, London, Oct. 28, 1647, Clar.SPB 30, fol. 153b.
80. Dyve to Charles I, Oct. 28, 1647, "TLB," p. 94.

the coming man and the publication of the Leveller manifestos *The Case of the Army Truly Stated* and *The Agreement of the People,* in the first of which Cromwell was attacked as a hypocrite and timeserver, were indications of his declining influence, not to say imminent danger. Faced by the growing ferocity of the Leveller attacks, Cromwell made a bid for the support of moderate elements in Parliament by a three-hour speech on October 20 in favor of monarchy and the restoration of the King. About the same time, however, he and his supporters seem to have attempted to create a new political post: "High Constable" for the kingdom, an office that would presumably have been filled by Cromwell and would have considerably limited the authority of any restored monarch. Marten led the opposition in the House to the scheme declaring in his usual style that such power was too great for one man and that he, "could not endure anything that looked like a King . . . "[81]

Cromwell's protestations in favor of the King were received with understandable skepticism in more than one quarter. His actions during the next week did little to allay suspicions. Although a few days after his speech he attempted to win Lilburne over by "making many large and fair promises to him," at the same time he was alleged to have been making overtures to the agitators of the mutinous five regiments, "promising a full compliance with them in all they desire and to relinquish all other interests whatsoever."[82] But by October 28, the date of the opening of the Putney debates, both Lilburne and the agitators remained hostile.

The debates have interested historians of political theory chiefly because the democratic political demands of the Levellers relating to matters like the franchise are regarded, rather patronizingly, as "ahead of their time." For the political historian, their main interest lies in their revelation of Cromwell's and Ireton's dangerous isolation. The debates were not so much between conservative officers and radical common soldiers, but between officers and agitators on the one hand and Cromwell and Ireton on the other. By his rapid changes of front and his negotiations with representatives of almost every shade of political opinion, Cromwell had forfeited the confidence of important sections of the army. These elements were now being united under his rival Rainsborough, who was almost ready to move against him. Despite the fact that he was himself by no means "the poorest hee" in England, Rainsborough had taken up the demogogic appeal of Lilburne and Wildman. The insolent assurance that he and lesser lights

81. *Merc. Prag.,* Oct. 19–26, 1647, BM, Burney Collection, 14.

82. Dyve to Charles I, Oct. 28, 1647, "TLB," pp. 93–94; newsletter, London, Oct. 22, 1647, RT, PRO, 31/9/46, fols. 137, 139, 140.

like Edward Sexby displayed during the tense confrontations at Putney demonstrated their confident belief that Cromwell's day was done.

Much constitutional theorizing was attempted during the debates, but, as Ireton realistically put it, the main point at issue was one of power: "whether such or such shall have the managing of the business."[83] That this was the crux of the matter was made sufficiently clear by Rainsborough. Marching into the council room at the head of the agitators, he demanded that justice be done on those persons of the army who had had "intelligence" with the King.[84]

Although at the outset Cromwell refused to be intimidated, and even supported further talks with Charles, he weakened considerably in the face of the bold and united opposition. As the debates proceeded it became increasingly clear that the issue was not whether the King should be negotiated with, but whether, by one means or another, he should be put out of the way. Ireton was notably more resolute than Cromwell, declaring that he would not join with those who sought "the destruction either of Parliament or the King . . . "[85] But it only required one day of debate to establish that the two senior officers were almost without support: of the remaining twelve persons who took part in the talks on that day, not one supported them on the issues at stake, and many were actively hostile.

In the debates that followed, the contrast between the attitude of Cromwell and that of his son-in-law gradually became more apparent. Ireton may not have been aware that Cromwell, by his overtures to the agitators, had already, in effect, abandoned the King. Whatever the explanation, the debates rapidly took on the character of a contest between Ireton and the agitators led by Rainsborough, with Cromwell adopting an attitude of near neutrality. By November 1 Cromwell was denying that anyone in the army had any intention to "set up" either the King or the House of Lords, adding significantly that, if the army were free to do what it wished, "we should set up neither." Ireton, by contrast, stuck to his guns, declaring roundly in the face of almost unanimous opposition that "the government of Kings or of Lords, is as just as any in the world, is the justest government in the world."[86]

On the following day the Rainsborough group made further gains. The recommendations of a committee appointed to compose matters went far to meet the demands of the agitators: all veterans of the parliamentary armed forces—property owners or not—were to be granted the franchise. "There were but three voices against this, your native

83. *Puritanism and Liberty*, ed. A. S. P. Woodhouse (London, Dent, 1951), p. 87.
84. Grignon to Brienne, London, Nov. 1, 1647, PRO, 31/3/85, fol. 155a.
85. Woodhouse, *Puritanism and Liberty*, p. 5.
86. *Ibid.*, p. 122; Salvetti to Gondi, Oct. 29, 1647, SC, BM, Add. MS. 27,962L, fol. 459b.

freedom," declared the agitators.[87] They were almost certainly Cromwell, Ireton, and Fairfax.

The tide against Cromwell and Ireton now became even stronger. On November 5 the Rainsborough group successfully dispatched a letter to Parliament stating that the army had no intention of putting pressure on Parliament to send new propositions to the King. This was a definite victory for Rainsborough; on the following day Ireton angrily withdrew from the council.[88]

The ascendancy of the Rainsborough group at Putney was reflected at Westminster. Rumors reached London of a demand for the execution of the King and of the imminent appointment of Rainsborough as general of the army. In the Commons, while moderates and old radicals closed ranks in the face of the common danger, the extreme radicals, led by Mildmay and Marten, seized the initiative.[89] Their influence could be seen in the appointment of a committee, on which they were well represented, whose purpose was to collect all the papers captured from the King at Naseby, "that they may be ready when the House has occasion to use them . . . "[90] The move was interpreted by some as a preparation for the trial of the King. By November 4 the influence of the Rainsborough group had reached the point where it was thought that "Cromwell and some of his party are like to side with them out of fear,"[91] and it was reported that the Mildmay-Marten faction was preparing to impeach Cromwell. But the attempt of the latter group to deprive the King of his negative voice, and thus to implement a proposal put forward by the agitators during the Putney debates, was blocked apparently by the combined forces of the moderates and the Vane-St.John party.[92]

The extent to which Parliament could offer continued opposition to the ascendant extremists in the army was now doubtful. Money alone, which was being scraped together to meet the demands for arrears, would not satisfy the Levellers, now said to be talking of "cauterizing the kingdom and reducing the subjects to a parity."[93] The freewheeling and metaphor-mixing author of *Mercurius Elencticus* gleefully recorded that the Parliament men were at their wits end: "the poor ani-

87. W. C. Abbott, *The Writings and Speeches of Oliver Cromwell*, 4 vols. (Cambridge, Mass., Harvard University Press, 1937–1947), I, 548.

88. Gardiner, *GCW*, IV, 8.

89. Letter of intelligence, London, Nov. 1, 1647, Clar.SPB 30, fol. 164a; Salvetti to Gondi, London, Nov. 22, 1647, SC, BM, Add. MS. 27,962L, fol. 463a; newsletter, London, Oct. 22, 1647, RT, PRO, 31/9/46, fol. 140.

90. *Merc. Prag.*, Nov. 2–9, 1647, BM, E.413(8), p. 63; newsletter, London, Oct. 29, 1647, RT, PRO, 31/9/46, fols. 191–192.

91. Letter of intelligence, London, Nov. 4, 1647, Clar.SPB 30, fol. 171a.

92. Newsletter, London, Nov. 11, 1647, Clar.SPB 30, fol. 180b.

93. Newsletter, London, Nov. 11, 1647, Clar.SPB 30, fol. 167b.

mals sail 'twixt Scylla and Charybdis, with their posteriora between two stools ready to fall on the floor."[94] On November 9 Sir Arthur Hopton wrote that the situation was so fluid that he might have to change his opinion before his letter was sealed. The reputed aim of the Levellers, that of "molding the Kingdom into parity," was, he said, "much feared by all rich men." The "Presbyterian" party had never been as violently opposed to the Cavaliers as they were to the Levellers, but, "to save their own stakes they sit still and hinder nothing."[95]

At Putney, meanwhile, Cromwell had rather mysteriously managed to emerge unscathed from a difficult and dangerous situation. On November 8 he and Ireton criticized both the extension of the franchise and the dispatch by the Rainsborough group of the letter to Parliament. Cromwell had also wanted to dissolve the Council for a fortnight "to prevent . . . further debate."[96] He attacked those who were attempting to divide the army and described the *Agreement of the People* as a manifesto that tended "very much to anarchy." He then succeeded in carrying a crucial motion in favor of the return of the agitators and officers to their quarters.[97]

With the support of Fairfax, he was now in a better position to deal with his opponents. A remonstrance signed by the general on November 14 may be regarded as Cromwell's answer to the Leveller demands. The soldiers were offered various concessions relating to pay and pensions, but although Fairfax (and Cromwell) were agreeable to setting a time limit for Parliament and for measures that would ensure "freedom and equality of elections thereto," nothing was said about extension of the franchise.[98]

But the most important demand of the agitators, and one underlying much in the Putney debates, was their determination to bring the King to trial, and even perhaps to the scaffold. Although adamant on the extension of the franchise, Cromwell was increasingly willing to compromise with respect to the King. When Colonel Thomas Harrison called for Charles's trial, he replied merely that the army must not "do the work when it is disputable and the work of others to do it, [but only] if it be an absolute and indisputable duty for us to do it."[99] Cromwell and his friends in Parliament were now taking a position of

94. *Mercurius Elencticus,* Nov. 5–12, 1647, BM, Burney Collection, 14/48, p. 11.

95. Hopton to Sir R. Graham, London, Nov. 9, 1647, Manuscripts of Sir R. Graham, *Sixth Report of the Royal Commission on Historical Manuscripts, Part I, Report and Appendix* (London, H.M. Stationery Office, 1877), pp. 329–330.

96. Woodhouse, *Puritanism and Liberty,* p. 453.

97. *Ibid.,* pp. 454–455.

98. *LJ,* IX, 529.

99. Abbott, *Writings and Speeches,* I, 551.

settled hostility to mass democracy, coupled with a growing readiness to compromise over the King. Charles's flight to the Isle of Wight on November 14 clarified the situation considerably. If there had been real danger of an assassination attempt, it had now passed. What was more important, Charles was now far from London and its potential assistance, and as long as Colonel Robert Hammond controlled Carisbrooke Castle there was little danger of a second flight to the Scots.

But the Rainsborough-Marten party had no intention of abandoning their campaign, and they carried the fight to the floor of the Commons where they attempted to impeach Cromwell and Ireton. On November 13 a letter from Cromwell containing an indirect attack on Rainsborough was read. Rainsborough then delivered some "hot expressions" against the two commanders and suggested that the King might still be hiding in Hampton Court, "there to be ready to act some great design."[100] Rainsborough also condemned the projected rendezvous of the army, despite the fact that he himself had first broached the idea in the apparent expectation that he could use the mass of the army to break Cromwell. The latter had, however, spoiled this plan by arranging to divide the army into three parts, each meeting in a separate place. Despite his efforts, Rainsborough failed to persuade the Commons either to impeach Cromwell or to cancel the rendezvous. A petition against the rendezvous presented on behalf of the agitators by Grey of Groby met the same fate.[101] The extreme agitators now turned to more direct methods and may even have plotted to murder Cromwell on the eve of the rendezvous.[102]

The dramatic scene at Corkbush Field when Cromwell, "with his naked waved sword,"[103] intimidated the mutinous soldiers, need not be detailed here. While his bold action checkmated Rainsborough and reestablished his ascendancy in the army, it did not succeed in breaking the power of his enemies. Cromwell survived what must have been a severe personal ordeal, but he saw clearly how close he had come to going under. He also realized that the policy he had adopted in the previous June had made him many enemies and few friends. He had wavered before in his support of a settlement with the King, and he was now on the verge of making the final break. As early as November 1 Grignon, the French ambassador, had written that Charles was rely-

100. *His Majesty's Declaration left by him on his Table at Hampton Court, 11 Nov., and directed to be communicated to the Lords and Commons. Together with a true relation of His Majesty's private departure* (London, 1647), BM, E.413(15), p. 7.
101. Memorandum of newsletters, Clar.SPB 30, fol. 181a, b.
102. *The Leveller Tracts, 1647–1653*, ed. W. Haller and G. Davies (New York, Columbia University Press, 1944), pp. 303–304.
103. *Ibid.*

ing too much on divisions among his enemies; three weeks later Cromwell was working out an alliance with Rainsborough.[104]

For the moment, however, there seemed reason to believe that Corkbush was the prelude to a more conservative program and that the "moderate men of both parties" would be able to effect a settlement.[105] Disillusionment set in quickly. It soon became apparent that Carisbrooke was more a prison than a royal residence. If, as some said, the move had saved the King from assassination, it had just as surely placed him completely under the control of Cromwell. Physical possession of the King was still an important advantage in the struggle for power. Charles, however, remained optimistic, if not overconfident. On November 16 he offered to surrender the militia during his lifetime and promised satisfaction concerning Ireland. In a proposal obviously aimed at Cromwell and the leading radicals, he suggested that an act be passed for the naming of privy councillors for the duration of his reign.[106] Although he would neither consent to the abolition of the office of bishop nor to the sale of the bishops' lands, he proposed to restrict their powers and to provide for tender consciences.

The moderates now made their last bid for a settlement prior to the vote of no addresses. They proposed that four bills be drawn up; their signing by Charles would be the prelude to a personal treaty. The King would be asked to grant the militia to Parliament for twenty years and indirectly for an indefinite period, to annul all antiparliamentary declarations, and to disable all peers created since his departure from London in January 1642. It is significant that nothing was said about religion.[107]

Although the radicals at first strongly opposed the bills,[108] by November 27 they had seemingly decided to make them their own. By December 1, however, they had altered them sufficiently to ensure the King's refusal and by so doing had cleared the way for the vote of no addresses. The bills, in their final form, called for a permanent alienation of the militia power from the Crown and the complete suppression of Anglicanism.[109]

The radicals' determination to crush the opposition in the Commons was made clear on December 1 when, after a petition from mod-

104. Grignon to ——, London, Nov. 1, 1647, PRO, 38/3/85, fols. 154b–155a.

105. Newsletter, London, Nov. 18, 1647, Clar.SPB 30, fol. 188b.

106. S. R. Gardiner, *Constitutional Documents of the Puritan Revolution, 1625–1666* (Oxford, Clarendon Press, 1906), pp. 328–332; newsletter, London, Nov. 26, 1647, RT, PRO, 31/9/46, fols. 157, 158.

107. *LJ*, IX, 541.

108. *The Moderate Intelligencer*, Nov. 25–Dec. 2, 1647, BM, E.419(3), p. 1390; newsletter, London, Dec. 2, 1647, Clar.SPB 30, fol. 211a.

109. *CJ*, V, 370; newsletter, London, Dec. 2, 1647, Clar.SPB 30, fol. 211a; see *LJ*, IX, 541, 544, for proposals of the Lords.

erate-minded Londoners had received strong support in the House, Vane threatened to use the army to purge Parliament of his opponents.[110] The threat was effective: a general exodus of moderate parliamentarians followed. The shift in the balance of power was apparent in a division of the House over the four bills. The moderates could muster no more than fifty votes as against eighty-four for the radicals.[111]

Royalist observers saw in all this evidence of a change more dangerous to the King's cause than any in the past. It was now known in London that the officers at army headquarters were "dancing after a new tune" and that the King was in a "hard strait."[112] On December 3 it was rumored that Parliament intended to send unacceptable propositions to the King and, on his refusal, "to bring about the total change of the present form of government."[113] News that officers and agitators had become reconciled caused general bewilderment in London, and it was expected in some quarters that a purge of some seventy moderate members of the Commons was a good possibility.[114]

The altered atmosphere in Parliament was a result of Cromwell's decision to abandon his support of Charles in favor of a working alliance with Rainsborough. Sir John Berkeley, who had delivered Charles's message to the army about November 28, perceived clearly that the die had been cast. He had been greeted "very coldly" by both Cromwell and Ireton, and he had noted that both men were quite changed toward him. That night Berkeley talked to a high-ranking officer who told him that it was now the intention of the army leaders "to destroy the King and his posterity." They intended to imprison him and "to bring him to trial, and I dare think no farther."[115]

Berkeley, like many others, was mystified as to why Cromwell, having apparently put down the Leveller threat, should now adopt the policies of their most extreme wing. He queried his informant about this and was told that, despite the scene at Corkbush Field, the Levellers were in fact far from crushed and that "two thirds part of the army" had been to see Cromwell and Ireton "one after another" to tell them that they intended to persuade the rest of the army to follow their ideas, and if all else failed, to bring about a division in the army. In the face of this situation Cromwell and Ireton were reported to have argued that, if the army divided, "the greatest part will join with

110. Newsletter, London, Dec. 2, 1647, Clar.SPB 30, fol. 211a.

111. *CJ*, V, 374.

112. Newsletter, London, Dec. 3, 1647, Clar.SPB 30, fol. 197a.

113. *Ibid.*

114. John Evelyn to Sir Richard Brown, London, Dec. 6, 1647, *Diary and Correspondence of Sir John Evelyn*, ed. William Bray, 4 vols. (London, 1898–1900), III, 6; Grignon to Mazarin, London, Dec. 13, 1647, PRO, 31/3/85, fol. 121b.

115. Berkeley, "Memoirs," *Harl. Misc.*, IX, 483–484.

the Presbyterians and will . . . prevail to our ruin," in which case they would be forced to turn to the King and "to crave rather than offer any assistance." They would then be fortunate to escape with a pardon. They concluded that since they could not defeat the Levellers they were forced to join them; "therefore Cromwell bent all his thought to make his peace with the party that was most opposite to the King." Cromwell made his own position more explicit on the following day. He told Berkeley that he would serve the King as long as he could do so without his own ruin, but that he should not expect him "to perish for his sake."[116] A few weeks later Lilburne told an audience that Cromwell's fear of assassination was a major factor in influencing his decision to abandon a bargain with the King by which he was to be made Earl of Essex, and Ireton, lord lieutenant or field marshal of Ireland.[117]

When Lord Broghill asked Cromwell some years later why the army had turned against the King, Cromwell told the famous story of how he and Ireton, dressed as troopers, had intercepted a letter from the King to the Queen at the Blue Boar Inn in Holborn about November 21. The letter was said to have contained a statement that the King was courted by both the Scots and the army and that "he thought he should close with the Scots sooner than the others." "Upon this," Cromwell said, "we took horse and went to Windsor, and finding we were not likely to have any tolerable terms from the King, we immediately, from that time forward, resolved his ruin."[118] The difficulty is not in the truth or falsity of the story, but in whether it really explains anything. As W. C. Abbott has pointed out, Cromwell was aware that the King was dealing with the Scots; thus the letter could tell him nothing that he did not know before. He was nearer the truth in the latter part of the statement where he talks of the improbability of getting "tolerable terms" from the King, if by "tolerable" he meant a settlement that would guarantee his own position against the ring of enemies that was closing around him.

As we have seen, Cromwell had unsuccessfully attempted to come to an agreement either with Lilburne or with the agitators in late October, just prior to the Putney debates. It seems likely that he made a second and successful attempt shortly thereafter. As early as November 5 moderate and royalist elements in London were alarmed by the fact that Lilburne had been permitted to walk about in the City. On

116. *Ibid.*

117. "A Declaration of some Proceedings," *Leveller Tracts,* ed Haller and Davies, pp. 97–101.

118. Thomas Morrice, "Biography of Orrery," in *A Collection of State Letters of . . . Roger Boyle, the first earl of Orrery, lord president of Munster in Ireland,* 2 vols. (Dublin, 1743), I, 219–228, quoted in Abbott, *Writings and Speeches,* I, 564.

November 9 the Commons ordered his official release. On the previous day the agitators, who only a few days before had treated Cromwell and Ireton with something very like contempt, meekly consented to return to their regiments. When news of this reached London, there was great speculation as to the reasons for the sudden détente: One royalist observer suspected it had resulted from some kind of secret agreement between the Cromwellian group and the Levellers and asserted that only those "who understand not the mystery" were optimistic. He himself was gloomy and asserted that if the Cromwellians had "continued in the fear they were in of the Levellers but one day longer, I know it for certain that the King had been on Wed. night last [November 10] at St. James, upon almost as good terms, as you and I could wish; but that conjuncture is almost, but not quite, past."[119] Clarendon also suspected that the release of Lilburne was part of some kind of bargain. A few weeks later he observed that, although the execution of the mutineer by Cromwell's orders at Corkbush Field on November 15 would seem to indicate that the Cromwellians "approved not their [the Levellers'] doctrine," nevertheless "letting John Lilburne walk the street . . . makes the other severely less understood."[120]

In a pamphlet published in early 1649 Lilburne seemed to confirm the existence of an agreement between himself and Cromwell during the Putney debates. Describing the attitude of Cromwell and Ireton toward the Agreement of the People and their subsequent change, he said: "The great officers very much oppose it awhile, as having set up another interest; but seeing the same take with the army, profess though at present their judgements could not so far close with it as to act for it, yet they would never oppose it. Hereupon the whole frame of design alters, and matters in projection with them, were how to disengage themselves, and be rid of the King, and how likewise to discountenance and keep under the discerning party in the army."[121]

But why did the alliance between Cromwell and Lilburne produce an attitude of hostility toward the King if, as seems well established, Lilburne was himself aiming at an understanding with Charles? The answer may lie in a consideration of the relationship between Cromwell, Rainsborough, and Lilburne.

The first two men were, at this point, attempting to destroy one another, and each needed the support of Lilburne if he was to succeed. Both made overtures to him before and during the Putney debates. Lilburne's hostility toward Cromwell was public knowledge, and so

119. Newsletter, London, Nov. 11, 1647, Clar.SPB 30, fol. 180a.
120. Hyde to Richard Harding, Dec. 15, 1647, Clar. SPB 30, fol. 180a.
121. John Lilburne, Richard Overton, and Thomas Prince, "Second Part of England's New Chains Discovered," *Leveller Tracts,* ed. Haller and Davies, p. 177.

Rainsborough had reason to be confident of winning his support. If he had succeeded, Cromwell's career would almost certainly have come to a sudden end in November 1647. The fact that he did not prompts the question as to why Cromwell gained either Lilburne's backing or at least his benevolent neutrality.

Lilburne's position vis-à-vis his own followers had become increasingly uneasy. He had greatly underestimated the difficulty of winning them over to a policy of cooperation with the King and was now viewed with some suspicion by the extremists.[122] When Rainsborough met Lilburne on October 31 (while the Putney debates were in progress) he did his best to make common cause with him, assuring him of his opposition to those agitators who had "evil intentions" toward the King and declaring that their own safety depended on the King's preservation.[123] That the person who was generally regarded as Charles's worst enemy should suddenly reverse his position caused general surprise and aroused the keen suspicion of the King himself.[124] It is likely that Rainsborough asked for Lilburne's cooperation in the elimination of Cromwell, probably promising in return to support Lilburne's project with respect to an agreement with the King. But Lilburne had reason to fear that if he assisted in the destruction of Cromwell on the grounds of his "treasonable" dealings with the King, he might well find himself the next victim, and on the same charge.

Rainsborough's attitude when he talked to Lilburne was sharply at variance with the statements he had been making at Putney: "it may be thought that I am against the King," he had declared, adding significantly, "I am against him or any power that would destroy God's people, and I will never be destroyed until I cannot help myself."[125] On the night of October 28 Rainsborough was in London, allegedly because of an indisposition, but perhaps in reality to lay the groundwork for his meeting with Lilburne on October 31.

During the debates on October 29, almost as if to justify the assurances concerning the King that he was to give Lilburne two days later, Rainsborough was considerably more moderate. Having accused Ireton of declaring in a former speech that in some cases Ireton would not care whether there was "a King or no King, whether Lords or no Lords, whether a property or no property," Rainsborough declared, "I do very much care whether there be a King or no King, Lords or no Lords, property or no property; and I think, if we do not all take care, we shall all have none of these very shortly."[126] On November 1, how-

---

122. Gregg, *Free-born John*, pp. 204–205.
123. Dyve, "TLB," pp. 95–96.
124. *Ibid.*, p. 96.
125. Woodhouse, *Puritanism and Liberty*, p. 33.
126. *Ibid.*, p. 55.

ever, the day after his meeting with Lilburne, he seems no longer to have found it necessary to exhibit undue piety toward the old constitution. He moved that the council debate whether or not a bill could become an act without the consent either of the Lords or of the King. Later in the debate he made significant references to the charges against Richard II, pointing out that he had not agreed with the laws offered him by the Commons. "If that were so great a right as did depose him," he argued, "it is in the Kingdom [still], and therefore let us go to the justice of the thing."[127] Disappointed, perhaps, at his reception by Lilburne, he had reverted to the hard line of the army agitators.

Rainsborough now pressed his attack, and by November 5 the fall of Cromwell and Ireton appeared to be imminent. On that day, however, Lilburne was permitted to leave the Tower during the daytime, and four days later he was virtually a free man.[128] Since Rainsborough's influence in the Commons was not strong enough to obtain this order in the face of Cromwell's opposition, it is likely that it was done with Cromwell's approbation if not at his request. This would indicate some kind of understanding between Lilburne and Cromwell.

Yet such an agreement could hardly have been to the advantage of the King. Lilburne, faced by the wreckage of his policy, was clearly forced to choose between Rainsborough and Cromwell. He may have found himself obliged to support his old comrade because he could not consent to his destruction. As for the King, both men had, to some extent, used him as a weapon against the other, which must have made it difficult for them to join forces with Charles.

Whether they also collaborated in prompting the King to make his escape from Hampton Court on November 11 is not known, but, although Lilburne later denied it, there is evidence that both played a part in it.[129] For both men the King's departure from the scene, perhaps even from England, would have had the effect of freeing them from any past obligations to him and of permitting them complete freedom of maneuver against their opponents.

The mutiny at Corkbush Field may be seen as Rainsborough's last attempt to unseat Cromwell. It is significant that although Lilburne went to Ware, he chose not to appear on the scene at Corkbush. But what appeared to be neutrality was, in effect, a decision of at least limited support for Cromwell. Lilburne's mere presence on the field, unless he chose to oppose Rainsborough and his brother Robert directly, would have strengthened their hand greatly against Cromwell. But because he was not with Rainsborough, he was, in effect, against him.

127. *Ibid.*, pp. 55, 114, 121.
128. Gregg, *Free-born John*, p. 202.
129. *Ibid.*, pp. 203–205; Abbott, *Writings and Speeches*, I, 550–555.

If, on the other hand, Lilburne had used his influence to persuade the agitators to return passively to their regiments on November 8 and had remained neutral in the second major crisis at Corkbush, Cromwell was remarkably ungrateful. On November 9 the Commons had declared the Agreement of the People to be "destructive to the meaning of Parliament and to the fundamental government of the Kingdom."[130] On November 14 Fairfax and Cromwell delivered their counterblast to the Leveller program in "a Remonstrance to the House of Lords." Lilburne, for his part, strongly protested the shooting of Private Richard Arnold at Corkbush Field.[131]

Whatever the character of Cromwell's relations with Lilburne may have been, there is no doubt that shortly after Corkbush he turned against both Lilburne and the King and assiduously pursued an alliance with Rainsborough.

Most moderates and royalists were at that time confidently expecting to witness the immediate trial of Rainsborough for treason. On November 16, after receiving a letter from Fairfax, the Commons had ordered Rainsborough "forthwith to attend the House."[132] On November 18 Fairfax sent the Commons a Leveller manifesto, "England's freedom, Soldiers' rights," and specifically singled out Rainsborough as a ringleader. A committee dominated by moderates was appointed to investigate "the proceedings of the London agents" mentioned in Fairfax's letter.[133] A resolution to issue a declaration against the Levellers was then carried by seventy-five votes to sixty-seven.[134] On the same day Rainsborough and his supporter, Major Thomas Scott, were suspended from the House, and it was confidently expected that Marten, Thomas Chaloner, and Mildmay, the last described as "the most bloody-minded against the King," would soon follow.[135]

But Cromwell, having checkmated his opponents, was ready as usual to reappraise the whole situation. By telling the House that the army was now "in a state of obedience,"[136] he seems to have been indirectly asking them to abandon the attack on Rainsborough. There was, at any rate, a sudden and notable improvement in the treatment of Rainsborough's supporters. Mildmay, who a few days before had been a candidate for expulsion, was now appointed to request the assistance of

130. *CJ*, V, 354.
131. Gregg, *Free-born John*, pp. 298–299.
132. *CJ*, V, 359.
133. *Ibid.*, 363.
134. *Ibid.* Sir John Bampfield and Herbert Morley and Sir John Evelyn and Sir James Harrington were tellers for the majority and the minority, respectively.
135. Newsletter, London, Nov. 18, 1647, Clar.SPB 30, fol. 189a.
136. *CJ*, V, 364.

the Lords in the preparation of propositions to be sent to the King.[137]

The London Levellers, by contrast, now received very rough treatment from the Commons. A petition on November 23 from the "Free-Born People of England," in which reparations were demanded for the death of the innocent agitator shot by Cromwell's orders on November 15, was declared seditious, and some petitioners were imprisoned. Cromwell appears to have led the assault on the Levellers, and his words echoed those of Ireton during the Putney debates. He had permitted these men freedom to speak to the army, he told the House, hoping that "their follies would vanish"; now that he saw them spread so widely, he thought it high time they were suppressed. He had permitted the council of war to discuss the question of a wider franchise, but when he realized that the "London agents," although agreeable to the exclusion of children and servants from the franchise, "insisted on" extending it to persons receiving alms and "persons which had no interest in estate at all," he had been forced to oppose them. Such propertyless persons, he went on, "being the most," were likely to choose "those of their own condition"; the result would be "a levelling and parity . . . " His opposition to the Levellers, he complained, had brought many "obloquies" on himself and the other officers, and he blamed them for the "calumnies raised upon the Army . . . "[138]

The Levellers, returning to the attack, again appeared at the door of the House on November 29. This time they rebuked the Commons for their treatment of the petitioners of November 23. The London civic government had warned the Commons about the petition and had even offered troops to protect the Houses.[139]

On December 2, the day after Vane had threatened to use the army against the moderates, the attitude of the House toward the Levellers changed dramatically. It was the subject's right to present petitions and Parliament's right to judge them, they declared mildly, adding that they hoped that the petitioners would accept this answer.[140]

Early in 1648 Wildman and Lilburne declared that their petition of November 23 "had made the Lords House to quake, and the Com-

137. *Ibid.*, 364–367; Whitelocke, "Annals," BM, Add. MS. 37,344, fol. 121b.
138. "The Parliamentary Diary of John Boys, 1647–8," ed. David Underdown, *Bulletin of the Institute of Historical Research*, XXXIX (1966), 152–153. The explicit character of Cromwell's words on this subject gives rise to serious reservations with respect to C. B. MacPherson's contention that almstakers were "consistently excluded" from the enfranchised groups by the Levellers. (See C. B. MacPherson, *The Political Theory of Possessive Individualism* [Oxford, Oxford University Press, 1962].) MacPherson has made some significant revisions of accepted interpretations of Leveller theory and practice, but I cannot accept his view (p. 158) that "they ought to be remembered as much for their assertion of a natural right to property in goods and estate as for anything else."
139. Whitelocke, "Annals," BM, Add. MS. 37,344, fol. 122a.
140. Rushworth, *Hist. Coll.*, II, pt. iv, 919–920; *CJ*, V, 375.

mons themselves to stink; and that before the petition was two days old, or had been two days abroad, the Lords . . . the greatest Earls of them in estate . . . sent to us a creature of their own to article with us . . . " This person, said Lilburne, had offered on behalf of the Lords, to agree to all the outstanding Leveller demands, if that party in turn would agree to leave the upper house with its present power. When the Levellers refused they were offered £30,000. Lilburne added that they had approached Wildman with similar offers.[141]

Whatever the character of the arrangement made or being made between Cromwell and Rainsborough, it was one from which Lilburne was definitely excluded. Cromwell's decision to break with the King and to ally with Rainsborough seems to have taken place sometime between November 18, when the Commons was still hostile to the agitators' hero, and November 28, the approximate date of Berkeley's visit to the army. It is worth noting that, at this time, the King was far from agreement with the Scots. As late as November 29 he had to defend himself against Scottish criticisms of his offers to Parliament, by telling the Scots that it was necessary "in many respects that I should seek to satisfy, as far as I can with conscience and honour, all chief interests."[142]

On December 8 Loudon, Lauderdale, and Lanark, after warning the King that "eminent persons" were organizing projects for his destruction and that discussions to this effect had gone on both in London and the army, proposed that he escape from Carisbrooke and make his way to Berwick.[143] In Parliament, meanwhile, the moderates, although greatly weakened by the exodus following Vane's threat to use military force against Parliament, were able to muster sufficient strength on December 10 to defeat an attempt by the radicals to permit Rainsborough to take up his command at sea. They won the division by sixty-one votes to fifty-eight, and during the debate they boldly pointed out that Rainsborough should clear himself of the serious charges against him before being entrusted with such an important command.[144] But this was their last show of strength, and between this date and the passage of the vote of no addresses on January 3, 1648, they put up no serious opposition to radical policy. The agreement between the two

141. "A Declaration of some Proceedings," *Leveller Tracts,* ed. Haller and Davies, pp. 97–101; newsletter, London, Nov. 26, 1647, RT, PRO, 31/9/46, fol. 160.
142. Charles I to Lanark, Nov. 29, 1647, *Letters of the Kings of England,* ed. J. O. Halliwell, 2 vols. (London, 1848), I, 448–449; see also Berkeley, "Memoirs," *Harl. Misc.,* X, 485–486.
143. Loudon, Lanark, and Lauderdale to the King, London, Dec. 8, 1647, Burnet, *Memoirs of the Hamiltons,* p. 330.
144. *CJ,* V, 378; newsletter, London, Clar.SPB 30, fol. 210a.

commanders was, meanwhile, made official on December 22 at a prayer meeting at Windsor.

At Westminster the radicals carried a resolution in favor of Rainsborough's naval command by eighty-eight votes to sixty-six.[145] The Lords opposed the move on the grounds that Rainsborough had shown himself sympathetic to the army mutineers. A person so poorly regarded by Fairfax, they argued, should not be given a position of trust. But at a conference, managed by radicals like Prideaux, Pury, Haselrig, Scott, and Rigby, the peers were told that Rainsborough had cleared himself of the charges against him and that the Commons had taken action on the request of Fairfax and the army Council of War.[146] At least one observer, however, regarded the rapprochement with Rainsborough as Cromwell's work, the latter being described as "now the ringleader in this way."[147] When Cromwell was asked how he could trust a man like Rainsborough, he had replied that the colonel had given him assurances "as great as could be given by any man" that he would follow the directions of Ireton and himself "for the management of the business at sea."[148] But it was soon clear that the agreement was concerned with more than merely naval matters. Two days later another ominous prayer meeting took place at Windsor during which it was decided that "the King should be prosecuted for his life, as a criminal person."[149] Both Cromwell and Rainsborough abandoned former positions in order to reach agreement. Cromwell dropped the King while Rainsborough deserted Lilburne. Six weeks later Rainsborough was described as one who was as obedient to the Cromwellian faction "as the nimblest of their creatures" and as having "quitted the title of Prince of the Levellers . . . "[150]

Relations between the radicals and the Scots were, meanwhile, steadily worsening, and the probability of a second civil war appears to have been widely accepted as early as mid-December.[151] But the radicals do not appear to have been unduly disturbed by the prospect.

145. *CJ*, V, 403–405. Haselrig and Ludlow were tellers for the majority; Sir Edward Hungerford and Sir Edmund Fowell for the minority.

146. *Ibid.*, 406; Whitelocke, "Annals," BM, Add. MS. 37,344, fol. 126a.

147. Newsletter, London, Dec. 30, 1647, Clar.SPB 30, fol. 233a.

148. Robert Huntingdon, "Sundry Reasons inducing Major Robert Huntington to lay down his Commission," *LJ*, X, 409.

149. Edward Hyde, Earl of Clarendon, *The History of the Rebellion and Civil Wars in England*, ed. W. D. Macray, 6 vols. (Oxford, 1888) [hereafter cited as Clarendon, *Rebellion*], IV, 282–283; R. H. Whitelocke, *Memoirs, biographical and historical, of Bulstrode Whitelocke* (London, 1860), pp. 284–285, quoted in Abbott, *Writings and Speeches*, I, 573.

150. *Merc. Prag.*, Feb. 1–8, 1648, BM, E.426; Salvetti to Gondi, London, Dec. 17, 1647, SC, BM, Add. MS. 27,962L, fols. 21b, 22a.

151. Nicholas to Edgeman, Dec. 16, 1647, Clar.SPB 30, fol. 218a.

They wasted no words in refusing the Scottish request that the four bills be sent to them for their perusal.[152] "They are fair asunder," exulted one royalist. "I hope gold shall not have the power to join them again."[153]

The Four Bills passed the houses on December 14. They were, in essence, a reversion to the old intransigence of Uxbridge and Newcastle and were probably intended from the start to be unacceptable. The militia power was to be taken from Charles, and in effect, from the Crown permanently. The Cessation in Ireland was to be voided, and the use of the *Book of Common Prayer* was to be forbidden "in any place whatsoever."[154] They were presented to Charles on December 24, and his signature was demanded without further discussion within four days.

The Scottish commissioners appeared at Carisbrooke about the same time with more acceptable proposals. Charles signed, after some discussion, the "Engagement," by which he undertook, in return for a promise of military support from the Scots, to establish Presbyterianism for three years and to confirm—but not impose—the covenant by act of Parliament and to suppress the sects, including the Independents. He also agreed to free trade between the two nations and promised to give at least one-third of important offices of state to Scots.[155] The commissioners were disappointed that they could not wring from Charles more enthusiastic support for Presbyterianism. Without it, they argued, the Kirk would be only too ready to listen to Argyle. Events in Scotland soon bore them out. As soon as the King's concessions were made known in Scotland many ministers began to protest against them. With Argyle's support, a special committee was set up by the Committee of Estates to correspond with the Commission of the Church and to "consider of the danger of irreligion and of the monarchy."[156] This was the beginning of close cooperation among Argyle, the Kirk, and Cromwell, designed to frustrate any invasion plans of the Hamiltonian party.

The intentions of the radicals became clearer on December 31 with the passage of a resolution for "the security of the King's person." The measure, which in effect made the King's imprisonment official, was carried to the Lords by Mildmay.[157]

---

152. *CJ*, V, 386; advices from London, *CSPV, 1647–1652*, p. 36.

153. Newsletter, London, Dec. 20, 1647, Clar.SPB 30, fol. 222a.

154. Gardiner, *Constitutional Documents*, pp. 335–347.

155. *Ibid.*, pp. 347–352.

156. *Memoirs of Henry Guthry, late bishop of Dunkeld, in Scotland: wherein the conspiracies and rebellion against King Charles I, to the time of the murther of that monarch are related*, ed. George Crawford (Glasgow, 1748) [hereafter cited as Guthry, *Memoirs*], pp. 256–257.

157. *CJ*, V, 413.

Events reached a climax on January 3 with the passage of the famous vote of no addresses, which ordained that there were to be no further overtures whatever to Charles for the settlement of the kingdom. On the same day, the committee of both kingdoms was abolished and its powers vested in a purely English committee of Parliament. The fateful measure was passed only after an all-day debate. In the first division, the radicals triumphed by 140 votes to 92, and by the same margin in the second.[158] John Maynard, member for Totnes, was one of the strongest opponents of the motion. It seemed to imply, he said, a determination to lay the King aside; he further characterized it as "a mask to carry other things under it." The danger was, he warned the Commons, "that you will totally subjugate yourselves to an army."[159]

Cromwell countered Maynard in a speech in which his inner conflicts were clearly evident. A Parliament man, a soldier, and a member of the "honest party," he was obviously finding it increasingly difficult, if not impossible, to reconcile the three positions: "we declared our intentions for monarchy," he began uncertainly, "and they are still so, unless necessity enforce an alteration." Suddenly he threw pusillanimity to the winds and began to bully the members: "Look on the people you represent," he barked, "and break not your trust, and expose not the honest party of the Kingdom, who have bled for you, and suffer not misery to fall upon them, for want of courage and resolution in you, else," he threatened, "the honest people may take such courses as nature dictates to them." It was a typical stacatto outburst of Cromwell in his best—or worst—form, and one can readily picture the mixture of resentment, fear, and grudging respect on the faces of his listeners.[160] He went on to accuse the King of untrustworthy conduct and of attempts to embroil the nation in another war and ended by placing his hand on his sword and shouting: "thou shalt not suffer an hypocrite to reign!"[161]

Among the nearly one hundred moderates who were courageous enough to take their seats in the House of Commons on that day and to record their votes against the measure was D'Ewes. He has left an account of the speech he delivered—or intended to deliver—on that occasion. He was shocked, he said, to hear of the House actually debating the deposition of the King, and he warned that although the King

158. *Ibid.,* 415. Haselrig and Evelyn of Wilts. were tellers for the majority; Hungerford and Sir Thomas Twisden for the minority.
159. "The Parliamentary Diary of John Boys, 1647-8," ed. Underdown, pp. 141–164.
160. *Ibid.,* p. 156.
161. *Merc. Prag.,* Jan. 4–11, 1648, BM, E.422, quoted in Abbott, *Writings and Speeches,* I, 576.

himself might perish, "I do very much fear that this will prove the ready means . . . to make his posterity more absolute in their rule than any of their ancestors." He observed that some of the members who were willing to pass the measure still favored reception of messages from the King and were opposed to his deposition or to alteration of the form of government, but "such things of necessity follow when this is passed." He refused to do evil that good might come of it, and he would not agree to it even if he were sure that "no intestine troubles, new wars, or other miseries would ensue upon it which I do too probably foresee must follow." At the beginning of the war, he said, Parliament had declared that it had no intention "to alter the frame of government," but now, when the King wanted to return, Parliament was not only about to vote against further addresses to him, "but depose him and change the government."[162]

Outside the House it was also widely believed that the radicals with the aid of the army intended to bring the King to trial, to depose if not to execute him, and to form a republican government. Many of the moderates retired to the country after their defeat. Any hope of a shift in the balance of power was lessened by the fact that many royalists and moderates distrusted the Scots because of their previous treatment of the King. If it were not for that, one writer affirmed, "The greatest part of his Kingdom would appear for them . . . "[163] For the moment there was no danger of this. The Rainsborough-Cromwell agreement had brought the army, temporarily at least, under control, and on January 9 the New Model explicitly declared itself in favor of settling the kingdom "without the King and against him, or any other that shall hereafter partake with him."[164] This was both the logical result and the necessary precondition of the vote of no addresses, a landmark in the history of the Revolution.

Despite these moves, Cromwell's position in January 1648 was by no means secure. During the crisis of 1647 he had emerged as the key figure, but his tortuous negotiation with different parties had produced accusations of bad faith from royalists, moderates, and extreme radicals in the Commons and the army. Threats of assassination were frequent, and Cromwell admitted more than once that he feared for his life. His alliance with the Levellers had been the prelude to the Holmby coup. But instead of following either the antimonarchical drift of the extreme Levellers or Lilburne's reforming constitutionalism, he had

162. Sir Symonds D'Ewes, "Journal of the Parliament begun November, 1640," BM, Harleian 166, fols. 284b, 285a.
163. Newsletter, London, Jan. 6, 1648, Clar.SPB 30, fol. 256b.
164. "A Declaration from the Army," Rushworth, *Hist. Coll.*, II, pt. iv, 962.

offered the King better conditions than many royalists had dared hope
for. The Heads of the Proposals was essentially a scheme to solve the
problems posed by the minority status of the radicals and was a bargain by which, in return for support of the monarchy, the leading
radicals would be assured of positions of power, coupled with a religious and political settlement palatable to them and to their supporters. The resultant animosity of the Levellers toward Cromwell
and Ireton had forced the radicals to conciliate the moderates, and it
was not until August 20 that the power of the New Model was finally
used to create a majority for the radicals in the Commons. Even then
Cromwell had been careful to prosecute only the most dangerous of
his opponents. Henceforth, and until his agreement with Rainsborough in late November, Cromwell attempted to create a parliamentary
consensus to counterbalance his rivals' strength in the army. In Scotland, meanwhile, Argyle had done good service for his radical English
friends by blocking any genuine efforts to support the King.

The Putney debates revealed the dangerous isolation of Cromwell
and Ireton. Rainsborough had seemed likely to oust Cromwell and
might have done so but for Fairfax's continued support of the lieutenant general. With the probable support of Lilburne, Cromwell rode
out the storm, and Rainsborough's challenge was turned aside at Corkbush Field. He then surprised royalists, moderates, and probably Lilburne himself by uniting with the extreme Rainsborough group who
had been heretofore calling for the trial and even the execution of the
King. It was a reversal similar in character to that which he had carried out in the previous June, but in the opposite direction. In this
connection it is worth noting that Cromwell's abandonment of the
King was not prompted by a prior agreement between Charles and the
Scots, but was itself the step that paved the way for such an agreement.

By mid-January it had become apparent that although Cromwell
had consolidated his position in one direction by the link with Rainsborough, he had, almost at the same time, lost the support of an old
and trusted friend, Sir Henry Vane, Jr. On December 10 Vane had requested permission to retire to the country for six weeks.[165] He was
absent during the debate on the vote of no addresses, and at his trial
in 1662 he declared that he had neither consented to nor voted for
that measure.[166] The cause of Vane's break with Cromwell remains obscure. It may be that he regarded the alliance with Rainsborough as a

165. *CJ*, V, 378.
166. William Cobbett, Thomas B. Howell, and Thomas J. Howell, *Collection of
state trials and proceedings for high treason and other crimes*, 34 vols. (London,
1809–1828), VI, 157–164.

step committing Cromwell to dependence upon the sword and to a course of action that was in essence hostile not only to the King but to Parliament itself.

Vane's defection was a foretaste of the difficulties that Cromwell was to encounter in the first six months of 1648 when the fragmentation of parties and groups both in Parliament and army made it almost impossible for him to find a firm footing.

XI] The Return to Violence

If 1647 had been grueling for Oliver Cromwell, 1648 brought little relief, and the first six months of that year were perhaps the most critical of his career. His alliance with Rainsborough had cleared the way
for the vote of no addresses and had temporarily stabilized his position. But it had been a somewhat desperate measure and may even
have compounded his problems, coinciding with, or perhaps produc-
ing, the alienation of Vane. It also presaged worsening relations with
Lilburne, who, together with his supporter Wildman, soon found himself back in prison. The embittered Leveller, ably assisted by Marten
in the Commons, now combined with Cromwell's enemies to make his
position almost completely untenable. The City continued hostile, the
counties rebellious, and the Hamiltonian Scots menacing. As his power
base in England narrowed dangerously, Cromwell was forced to de-
pend for stability on a rather incongruous alliance with Argyle and
the ministers of the Scottish Kirk. By late April 1648 he had not only
virtually lost control of the Commons, but was far from secure in the
army. With the outbreak of royalist risings in Wales, Essex, and Kent,
however, his prospects brightened. The terms of power were once
again converted from political to military ones, and Cromwell was
able to extricate himself from the mare's nest at Westminster by taking
the field as a military commander.

The atmosphere in London after the historic vote was one of fear
and foreboding. It was freely predicted that the radicals intended to
abolish both monarchy and Lords and to establish a republic. The
more conservative peers, understandably disturbed by these possibilities, opposed the vote of no addresses and did their best to delay its
passage.[1] Their position was certainly shaky. The rather startling radical assertion that the peers really wished to sit as members of the Commons did little to restore confidence. Fears persisted that the upper
chamber would be abolished despite the army's explicit repudiation of
any such intention.[2] By January 17 the Lords, under the leadership of

1. Grignon to Brienne, London, PRO, 31/3/86, fol. 26a, b.
2. Newsletter, London, Bodleian Library, Clarendon State Papers [hereafter cited
as Clar.SPB], 30, fol. 261b; Bulstrode Whitelocke, "Annals," BM, Add. MS. 37,344
[hereafter cited as Whitelocke, "Annals," BM, Add. MS. 37,344], fol. 130a.

Salisbury, and despite the protests of Northumberland, Rutland, Warwick, Manchester, and Delaware, had passed the vote of no addresses. Northumberland had led the opposition, and although the resentful radicals considered arresting him as an enemy of the state, he retired unscathed to Petworth. Salisbury, on the other hand, received his due reward when the upper house sent a message to the Commons approving of his purchase of Worcester House.[3]

Cromwell was now ready to move against Lilburne and Wildman and found the peers more than pleased to cooperate in bringing the Leveller terriers to heel. At a conference with the Commons on January 18 the Lords accused the Levellers of organizing a petition hostile to both houses, and a few days later Lilburne was back in the familiar confines of the Tower.

The radicals were now described as falling into three groups: those who demanded the immediate abolition of the monarchy and the establishment of a republic; those who opposed any such precipitate move on the grounds that the people should first become accustomed to government by Parliament alone; and those who favored offering the crown to the Prince of Wales. There appears to have been little support for the King himself, and at least one observer believed that the majority in Parliament would have been happy to see him deposed.[4]

Cromwell's alliance with Rainsborough had committed him to the extremist position. He was soon to press for the trial of the King on such charges as complicity in the alleged murder of his father, a step that would seem to have precluded any offer to the Prince of Wales. But, judging from his subsequent actions, he was not likely to have favored a republic, a course that, in any case, would not have pleased Argyle. It is probable that, like many others, he knew better what he opposed than what he favored. He could still count on the backing of old radicals like St. John and Haselrig, but the defection of Vane had been a heavy blow and had introduced new divisions. The old party of 1644 was now splintered into three fragments: Levellers, Cromwellians, and Vanists. Cromwell's treatment of Lilburne and Wildman had earned him the cordial hatred of Marten, and it was not long before Marten, in conjunction with the moderates, was making it almost impossible for Cromwell to control the Commons. The embattled gen-

3. *Mercurius Pragmaticus* [hereafter cited as *Merc. Prag.*], Jan. 19–25, 1648, BM, Burney Collection, 14.

4. Salvetti to Gondi, Feb. 4, 1648, Salvetti Correspondence, Transcripts from archives at Florence of correspondence of Florentine ambassadors in England, 1616–1679, BM, Add. MS. 27,962L [hereafter cited as SC, BM, Add. MS. 27,962L], fol. 47a.

eral could find a measure of support only in the army, and even in
that quarter he was losing his grip. The Leveller-moderate connection
was further strengthened by a remarkable friendship between Lilburne
and Sir John Maynard. The moderate leader had been imprisoned in
the Tower after the flight of the eleven members in August 1647. The
link between the two men was an important factor in the politics of
the summer and autumn of 1648, and Maynard continued to be a
friend to Lilburne until the latter's death as Cromwell's prisoner in
Dover Castle in 1657.

Lilburne could and did make things difficult for Cromwell both in
Parliament and in the army, with the result that he felt more and more
pushed to extremes. "They cannot show mercy upon any consideration," wrote one observer, "so many of their own creatures daily fall
from them . . . "[5] Although 141 votes had been mustered in favor of
the vote of no addresses, the unreliability of this majority is indicated
by Cromwell's unsuccessful attempt, only two weeks later, to pass a
measure requiring all members to swear to abide by it.[6] Shortly thereafter members of the Commons were telling friends of their "remorse
of conscience" for having supported the measure.[7]

Secretary Nicholas regarded the dissension among the radicals as so
serious, both in Parliament and in the army, that if the royalists had
patience, "they would fall with their own weight."[8] One royalist reported hopefully that the split in the army might yet bring the radicals to disaster. The "Agitators and Levellers," he wrote, "are not yet
dead though asleep . . . "[9]

Cromwell's policy in the first half of 1648 was exertmely confused.
Attempts to conciliate the Scots and the Londoners were combined
with moves against the King, the House of Lords, and the Levellers.
The King's position was generally thought to be desperate. It was expected that he would soon be brought to the Tower either to prevent
the Scots from negotiating with him further or for purposes that one
writer was "afraid to think of . . . "[10] In mid-January, D'Ewes, Selden,
and Wheeler were supervising the removal of the King's library from
Whitehall to St. James "to remain for public use."[11] The locks on
the Queen's chapel at Somerset House were ordered broken and the
chapel fitted with a pulpit. These moves met with little or no opposi-

5. Newsletter, London, Jan. 13, 1648, Clar.SPB 30, fol. 261b.
6. *Ibid.*
7. Newsletter, London, Jan. 27, 1648, Clar.SPB 30, fol. 276.
8. Nicholas to Edgeman, Jan. 17, 1648, Clar.SPB 30, fol. 262.
9. Newsletter, London, Jan. 20, 1648, Clar.SPB 30, fol. 268.
10. Newsletter, London, Jan. 24, 1648, Clar.SPB 30, fol. 273b.
11. *Journals of the House of Commons* [hereafter cited as *CJ*], V, 436.

tion, and it was thought that the Cromwellian radicals, if they wished, could bring the King to trial with impunity.[12] On January 25 the House ordered the Committee of the Revenue to "retrench the King's family" and to use the money thus saved to pay his jailers. About the same time Marten moved that the King be transferred to the Tower,[13] and by February 3 the Commons had drawn up an impeachment against him for the murder of his father and the loss of La Rochelle and the Isle of Rhé.[14]

The King's execution was freely predicted. Even Clarendon, who still felt that it was in the interests of Cromwell and the senior officers to support the King, was puzzled and worried by the turn of events: "the safety of the King's person from violence is that I now most apprehend."[15]

The declaration against the King, said to have been drawn up by William Pierrepont, was, after a furious debate, finally approved on February 11, the radicals counting eighty votes as against fifty for their opponents. Cromwell led the radicals and delivered what was described as "a severe invective against monarchical government."[16] John Selden, a man who commanded the respect of all factions and who had been a member of the original committee of inquiry into the alleged poisoning of James I, declared that the committee had been unable to find anything "reflecting upon this King." He therefore moved that the article in question be deleted from the declaration. Cromwell now exhibited his worst side. Enraged by this unexpected opposition, he demanded that the House expel Selden as "not fit to sit any longer . . ."[17] D'Ewes ventured some rather timid criticisms, remarking that he had prepared a speech to support Selden, but since that member was "like to speed so ill for declaring his mind" he asked that he might be permitted to sit down and say nothing, which, remarked one sardonic commentator, "was his wisest course."[18]

D'Ewes has left us an account of a speech written about this time in which he protested against the infringement of "freedom of speech," and declared that a certain noble gentleman "rather deserved thanks

12. Newsletter, London, Jan. 24, 1648, Clar.SPB 30, fol. 272a.

13. *Mercurius Elencticus* [hereafter cited as *Merc. Elenc.*], Jan. 26–Feb. 2, 1648, BM, E.414(4); *CJ*, V, 443.

14. Newsletter, London, Feb. 3, 1648, Clar.SPB 30, fol. 279b.

15. Hyde to Hopton, Feb. 4, 1648, Clar.SPB 30, fol. 284a; Salvetti to Gondi, Jan. 21, 1648, SC, BM, Add. MS. 27,962L, fol. 39a.

16. Newsletter, London, Feb. 10, 1648, Clar.SPB 30, fol. 290a; *CJ*, V, 462; Salvetti to Gondi, Feb. 11, 1648, SC, BM, Add. MS. 27,962L, fol. 49b. Haselrig and Sir Peter Wentworth and Sir John Evelyn of Surrey and John Bulkeley were tellers for the majority and the minority, respectively. (*CJ*, V, 462.)

17. Newsletter, London, Feb. 17, 1648, Clar.SPB 30, fol. 292b.

18. *Ibid.*

than blame" for saying that "by the same rule that you take upon you here to judge the King for breach of trust, the people may take upon them to give their judgment of us also, whether we have not broken our trust . . . I cannot but much wonder that this new doctrine of the people's power should now seem so strange to us who have heard it formerly broached in this House over and over again . . . " The King should be given the right to defend himself, he urged, and concluded by asserting that the declaration and the vote of no addresses were as much as "to abolish all regal government for the future."[19]

Cromwell seems to have been prepared to use force against his opponents, and a general purge of the moderates was averted only by Marten's refusal to cooperate. Cromwell had apparently considered a purge in January and may have abandoned the idea because of his fear that he and his party would find themselves the sole target of Marten's agitation inside the House and Lilburne's troublemaking outside it. "This was our chiefest end in not purging the House," one anonymous writer later claimed, "that those members might be as a screen betwixt us and the people's hatred."[20] By the end of January the radicals were described as toying with the alternative plan of adjourning Parliament and placing all power in the Derby House Committee, the successor to the committee of both kingdoms.[21] The opposition Cromwell encountered during the debate prompted him once again to take up the idea of a purge. When he approached Marten to ask for his cooperation, however, he received a blank refusal, and the two men were reported to have parted "much more enemies than they met."[22]

Cromwell had good reason to fear a coalition of his enemies in Parliament and the army. He was also aware that there could be no real settlement in England as long as the threat of a Scottish invasion remained, and while he made threatening moves against the King he did everything possible to frustrate the plans of the Hamilton party in Scotland by strengthening his alliance with Argyle and the Scottish Kirk. On January 20, 1648, the Commons resolved that they intended to pay the Scots the £100,000 still owing to them, although one skeptical observer felt that they had no intention of letting the Scots have "a

19. Sir Symonds D'Ewes, "Journal of the Parliament begun November, 1640," BM, Harleian 166 [hereafter cited as D'Ewes, "Journal," BM, Harl. 166], fols. 285a, 286b.
20. *Westminster Projects; or the Mystery of Iniquity of Darby House discovered*, No. 5. (London? 1648), BM, E.446(5).
21. Salvetti to Gondi, Feb. 4, 1648, SC, BM, Add. MS. 27,962L, fol. 48a.
22. *Westminster Projects*, p. 9; ―― to Lanark, London, Feb. 22, 1648, *The Hamilton Papers; being selections from original letters in the possession of His Grace the Duke of Hamilton and Brandon relating to the years 1638–1650*, ed. S. R. Gardiner (London, 1880), p. 154.

penny, unless they can disengage them from their late declaration."[23] By February 3 the radicals were said to have been "very confident the Scots will not come in . . . "[24] and to have been trying desperately to avoid war because they doubted their capacity to stop the Scots and at the same time to control London. Large sums were reportedly offered to Argyle and to others in Scotland, in order to impede the offensive plans of the Hamilton party. They apparently hoped by the same means to gain the support of the ministers of the Kirk. One of Lanark's correspondents described Stephen Marshall as having been sent to Scotland by the radicals "with fifty thousand pounds to clear your clergymen's lungs."[25] But the mixed reception accorded Marshall by the Kirk indicated that many of its members were still reluctant to ally themselves with the "Great Independent." It is significant, however, that the Reverend George Gillespie, a close associate of Argyle who had already done good service for the radicals in England, extended the hand of friendship.[26]

Despite the critical state of parliamentary finances at this time, the Cromwellian radicals displayed an unaccustomed spirit of generosity toward the Scots and were particularly attentive to the needs of Argyle. Mildmay, once again a strong Cromwellian, after praising the Marquis and telling the House that his party "and the Scottish clergy, were the only men that upheld the English interest in Scotland . . . ," moved that he should be provided with the sum of £10,000. The amount might have been even greater, it was said, but for the fear of rendering Argyle suspect in the Scottish Parliament.[27] In Edinburgh, meanwhile, one of the English commissioners was assuring Montereul that the radicals would be able to retain Scottish support because they had decided not only to establish Presbyterianism but also "to give them money," which, the Frenchman was unkind enough to add, "they like still better than their religion." The Duke of Hamilton declared that Argyle had a man in London "simply to receive money there."[28] The

23. Newsletter, London, Jan. 24, 1648, Clar.SPB 30, fol. 273a.
24. Newsletter, London, Feb. 3, 1648, Clar.SPB 30, fol. 279b.
25. —— to Lanark, Feb., 1648, Hamilton Papers, p. 163.
26. Memoirs of Henry Guthry, Bishop of Dunkeld, ed. George Crawford (Glasgow, 1748) [hereafter cited as Guthry, Memoirs], pp. 58–59.
27. Clement Walker, History of Independency (London? 1648), BM, E.463(19), p. 79; Robert Monteith, The history of the troubles of Great Britain, containing a particular account of the most remarkable passages in Scotland, from the years 1633 to 1650 (London, 1735), p. 354.
28. Montereul to Mazarin, Edinburgh, Feb. 28, 1648, The Diplomatic Correspondence of Jean de Montereul and the Brothers de Bellièvre, French Ambassadors in England and Scotland, 1645–1648, ed. J. G. Fotheringham, 2 vols. (Edinburgh, 1898–1899) [hereafter cited as MC], II, 409.

English parliamentary commissioners in Edinburgh, led by Sir Arthur Haselrig, were described as having seen practically no one but Argyle with whom they kept up "a very extraordinary correspondence . . . "[29] The Earl of Lanark was surprised to learn that the English commissioners, far from being difficult about the church, mentioned neither religion nor the treatment of the King. Instead, he reported, they had confined themselves to emphasizing their readiness to give the Scots "a hundred thousand pounds sterling at present and the interest of what remained . . . at eight per cent . . . "[30]

Far from quarreling with the Scots about religion, the radicals were now making distinctly Presbyterian noises. On January 12, 1648, a fresh appeal was made to the counties to set up the Presbyterian system, and about two weeks later all members of Parliament who had not taken the covenant were urged to do so.[31] The merciless ordinance of February 11 against stage plays can be taken as additional evidence of anxiety to please the Scottish Kirk. It provided, among other things, that the unfortunate actors should be "openly and publicly whipped" in the marketplace.[32] At least one observer feared "a marriage between a Presbyterian incubus and an Independent succubus, to beget a new generation of devils of the next parliament."[33] The radicals certainly had no intention of binding themselves to the Presbyterianism that they seemed about to fasten on the country, and there was some justification in the complaint of *Mercurius Aulicus* that "though they tie our consciences in the devil's chains, they walk at liberty as the Lord's free men."[34]

By mid-April 1648 the radicals had apparently decided to cement relations with the Kirk even more tightly. They were described as having instructed their emissaries in Edinburgh "to give the Presbyters all the hopes that may be . . . " in order, it was said, that the Kirk might be "a stalking horse to carry on the design of Independency . . . "[35] The radicals were also accused of deliberately choosing commissioners with a Presbyterian background and reputation and of bribing them to act in the radical interest.[36] By mid-April Haselrig was reporting good

29. Montereul to Brienne, Edinburgh, Feb. 15, 1648, *ibid.*, 400.
30. Montereul to Mazarin, Edinburgh, Mar. 1, 1648, *ibid.*, 415.
31. *Journals of the House of Lords* [hereafter cited as *LJ*], IX, 657; *CJ*, V, 443.
32. *LJ*, X, 41.
33. Sir Thomas Knyvett to Sir John Hobart, Feb. 11, 1648, *Memorials of the Great Civil War, 1646–1652*, ed. H. Cary, 2 vols. (London, 1842), I, 377.
34. *Mercurius Aulicus* [hereafter cited as *Merc. Aul.*] ed. John Berkenhead, Jan. 25–Feb. 3, 1648, BM, E.425.
35. Knyvett to Hobart, Feb. 11, 1648, Cary, *Memorials*, I, 377.
36. Montereul to Mazarin, Edinburgh, Mar. 8, 1648, *MC*, II, 420–421.

progress to his masters in London: "the ministers . . . oppose [Hamilton] really and Argyle strives to the utmost . . . "[37]

The joint efforts of Cromwell, Haselrig, and Argyle were crowned with success in early March when the Kirk issued a manifesto against the Engagement and against assisting the King in any fashion. A substantial minority of ministers opposed the declaration, and only four lay members voted for it. One of the four was Argyle, now described as "daily more and more openly opposed to the restoration of the King . . . "[38] In the light of this, Argyle's statement at his trial in 1661 makes strange reading: ". . . I never saw that monstrous usurper Oliver Cromwell in the face, nor ever had the least correspondence with him, or any of that sectarian army, until the commands of the Committee of estates sent me . . . to the border in anno 1648, to stop his march into Scotland . . . "[39]

But Cromwell failed to match his diplomatic successes in Scotland with equivalent gains closer to home, particularly in London. Dissension within the parliamentary ranks and increased restiveness in the counties combined to erode confidence; this was reflected in the unwillingness of London financiers to lend money to Parliament, except at exorbitant rates of interest. Significant moves were made, however, to placate the London money men, particularly those concerned with the Irish interest. On November 13, 1647, the advantages of the Irish Adventurers' "Doubling Ordinance" of July 1643 had been made more attractive. A second ordinance on January 13, 1648, was designed to please both those who had already advanced large sums to Parliament and were beginning to have second thoughts and the London Irish Adventurers who had long clamored for better terms. All such could now be credited with double their total loans, to be repaid by the sale of all rebel property in Dublin, Cork, Kinsale, Youghal, and Drogheda.[40]

The response in political terms was disappointing and seems to have been confined to "the factious part" of the Common Council who

37. Haselrig to the Derby House Committee, Apr. 18, 1648, Bodleian Library, Tanner Manuscripts, 57, fol. 16a.

38. Guthry, *Memoirs*, p. 259; Montereul to Mazarin, Edinburgh, Mar. 8, 1648, *MC*, II, 420–421; Gilbert Burnet, *Memoirs of the lives and actions of James and William, Dukes of Hamilton* (London, 1677) [hereafter cited as *Memoirs of the Hamiltons*], p. 343; newsletter, London, Mar. 24, 1648, Roman transcripts, PRO, 31/9/47 [hereafter cited as RT], fol. 118.

39. Speech of Argyle at his trial, William Cobbett, Thomas B. Howell, and Thomas J. Howell, *Collection of state trials and proceedings for high treason and other crimes*, 34 vols. (London, 1809–1828), V, 1426; Salvetti to the Secretary, Feb. 25, 1648, SC, BM, Add. MS. 27,962L, fol. 63b.

40. *Acts and Ordinances of the Interregnum, 1642–1660*, ed. C. H. Firth and C. S. Rait, 3 vols. (Oxford, 1906–1911), I, 1027–1029.

visited the House and declared their support of the vote of no addresses. Delegations from various counties did likewise, but the majority were described as afraid to make their opinions known "for fear
of being imprisoned . . . "[41]

The radicals were far from sure either of London or of the counties,
as their measures for the defense of Parliament attest. Artillery was
emplaced in Scotland Yard, and new fortifications were erected in
Whitehall.[42] There were persistent reports of mutinies in the army
and disorders in Gloucester City and county. Revolts against Parliament erupted in early March at Pembroke Castle and elsewhere in
Wales. In the western counties some towns, including Plymouth, refused to obey Fairfax's orders and declared for "the Presbyterian
party."[43] Some of the western garrisons, ordered to disband by Parliament—probably because their loyalty was suspect—refused to do so
while their arrears remained unpaid. According to Grignon, only igno-
rance of their own strength and fear of the New Model prevented a
successful rising by the discontented populace.[44] Relations with the
City continued to deteriorate. On February 4 when Cromwell was
preparing the declaration against the King, Fairfax and his chief officers dined with the lord mayor and some of the aldermen. The occasion cannot have been an unqualified success, however, since only three
days later the radicals were apparently on the point of disarming the
City and purging the Common Council. On February 23 the impeachment of City aldermen was still expected, and Haselrig was said to be
pressing it violently.[45]

Fragmentation of parties in the Commons made it impossible for
Cromwell to control that body except by threats of military force. But
he had yet to regain his prestige in the New Model, and indeed the
threat from that quarter was more dangerous than from the Commons
itself. The alliance with Rainsborough had done little to improve the
situation. The latter had now taken up his naval command and was
thus of no use to Cromwell in helping to control the army. Lilburne
and Marten were thus handed an opportunity they did not hesitate to
exploit. Many of the rank and file of the army could no longer be
trusted, and lack of pay was still an important cause of discontent
among them. There were even demonstrations against Cromwell. Fairfax's life guard mutinied, and "a whole gang" of mutinous soldiers

41. Newsletter, London, Jan. 27, 1648, Clar.SPB 30, fol. 273b.
42. *Ibid.*
43. Clar.SPB 30, fol. 273a.
44. *Ibid.*; Grignon to Brienne, Jan. 24, 1648, PRO, 31/3/86, fol. 45b.
45. Newsletter, London, Feb. 10, 1648, Clar.SPB 30, fol. 290a; —— to Lanark,
London, Feb. 23, 1648, *Hamilton Papers*, p. 156; Grignon to Brienne, London,
Feb. 7, 1648, PRO, 31/3/86, fol. 78b.

followed Cromwell, "railing to the very door of the House." The soldiers had apparently gone to Cromwell's house, shouted for their arrears, and protested against their disbandment before the discharge of the remainder of the army. Cromwell argued with them, and "the contest . . . grew very high" before the ringleaders were finally arrested.[46] Although one trooper was sentenced to death, a further demonstration in which the soldiers shouted that "if one suffered, they would all suffer," was persuasive in staying execution.[47]

After the Putney troubles the radicals had attempted to eliminate some of their opposition in the army by discharging all those soldiers suspected of royalist or moderate sympathies. The difficulty was that they were so numerous that they could rid themselves of all suspects only at the price of seriously weakening the army.[48] Men of good judgment in London, wrote one observer, were confident that the New Model could "never be brought unanimous to a rendezvous to engage against that party which will declare for Monarchy." Much money had been raised for the army pay, he said, "yet the distempers and discontents of their army are so many, that they dare not pay the soldiers any part of the arrears, fearing that they would desert the services."[49]

Meanwhile, the split between Cromwell and Fairfax, already of long standing, deepened. On March 21 a definite break between the two men was rumored. Cromwell's actions "reflected on the general and the whole army . . . ," and it was predicted that before long the commander of the New Model, whom Cromwell was allegedly treating as a figurehead, would reveal the lieutenant general's "knavery" and "crush his faction . . . "[50]

Cromwell's enemies in the Commons were quick to take advantage of his obvious weakness in the army. He was regarded, moreover, as having the real support of but a small minority in the House. One observer predicted confidently that the mere danger of a Scottish invasion would be enough to tip the balance of power completely in favor of the moderates. The Cromwell faction, which "run altogether upon extremes," would in consequence be "quelled utterly."[51] Another royalist was equally certain that both the northern counties and Lon-

46. Newsletter, London, Clar.SPB 29, fol. 134a; —— to Lanark, Mar. 7, 1648, *Hamilton Papers*, p. 161; 282 to Lanark, Mar. 7, 1648, *Hamilton Papers Addenda*, ed. S. R. Gardiner, *Camden Miscellany*, IX (London, 1895), 20; newsletter, London, Mar. 2, 1648, Clar.SPB 29, fol. 134b.

47. Newsletter, London, Mar. 2, 1648, Clar.SPB 29, fol. 134a, b.

48. Grignon to Brienne, London, Mar. 6, 1648, PRO, 31/3/87, fol. 34b.

49. —— to Lanark, Mar. 14, 1648, *Hamilton Papers Addenda*, p. 25.

50, Newsletter, London, Mar. 21, 1648, Clar.SPB 31, fol. 6a, b.

51. *Ibid.*

don would support a Scottish invasion and would bring about a restoration of the old constitution in church and state "after a little struggling for Presbytery on Covenant pretences."[52] The essential weakness of the Cromwellians and their fear of a popular rising were starkly revealed in a debate over the dispatch of reinforcements to the parliamentary forces at the siege of Pembroke Castle. Cromwell opposed sending the troops on the interesting grounds that "other parts" of the kingdom would be "much weakened and left naked."[53] The troops were not sent.

The situation of the radicals was made even more difficult and dangerous by continued dissension among their leaders. Vane was described on February 1 as having returned to the House "unsatisfied, notwithstanding that Cromwell hath bestowed two nights oratory upon him."[54] The two were still estranged on February 13 when the radicals were said to have been torn with fears and suspicion "in so much as Sir Henry Vane, jr. hath left them."[55] Ten days later Vane was still at odds with his old friends: "while Cromwell makes applications to him," wrote one reporter, " . . . he at heart seems coy."[56]

The Levellers meanwhile continued hostile. Marten was willing to make temporary alliances with almost anyone, if by doing so he could embarrass the lieutenant general. Cromwell had attempted a reconciliation about February 20, but the outspoken republican had remained implacable. Three weeks later Marten informed the well-known moderate, Lionel Copley, that he and his faction were now even willing to support monarchy if this would destroy Cromwell and his party, "the falsest of mankind . . . "[57] This could be done, he affirmed, if the Scots would promise to support his actions in Parliament. His claim to control four regiments of the New Model was supported by Lanark's informant, who remarked that Marten's party in the army was "very mutinous, and expects a fair opportunity to decline Cromwell's commands . . . "[58]

Faced by growing opposition and plagued by internal dissension, the Cromwellians began to reconsider their policy toward Charles. The parliamentary declaration against the King, filled as it was with incredible accusations, had failed to win popular support and was

52. Newsletter, London, Mar. 6, 1648, Clar.SPB 31, fol. 31b.
53. Newsletter, London, Mar. 30, 1648, Clar.SPB 31, fol. 38a, b.
54. —— to Lanark, Feb. 1, 1648, *Hamilton Papers*, p. 148.
55. Newsletter, London, Feb. 13, 1648, Clar.SPB 30, fol. 291a.
56. —— to Lanark, Feb. 23, 1648, *Hamilton Papers*, p. 156.
57. —— to Lanark, London, Mar. 14, 1648, *Hamilton Papers Addenda*, quoted in Gardiner, *GCW*, IV, 86.
58. *Ibid.*

quietly laid aside.[59] Cromwell and his party, wrote one observer, because of their fear of the Scots "and finding their own weakness, intend again to court the King."[60] About February 28 Cromwell, Prideaux, Francis Allen, and other radicals met in a house in Fleet Street to discuss the dispatch of new propositions to Charles with, it was said, the primary objective of driving a wedge between him and the Scots.[61]

Cromwell was also painfully aware of the need to weaken the alliance between Marten and the moderates, which was now strong enough to challenge him severely in the Commons. Evidence of a developing struggle for power was provided by a message the Lords sent to the Commons on March 4. It comprised an explicit approbation of the Engagement signed by those members of Parliament who had fled to the army in July 1647. The measure appears to have been designed to counteract a plan, allegedly hatched in Scotland, for the impeachment of the leading radicals. The Scottish Convention of Estates was reported to have drawn up a charge that, after approval by the Scottish Parliament, was to have been sent in the name of the whole kingdom to Westminster against such persons as Lord Saye and Sele, Cromwell, Marten, Lenthall, St. John, Vane, Haselrig, Pierrepont, and Nathaniel Fiennes.[62] They were to have been charged with subverting religion, destroying monarchy, dividing the House in July 1647, and disturbing the peace between the two kingdoms. Lord Saye reportedly found out about the scheme and, in order to frustrate it, originated the ordinance for indemnity in the upper house.

The Lords' message provoked a furious debate in the Commons, so much so that Saye was apparently forced to summon Cromwell, "whose appearance did somewhat allay their fury."[63] The moderates then attempted to have the measure laid aside for a month, apparently hoping to give the Scots time to make their move, but after Cromwell once again threatened a purge they were defeated in a division by ninety-nine votes to fifty-two.[64] When the question was taken up again on March 9 the moderates, although they mustered considerable strength, in an effort to avert what was now regarded as a prelude to their own expulsion, were after "much dispute" defeated by ninety-nine votes to ninety.[65]

59. Newsletter, London, Feb. 24, 1648, Clar.SPB 31, fol. 301a.
60. —— to Lanark, London, Feb. 28, 1648, *Hamilton Papers*, p. 16.
61. Newsletter, London, Mar. 2, 1648, Clar.SPB 30, fol. 134a.
62. *Merc. Elenc.*, Mar. 1–8, 1648, BM, E.431; *Merc. Prag.*, Mar. 14–21, 1648, BM, E.432.
63. *Merc. Elenc.*, Mar. 1–8, 1648, BM, E.431; *Merc. Prag.*, Mar. 14–21, 1648, BM, E.432.
64. *Merc. Prag.*, Mar. 14–21, 1648, BM, E.432; *CJ*, V, 479. Haselrig and Evelyn of Wilts. were tellers for the majority; Sir Walter Erle and Tate for the minority.
65. *CJ*, V, 489. Haselrig and Evelyn of Wilts. and Sir Walter Erle and Tate were tellers for the majority and the minority, respectively.

There was a significant difference between the original resolution sent down from the Lords on March 4 and its final form as passed by the Commons on March 9. The former measure—apparently designed to gain broad support—would have indemnified both the members who went to the army and those who stayed in the Commons in London. The resolution of March 9, by contrast, protected the radicals only and, in effect, rendered the moderates liable to prosecution for their support of the coup of July 1647.[66] One observer predicted that after its passage "the House would be ready for another purge whensoever the army shall think fit to administer it."[67] Nonetheless, the fact that ninety moderates were bold enough to appear in the House at all was a sign that the internal weakness of the radicals was no secret.

Despite the precarious position of the moderates, their stock continued to rise. There were reports that their strength in the counties was growing, as more people became convinced that agreement with the King was to be preferred to the chaos and ruin of a new war.[68] The Cromwellians, aware that in the event of a Scottish invasion they could be swamped by an influx of their opponents, once again entertained the idea of adjourning the House and ruling through a committee.[69]

Cromwell's inability to control the Commons, largely owing to Marten's continued refusal to cooperate, was obliging him to choose between eliminating his parliamentary opponents by military force or outmaneuvering them by renewed negotiations with Charles. Although he was described in mid-March as opposed to further dealings with the King, he appears a short time later to have given way to the Vane-Saye group who favored a strategic retreat from the policy embodied in the vote of no addresses.[70] On March 18 the Commons debated the question of reopening talks with the King in the Isle of Wight, and it was also reported that the plan for crowning the Duke of Gloucester was "freshly thought upon."[71] Saye appears to have gone to the Isle of Wight in the last days of March to open negotiations, and it was confidently reported in London that the leading radicals would settle with

66. —— to Joachimi, Mar. 10, 1648, Dutch transcripts [hereafter cited as DT], BM, Add. MS. 17,677(a), fol. 53a.

67. —— to ——, London, Mar. 7, 1648, *Hamilton Papers*, p. 166; Grignon to Brienne, Mar. 13, 1648, PRO, 31/3/87, fol. 47a.

68. Grignon to Brienne, London, Mar. 20, 1648, PRO, 31/3/87, fol. 58a, b.; —— to Lanark, Mar. 14, 1648, *Hamilton Papers Addenda*, p. 24; Salvetti to the Secretary, Mar. 10, 1648, SC, BM, Add. MS. 27,962L, fol. 69b.

69. *Westminster Projects*, p. 8.

70. Newsletter, London, Mar. 20, 1648, Clar.SPB 31, fol. 4b.

71. *Merc. Elenc.*, Mar. 15–22, 1648, BM, E.433; 143 to Lanark, c. Mar. 20, 1648, *Hamilton Papers Addenda*, p. 28.

the King rather than "have the Scots invade."[72] Cromwell's Derby House Committee was also reported to be debating as to the best way "to salve up the business with his Majesty . . . "[73]

Marten chose this moment to embarrass Cromwell further. He attacked the policy of drift, which, in view of the temper of the country and of London in particular, he viewed as the most dangerous of all. On March 27, aware that many of the Cromwellians would have opposed Saye's mission, he moved that Parliament depose the King, declaring that "the rude multitude" would continue to be restless until they knew "what they must trust to." This provoked a "high scuffle" in the House, with members speaking heatedly for and against the King. Marten's opposition was understandable. It was typical that he had chosen the anniversary of the King's coronation to make his suggestion. But the Londoners, who in January 1642 had virtually driven the King out of their city, were now of a different mind. They had made the anniversary the occasion for a striking demonstration of their support, not only for the monarchy, but for Charles I himself. That night the London sky was lit by more bonfires than had been seen in the City for the previous twenty-five years. It was said that if the City gates had not been kept shut the London mob, once such a ready instrument in the hands of Pym, would have "gone from their bonfires to the beating the saints out of Westminster Hall."[74]

About this time a group of Parliament men of varying degrees of radicalism, including Pierrepont, St. John, Lord Saye, his son Nathaniel Fiennes, Evelyn, and Marten, met to consider the situation. They discussed the various alternatives before the kingdom. A republic was considered but rejected, whereupon Marten argued that if the monarchy must be continued, "we had better have this King and oblige him, than to have him obtruded on us by the Scots, and owe his restitution to them."[75] Marten's apparent indecision may have reflected concern to preserve a working alliance with the moderates. The Commons' grant of a weekly allowance of forty shillings to Lilburne may also have been part of this pattern.[76] The majority of this group seemed to favor renewed negotiations with the King, for which John Ashburnham and "the clergy of England" were reportedly working.[77] It was finally agreed that a treaty should be entered upon with Charles, the purpose of which would be "to disengage him from the Scottish in-

72. Newsletter, London, Mar. 21, 1648, Clar.SPB 31, fol. 7a.
73. *Ibid.*
74. Newsletter, London, Clar.SPB 31, fol. 42.
75. —— to Lanark, London, Mar. 29, 1648, *Hamilton Papers,* p. 170.
76. Joseph Frank, *The Levellers* (Cambridge, Mass., Harvard University Press, 1955), p. 161.
77. Mungo Murray to Lanark, Mar. 15, 1648, *Hamilton Papers Addenda,* p. 26.

terest . . . " If this did not succeed, they were said to prefer a plan whereby the King would be killed during an "attempted escape."[78] In this meeting Lord Saye, Fiennes, and perhaps Pierrepont were by now "moderate radicals"; St. John and Evelyn represented the Cromwellian point of view, and Marten that of the extreme radicals or republicans.

The change in policy may have been prompted by a report that the Scots Parliament intended to send commissioners with demands concerning the safety of Charles. In order to forestall this, the radicals decided to offer "fairer terms" to the King, which, if accepted, would have led to a personal treaty, and to adjourn the House for one week to allow time for his answer to arrive before Parliament was obliged to deal with the Scottish demands.[79]

The radicals now attempted to prepare public opinion for the new approach to the King. On April 2 a petition from Essex in favor of a personal treaty arrived in Westminster. It was said to have been organized in order that the Cromwellians might have "some plausible ground to retreat from their former votes of non addresses."[80] But an attempt to persuade the City of London to petition in the same way met with a blank refusal.[81] The radicals had no better success when they suggested that the Londoners agree to buy all the bishops' lands in the north of England, "the further to engage them" in the radical cause. Angered by the Londoners' refusal, they retaliated by pressing the charges against the former lord mayor, Sir John Gayer, and a number of moderate aldermen,[82] and on April 3 Mildmay went to the upper house to request greater speed with the London impeachments.[83]

The terms Cromwell offered the King are unknown, but it seems likely that they included restoration to a titular crown with retention of the decisive militia power in radical hands. From Charles's point of view there were few good arguments for accepting this rather dubious olive branch from the man who had so recently abused him with the accusation of patricide. He was also aware that Cromwell's position in London, the counties, Scotland, and Ireland was deteriorating rapidly and that his party's total collapse could be imminent. Accordingly, in early April he rejected their offers, declaring that they had never kept faith with him, that he could not trust them, and that he would not

78. —— to Lanark, London, Apr. 4, 1648, *Hamilton Papers*, p. 174.

79. *Merc. Elenc.*, Apr. 5–12, 1648, BM, E.435; *Merc. Prag.*, Mar. 21–28, 1648, BM, E.433.

80. Newsletter, London, Apr. 2, 1648, Clar.SPB 31, fol. 43a; Salvetti to the Secretary, Mar. 31, 1648, SC, BM, Add. MS. 27,962L, fol. 82a.

81. Salvetti to the Secretary, Mar. 31, 1648, SC, BM, Add. MS. 27,962L, fol. 82a.

82. Newsletter, London, Mar. 9, 1648, Clar.SPB 30, fol. 310b.

83. *LJ*, X, 125.

negotiate with them without the consent of Scotland.[84]

The King's refusal seems to have demoralized the radicals. They were variously described as "in a pitiful state"; "at their wit's end"; so struck with "panic fear . . . that they are in a manner distracted . . . and know not which way to proceed . . . "; "their resolution ebbs and flows seven times a day . . . "[85] Having failed to enlist support in London and the counties, they turned finally to the ministers of the Westminster Assembly and, despite the ministers' bitter memories, managed to extract a promise from them to remain at least neutral in their sermons, "if they cannot declare point blank against the Scots . . . "[86]

Fear of the rising power of the royalists and of the moderates may be seen in a bitter exchange between Lord Saye and Major General Browne, long known to his political opponents as "the Woodmonger." Saye, who was attempting to curry favor with the moderates, did his best to be ingratiating, but Browne was not in a forgiving mood and told him bluntly that he had better talk to someone else, because he might need his friends "before five weeks were at an end . . . "[87]

Meanwhile, Cromwell in early April was desperately attempting to forge a coherent party out of the disparate factions in Parliament, army, and City. In the Commons he called for a united stand, and at a "Common Hall" (an assembly of all the London Livery companies) he again attempted to get the backing of the Londoners. When his proposals were coldly rejected, he angrily demanded to know by what authority the Tower and militia had been restored to London. The civic fathers produced a warrant signed by Fairfax, Vane, St. John, and himself, whereupon he had "the impudence to put it in his pocket." According to his enemies, Cromwell now made use of his supporters in London to stir up disturbances that would give the army the excuse to intervene in the City.[88] The Roman correspondent, on the other hand, reported that the April uprising of the apprentices, in which Cromwell himself narrowly escaped injury, was an unplanned, largely spontaneous affair.[89]

Serious internal divisions were to continue to plague the radicals.[90]

84. *Merc. Elenc.,* Apr. 5–12, 1648, BM, E.435; newsletter, London, Apr. 22, 1648, RT, PRO, 31/9/47, fol. 142.

85. Newsletter, London, Apr. 22, 1648, RT, PRO, 31/9/47, fol. 142; *Mercurius Bellicus,* Apr. 11–18, 1648, BM, E.436, p. 3; newsletter, London, Apr. 6, 1648, Clar. SPB 31, fol. 43b; —— to Lanark, London, Apr. 1648, *Hamilton Papers,* p. 177.

86. Newsletter, London, Apr. 6, 1648, Clar.SPB 31, fol. 43a, b.

87. *Ibid.*

88. Clement Walker, *History of Independency* (London? 1648), BM, E.463(19), pp. 84–86.

89. Newsletter, London, Apr. 14, 1648, RT, PRO, 31/9/47, fols. 199–201.

90. Newsletter, London, Apr. 14, 1648, RT, PRO, 31/9/47, fols. 221–222.

Pierrepont had joined Vane in opposition to Cromwell, and, when the Commons discussed a proposal on April 15 to sell "unnecessary" hangings in the royal wardrobe in order to raise £1,500, Vane opposed the measure with the uncharacteristic declaration that the hangings were "the marks of regality which yet they might live under, and therefore not wantonly to be sold . . ." Appropriately enough—from the ironic point of view of the historian—"all the old courtiers were for the sale of them."[91] But an attempt by the extreme radicals on the same day to require all members to swear to uphold all the measures already taken, including the vote of no addresses, was defeated. Pierrepont reportedly led the opposition, declaring that such an oath was "against that freedom they pretended due to all men and a distrust of themselves . . ."[92] A few days before, the radicals had been depicted as split "in their counsels and ends . . . ," so much so, in fact, that one of them had pointed out that unless they united quickly "the King would come without clogs and fetters and act his own part."[93] Royalist pamphleteers viewed the scene with unconcealed relish; one confidently looked forward to seeing "the Houses sit in several prisons, and their politic pates to meet in consultation on London Bridge."[94]

Disturbances in the counties were becoming more widespread, and sympathy for the King was growing noticeably. The financial position of Parliament was, moreover, deteriorating rapidly. It was becoming increasingly difficult to collect assessments in old parliamentary strongholds like Surrey and Kent,[95] and parliamentary credit was almost nonexistent, the value of the pound having fallen drastically in terms of other currencies.[96] On April 18 county committees were empowered to arrest all persons suspected of disloyalty to Parliament, a measure that passed over the strong opposition of those who regarded it as "a thing of ill consequence and example, especially by those who professed to be so highly for the liberty of their nation."[97]

The situation in Ireland, meanwhile, had grown worse, and the defection of the Earl of Inchiquin from the parliamentary cause had made the radicals uncomfortably aware of the possibility of an invasion from both Ireland and Scotland.[98] At the same time they dared not send too many troops into the north of England as long as there was

91. —— to Lanark, Apr. 18, 1648, *Hamilton Papers*, p. 185.
92. *Ibid.*
93. —— to Lanark, London, Apr. 11, 1648, *Hamilton Papers*, p. 181.
94. *Mercurius Criticus*, Apr. 6–13, 1648, BM, E.435(23).
95. Derby House Committee for Irish Affairs to committees of Kent and Surrey, Apr. 17, 1648, Committee Letter Book, PRO, State Papers, 21/27.
96. —— to Joachimi, DT, BM, Add. MS. 17,677(T), fol. 65b.
97. Whitelocke, "Annals," BM, Add. MS. 37,344, fol. 146b.
98. Newsletter, London, Apr. 6, 1648, Clar.SPB 31, fols. 43b, 44a.

danger of losing control of the south.[99] Their nervousness was reflected in the passage of an ordinance on April 21 for the arrest of "tumultuous persons and delinquents." Although the moderates succeeded in amending the measure by seventy-four votes to seventy-one, the radicals pushed through a resolution for the sequestration of the estates of those offending under the first ordinance. The radicals won this division by eighty-two votes to seventy-nine, but the narrow majority reflected the growing boldness of the moderates and their increased willingness to appear in the House.[100]

Cromwell, who must have been close to desperation, appears at this point to have given the King a direct choice between negotiation and deposition and to have considered crowning the Duke of York.[101] April 24 was appointed as the date for the "calling" of the House, and it appeared that the stage was being set for a historic change. But if plans existed for the installation of the Duke of York as a kind of puppet monarch, they were effectively frustrated on April 21 by his escape.[102]

The calling of the House brought in 306 members and gave the moderates a comfortable majority. Faced by an untenable situation, the Cromwellian radicals adopted a policy reminiscent of their strategy in the first six months of 1647. They withdrew into the background, and during the next six weeks there was a kind of truce between the parliamentary parties. Cromwell had no choice but to abandon parliamentary maneuvering in favor of renewed dependence on the army and the adoption of a plan of action that could end only with the subjugation of Parliament.

It was soon apparent that a moderate majority did not necessarily mean cooperation with the Hamiltonian Scots and their projected invasion. When, on April 25, the Commons heard of a Scottish resolution to raise an army, they immediately resolved to strengthen the fortifica-

99. Grignon to Brienne, London, Apr. 17, 1648, PRO, 31/3/87, fols. 101b, 102a.
100. CJ, V, 539. Sir Michael Livesay and Denis Bond and Sir W. Erle and James Herbert were tellers for the majority and the minority, respectively.
101. Advices from London, Calendar of state papers and manuscripts relating to English affairs existing in the archives and collections of Venice and in other libraries of northern Italy, vols. 10–38 (1603–1675) [London, H. M. Stationery Office, 1900–1940] [hereafter cited as CSPV], 1647–1652, pp. 56–57; newsletter, London, Apr. 20, 1648, Clar.SPB 31, fol. 56b; Salvetti to Gondi, Apr. 21, 1648, SC, BM, Add. MS. 27,962L, fol. 92a; Evelyn to Sir R. Brown, London, Apr. 21, 1648, Diary and Correspondence of Sir John Evelyn, ed. William Bray, 4 vols. (London, 1898–1900) [hereafter cited as Evelyn, Diary], III, 8; S. R. Gardiner, History of the Great Civil War, 1642–1649, 4 vols. (London, 1893) [hereafter cited as Gardiner, GCW], IV, 99–100.
102. Walker, History of Independency, p. 107; Colonel Joseph Bamfield's Apologie written by himself and printed at his desire (The Hague? 1685).

tions of Newcastle and to proceed without delay to the question of the settlement of the kingdom. Three days later, after a full-scale debate, the House voted by a majority of 165 to 99 that they would not "alter the fundamental government of the Kingdom, by King, Lords, and Commons," and that any member should be free to make any suggestion for that settlement.[103] The fact that Vane, Pierrepont, and other leading radicals supported the moderates in this division indicated that the split persisted in the radical party. It is probable that the ninety-nine who voted against the resolution were divided between the Marten faction and old-line radicals. Although it could be regarded as a vote of no confidence in Cromwell, it could not be construed as an indication of support for the King. The opportunity to accord him explicit recognition was passed over. It appears that although a parliamentary consensus was possible on the question of the monarchy, no such solid majority was obtainable for Charles himself. The temper of the House was further indicated by a declaration of May 6 in favor of maintaining the covenant and of joining the Scots in the presentation of the Hampton Court propositions (in effect, the Newcastle propositions) to the King. This new coalition of anti-Cromwellian radicals and moderates appears to have attempted to steer a course between Charles and the Hamiltonian Scots. Their revival of the much-rejected propositions had a number of advantages. There was no danger that the King would agree to them, and yet their espousal might help to end the threat of a Scottish invasion.[104]

The rapprochement between radicals and moderates did not include Cromwell. He was now with the army, where the situation was hardly more stable than that in London. Except for one brief interval, he was not to resume his seat until the New Model had finally cleared his political opponents from the House. One may believe Burnet when he says that if "the stirs over England had not given him other employment, he would have made a journey to London with his army for the purging of the House anew."[105] With news of the deteriorating situation in Wales, Cromwell was ordered into that region at the head of a force of cavalry and infantry. But before the news of a general revolt in Wales arrived, a meeting of officers and agitators had been held at Windsor from April 29 to May 1 to discuss the political situation. On the last day of the talks, after much soul-searching, there was general agreement that after they had subdued their enemies they should "call

103. *CJ*, V, 547.
104. Burnet, *Memc rs of the Hamiltons*, p. 345.
105. *Ibid.*

Charles Stuart, that man of blood, to an account for the blood he had shed . . . "[106]

From the point of view of the King, the attitude of Parliament was only a slight improvement over that of the army. In the arguments put forward during the April 28 debate on the settlement of the kingdom there was little to cheer the royalists. "The best of them," said one, "have been little favourable for the King, and the worst of them more insolent than ever."[107] Even if the monarchy were to be restored, there were indications that it would be in the person of the eight-year-old Duke of Gloucester rather than in that of his father.[108] At least one royalist still looked to the radicals as the King's best hope and argued that it was in his interest to come to an agreement with them.[109] That there may have been some such attempt on the basis of the Heads of the Proposals is indicated by a report of May 8 of a "strong endeavour by the Independents to close with the King."[110]

For the more extreme radicals London was evidently becoming a rather uncomfortable place. But if, as some said, they contemplated another flight to the army, they had chosen a dubious place of refuge. By mid-May it was reported that Cromwell had been forced to shoot three mutinous soldiers with his own pistol, and Evelyn described Cromwell as "not in such grace with his soldiers as to make that force . . . to accompany him into Wales."[111] Another account of the incident blamed the Levellers, "who will not fight being extremely discontented . . . "[112] On May 11 the soldiers in the Mews were so mutinous that their commander, Colonel Rich, resigned his commission. The navy was in no better condition: an indignant Rainsborough told the House that the sailors were so rebellious that he dared not put to sea.[113]

If at this juncture the parliamentary moderates had wholeheartedly espoused the cause of the Hamiltonian Scots and had encouraged the smouldering counties to rebel, it is difficult to see how Cromwell and his followers could have survived. They were saved not only by a

106. "Allen's Narrative," *Collection of scarce and valuable tracts selected from public as well as private libraries, particularly that of the late Lord Somers*, 16 vols. (1748–1751), later ed. Sir W. Scott, 13 vols. (1809–1815), quoted in Gardiner, *GCW*, IV, 120.

107. Newsletter, London, May 4, 1648, Clar. SPB 31, fol. 67b.

108. Advices from London, May 4, 1648, *CSPV, 1647–1652*, p. 60.

109. Newsletter, London, May 4, 1648, Clar.SPB 31, fol. 67a.

110. Newsletter, London, May 8, 1648, Clar.SPB 31, fol. 72a.

111. Evelyn, *Diary*, III, 12.

112. Newsletter, London, May 11, 1648, Clar.SPB 31, fol. 72b.

113. Clar.SPB 31, fol. 71a. Abbott's statement that at this time " . . . Cromwell's ascendancy among the soldiers was unshaken" is difficult to substantiate in terms of contemporary evidence. (See *Writings and Speeches*, I, 603.)

combination of English nationalism and distrust of the Scots, but also by the well-founded fear that support for the monarchy and for Charles had become so widespread as to threaten a full-blown royalist reaction. There was, as a result, much more cooperation between the moderates and radicals at Westminster than between the moderates and Scots. Even among Argyle's enemies in Scotland there was concern that a Scottish invasion might trigger a royalist reaction in England. The very strength of conservative feeling in the England of 1648 may have prevented a restoration.

A vengeful royalist counterrevolution with a revival or even extension of all the old prerogatives was distasteful to parliamentarians of all shades and doubtless even to many royalists. Six years of accumulated hatred made it impossible to predict the results of a royalist victory. The Scottish demands presented to the Commons on May 3 were, moreover, not such as to arouse enthusiasm at Westminster. They required that the King go to London for a personal treaty, that the New Model be disbanded, that the *Book of Common Prayer* be abolished, and that Presbyterianism be established with no toleration.[114]

The English parliamentarians were, nevertheless, much more uneasy about the ultimate objectives of Hamilton and his supporters than they were about their professions of Presbyterianism, which they recognized as a political and religious expedient. But although they regarded Hamilton as essentially royalist and tended to reject him as such, Montereul, who was in Edinburgh, was gloomy precisely because he was convinced that a victory for Hamilton in England would be the prelude to the triumph of the parliamentary "Presbyterians."[115]

At that very time the English "Presbyterians" themselves were being described in London as discontented and anxious to be rid of "their new masters" and as preferring to do nothing rather than "hazard the coming of the cavaliers and reduction [to] Episcopacy . . . "[116] Some royalists feared that the Scots and the moderates in Parliament might "agree both together in desertion of the rest . . . " Fear of the royalists, who were "beginning to appear so formidable . . . in every corner of England . . . " would, it was predicted, be the important factor in bringing about such a union.[117] Lanark's correspondent wrote: "I fear the moderates [more] than the Levellers. I think Argyle's designs were never so dangerous as at this present . . . If the Parliament of England can engage your nation upon such demands as they know the King

114. John Rushworth, *Historical Collections*, 7 vols. (London, 1654–1701), III, pt. iv, 1100.
115. Montereul to Henrietta Maria, May 3, 1648, *MC*, II, 475–476.
116. Newsletter, London, May 1, 1648, Clar.SPB 31, fol. 64b.
117. Evelyn to Brown, London, May 4, 1648, Evelyn, *Diary*, III, 10–11.

will never grant I am sure he neither hath nor can ever have any thing to help him."[118]

The moderates were described in early May as lukewarm about Charles's restoration, but willing to cooperate with the Scots in setting up some kind of interim government pending his acceptance of their terms. The royalists, on the other hand, were greatly shocked and disappointed by the withholding of moderate support and as a result were said to have been in a "miserable condition."[119]

This state of affairs was, of course, very much to the liking of the Cromwellian radicals. That party was playing two games. While they continued to make dubious overtures to the King, they maintained close relations with Argyle in Scotland and effected a working agreement with the parliamentary moderates. Argyle appears to have inspired the parliamentary declaration of May 6 by sending Stephen Marshall to London with the message that nothing would be so apt to divide the Hamiltonian Scots as a parliamentary declaration in favor of the covenant and the propositions of Newcastle. After Marshall's arrival he did his best to reconcile the two parliamentary factions, with the result that the declaration was produced and the parliamentary moderates effectively deflected from an alliance either with the English royalists or with the Scots of the Hamilton party.[120] By May 11 it was generally agreed that the moderates and the radicals were working together. Even the Londoners had been prevailed upon to remain neutral. The radicals reportedly aimed "to keep the English Presbyters at least neutral to the Scottish design." The moderates, on the other hand, did not feel strong enough to exploit the split in the radical ranks.[121] "We cannot but fear . . . ," wrote one commentator on the radicals, "that this patience of theirs is but counterfeit."[122]

Thus the radicals, despite their minority position, still contrived to control affairs. The moderates in their reluctance to link up with the Hamiltonian Scots were following a policy apparently inspired by Argyle and the leaders of the Kirk. One observer summed up the situation by declaring that the Londoners and the moderates were "led by the nose with their own principles by the Kirk of Presbyters in Scotland by whose direction it is that they comply thus with the Independent party."[123]

---

118. Lord Byron to Lanark, London, Apr. 28, 1648, *Hamilton Papers,* p. 190.
119. Newsletter, London, May 4, 1648, Clar.SPB 31, fol. 67b.
120. Burnet, *Memoirs of the Hamiltons,* p. 350.
121. Newsletter, London, May 11, 1648, Clar.SPB 31, fol. 72a.
122. *Ibid.*
123. Newsletter, London, May 22, 1648, Clar.SPB 31, fol. 85a; Guthry, *Memoirs,* pp. 270–271; —— to Lenthall, Edinburgh, May 14, 1648, Bodleian Library, Tanner MS. 57(1), fol. 80a.

On the eve of the Kentish rising the radicals were confident that their influence in Scotland, through Argyle and the Kirk, was sufficient to prevent any full-scale invasion of England. But to make sure, they intended to remove the pretext for invasion by starting negotiations with the King, the ostensible object being a personal treaty. In the opinion of one Scottish observer in London, this policy was inspired by Argyle. Whatever might be done on paper by Parliament, he wrote, the Cromwellians intended when the time was ripe "to depose [the] King and pursue their anarchical design . . . " Argyle, he said, was in communication with the leaders of both moderates and radicals. His object, in which he had now nearly succeeded, was to terrify the moderates by the suggestion that Hamilton was a complete royalist and intended to destroy "Covenant, Presbytery and Parliament of England and their adherents . . ."[124] Fear of such an eventuality prompted Marten to declare that, since it was impossible to settle the kingdom without the King, it was better to join with him and his party than to permit the Scots to prevail in England.[125]

The day the Commons heard the news of the Kentish rising (May 24), they voted by a majority of 169 to 86 for a personal treaty with Charles.[126] But the royalist Sir John Evelyn was skeptical and regarded the projected treaty as a mere blind. He told a friend that if he never slept until a genuine treaty was begun " . . . I shall never lay mine eyes together . . . "[127] The votes on the treaty were described as "Argyle, his masterpiece."[128]

Proceedings of the Commons virtually ceased during the Kentish rising. The revolt itself was doomed from the outset, not only by its lack of leadership and coherent planning, but also by the inaction of the parliamentary moderates, the Londoners, and, above all, the Scots. The moderates noted with apprehension the fact that many radicals had deserted the House and had gone to the army and feared "that the House shall be purged if the army prevail . . . "[129] The moderates, and especially "rich men of the Houses," were described as feeling that they had allowed themselves to be led too far by men "of desperate fortunes."[130] As usual, they had no coherent policy of their own.

Before the actual defeat of the Kentish men the moderate groups

124. —— to Lanark, London, May 19, 27, 1648, *Hamilton Papers*, pp. 198, 202–203.
125. Thomas Smyth to ——, Paris, May 13, 1648, Clar.SPB 31, fol. 67a; 282 to Lanark, London, May 9, 1648, *Hamilton Papers Addenda*, p. 34.
126. *CJ*, V, 572.
127. Evelyn to Brown, London, c. May 25, 1648, Evelyn, *Diary*, III, 20.
128. —— to Lanark, London, May 30, 1648, *Hamilton Papers*, pp. 204–205.
129. Newsletter, London, June 1, 1648, Clar.SPB 31, fol. 105b.
130. *Ibid.*

in London and elsewhere gained greatly in strength, and it appeared for a time that the Londoners might decide to support Kent. The City moderates petitioned the Commons for a personal treaty with the King in London, the release of their aldermen, and the creation of an association with Kent, Essex, Middlesex, Hertfordshire, Surrey, and Sussex. This demand was, in Evelyn's words, "a breakfast more hard than they could digest at that time."[131] But some royalists were optimistically expecting an early restoration of the monarchy on the grounds that the kingdom was "weary of the war" and "desires peace more than the Parliament."[132]

Everything hinged on the outcome in Kent. If the Kentish men had been able to win one victory, the Londoners would probably have supported them.[133] But the radicals were still in control and in close liaison with Argyle and the Kirk in Scotland, where the preachers were doing their best to prevent the invasion of England, "holding forth from their pulpits and influencing whole towns from providing assistance."[134] The gratitude of the radicals produced an order of June 2 for a "brotherly union" between the two countries and the maintenance of the covenant "according to the example of the Kirk of Scotland."[135]

As the Kentish men approached the City, Parliament hurriedly passed various measures designed to retain the loyalty of the Londoners. The charges against the impeached aldermen were dropped, and some important future land confiscations in Ireland were assigned to the trusteeship of the Irish Adventurers of London.[136] Whether or not these measures tipped the scales is, of course, not known, but London remained on the side of Parliament, and what appeared to be a formidable royalist rising dwindled rapidly to a few skirmishes. By June 5 the forces under Norwich had been defeated at Maidstone, and the crisis had passed. On the same day the Commons voted £35,000 to the Marquis of Argyle.[137] It was a fitting consummation of a policy that had been assiduously pushed for the previous six months. On June 7 the House approved of a letter from the assembly of divines to the Scottish Kirk "to strengthen the amity and union of both kingdoms."[138]

131. Evelyn to Brown, London, June 1, 1648, Evelyn, *Diary*, III, 24.
132. Newsletter, London, June 1, 1648, Clar.SPB 31, fol. 100b.
133. Newsletter, London, June 1, 1648, Clar.SPB 31, fol. 105b.
134. Advices from London, June 1, 1648, *CSPV, 1647–1652*, p. 64.
135. Whitelocke, "Annals," BM, Add. MS. 37,344, fol. 155b.
136. J. R. MacCormack, "Irish Land and the English Civil War," *Canadian Catholic Historical Association Report*, no. 25 (1958), p. 65.
137. *CJ*, V, 586, 603.
138. Whitelocke, "Annals," BM, Add. MS. 37,344, fol. 157a.

XII] Pride's Purge

The summer of 1648 was a time of confusion and contradiction when Englishmen of goodwill oscillated desperately between two almost equally unpalatable alternatives: a Scottish-royalist restoration on the one hand, and a military dictatorship on the other. Although holding the balance of power, the parliamentary moderates were acutely conscious that in either eventuality they would be losers. A firm agreement between the moderates and the King might well have tipped the balance in London and have enabled the Kentish-Essex rising to have become general. But the memory of his treatment at Holles' hands was still fresh in the King's mind. The moderates, for their part, knew from long experience that Charles preferred to deal with their parliamentary enemies. Decisive leadership was, moreover, lacking, and by the time Holles returned to his seat on the eve of Preston, the terms of power had changed almost irrevocably.

"The Presbyters do want good leaders, and . . . courage to do anything of themselves,"[1] wrote one observer in early June, and the comment held good for virtually the whole period between the suppression of the Kentish rising in June 1648 and the return of Holles in mid-August. It was the Londoners, for whom discretion had been very much the better part of valor during the Kentish rising, who now led the movement in favor of a treaty with the King. By the end of June, enthusiasm for the project was strong in both London and the House of Lords. It was otherwise in the Commons, where some moderates were distinctly unwilling to commit themselves and were even regarded as ready to make their peace with the radicals. Many of the eleven members were now returning to the House, but were described as leaning toward the Prince of Wales and "not at all for the King."[2]

If the moderates were indecisive, the radicals appeared ready to follow the extremist lead. When the masters of Trinity House petitioned in support of a treaty with the King on June 29, they were attacked by hotheads like Thomas Scott, John Venn, and Miles Corbet.

1. Newsletter, London, June 1, 1648, Bodleian Library, Clarendon State Papers [hereafter cited as Clar.SPB], 31, fol. 105b.
2. Denton to Edmund Verney, London, June 26, 1648, Sir H. Verney Manuscripts, BM, microfilm 636/9 [hereafter cited as Verney MSS, BM, M,636/9].

"He that draws his sword upon his King must throw his scabbard into the fire," proclaimed Scott.[3] Cooler heads recognized that the idea of a treaty had gained widespread popular support and were anxious to avoid the stigma attached to its opponents.[4]

Baillie, viewing the world from Glasgow, and now much more inclined to support the King than he had been in 1644, was very gloomy. He attributed the failure of the English risings to the delay of the Scottish invasion. The English, he said, were now being crushed at leisure, while in London "great pains are taken to join the Presbyterians and the Independents against all the risers in the shires . . . If this conjunction go on, both the King and our nation is in a hard taking."[5] Marchamont Needham, the irrepressible author of *Mercurius Pragmaticus,* agreed: "At Westminster all quarrels and caterwauls of opinions are laid aside, and care taken to tie a true lover's knot betwixt both the factions . . . "[6] Marten was a notable exception to the prevailing atmosphere of détente. Having withdrawn into Berkshire, he appears to have been attempting to raise a republican force opposed to Parliament and army alike.[7]

The political situation was confused and is difficult to assess with certainty. At the extreme left were the Levellers, but even this group appears to have been divided. Lilburne was still in the Tower and remained favorably disposed to moderates like Sir John Maynard. To the right of Marten and his republicans was Cromwell, with the officers of the army loyal to him, the troops whom they could control, and a faction in the Commons. Another group of "moderate radicals," led by Lord Saye, Vane, and Pierrepont, occupied a key position in the Parliament. They appear to have preferred a settlement based on some of the principles of the Heads of the Proposals and may have drawn support from a variety of sources. Still further to the right were the "old" moderates, those who had supported Holles since 1644. They too were divided between a group who favored the Prince of Wales and those still willing to deal with Charles. Since many of the extremists were Marten men, the number of members still loyal to Crom-

3. Clement Walker, *History of Independency* (London? 1648), BM, E.463(19) [hereafter cited as Walker, *History of Independency*], pp. 108–109; *The Hamilton Papers; being selections from original letters in the possession of His Grace the Duke of Hamilton and Brandon relating to the years 1638–1650,* ed. S. R. Gardiner (London, 1880), pp. 212–213.

4. Grignon to Brienne, London, June 26, 1648, PRO, 31/3/88, fols. 35b, 36a.

5. Baillie to Spang, Glasgow, June 26, 1648, *The Letters and Journals of Robert Baillie,* ed. David Laing, 3 vols. (Edinburgh, 1841–1842) [hereafter cited as Baillie, *Letters*], III, 46–47.

6. *Mercurius Pragmaticus* [hereafter cited as *Merc. Prag.*], June 6–13, 1648, BM, E.447.

7. *Ibid.*

well must have been very small indeed. Over all hung the threat of the complete subjugation of Parliament and the establishment of a military dictatorship, a prospect that had a hypnotic and almost paralyzing effect on the politicians at Westminster.

The Commons rescinded the vote of no addresses, but insisted that the King agree to Presbyterianism for three years, the recalling of royal declarations against Parliament, and parliamentary control of the militia as a precondition of any treaty.[8] They were notably cool to the demand of London that the King be permitted to come to the City without conditions.[9] The Lords, however, protested that the Commons' terms would delay matters and were also contrary to the wishes of the Parliament of Scotland.[10] In the Commons, Philip Skippon, commander of the London trained bands since early May and now firmly in the Cromwellian camp, attacked the London petition, and after some debate the House rejected it. The Commons then proceeded to demonstrate their determination to keep London firmly under control, by giving Skippon permission to raise 1,000 horse in the City without reference to the London militia committee.[11] The resentful Londoners made their feelings clear a few days later, when a Commons committee questioned the Common Council about their petition. At one point, Recorder John Glyn, one of the eleven members recently released from captivity but now opposed to City policy, asked the Common Councillors whom they would support in case the treaty failed. He was greeted with complete silence.[12] Shortly after this, however, the council appears to have agreed that should a personal treaty in London fail they would surrender the King to the discretion of Parliament.[13]

It was thought in some quarters that the radicals were merely delaying matters until the time was ripe and the position of the New Model strengthened, after which they would refuse to negotiate.[14] Certainly they were determined that the King not be given the opportunity to make effective use of the potential support for him in London. On this issue Vane made common cause with the extreme Cromwellian,

8. *Journals of the House of Commons [hereafter cited as CJ]*, V, 622.

9. *Journals of the House of Lords* [hereafter cited as *LJ*], X, 363–365; Grignon to Brienne, London, July 6, 1648, PRO, 31/3/88, fol. 55; Woodhead to Denman, July 8, 1648, Clar. SPB 31, fol. 149a.

10. *LJ*, X, 368.

11. *Merc. Prag.* July 4–11, 1648, BM, E.453.

12. *Ibid.*

13. *Merc. Prag.*, July 11–18, 1648, BM, E.453.

14. Grignon to Brienne, July 10, 1648, PRO, 31/3/88, fol. 60a; Bulstrode Whitelocke, "Annals," BM, Add. MS. 37,344 [hereafter cited as Whitelocke, "Annals," BM, Add. MS. 37,344], fol. 167b; John Rushworth, *Historical Collections*, 7 vols. (London, 1654–1701) [hereafter cited as Rushworth, *Hist. Coll.*], II, pt. iv, 1185–1187.

Mildmay. The King was "a perjured man" and ought not to be trusted, they declared. D'Ewes took strong exception to this. Parliament, he told his listeners, was in a weak financial position: the navy had rebelled, the Scots had organized against it, and the affections of the City and of the kingdom were alienated. It was high time, he concluded, that a settlement was reached with the King.[15]

The Londoners, meanwhile, were complaining bitterly that the horse that Skippon had been permitted to raise in the City were being sent secretly to the New Model. The Commons backed Skippon, and once again the Londoners found significant support only in the Lords, who not only recalled their own consent to the ordinance authorizing Skippon's action, but voted that the measure should be completely nullified and that his authority should rest on the consent of the Common Council and militia committee of London. The Commons, however, continued to stand by Skippon, and, despite the determined efforts of the Lords and the Common Council, he retained his key position.[16]

By late July the military situation was, from the radical point of view, considerably improved: Kent had been crushed; the surrender of Colchester was but a matter of time; Pembroke Castle had fallen; and the royalist rising under the inept leadership of Holland and Buckingham had been easily snuffed out. But the Scots were still the all-important factor, and the political complexion of groups at Westminster could be at least partially gauged by their respective attitudes toward the Duke of Hamilton and his opponents in Scotland.

With the siege of Pembroke Castle successfully concluded, Cromwell returned to the Commons on July 17 "to revive the courage of his party." On the following day the Lords rejected a Commons' declaration condemning the Hamilton faction in Scotland and proclaiming them to be enemies and ordered the publication of the declaration of the Scottish Committee of Estates against toleration either of the sects or of the *Book of Common Prayer*.[17] The Commons promptly countered this by publishing their own anti-Hamiltonian declaration.

The Scots, in their public declaration, had made the rather impolitic statement that they had been invited into England by several eminent persons of that kingdom. The extreme radicals seized the opportunity to attack the moderates, Prideaux singling out Maynard for special attention. Maynard admitted that he had written letters, but asserted that they were not intended as invitations "but only to bemoan the

15. *Merc. Prag.*, July 11–18, 1648, BM, E.453.
16. *Ibid.*, July 18–25, 1648, BM, E.454.
17. Declaration of the Committee of Estates, BM, E.453(32), cited in S. R. Gardiner, *History of the Great Civil War, 1642–1649*, 4 vols. (London, 1893) [hereafter cited as Gardiner, *GCW*], IV, 169, n. 1.

pitiful tossings and tumblings of the Kirk."[18] Some other moderates found themselves under fire before the radicals temporarily dropped the matter.[19]

The radicals had, of course, their own connections in Scotland which they were careful to cultivate, and they now made a number of moves calculated to please the governors of the Kirk. On July 21 the Commons ordered a letter sent to the General Assembly informing them of the zeal of Parliament in "settling religion and church government."[20] A few days later Samuel Browne, St. John's close associate, was appointed to frame an ordinance for the better observation of the Sabbath. The playhouses of London were now ordered pulled down, Skippon being directed to assist the project with his cavalry.[21]

The radicals were aware that rising tensions in London might produce an explosion that could provide the basis for a moderate or even royalist coup timed perhaps to coincide with Hamilton's advance. Skippon was the Cromwellian watchdog in the City, and by late July the radicals appear seriously to have considered employing his forces to purge both City and Parliament of their opponents. According to one report, Aldermen Langham and Bunce, other leading men of the City, and a number of parliamentary moderates were to be seized. Word of the plot leaked out, and the moderates countered with a motion forbidding Skippon to arrest any Parliament man or civic official without an order from the Commons. Nothing more was heard of the scheme.[22]

Up to this point the radicals had insisted that the King accept the three propositions prior to any treaty. On July 28, however, perhaps as a result of the abandonment of the plan to purge the House, they reversed themselves and voted for negotiations, without prior conditions, provided that the treaty were held on the Isle of Wight.[23] This strategic retreat executed by the leading radicals alienated extremists like Richard Weaver, Wentworth, Scott, and Blakiston, but seems to have won the support of some moderates.[24] Sir Edmund Verney wrote that the radicals "with threats and promises have wrought to their party many considerable Presbyterians as Sir Gilbert Gerard, Crewe, Knightley, Swinfen and others."[25] Colonel Edmund

18. *Merc. Prag.*, July 18–25, 1648, BM, E.454. This was Sir John Maynard.
19. *Ibid.*
20. *CJ*, V, 631, 648.
21. *Ibid.*
22. *Merc. Prag.*, July 25–Aug. 1, 1648, BM, E.456.
23. *CJ*, V, 650.
24. *Merc. Prag.*, July 25–Aug. 1, 1648, BM, E.456.
25. Sir E. Verney to Sir R. Verney, St. Germain, July 30, 1648, Verney MSS, BM, M,636/9.

Harvey, "once a plant of Presbytery," was now described as having switched his support to the radicals.[26]

The moderates, perhaps emboldened by the failure of the radical plan to purge the House, launched a counterattack against Cromwell himself. They were relying for the success of their project on the assistance of Lilburne with whom they had maintained an unlikely relationship since the previous January. Maynard demonstrated the strength of his friendship with his old fellow prisoner by delivering a speech on July 27 in which he demanded Lilburne's release. On August 1, after a pro-Lilburne petition of moderate tone signed by 10,000 persons was presented to the Commons, a committee heavy with prominent moderates like Lionel Copley and Maynard was appointed to consider how Lilburne might have compensation granted to him "for his sufferings." On the same day Major Huntingdon delivered his famous attack on Cromwell in the Lords, and *Mercurius Pragmaticus* predicted confidently that Lilburne would be "a brave second to Major Huntingdon."[27]

The moderates suffered a nasty reverse, however, when the unpredictable Lilburne turned on them. He attacked Huntingdon as a traitor and strongly supported Cromwell, to whom he wrote a remarkable letter on August 3 assuring him of his loyalty.[28] Despite this setback the Lords ordered Huntingdon's charge delivered to the Commons. This move was frustrated by Lord Wharton, who followed the Lords' messenger to the door of the lower house and sent a warning to Lenthall, with the result that the messengers were never called in.[29]

In the weeks preceding the Battle of Preston the mood of the Londoners was extremely rebellious, and a rising directed against the Cromwellian radicals, both within and without Parliament, seemed a distinct possibility. While Skippon continued to raise cavalry, the purpose of which, the Londoners claimed, was to overawe the City rather than to defend it, the City men themselves enlisted forces secretly. On August 8 the Common Council petitioned Parliament demanding that the King be freed, that he be invited to participate in negotiations leading to a treaty, and that the Self-Denying Ordinance be observed.[30] On the same day approximately 8,000 former soldiers petitioned for a personal treaty. The radicals, led by Aldermen Isaac Pennington and Venn, countered by accusing all petitioners of disloyalty to Parliament.[31] When the radical-dominated committee brought

26. *Merc. Prag.,* Aug. 1–8, 1648, BM, E.457.
27. *Ibid.*
28. Gardiner, *GCW*, IV, 176–178.
29. *Merc. Prag.,* Aug. 1–8, 1648, BM, E.457.
30. Rushworth, *Hist. Coll.,* II, pt. iv, 1220.
31. *Merc. Prag.,* Aug. 8–15, 1648, BM, E.458.

in what was to be the Commons' reply to the petition of the City, one member objected that the answer covered only four of the twelve points raised by the City men. "Mr. Weaver" (probably John) defended the answer on the grounds that "the citizens did now adhere to the Lords and neglect the House of Commons."[32]

On the following day a confrontation between the Commons' committee and the Common Council took place in the City chambers. The parliamentary delegation was led by John Swinfen who, although he was later to be purged, could at this point be counted as a radical supporter, Prideaux, the well-to-do member for Lyme Regis and a veteran of the radical ranks, Pennington, Venn, and Thomas Atkins, a former warden of the Mercers' Company. The Common Councillors, when they heard the committee's answer, suggested sarcastically that the Commons must have answered the wrong petition because there was no mention of their points about the Self-Denying Ordinance, the disbanding of armies, and the establishment of the laws. Swinfen, backed by Prideaux, then instructed them that the business of Parliament was too urgent to permit them to dally with such trivial matters. This only stiffened the opposition. When the committee clumsily attempted to divide the Common Council by suggesting that they should put all the horse that they themselves had listed under the command of Skippon, only two Councillors, Fowke and Gibbs supported the move.[33]

By August 10 Holles had resumed his seat in the Commons, but all factions were highly conscious of the fact that everything now hinged, not on votes, but on an appeal to arms.[34] One might have expected that at this juncture the moderates in the Commons would have cooperated closely with the City. Such, however, does not seem to have been the case. On August 17 the radicals, fearing an uprising in the City and with no apparent opposition from the moderates, appointed a committee dominated by their own supporters, to "seize upon horses, arms, ammunition and other habilements of war" in London.[35]

Holles apparently advised the King to treat in the Isle of Wight in order to get negotiations started before it was too late. To the surprise of the radicals, Charles promptly consented, and by August 17 the moderates were able to muster ninety-five votes against eighty in a division over negotiations.[36] But on the morning of August 21 came

32. *Ibid.*
33. *Ibid.*
34. Grignon to Brienne, Aug. 10, 1648, PRO, 31/3/88, fols. 77b, 80a.
35. *CJ*, V, 673; Roman transcripts, PRO, 31/9/47 [hereafter cited as RT], fols. 256, 257.
36. *CJ*, V, 674.

the news of the total defeat of the Scots at Preston—an almost fatal blow to any hopes for a negotiated settlement.[37]

The period between the Battle of Preston and Pride's Purge was outwardly dominated by the abortive negotiation known to historians as the Treaty of Newport. It was, in many respects, a kind of dumb show; only a very optimistic observer could have viewed it as anything else. The appeal to arms had been made, and the verdict had gone against both royalists and moderates. But all issues were by no means decided. The decisive question was whether or not Cromwell, now busy in the north, could reestablish his former dominance over both army and Parliament.

It is curious that the victory at Preston appears to have had the effect of strengthening Holles and his supporters and of further dividing the radicals. It was as if it suddenly became clear to many men that the destruction not only of the King but of Parliament itself might now be imminent. At least one contemporary noted that a group in Parliament, described as "the more severe part of the Presbyterians," who had supported Cromwell's policy at the time of the vote of no addresses, fearing "the total subversion of the ancient government . . . forsook the Army party, and joining themselves to the Moderate Presbyterians (who in truth and reality were strong Protestants, but no Presbyterians) were by much the most numerous in both Houses . . . "[38]

Observers in London were unsure whether the Cromwellian radicals would permit the treaty to begin with the object of breaking it off "or would establish a republic immediately." Scott, Cornelius Holland, and Mildmay were reported to be "so puffed up" by the news of the victory that "they began to swell with disdain and malice against the . . . treaty . . . " This faction doubtless was encouraged by Cromwell's well-known letter to Lenthall on August 20, in which he declared that the victory was a confirmation of God's favor and approval of "his people . . . for whom even kings shall be reproved . . . " He called upon Parliament "to do the work of the Lord so that those persons who would not leave off troubling the land may speedily be destroyed out of the land . . . "[39] But Cromwell was to find that not all his old followers were willing to obey orders; a significant number were acutely conscious of their growing unpopularity among the general populace and of the exasperation of the people with heavy taxation. They pre-

37. Grignon to Brienne, London, Aug. 21, 1648, PRO, 31/3/88.
38. *Colonel Joseph Bamfield's Apologie written by himself and printed at his desire* (The Hague? 1685), p. 49.
39. W. C. Abbott, *The Writings and Speeches of Oliver Cromwell,* 4 vols. (Cambridge, Mass., Harvard University Press, 1937–1947), I, 638.

ferred negotiation.[40] They were now ready to admit, it was said, that they had made a mistake in refusing to come to an agreement with the King in 1647. They were aware, too, that if Preston had gone against them they would have been completely ruined.[41] Above all, they included many men who could look back on long years of defending what they had considered to be the rights and privileges of Parliament against arbitrary rule. They were understandably outraged by the thought that the whole struggle could end with the spectacle of that same Parliament brought to heel by military force and held in general contempt.

By September 1 it was apparent that the alternatives facing Parliament were not so much between a radical- or a moderate-dominated negotiation with the King, but a choice between a treaty that might preserve both King and Parliament on the one hand and the dissolution or purging of Parliament followed by the trial of the King on the other. The Cromwellian radicals were reportedly confident that they could control the moderates as the result of the capture of the Duke of Hamilton, who they asserted, had admitted that he had been invited into England by "more than half of the members of the House of Commons" and had even named some of them. The groundwork, it seemed, was being laid for the purging of the Commons. In any case, a committee began interrogating prisoners with a view to gathering further evidence.[42]

Both in the debates that preceded the treaty and those that were carried on in the Commons during the negotiations a certain realignment of forces was apparent. To the great annoyance of Cromwell, Vane emerged as one of the strong supporters of the treaty. The most vehement opposition to the King in the Commons came from a relatively small group of extremists.

In the debate on the treaty John Boys, supported by Prideaux, suggested that unless the King agreed to certain preliminary propositions there be no further treaty on other items. The motion failed, but another was substituted, which was designed to divide the allotted time into sections, with a number of days for each item. The moderates opposed this strongly, stating that it would limit debate on the most important subjects and make agreement upon them more difficult. Certain members, notably Thomas Hoyle, a veteran radical supporter, continued to reject the whole idea of a treaty.[43] The influence of the Cromwellian radicals in the House was now far out of proportion to

40. Walker, *History of Independency*, p. 141.
41. Grignon to Brienne, London, Aug. 24, 1648, PRO, 31/3/88, fol. 100a.
42. Grignon to Brienne, London, Aug. 28, 1648, PRO, 31/3/88, fol. 104a.
43. *Merc. Prag.*, Aug. 29–Sept. 5, 1648, Beineke Library Collection.

their numbers, so much so, in fact, that debate was seriously inhibited.[44]

Even more ominous for the future were signs that the split between Cromwell and the Levellers had been at least partially healed and that both Marten and Lilburne were beginning to cooperate with the army leaders. A sign of the times was the vote of September 5 awarding £3000 to Lilburne in recompense for the Star Chamber sentence against him.[45] The intention of the Cromwellians to employ the Leveller group as a stalking horse for their own policies was apparent by the early weeks of September. Grignon predicted that Cromwell would use the Levellers once again as an excuse to break off negotiations on the treaty, as he had allegedly done late in 1647.[46] The effects were seen as early as September 10 when a large group of Levellers appeared at the door of the Commons with a lengthy petition. Most significant was their demand that the House think of the "innocent blood that hath been spilt . . . by express commission from the King . . . "[47] They queried whether justice would be served by a mere act of oblivion. There were significant omissions in the petition, indicating a retreat from the Leveller policy embodied in the Agreement of the People of 1647 and a closer approximation to the position adopted by Cromwell and Ireton in the Putney debates. Thus no mention was made of the will of the people as the basis of the constitution, of parliamentary reforms, of the decentralization of government, of the election of magistrates, or of the codification and simplification of the laws in English.[48] The Commons carefully thanked the petitioners for their "great pains and care to the public good" and promised to consider their demands. Two days later a group of Leveller supporters demanded that the Commons consider the petition before proceeding with the treaty.[49] Lilburne boasted later that this pressure had been "no small piece of service to Cromwell and his great associates."[50]

The confidence of the Cromwellian radicals was now such that they felt able to permit negotiations with the King in the knowledge that when the time was ripe they could use the power of the New Model

---

44. *Ibid.*
45. Whitelocke, "Annals," BM, Add. MS. 37,344, fol. 191.
46. Grignon to Brienne, Sept. 4, 1648, PRO, 31/3/88, fol. 109b.
47. Rushworth, *Hist. Coll.*, II, pt. iv, 1257–1258; newsletter, London, Sept. 1648, RT, PRO, 31/9/47, fol. 283.
48. H. N. Brailsford, *Levellers and the English Revolution*, ed. Christopher Hill (London, Cresset, 1961), pp. 352–353.
49. Grignon to Brienne, London, Sept. 11, 1648, PRO, 31/3/88, fol. 114a; Rushworth, *Hist. Coll.*, II, pt. iv, 1257–1258, 1261.
50. "Legal Fundamental Liberties," *The Leveller Tracts, 1647–1653*, ed. W. Haller and G. Davies (New York, Columbia University Press, 1944), pp. 399–449. The Levellers were supported in the Commons by Thomas Scott, Blakiston, John(?) Weaver, and Brian Stapleton. (*Merc. Prag.*, Sept. 19, 1648.)

to bring the majority into line. Despite the fact that a well-attended House meant a moderate majority, they took steps in early September to force more regular attendance upon members. The veteran radical Blakiston moved on September 5 that the House be called; he was strongly supported by the radicals who favored a fine of £100 for absentees.[51]

Although the majority in Parliament apparently preferred a settlement with the King, they were also anxious to retain their seats, and it was widely believed, as early as September, that any attempt by the majority to use their strength would bring in the soldiers.[52] In London fear of the New Model had brought about another revolution in the civic government. Cromwell's old friends were once again in control and were searching assiduously for evidence of collusion between the moderate Londoners and the Hamiltonian party in Scotland.[53] Meanwhile Cromwell was headed for Scotland with the object of bolstering the authority of his ally, Argyle, and of concluding agreements with him that were the necessary preliminaries to any decisive steps in England.[54]

The radicals made no moves to prevent negotiations for the treaty, which opened on September 18 at Newport. The parliamentary delegation was headed by Holles, Vane, and Lord Saye. Vane's continuing advocacy of some kind of agreement with Charles placed him at odds with Cromwell and Ireton, as Cromwell's letters and Ireton's activities indicate. St. John had remained loyal to Cromwell, and in a letter to him the lieutenant general expressed the hope that Vane would have a change of heart as a result of the victory at Preston, that he would, in fact, regard it as a manifestation of divine approbation of Cromwell's policies. Vane recalled some years later that Cromwell had criticized him for his "passive and suffering principles" at this time.[55] Cromwell complained that the significance of the victory was not appreciated at Westminster. It was, he declared, a "great mercy . . . much more than the House expresseth."[56]

Meanwhile a deep split was developing in the army between a group of officers headed by Ireton and another under the leadership of Fairfax. Shortly after the news of the Battle of Preston, Colonel Edmund Ludlow attempted to persuade Fairfax to back a plan to sabotage the treaty and to bring the King to trial. Finding the general cool toward the project, he turned to Ireton who gave him a much more sympa-

---

51. *Merc. Prag.*, Sept. 5–12, 1648, BM. E.462; *CJ*, VI, 6.
52. Grignon to Brienne, London, Sept. 7, 1648, PRO, 31/3/88, fol. 111a.
53. Grignon to Brienne, London, Aug. 31, 1648, PRO, 31/3/88, fol. 106a.
54. Grignon to Brienne, London, Sept. 18, 1648, PRO, 31/3/88, fol. 114a.
55. Sir Henry Vane, *The Proceedings of the Protector* (London, 1656), p. 7.
56. Abbott, *Writings and Speeches*, I, 644, n. 99, 646.

thetic hearing. Ireton agreed that the army must intervene, but thought that it would be wiser to wait until the treaty had been concluded. Ludlow pointed out, however, that once agreement had been reached the moderates would immediately attempt to disband the New Model, ostensibly to reduce taxes. If the military then stepped in, they would incur the hatred of the general public.[57] Ludlow's arguments may have influenced Ireton's thinking. Ludlow was associated with the Leveller petitioners of September 11; his interview with Ireton illustrates the sudden improvement in relations between the Cromwellians and some Leveller elements.[58] Shortly after the middle of September, or about the time of the beginning of negotiations for the treaty, Ireton began work on the famous army remonstrance, in the name of which the army was eventually to seize power. Fairfax had evidently broken with Ireton over this issue, and on September 27 the latter threatened to resign immediately if the general would not agree to the purging of Parliament.[59] About two weeks later Ireton took his seat in the House. When a Commons delegation asked Fairfax whether, in case the army should be pitted against the Parliament, he would take a public stand on the issue, Fairfax refused to commit himself.[60]

Despite Ludlow's talks with Ireton, there were signs that many of the Levellers were strongly opposed to any policy that might elevate the position of the military at the expense of parliamentary authority. This group, including Lilburne himself, leaned toward a coalition of parliamentarians and Levellers, which, they hoped, would begin the implementation of the Leveller program while preserving what Lilburne regarded as the essentials of the ancient constitution. Their policy with respect to Charles was also notably more moderate than that being adopted by Cromwell and Ireton.

Fairfax found himself under pressure from both sides. Sometime in September Lieutenant Colonel John Jubbes, who had been closely associated with the Levellers, approached him with a plan for the settlement of the kingdom. The King should be declared guilty of having caused the two civil wars, he suggested, but should be restored to his throne provided he accept the Agreement of the People, which, among other things, would deprive him of his negative voice and of his right to make appointments without the consent of the Commons. In addition, the Long Parliament should be dissolved and the country

---

57. *Memoirs of Edmund Ludlow*, ed. C. H. Firth, 2 vols. (Oxford, 1894) [hereafter cited as Ludlow, *Memoirs*], I, 203–204.

58. *Ibid.*

59. Gardiner, *GCW*, IV, 215, n. 3.

60. —— to Joachimi, Oct. 13, 1648, Dutch transcripts, BM, Add. MS. 17,677(T) [hereafter cited as DT], fol. 241b.

governed through a "Committee of State," which would include all shades of the parliamentary political spectrum. There are a number of interesting aspects to this proposal. If it had been implemented it would not only have dissolved the Long Parliament, but would have frustrated any attempted take-over by the army. It was thus very much in line with Lilburne's oft-stated aims. The inclusion of the name of Lilburne's old friend Maynard in the list of persons on the projected Committee of State suggests that Lilburne himself may have had a hand in it. If this is so, a rapprochement between Rainsborough and Lilburne may have taken place about this time, since there is evidence that Rainsborough, Harrison, and other colonels were prepared to accept the scheme while Ireton and Cromwell remained strongly opposed to it.[61] It is also worth noting that despite Lilburne's letter to Cromwell in August assuring him of his support, relations between the two men after the Battle of Preston were not good. Cromwell was expected, in some quarters, to support the Levellers. Sometime in September, on the other hand, Lilburne had journeyed north to confer with Cromwell and had returned profoundly dissatisfied with his attitude, which, he declared, tended more to "self-exalting" than to the good of the commonwealth.[62] Whether or not Jubbes's proposal was brought forward as a result of Lilburne's dissatisfaction with Cromwell is uncertain. But it seems clear that by late September 1648 an anti-Cromwellian alliance was in the making, composed of parliamentary moderates, Levellers, and army elements including Rainsborough.

Not all the London Levellers shared the constructive attitude reflected in the Jubbes proposals. Some, who perhaps leaned toward Cromwell, were behaving as though they had little to fear from their opponents in the Long Parliament. On October 6 a group appeared at the door of the Commons calling for support for their "Large Petition" and jeering at the members as they came and went. When one of the more fashionable of the Parliament men emerged clothed in a scarlet cloak with silver lace, "They abused him most grossly to his face and said he was some black malignant parboiled, and that made him look so like a lobster."[63]

The Cromwellians were said to be aiming at a purge of Parliament and a complete revolution in the state. To that end the army was organizing continuous petitions that demanded action against the King and suppression of monarchy.[64] Secret conferences were going on between the army extremists and their opposite numbers in Parlia-

61. Brailsford, *Levellers*, pp. 357–358.
62. Pauline Gregg, *Free-born John: A Biography of John Lilburne* (London, G. G. Harrap, 1961), p. 249; Brailsford, *Levellers*, p. 361.
63. *Merc. Prag.*, Oct. 3–10, 1648, BM, E.466.
64. Grignon to Brienne, London, Oct. 5, 1648, PRO, 31/3/88, fol. 149b.

ment.[65] By October 5 it was reported that they had agreed "to dispose of his Majesty" and that a message to this effect had been sent to Cromwell.[66]

At Westminster, meanwhile, the moderates were showing surprising vitality. The calling of the House had given them a majority, and on September 26 they won an important test of strength. The King had agreed to recall all his declarations against Parliament as a necessary precondition to the negotiation, but he had added that the promise depended on a successful end to the negotiation. Despite strong opposition from the radicals, the moderates had succeeded in carrying a motion in favor of the King's position. Two days later, however, there was an attempt to reverse this decision. A group of extremists, including Nathaniel Stephens, Mr. (Luke?) Hodges, Thomas Pury, and Cornelius Holland, were said to have met at the house of John Lisle early on the morning of September 28 in order to plan strategy. In the ensuing debate Lisle, Stephens, Pury, and Holland led the attack, with Lisle declaring that the treaty was of no use and was intended "but to the destruction of them [the well affected of the kingdom] and us." In spite of their best efforts the motion was once again put to the question and was carried.[67]

Those who wanted a settlement with the King were now urging Charles to make sweeping concessions in order to frustrate the army's intentions. The King, now more concerned to gain time in which to make his escape than to negotiate in good faith, had by October 9 agreed to surrender the militia to Parliament for twenty years, to limit the authority of bishops, and to settle Ireland by the will of Parliament. The King's determination to retain episcopacy, coupled with the fact that many parliamentary members had already invested in episcopal lands made agreement on church government extremely difficult. Royal intransigence on this point was widely regarded as politically disastrous. It was asserted that many of his own clergy did not support Charles's stand and that "many others of his party" were of the same opinion, "few of his nobility or gentry being bound in it."[68] On October 16 the Londoners petitioned for the sale of the remaining episcopal lands. This again demonstrated, as one observer put it, the interest many people had in preventing the revival of episcopacy. If the King remained stubborn on the issue he would be blamed for the

---

65. Grignon to Brienne, London, Oct. 16, 1648, PRO, 31/3/88, fol. 158a, b.
66. "Helen" to ——, c. Oct. 5, 1648, Thomas Wagstaffe, *A Vindication of King Charles the Martyr, proving that his Majesty was the author of Eikon Basilike* (London, 1711), pp. 159–160.
67. *Merc. Prag.*, Sept. 26–Oct. 3, 1648, BM, E.465.
68. John Swinfen to Crewe, Oct. 13, 1648, PRO, State Papers, 16/516/98.

rupture of the treaty, which, in any case, was what his enemies were seeking.[69]

Colonel Edmund Harvey, who had acquired sufficient episcopal lands to earn the title "Lord Bishop of Fulham," led the protest. With engaging honesty he declared that if the bishops were not extinguished "root and branch," the purchasers of their lands would be left without any guarantee of enjoying their new properties. Supported by Blakiston and Pennington, he argued further that the state could sell the lands more quickly and at better rates if the purchasers were assured that episcopacy could never be restored.[70]

The importance of the issue of episcopal lands was further emphasized on October 30 when the Commons refused a request of the Lords that the dispute be temporarily shelved. The Lords had argued that bishops' lands were beginning to be a serious stumbling block to the successful conclusion of the negotiation and suggested that some other way be found to satisfy the purchasers as well as the King's conscience. In the Commons' debate that followed Harvey declared that the Lords' reasons were "hatched under a malignant planet." Edward Ashe suggested that the Commons carry on the negotiation without further reference to the Lords,[71] while the more moderate John Crewe warned against creating the impression among the general public "that there is too much eye upon their lands."[72]

Irish land was also an issue of some importance in the negotiations. Charles, despite outward concessions, still regarded Ireland as one of his few remaining sources of strength, an asset that gave him a real if tenuous bargaining position. The Irish Adventurers in London and Parliament were equally determined that Parliament should be given a free hand in any settlement in that country. By October 28, after Charles had made sweeping concessions to the parliamentarians, progress toward some kind of peace, barring the intervention of the army, seemed more possible. On that date, however, the Commons heard that the King's agent, Ormonde, was negotiating with the Irish, and they demanded a clear-cut repudiation of his activities.[73] As one observer put it, "the Houses are much staggered at the proceedings in Ireland and do almost give all their part for lost there."[74] The King's answer was evasive and, as the parliamentary commissioners pointed

69. Grignon to Brienne, London, Oct. 16, 1648, PRO, 31/3/88, fol. 158a, b.

70. *Merc. Prag.*, Oct. 3–10, 1648, BM, E.466.

71. *Ibid.*, Oct. 31–Nov. 14, 1648, BM. E.470–471.

72. Crewe to Swinfen, London, Nov. 6, 1648, PRO, State Papers, 16/516/108; Rushworth, *Hist. Coll.*, II, pt. iv, 1310.

73. *LJ*, X, 569.

74. Newsletter, London, Nov. 9, 1648, Clar.SPB 31, fol. 290a.

out, could be interpreted as a "countenancing and approving of those proceedings . . . "[75] That the parliamentary suspicions were justified is demonstrated by Charles's letter to Ormonde on October 28 in which he assured him that his concessions regarding Ireland "will come to nothing."[76]

By mid-October it was clear that the extreme radicals in the Commons were more than ever determined to bring the King to trial. On October 10 Cornelius Holland, Thomas Hoyle, and John Wilde brought in petitions against any settlement with the King and called for justice upon all delinquents "from the highest to the lowest without exception."[77] Moderate opposition to the petitions was countered by radicals like Venn, Harvey, Hoyle, and Weaver, who are said to have argued that, since the blood of the people had been shed, some recompense would be required. This group also urged that more names be added to the list of the seven delinquents already exempted from pardon. Dennis Bond declared that he hoped "to see the day when we may have power to hang the greatest lord of them all (if he deserve it) without trial by his peers; and doubt not that we shall have honest resolute judges to do it, notwithstanding Magna Carta."[78] Bond's boldness shocked the House, but he was supported by Colonel William White, who urged that all delinquents be tried by martial law. A moderate member struck a different note by his suggestion that members of Parliament and officers should be called to render account for all public moneys received and sequestered. That type of justice, he observed dryly, "would please the people better than the shedding of blood."[79]

Cromwell, meanwhile, had returned from Scotland, where he had left Argyle very much in control of affairs. Whether, as Guthry claims, he had actually obtained Argyle's approval of the trial of the King is uncertain.[80] His decision to remain near Pontefract, rather than to return to London, must have been made on political rather than on military grounds. Cromwell appears to have chosen Ireton to be the executor of a strategy, the main outlines of which he had himself determined.

75. *LJ*, X, 597.
76. Charles to Ormonde, Oct. 28, 1648, Thomas Carte, *Life of Ormonde*, 6 vols. (Oxford, 1851), V, 24, quoted in Gardiner, *GCW*, IV, 225.
77. *Merc. Prag.*, Oct. 10–17, 1648, BM, E.467.
78. *Ibid.*
79. *Ibid.*; Salvetti to the Secretary, London, Oct. 27, 1648, Salvetti Correspondence, Transcripts from archives at Florence of correspondence of Florentine ambassadors in England, 1616–1679, BM, Add. MS. 27,962L [hereafter cited as SC, BM, Add. MS. 27,962L], fol. 201b.
80. *Memoirs of Henry Guthry, Bishop of Dunkeld,* ed. George Crawford (Glasgow, 1748) [hereafter cited as Guthry, *Memoirs*], p. 298.

It was soon clear that the Treaty of Newport was to be further sabotaged and that religion was to be one of the main weapons. Cromwell had long since realized the importance of placating the Kirk, and he was now willing to push such a policy, even at the risk of being called a traitor to his own principles. The field of Preston was scarcely cold before the Commons, on August 29, had voted to establish Presbyterianism without toleration. Vane had strongly opposed this because he favored a religious settlement based on the Heads of the Proposals and because he recognized the move for what it was: a roadblock in the way of any agreement.[81] But despite the doubtful auspices, the policy won the approval of many genuine, if naïve, Presbyterians; their consequent defection from the Holles ranks seriously weakened that group. The King countered with an offer of toleration for tender consciences. This not only failed to impress the extreme radicals whose consciences, in any case, do not appear to have been unduly tender, but alienated an element among the moderates who associated such phrases with memories of secret arrangements between the King and their enemies. Now, once again, that tired old workhorse, the covenant, was to be pressed into service, Cromwell having apparently agreed that the Scots should not only make it a *sine qua non*, but that the King should be required to subscribe to it personally.[82]

Cromwellian stalwarts at Westminster had little difficulty in adjusting to the new order. They carried a vote in favor of Cromwell's actions in Scotland on October 17, and they demanded that the King must satisfy the Scots in the matter of the covenant before he could be restored.[83] The spectacle of the "Independents" demanding that the King take the covenant was electrifying. That party was described as urging it "strongly (though many of themselves and of the Army have not taken it) . . . "[84] "I presume you have heard of the gracious compliance between Cromwell, his holiness, and the reverend Presbyters of Scotland," wrote one sarcastic observer, "and such letters commendatory pass from them both to the Parliament here of one another that beget amazement in every one that hears of it; considering how small a Presbyterian he was not long since. But we can upon occasion change our shape."[85] The measure encountered no strong opposition in the House largely because the moderate leaders could oppose it

81. Gilbert Burnet, *Bishop Burnet's history of his own time*, ed. O. Airy, 2 vols. (Oxford, Clarendon Press, 1897–1902), I, 44.
82. Grignon to Brienne, London, Oct. 9, 1648, PRO, 31/3/88, fol. 151b; Salvetti to Gondi, Oct. 20, 1648, SC, BM, Add. MS. 27,962L, fol. 201b.
83. Grignon to Brienne, London, Oct. 26, 1648, PRO, 31/3/89, fol. 4a, b.
84. Pulford to Denman, Oct. 27, 1648, Clar.SPB 31, fol. 287a.
85. Burgoyne to Verney, Oct. 19, 1648, Verney MSS. BM, M,636/9.

publicly only at the risk of alienating the genuine Presbyterians among their followers.

Cromwell paid a definite price for his policy of expediency. Vane was not alone in his resentment; he and others were sharply critical of Cromwell's role in the agreement with the Scots. Cromwell's letter of November 6 indicates his sensitivity to this criticism. Arguing that the King could less easily "tyrannise" if Presbyterianism were established, he added a word of warning to Vane: that he had gone too far toward the moderates and must make "an honorable retreat." He also protested against the accusation that he and an associate had "turned Presbyterians." In a pointed allusion to the King, he called upon Vane and his friends to "keep their hearts and hands from him, against whom God hath so witnessed . . . "[86]

Whatever disagreement existed over the covenant, there was general agreement at Westminster that there should be no toleration of Anglicanism or Catholicism. The House resolved on October 27 to proscribe that "abominable idol," the Mass, and voted against any special provision for the use of the *Book of Common Prayer,* even in the King's chapel, declaring that the King's answers on the covenant and the bishops' lands were unsatisfactory.[87] A committee consisting of a majority of moderates and headed by the Presbyterian, Sir Robert Harley, was appointed to consider how the covenant "may be so framed" as to be presented to the King and taken by him.[88]

Meanwhile, the division in the army between those officers who wanted some kind of settlement with Charles and the Cromwellians who demanded his trial and, by implication, his execution had deepened swiftly. On October 18 Ireton forwarded a petition to Fairfax. Justice must be done on those who had shed "innocent blood," it demanded; the same faults should have the same punishment "in the person of a King or Lord as in the person of the poorest commoner." Anyone who so much as spoke in favor of the King before he had been "acquitted of the guilt of shedding innocent blood" should be treated as a traitor.[89]

On November 10 Ireton presented the army remonstrance to the

86. Cromwell to Colonel Robert Hammond, Knottingley, Nov. 6, 1648, Abbott, *Writings and Speeches,* I, 677. David Underdown argues, partly on the basis of this letter, that Cromwell was still ready to come to an agreement with the King and that the real political leadership at this time was in Ireton's hands. This interpretation is not only inherently improbable, but is unsupported by firm evidence and—to my mind—is contradicted by Cromwell's own letters.

87. *CJ,* VI, 62.

88. *Ibid.* Gardiner attributes this policy to "the Presbyterian majority." (*GCW,* IV, 222.) It would be closer to the truth to say that it was effected by a coalition of Cromwellian radicals and genuine Presbyterians of the Harley type.

89. Whitelocke, "Annals," BM, Add. MS. 37,344, fol. 203b.

council of officers, but ran into strong opposition from Fairfax who, despite pressure in the form of petitions from the regiments of Fleet-wood, Whalley, and Barkstead, continued to insist on a parliamentary settlement.[90] Nor was he by any means isolated in his defense of con-stitutionalism. With but six dissenting, the council voted to accept the results of the treaty.[91]

The remonstrance demonstrated once again that the radicals were at least as disturbed by the prospect of a hostile House of Commons after a peace settlement as by a restored Charles I. Ireton frankly ad-mitted that the popular support that the King would enjoy after a settlement would make it necessary to keep the army in existence. But the very cost of maintaining such an army would necessarily increase the unpopularity of the parliamentarians and afford the King greater opportunities of exploiting the differences among them. Thus, even without new elections, he would easily be able to win the support of the majority of the Long Parliament. If Parliament were dissolved and a new Parliament elected, Charles would still have a majority at his disposal through royal influence in the smaller boroughs, and be-cause each party would want to have the royal favor. He would thus be free to take revenge upon his former enemies.[92] What Ireton failed to point out was that in any reconstituted Parliament the Cromwel-lians, who were now a splinter group of what had always been a minority party, would be hopelessly outnumbered even without royal influence. The point had been emphasized in a pamphlet written by a Cromwellian in mid-October, which frankly admitted that "every-where the greater party are for the King," in cities as in villages. But, he argued, "it is not *vox* but *salus populi* that is the supreme law . . . If the common votes of the giddy multitude must rule the whole how quickly would their own interest, peace and safety be dashed and broken?" The "scum of the people," he declared, had always been against the Parliament.[93] The sword was the only hope of the Crom-wellians; they frankly recognized the fact. The King, concluded the framers of the remonstrance, a trifle inconsequentially, was a traitor in the highest degree and ought to be punished accordingly.[94]

An event had taken place, meanwhile, that deepened the distrust long felt by Lilburne and his friends toward the Cromwellians: the

90. Gardiner, *GCW*, IV, 237.

91. *Ibid.*

92. *A Remonstrance of Lord Fairfax and of the General Council of Officers held at St. Albans. Presented to the Commons in Parliament, 20 Nov.* (London, 1648), BM, E.473(11), pp. 37–47.

93. *Salus Populi, Solus Rex, the People's Safety is the sole Soveraignty; or, the Royalist out-reasoned* (London, 1648), BM, E.467(39), quoted in Brailsford, *Level-lers,* pp. 345–346, n. 8.

94. *Remonstrance,* p. 62.

murder on October 29 of Colonel Thomas Rainsborough. The circumstances of his death were mysterious and aroused considerable suspicion at the time.[95] By November 10 there was widespread skepticism in London in the face of the official—and apparently true—story that Rainsborough had been murdered by royalists from the garrison at Pontefract.[96] "There is great doubt if the aforesaid garrison is the reason for Rainsborough's death," wrote one Dutch observer.[97] Some of the Levellers even suspected that Rainsborough's demise was not unwelcome to the Cromwellians;[98] four months later they made their suspicions public. Rainsborough, they declared, had been appointed commander at Pontefract against his will and had gone there with great reluctance and foreboding. "But that which gives greatest cause of grief and suspect to his friends," they charged, was "that his brother receives no furtherance, but rather, all discouragement that may be, in searching after, and prosecuting the causes of that so bloody and inhumane a butchery."[99] That the murder was the work of royalists may have appeared improbable in view of the fact that Rainsborough, by giving his support to Colonel Jubbes's proposals, had placed himself once again in opposition to Cromwell. It was in the interests of the royalists to nurture the potential hostility between the two officers rather than to eliminate it.

On the other hand, relations between Lilburne and Cromwell appear at this point to have been reasonably good. About the time of Rainsborough's murder, Lilburne had sent a Mr. Hunt to Cromwell at Pontefract, probably to sound him out as to his support for Leveller policy; Cromwell, in reply, had proposed that the Levellers meet with his supporters to work out a common program.[100]

The first meeting which took place early in November at the Nagshead Tavern in London, was stormy. The Cromwellians, who probably included Commons members like Cornelius Holland, Thomas Scott, and Thomas Chaloner, were enraged to discover that Lilburne was completely opposed to their simple and straightforward solution of the country's problems: the purging of Parliament and the execution of the King. But with characteristic boldness, Lilburne told them that since the army had already cheated them a year previously, they had

---

95. H. Ross Williamson, *Historical Whodunits* (New York, Macmillan, 1956), pp. 142–163; Gregg, *Free-born John*, pp. 247–248.

96. —— to Joachimi, Nov. 10, 1648, DT, BM, Add. MS. 17,677(T), fol. 270a, b.

97. Secretary to Joachimi, Nov. 17, 1648, DT, BM, Add. MS. 17,677(T), fols. 281a, 282a; —— to Joachimi, Nov. 17, 1648, DT, BM, Add. MS. 17,677(T), fols. 284b–285a.

98. Gregg, *Free-born John*, p. 247.

99. John Lilburne, Richard Overton, and Thomas Prince, "Second Part of England's New Chains Discovered," in *Leveller Tracts*, ed. Haller and Davies, p. 181.

100. Brailsford, *Levellers*, pp. 361–362.

no more reason to trust them than anyone else. Even if the King and Parliament were as bad as the Cromwellians painted them, it was in the interests of the Levellers to "keep up one tyrant to balance another."[101] The prospect of being frustrated, not by parliamentary moderates or royalists, but by the man who had so often been depicted as the leader of a lunatic fringe must have maddened the Cromwellians. But Lilburne's position was consistent, politically adroit, and even statesmanlike. The years of poring over the tower records and the association with men like Sir Lewis Dyve, Sir John Maynard, and Judge Jenkins had converted him into something of a constitutional theorist. He had long since learned to fear the tyranny of Parliament as much as the tyranny of the King, and his demand for a written constitution, which could control both, foreshadowed the attitudes of the American revolutionaries a century later. At the same time he was concerned that this not be the work of a mere faction. Lilburne was anxious to keep open the door to the parliamentary moderates and continued to envisage an agreement of the people that would be the product of a consensus of all major groups. Ireton and his supporters, on the other hand, looked not to a meeting of minds, but to an expulsion of bodies from Parliament, as the first step toward a solution. The tensions generated at the first meeting at the Nagshead Tavern were all but disastrous, but the Cromwellians knew that they needed Lilburne and they agreed to hold another meeting at the same place on November 15.

At the second meeting Ireton was ready to compromise. The two groups agreed that a kind of constituent convention should be called in order to draw up an agreement of the people; that Parliament should not be dissolved immediately; and that Ireton's remonstrance should be modified to include points raised in the Large Petition of the Levellers of September 1648. Ireton revised the remonstrance accordingly and made ready to persuade the council of officers to support it.

The group of officers around Fairfax were, meanwhile, preparing their final offer to Charles, which was, in the circumstances, eminently reasonable. In essence it envisaged an alliance between Charles and the council of officers against the Long Parliament, the Cromwellian radicals, and the Levellers. No mention was made of religion; nor was there any demand that Charles abandon his veto on parliamentary legislation, and only five royalists were to be exempted from pardon. A date was to be fixed for the dissolution of the Long Parliament, and the control of the militia was to be placed in the hands of a Council of

101. John Lilburne, "Legal Fundamental Liberties," in *Leveller Tracts,* ed. Haller and Davies, p. 416.

State. The great officers of the Crown were to be named by Parliament for the next ten years, but this prerogative was to revert to the Crown at the end of that time. Biennial Parliaments were to be established and the army was to be retained, at least until two months had elapsed after the calling of the first Parliament.[102]

When Charles considered this proposal, his mind must have gone back to August 1647 when Cromwell and Ireton had advised him to accept the army proposals in preference to Parliament's propositions. He knew that to come to an agreement with Fairfax was, at least temporarily, to raise the army once again above Parliament and thereby to lose its support. Whatever the King's motives, he rejected this last chance to avoid the fate that Ireton was preparing for him. In his reply, read in the council of officers on November 18, Charles ignored the proposal for a Council of State and contented himself with assuring the officers that some of their ideas would be submitted to Parliament. Fairfax must have marveled at the casual manner in which Charles had dismissed his offer and decided to discontinue his efforts. Ireton's remonstrance was accepted by the council with only two dissenting votes. Two days later Colonel Isaac Ewer presented the ominous document to the assembled Commons at Westminster. Ireton, who had been beset by the twin dangers of Fairfax and Lilburne, had now cleared one obstacle and was well on his way to negotiating the second.

Did Cromwell play a decisive role in those few critical days? Historians have heretofore assumed that he remained near Pontefract until just before Pride's Purge. But there is evidence that he was present at St. Albans between November 15 and 18. *Mercurius Pragmaticus* reported that Cromwell had arrived at St. Albans on November 15 and had been present at the council of officers on the following day. He had indeed "so shuffled and cut the cards since he came into the General Council, that the tide is turned with those that seemed friends unto the treaty, that they all run now upon the Levelling strain . . . "[103] Joachimi's informant wrote on November 17 that he had it on good authority that Cromwell had been present at the council of officers at St. Albans, presumably on the previous day.[104] Also

102. Gardiner, *GCW*, IV, 241–242.
103. *Merc. Prag.*, Nov. 14–21, 1648, BM, E.472.
104. BM, Add. MS. 17,677(B), fol. 281b; see also Nathan Drake, *Journal of the . . . sieges of Pontefract Castle*, ed. W. H. D. Longstaffe (Surtees Society, XXXVII, pt. ii, 1861), p. 102; Thomas Carte, *Ormonde Papers, a collection of original letters and papers concerning affairs of England, 1641–1660, found among the Duke of Ormonde's papers*, ed. Thomas Carte, 2 vols. (London, 1739), I, 192–193; newsletter London, Nov. 17, 1648, RT, PRO, 31/9/47, fol. 221.

on November 17 Ireton wrote a letter to the King's jailer Hammond, the tone of which indicated that some kind of shift in the balance of power in the council of officers had already taken place. Warning Hammond against permitting "that person" to escape, he intimated that within a few days Fairfax and the whole army would be united against the King.[105] A less likely report of November 23 stated that Cromwell had been in Windsor the day before and had taken with him the assurance that officers under him, with a few exceptions, supported the remonstrance.[106]

Since two of Cromwell's letters from Knottingley are dated November 15 and 20, it is quite possible that he could have left Knottingley on November 15 and have been present in the council and have returned in time to write a letter on November 20. Some of Cromwell's statements in his letter to Fairfax of November 20 indicate, moreover, that he may have been at army headquarters a short time before. He told Fairfax that he found "a very great sense in the officers of the regiments of the sufferings and the ruin of this poor Kingdom, and in them all a very great zeal to have impartial justice done upon offenders . . . " Again, in a letter to the Committee for Compounding written on the same day, Cromwell complained of the lenient treatment of royalists: "I find a sense among the officers concerning such things as these, even to amazement . . . "[107]

The remonstrance put the House of Commons into "a very sad confusion." Cromwellian radicals like Wentworth, Scott, and Holland supported the army strongly, but Maynard and Prynne attacked the document. One opponent of the army declared that it was unbecoming that the Commons should "be proscribed, regulated and baffled by a Council of petty sectaries in arms."[108] Another urged that the treaty be pursued in spite of the army declarations. Sir Ralph Assheton's demand that the doors be locked and that each member swear whether or not he had anything to do with the remonstrance was opposed by "the Levelling faction" and was defeated.[109] The Cromwellian radicals were strong enough to force postponement of further debate on the measure for one week, by which time complete agreement with Lilburne should have been reached and the army have occupied London. They would then "impeach and expel divers Members . . . they will have no

---

105. Ireton, *et al.* to Hammond, Nov. 17, 1648, *Letters between Hammond and the Committee at Derby House . . . relating to King Charles I while he was confined at Carisbrooke Castle,* ed. T. Birch (London, 1764), p. 87, quoted in Gardiner, *GCW,* IV, 243–244.

106. Newsletter, London, Clar.SPB 31, fol. 313a.

107. Abbott, *Writings and Speeches,* I, 690–692.

108. *Merc. Prag.,* Nov. 21–28, 1648, BM, E.473.

109. *Mercurius Elencticus,* Nov. 22–29, 1648, BM, E.473.

more Lords, and [will] level every man to themselves . . ."[110] Most of the members, anxious to retain their seats, remained silent.[111]

At Newport, meanwhile, the treaty negotiations were continuing. The commissioners, ignorant of an army order to Hammond "to clap up the King," were optimistic in their reports.[112] Postponement of the debate on the remonstrance, although it gave the army time to occupy London, also afforded an opportunity to complete the treaty. Accordingly, moderates and like-minded radicals, aware that it would be more difficult for the army to purge Parliament after a settlement had been reached, worked desperately to bring the negotiation to a successful conclusion.[113]

The policy expressed by the remonstrance split the radicals. Many of them balked at the idea of a purge of the House and the trial of the King. The strength of the combined forces of the moderates and dissident radicals can be seen in the divisions in the House before the final purge. They carried a resolution to end the negotiations on November 27 by ninety-four votes to sixty.[114]

Both parties were now making frantic efforts to recruit as much support as possible. The extreme radicals, anxious to avoid the future accusation that their authority rested on force alone, tried desperately to carry matters by majority vote.[115] But the combination of moderates and anti-Cromwellian radicals was too much for them. Although this coalition carried a resolution on November 29 to condemn the army for its imprisonment of the King,[116] it was soon brutally clear that—in Bismarckian language—the issues of the day were not to be decided by resolutions and majority votes.

At Windsor Ireton had just concluded an agreement with Lilburne that cleared the way for the army's march on London. Lilburne, Wildman, and two associates had gone to Windsor on November 27 to urge the officers to accept a modified Agreement of the People as the only safeguard against either royal or military despotism. By November 28 Lilburne felt it necessary to warn Ireton that if he marched on London without a prior agreement with the Levellers, Lilburne would mobilize all his supporters to resist him.[117] That night Colonel Harrison conferred with Lilburne and Wildman, and although he admitted

110. Newsletter, London, Nov. 20, 1648, Clar.SPB 31, fol. 312a.
111. Whitelocke, "Annals," BM, Add. MS. 37,344, fol. 227a.
112. Newsletter, London, Nov. 23, 1648, Clar.SPB 31, fol. 313a.
113. Grignon to Brienne, London, Nov. 23, 1648, PRO, 31/3/89, fol. 25b.
114. Arthur Annesley and either Francis or Sir Gilbert Gerard were tellers for the majority, and Ludlow and R. Goodwin for the minority. (*CJ*, VI, 86.)
115. Grignon to Brienne, London, Nov. 27, 1648, PRO, 31/3/89, fol. 27a.
116. Whitelocke, "Annals," BM, Add. MS. 37,344, fol. 230a.
117. *Leveller Tracts*, ed. Haller and Davies, p. 418.

that the army planned to "destroy the King" and to "root up" Parliament, he promised that the generals and cooperative members of Parliament would then implement the Agreement of the People. Lilburne refused, however, to accept this and again threatened a rising in London. Harrison countered with the argument that both army and Levellers would be destroyed should the treaty be approved, because the inevitable result would be the disbanding of the army, "so that you will be destroyed as well as we."[118]

Agreement was finally reached on a compromise plan, reminiscent of the earlier one of Colonel Jubbes: a council of sixteen would be set up that would be, in effect, a coalition of parliamentary Cromwellians, army representatives, Independents, and Levellers, to which Lilburne, at least, was willing to add four members of the "Presbyterian party." This group was to draw up the Agreement of the People to which all parties would submit. According to Lilburne, Ireton sent word that he heartily approved of the proposal. Lilburne returned to London, confident that no drastic steps would be taken by the army until the Agreement of the People had been ratified. He was soon to discover that Ireton did not intend to be impeded by the Levellers. On November 30 the long-expected blow fell. The army instructed Parliament to exclude "all such corrupt and apostasised members as have obstructed justice . . . "[119] The Commons, however, refused to bow, and when the emboldened Cromwellians attempted to pass a resolution to debate the remonstrance they were crushed by a combination of moderates and radicals.[120]

On December 1 Holles, once again the leader of the moderates, defied the army and presented the results of the treaty negotiations to the Commons. Formal debate on the King's answer was postponed, but Nathaniel Fiennes provided the House with an unexpected defense of the King's position on religion. After upholding the King's refusal to consent to the punishment of former royalists except by due process of law, Fiennes turned to the subject of bishops. Pointing out that their reinstatement would require the consent of Parliament after a three-year period, Fiennes argued—perhaps not too cogently—that this amounted to "putting them down forever." The radicals were said to have been "extremely enraged at the carriage of their quondam brother . . ."[121]

If the radicals had lost Fiennes, they had temporarily won back

118. *Ibid.*, p. 419.
119. Whitelocke, "Annals," BM, Add. MS. 37,344, fol. 230b.
120. *CJ*, VI, 91; Grignon to Brienne, London, Nov. 30, 1648, PRO, 31/3/89, fol. 32a. The resolution was defeated by 125 votes to 58. (*CJ*, VI, 91).
121. Newsletter, London, Dec. 4, 1648, Clar.SPB 34, fol. 7b; *Merc. Prag.*, Dec. 5–12, 1648, BM, E.476.

Vane, whose changes of front late in 1648 present some problems to the historian. He had consistently opposed Cromwell since the vote of no addresses and, according to Edward Walker, had been favorably impressed by the King during the discussions at Newport. On one occasion he told Walker that he had always thought of the King as a weak person, and the opinion had been shared by the other commissioners, "but now they found him far otherwise, and that he was a person of great parts and abilities."[122] But toward the end of the discussions, Vane intimated to Walker that the time for such things was past and that he and his friends "must consider their own securities."[123]

It seems clear that Vane was against both the purge of Parliament and the execution of the King. At his trial in 1662 he asserted that he had been so strongly opposed to these acts that he had refused to attend Parliament for a ten-week period from December 3, 1648, to mid-February 1649.[124] Vane may have hoped to avoid the humiliation of Parliament and the establishment of a military dictatorship by reverting to the position that had been attributed to him as far back as July 1644: that of a republican. It is possible to view his actions in the Commons on December 2 as an attempt to unite the House behind a program he had advocated in 1644: the deposition of the King and the establishment of a republic. Whether that republic would have been to the liking of Lilburne is another question; Vane's thinking on the subject tended to be oligarchic rather than democratic.

The Commons should debate the King's last answer, he declared, because the debate would reveal "who are the King's party in the House, and who are for the people." To this, one member replied—with a thrust at the two Vanes, who were believed to have done well financially during the wars—that the House should be rather divided between those who favored a settlement and those who opposed it. Those who wanted peace, he declared, were the same people who had lost money during the wars, while those who had profited opposed peace. He then moved that those who had gained contribute to those

122. Sir Edward Walker, *Historical Discourses upon Several Occasions* (London, 1705), p. 319.
123. *Ibid.* While it is true that Vane was regarded in some quarters as strongly opposed to a treaty in the summer of 1648 and in league with Cromwell, I cannot accept Dr. Violet Rowe's view that he was in any sense "the spokesman for Cromwell and the army" in that year. (See Violet Rowe, *Sir Henry Vane the Younger* [London, Athlone Press, 1970], p. 114.) The preponderant weight of evidence indicates that the breach between the two men, which began in December 1647, was not healed before Pride's Purge and may even have been widened by that act.
124. William Cobbett, Thomas B. Howell, and Thomas J Howell, *Collection of state trials and proceedings for high treason and other crimes*, 34 vols. (London, 1809–1828), XXX, 164. Gardiner wrote that Vane approved of the purge, but gave no supporting evidence and apparently overlooked Vane's own statement. (*GCW*, IV, 287.)

who had lost. After Wentworth had taken up the fight for the radicals, the debate ended with William Prynne's suggestion that all consideration of the King's answer be postponed until they were a free Parliament, an allusion to the fact that the army had now occupied London.[125]

As late as December 4 there were those in London who still hoped that Parliament might make (or be allowed to make) some kind of settlement. The commissioners, who had returned from the Isle of Wight, had been so favorably disposed toward the King, Vane excepted, that the army had reportedly attempted to kidnap them on the way to London. They had eluded their would-be captors by travelling "by night through by-ways."[126]

Once again on December 4 and 5 the moderate-radical coalition defied the army by passing a resolution by 136 votes to 102 stating that the removal of the King from Carisbrooke Castle had been without the consent of the House.[127] Finally, after the all-night session had worn on into the morning of December 5, the fateful division took place. The Commons declared by 129 votes to 83 that the King's answers were "a ground for the House to proceed upon for the settlement of the peace of the kingdom."[128] At Whitehall, meanwhile, Ireton was discussing with officers and some members whether the House should be completely dissolved, which he preferred, or merely purged. He was at last unwillingly persuaded to take the latter course.[129]

On the morning of December 6 the army moved to crush the parliamentary majority. Colonel Thomas Pride, who still had fresh memories of March 1647, when at the behest of Holles he had knelt at the bar of the House, was now in a position to settle old scores. Assisted by Lord Grey of Groby and armed with a list of those members to be arrested or barred from entry to the Commons, Pride stood at the door and carried out his orders with promptness and dispatch. Forty-one members were arrested and imprisoned for varying lengths of time; 143 members were excluded.[130] The reaction of those members who were permitted to enter the Commons indicated that the tradition of parliamentary privilege was strong enough to make even this group

125. *Merc. Prag.,* Dec. 5–12, 1648, BM, E.476.

126. Newsletter, London, Clar.SPB 34, fol. 7b.

127. Sir R. Pye and Sir S. Luke and John Ashe and Thomas Chaloner were tellers for the majority and the minority, respectively. (*CJ,* VI, 93.)

128. *Ibid.* Lord Cranborne and Ralph Assheton and John Lisle and Mr. Stephens were tellers for the majority and the minority, respectively.

129. John Lilburne, "Legal Fundamental Liberties," in *Leveller Tracts,* ed. Haller and Davies, pp. 421–422; Gardiner, *GCW,* IV, 269.

130. See David Underdown, *Pride's Purge* (Oxford, Clarendon Press, 1971). I am very grateful to Professor Underdown for permitting me to read portions of his book in manuscript.

unreliable from Cromwell's point of view. Some were indeed excluded on December 7 for their opposition to the purge of the previous day.[131] When the remnant of the Commons heard that some of the members were under arrest, they ordered the sergeant at arms to go to the captain of the guard and release them. On his return the sergeant informed the Commons that the captain had been ordered to secure the members, which "he was to obey before any other command."[132]

Almost exactly seven years before, in January 1642, another historic command had been issued. On that occasion, in direct opposition to the King, London had provided a guard for Parliament and instructions had been issued to those soldiers not to fail in their duty "upon any command . . . whatever, without further command of Parliament." In the contrast between these two orders the course of the Revolution is epitomized.

On the evening of December 6 Cromwell rode into Westminster. After listening to an account of the events of the morning, he remarked that, although he had not been told of the plan, he was pleased with what had been done and would "endeavour to maintain it."[133] Early the next morning, arm in arm with Henry Marten, the member for Huntingdon entered the House of Commons and took his seat.

131. Newsletter, London, Dec. 10, 1648, RT, PRO, 31/9/47, fols. 236–237.
132. Rushworth, *Hist. Coll.,* II, pt. iv, 1353.
133. Ludlow, *Memoirs,* pp. 211–212.

Conclusion

One of the problems this work set out to explore related to the legitimacy of the term "party" to describe the groups into which the Long Parliament was divided. Since the work of L. B. Namier, the historian has been properly chary of using this word loosely. But with all due respect to the memory of the historian whose pioneer work provided a pattern for others to follow, there now seems every justification for retaining a word that contemporaries had no hesitation in using.

The parties in the Long Parliament lacked the coherence and discipline of their modern counterparts, but, up to September 1647 at least, they were quite recognizable formations. With the rise of the Levellers, the distinction between the older parties became increasingly blurred. In 1648, when both radicals and moderates were equally threatened by resurgent royalists and discontented Levellers, the common danger appears to have had the effect of almost welding the two groups together. But between December 1643 and August 1647 there was a clear-cut party conflict between the moderates led by Holles and Stapleton and the radicals under Vane and St. John.

Pym had held the balance between the extremes of war and peace parties. He was able to gain the support of a substantial group of members who were not irrevocably committed in either direction, and to which J. H. Hexter has given the name "middle party." On Pym's death the "middle party" disappeared, and, despite the power and prestige of the Earl of Essex, Vane and St. John seized the initiative and never really lost it.

The fall of the Earl of Essex and the "Accomodation Order" in September 1644 set the stage for the Self-Denying Ordinance, which, in turn, finally ended the preponderant influence of the moderates in the army. After Uxbridge the radicals further consolidated their position by a judicious selection of officers for the New Model. With Naseby won, they were ready to attempt the impeachment of Holles and to carry out new elections, by which they hoped to assure themselves of a comfortable majority in the Commons. At the end of 1645, despite the growing opposition of the Scots and the moderate Londoners, they felt confident enough to ignore the King's peace overtures. By December 1646, however, the moderates, supported by many of the "recruiters," commanded overwhelming voting strength, and the radicals, after apparently considering the use of the army to overawe their political rivals, in the end thought better of it. By early 1647, however, the first signs of internal division appeared in the radical party, which up to that point had demonstrated remarkable cohesion.

The radicals divided into three sections. The first group favored some kind of arrangement with the King in order to counter the Holles policy of overtures to the Prince of Wales; the second were prepared to cooperate with Holles in his policy; the third, and probably the most numerous, separated completely under the leadership of Marten. The radicals never really regained their equilibrium, and Cromwell's policies were to put further strains on party unity. As early as June 1647 there were signs that St. John resented the emergence of Cromwell and Ireton as policy makers, and by the end of the year, Vane had broken with the lieutenant general.

From mid-1647 onward, the radicals had many serious difficulties, both from an increasing number of external enemies and from internal dissension. They had lost their revolutionary élan and were primarily concerned with self-preservation in an increasingly hostile world. Fear of the Levellers brought on a disposition to forget old differences and to make common cause with the moderates. In the autumn of 1647 Cromwell shuttled back and forth between moderates and Levellers in an effort to find a winning combination. Finally, like a man with a tiger by the ears, he decided that he must continue to ride the beast. The vote of no addresses was the result.

The period from January to June 1648 must be accounted the most critical of Cromwell's career. He could rely only on a small group of extreme radicals in the Commons, and his enemies were rapidly gaining strength. Marten and his followers had made common cause with the moderates against him, and Vane led a revolt within his own party. In an effort to solve his problems he executed a bewildering succession of policy shifts: at one moment the trial of the King seemed imminent; at another the purging of the Commons seemed possible. There was talk of renewed negotiations with the King and of offering the crown to the Prince of Wales or the Duke of York. The outbreak of war in Wales proved to be the catalyst, and before Cromwell took his forces west he had reaffirmed the extremist policy toward the King. Even after Preston, Cromwell did not regain complete control of the Commons. Vane and William Pierrepont still preferred a conciliatory policy toward the King. The votes in the Commons just before the purge revealed that Cromwell could count on the support of only a small minority, despite the fact that many moderates were absent from the House. It was significant too that the opposition included many who had been strong supporters of Cromwell in previous years.

By the time of the purge the old radical party had disintegrated. Vane momentarily rejoined the radical fold, but neither he nor St. John supported Cromwell's policy. Pierrepont was ejected with the rest on December 6. Cromwell was left in the Commons with his officers and a tiny remnant of his former supporters. The radical party, as it had existed in 1644, was no more.

The disintegration of the radical party structure was paralleled by increasing confusion concerning political aims. In the first years of the period covered by this study the party really deserved the name "radical," but by the end of 1648 many of the erstwhile firebrands had grown considerably more conservative. In 1644 they were generally reported to be republican in their objectives or, at the very least, to be aiming at the desposition of Charles I. In the early years, too, they were hostile to the House of Lords and were inclined to make thinly veiled threats to abolish that branch of Parliament. Moreover, they allied themselves with the "meaner sort" in the county committees and followed what was regarded as a popular, if not demogogic, policy both in politics and religion. As time passed, however, they became aware that their republican ideas were not acceptable to the vast majority of Englishmen. Those who did share them, they discovered, were not content with a republican oligarchy run by the "grandees" of the parliamentary party, but demanded a more rational and more democratic constitution than the "silken Independents" found palatable. The result was a gradual retreat from the republicanism of 1644 to the relatively conservative position represented by the Heads of the Proposals of 1647. In the light of this change, the sense of betrayal evident in much Leveller writing is understandable.

The radicals were trapped by their own early extremism, which was enough to alienate the moderate parliamentarians, and even many of the recruiters. When the Vane-St. John group recoiled from the logical extension of their own policies as exemplified by the Levellers, they were virtually isolated. If they were a minority in the Long Parliament, what would their position be in a reconstituted Parliament after a peace settlement? Clearly this thought gave the radical leaders some very uncomfortable moments. As early as the spring of 1645 they were beginning to realize this, as is indicated by the character of the proposals they made to the King at that time. Their demand for partisan rather than parliamentary control of the armed forces, and by implication the key positions of power in the state, was to be repeated late in 1645 and again in the autumn of 1646 before it was incorporated in the better-known Heads of the Proposals in the summer of 1647.

When it suited them, the Vane-St. John group were quite willing to use religion, and indeed the covenant, as a weapon against their enemies. In the summer of 1644, for instance, they did not hesitate to press the covenant on the Lords, to order Roger Williams' pamphlet on toleration to be burned, and to arrest a number of Anabaptists. Nor does there appear to have been a division along the usual party lines over the issue of toleration. Moderates like D'Ewes, for example, opposed the persecution of dissenters. This is not to say that there was complete agreement between the two parties over toleration, but simply that it was not the great issue dividing them.

The radicals could sometimes work up considerable enthusiasm for Presbyterianism. Their connection with Argyle, and through him with the Kirk, was a striking illustration of the old adage that politics makes strange bedfellows. In the spring of 1648, when this link was vital, the Commons assumed a notably Presbyterian tone. Later, in the autumn of 1648, it was Cromwell, according to report, who suggested that the Scots should require the King to take the covenant.

It would be unjust, however, to suggest that religion, and specifically liberty for "tender consciences," was nothing more than a tool of the radicals that they employed to further their own political aims. Vane and, despite his tergiversations, Cromwell himself were not men whose actions and influence are explicable solely in terms of expediency or hunger for power. Being human, they defy the historian's ready categories. They were complex personalities, deeply involved in a bitter and confused struggle for the highest stakes.

Although the moderates did not deserve the name "Presbyterian," they did include a number of committed Presbyterians who, precisely because of that fact, tended to be politically unreliable. When the King's offer via Murray arrived in London in October 1646, it was partly an attempt to win the support of the parliamentary moderates for the eventual return of a limited episcopacy. The issue split the moderates, with the genuine Presbyterians siding with the radicals and opposing acceptance of the offer. Once again, in the summer and autumn of 1648, the strong "Presbyterian" policy adopted by Cromwell and his followers in the Commons had the effect of weakening the moderates, by attracting to the radicals the support of this element.

The moderates were hampered throughout the period by the lack of a positive program of action. The fact that they continued to sit in Parliament made them traitors in the eyes of royalists; on the other hand, their periodic attempts to bring about peace were regarded as treasonable by those who had thrown themselves wholeheartedly into the fight and for whom there was no turning back. The fall of the Earl of Essex in 1644 was a disastrous blow because it forced the moderates into the arms of the Scots. An outward enthusiasm for Presbyterianism was henceforth a minimal requirement if the support of the Kirk was to be retained. Thus, despite the fact that many moderates would have accepted a limited episcopacy, they became irrevocably identified with a form of Christianity that was anathema to Charles I. Accordingly, they incurred the enmity of the radicals and their supporters without having gained either the confidence or support of the King.

By early 1647 Holles had not only lost interest in dealing with Charles, but apparently wanted to replace him with his eldest son. In this, Holles was following a more statesmanlike line of action than he has usually been given credit for, and for a time he appears to have gained the support of London, the Argyle Scots, and a number of radicals. The army crisis, and perhaps the unwillingness of the Prince himself to cooperate, ended the possibility of this type of restoration. When Cromwell, on whom Holles was forced to rely for support in the army crisis, decided to throw in his lot with the soldiers, the moderates could only bow to the inevitable.

By July 1647 the Leveller threat was effecting a kind of merger of the two older parties in Parliament, and Holles may even have lent support to the type of settlement envisaged by Cromwell and Ireton, in the hope that Parliament rather than the army would emerge supreme. This hope faded, and the take-over of Parliament by the moderates, after the flight of the radicals to the army, was nullified by the occupation of London and the consequent departure of the eleven members in August.

The disposition of the moderates to make common cause with Cromwell became evident once again in September and October 1647. After the vote of no addresses, however, they showed an increasing tendency to ally themselves with Marten and Lilburne in order to avoid the possibility of their own wholesale expulsion from the House. This connection was maintained until August 1648, when the attempt to gain Lilburne's support for the impeachment of Cromwell failed. Once again in the autumn of 1648, when Lilburne's relations with the army leaders became strained, there were indications of some friendliness between Levellers and parliamentary moderates. Maynard attempted to cement this relationship, but after Holles' return to the Commons in mid-August, little appears to have been done. The initiative, indeed, appears to have come thereafter from Lilburne, who would have permitted moderates to assist in drafting the second Agreement of the People. If the moderate leaders had reciprocated by espousing all or part of the Leveller program—by that time considerably more conservative than it had been in 1647—a significant political force might have emerged. But Holles, like Cromwell, was apparently incapable of extending his beloved principles of liberty beyond the narrow confines of his own class.

By the spring of 1647 a new parliamentary faction led by Henry Marten had appeared. It was soon to be a factor of some importance in the politics of the Long Parliament. Marten seems to have worked closely with Lilburne until the autumn of 1647, when the latter's overtures to the King resulted in a temporary estrangement. By the spring of 1648, however, they were again on good terms, and Marten's willingness to cooperate with the parliamentary moderates probably resulted from the growing friendship between Lilburne and Maynard in the Tower. But Lilburne's attempt to work out a modus vivendi with the King and the parliamentary moderates provoked a division within the ranks. By the autumn of 1648 Marten, who, in early 1648 had actually given a qualified approval to Charles's restoration, had reverted to his old position. His distance from Lilburne was indicated by the fact that, on the morning of December 7, he entered the House of Commons on the arm of Cromwell.

The last years of the Long Parliament were dominated by the personality of one of its members: Oliver Cromwell. His precise role in the purge itself remains obscure, but it is safe to say that his original intention was that Parliament should be completely dissolved and that the decision to limit the action was Ireton's. The split among Cromwell's old comrades, which had been evident as much as a year earlier, became even more obvious. Prominent in the list of those purged were the names of many men who had once been counted among the "honest party." It was soon evident that Cromwell could place little confidence even in the pitiful remnant of the proud assembly that eight years before had counted 524 members. Before the blow fell, Ireton had encountered strong opposition to his plan for complete dissolution, even from extremists like Chaloner and Scott.

When sittings resumed, many of the surviving radicals absented themselves, and a quorum was obtained only with difficulty. Moreover, the remaining members demanded that Fairfax state the grounds upon which their colleagues were prevented from attending the House.

With each successive step in the weeks preceding the execution of the King, Cromwell lost the support of more of his old friends. By mid-December both Vane and William Pierrepont were strongly opposed to the new direction of events, and men like Whitelocke and Sir Thomas Widdrington were no longer sitting in the House. St. John, recently elevated to the bench, had opposed the purge and when named one of the King's judges had refused to serve. As late as December 25 Cromwell had favored the trial but not the execution of the King. Sometime between January 1 and January 3, however, when the second ordinance for the King's trial was introduced, he seems to have approved of Charles's execution. The refusal of St. John and the other judges to serve may have been the result of this change.

By January 1, 1649, Lilburne had also left London in disgust, having come to the final and irrevocable breach with his old hero. He had hoped that all factions would unite behind the program envisaged in the second Agreement of the People and had supported Ireton on the understanding that no steps would be taken against Parliament or the King until the agreement had been ratified by the people at large. By early December, however, he had begun to suspect that he had been deceived. He was shortly to see the Commons purged and the Agreement of the People handed over to the council of officers, who mangled it beyond all recognition. Lilburne's beloved principle of popular sovereignty, according to which Parliament itself would be limited by a written constitution, was contemptuously brushed aside and the agreement presented not to the people but to the despised Rump for ratification. "An Agreement of the People is not proper to come from the Parliament," protested the embittered Levellers, "because . . . that which is done by one Parliament . . . may be undone by the next Parliament." Lilburne was never again to make his peace with the men who now guided the destinies of England and whom he castigated as "a pack of dissembling, juggling knaves."

When one reflects on the situation in December 1648 and January 1649, it is difficult to avoid the conclusion that both Charles and Cromwell were the unwilling protagonists in a tragic denouement that unfolded with something of the grim inevitability of a drama of Aeschylus. But of the two men, it is Cromwell rather than the King who appears as the truly tragic figure. When Charles stepped onto the scaffold on the afternoon of January 29, he did so in the complete confidence that he was dying in the name of the cause for which he had fought and that whatever his past failings might have been, the inner consistency of this act could not be called into question. With Cromwell it was far otherwise. He had, it is true, taken up arms against his King. In the eyes of some, the events of that day were looked upon as the logical, and indeed satisfying, culmination of a long and bloody struggle against a man who combined an unsatisfactory weakness of character with the methods of an autocrat. But the congratulations and forced humor of such persons must have been cold comfort to the lieutenant general. The events of the previous two years and his personal contact with the King had tended to undermine the validity of the old slogans, so effective in inspiring his men and himself in the early days. For Cromwell the vigorous, single-minded hatred felt by a man of Colonel Harrison's stamp was no longer possible. If the story of his uttering the words "cruel necessity" on viewing the King's body was apocryphal, it was, nevertheless, an accurate expression of his inner conflicts.

But if his feelings about the King were mixed, his reflections on Parliament must have been gloomy indeed. It was impossible to reconcile his actions against Parliament with the principles for which he had fought, and to both the royalist and moderate members of the Parliament summoned in November 1640 his name was anathema. Worse still was the alienation, not only of many of his old supporters in the Commons like Vane and St. John, but of Lilburne, who only a few months before had still been ready to be his staunch ally.

Cromwell could have chosen to espouse the principles of the Levellers and to follow the path mapped out by Lilburne. If he had done so, and if the King had been brought to trial and even executed, it would have been in the name of an extension of the principles that had launched the Revolution and Civil War in the first place. Even the forced dissolution of Parliament might have been justified in the name of the same principles.

Cromwell had not only been a successful military commander, but in the first five years of the Revolution had been a genuine popular hero, known for his sturdy equalitarianism and admired for such qualities by men like Lilburne and Vane. But when the prospect of the conversion of the Revolution into something much more democratic than he had ever envisaged became real, he had drawn back. The events of 1647 had also made him much more conscious of the need to preserve the shreds of constitutionality, if the rule of the sword was to be avoided. By 1648, then, the radical current had swept past him, with the ironic result that the most revolutionary act carried out in the seventeenth century—the execution of a reigning King—was directed by a man whose stance had become essentially conservative if not reactionary. It was thus unredeemed by that type of revolutionary élan which can lend to the most ruthless actions a kind of justification. Herein lay Cromwell's tragedy.

It was England's tragedy that the attempt to extend liberty by violent means had ended in social and political disintegration and in the undermining of those unspoken premises of politics without which liberty itself disappears.

Appendix and Index

Appendix

The information relating to the political activities of the members of the Long Parliament contained in the following table is based on the record of individuals as revealed by their appearance in parliamentary diaries, the Journals of both houses, manuscript and printed sources, and the work of W. D. Pink, Douglas Brunton and Donald Pennington, Mary F. Keeler, Lotte Mulligan, George Yule, David Underdown, Valerie Pearl, and Lawrence Kaplan.

A word about method may be in order. When this study of the Long Parliament was begun, the two-step procedure according to which biographies of the members are compiled preparatory to an analysis of party conflict was rejected in favor of a two-pronged approach. Previous interpretations of the period were so confused and erroneous on the most basic aspects of party or factional conflict as to be almost worthless. Accordingly, it was imperative to provide the political context in relation to which individual actions of members might be judged. The impracticality of the alternative approach can readily be seen when one considers that a member's service on a particular committee is virtually meaningless without an appreciation of the political situation that produced that committee. On the other hand, such knowledge can invest an otherwise isolated fact with great significance.

With these considerations in mind, I gathered material and employed a cross-reference system with the twofold purpose of clarifying the politics of the Parliament and of compiling material for individual records of members. This appendix is based on this record, which includes not only all appearances known to me in the manuscript sources and the pamphlet literature but also committee membership and mentions in the Journals. The record is unique in that previous historians have either concentrated on earlier or later periods or have restricted themselves to sources other than the accounts of the parliamentary proceedings themselves. I would, of course, be the last to claim infallibility with respect to the behavior of the hundreds of individuals who sat on the benches of St. Stephen's Chapel 340 years ago. To paraphrase Georges Clemenceau, it is the grandeur and misery of historical judgments that they can be questioned, and these are no exception. Nevertheless, the scope of the study and the relative wealth of material on the more active members make it possible to repose considerable confidence in the general conclusions.

The members have been divided into two major categories, radical (R) and moderate (M); those categories have been subdivided into core (C), fringe (F), latent (L), and secluded (S), with the further qualification of the word probable (P) in some cases.[1] In 1647 an additional category of Marten radical (MR) has been used to designate those members who supported Henry Marten in that year. In December 1647 the category core Cromwellian (CC) has been employed to indicate those members who supported Cromwellian policies in December 1647 and January 1648. The evidence for the politics of the members of the core of either group is usually ample enough to produce a confident judgment; for the fringe and latent groups it is frequently scanty and ambiguous, and the judgment must be correspondingly tentative.

Three periods have been selected for special attention. The first is the year 1644, a time of sharp political conflict when members ranged themselves on either side of the struggle over the control of the army, and one particularly rich in source materials. The second is the crisis of 1647, a peculiarly revealing time when the balance of power swung to Holles and the moderates in the first six months and to Cromwell in the last three. The third is the final denouement of December 1648.

The criterion of a radical or a moderate depends on the political situation and the response to it by the individual member insofar as this can be judged by statements in the Commons recorded in the diaries, patterns of committee activity, actions in the House recorded in the Journals, or in newsletters and pamphlets. In 1644 two main issues were in dispute: the control of the army and the conditions of peace. A typical radical in this period was a man who supported projects such as purging the army and the navy of "unreliable" officers, participated in campaigns designed to undermine the influence of moderate commanders on the local level, and opposed any compromise peace. A typical moderate was a member who followed the lead of Holles and Stapleton in the support of Essex, opposed draconic measures against royalists, and worked for a compromise peace.

The table provides striking evidence of the contrast between the declining fortunes of the radicals on the one hand and the steadily increasing strength of the moderates on the other. In 1644 the radicals enjoyed a slight preponderance made more effective by their superior discipline. By 1647 the situation had been dramatically reversed, the radicals having been reduced to marked numerical inferiority, accentuated by internal divisions.

1. See the first page of the table for a complete list of abbreviations.

The radicals of all shades of intensity in 1644 totaled 135 members. Although the figure for core radicals (68) was arrived at independently, it corresponds closely with the maximum number counted by the radicals in divisions in 1644.

By 1647 the radicals (including Marten's followers) had added 104 recruiters, or slightly over 50 percent of their total strength. They had, however, retained the support of only 96 original members; of these only 82 had been identifiable radicals in 1644. The attrition of veteran radicals continued thereafter at a slower rate, and by December 1648 the number of 1644 radicals still active in that cause had been reduced to 62, or 45.9 percent of the 1644 group. Of these some 34 became core Cromwellians. When to the picture of numerical decline the facts of internal division are added, the reasons for Holles' control of the Commons in the first six months of 1647 become clear.

The picture is different when one turns to the moderates. A total of 95 members may be counted as moderates in 1644, of whom 22 were CMs or PCMs, 48 were FMs or PFMs, and 25 LMs or PLMs. The moderate potential was, however, probably considerably greater. Some 39 members eligible to sit in 1644 remain politically unclassified in that year. Their politics can only be guessed at, but in most cases their inactivity probably signified disapproval of the proceedings at Westminster. The subsequent record supports this assumption. Some 26 were still living at the time of the purge, of whom 20 were either secluded or ceased to sit in Parliament. On this basis 30 members might be added to the moderates' potential in 1644. This would give them a maximum of 126 members as against 144 for the radicals.

The recruiting of the House—ironically a radical project—coupled with the defection of many radicals and radical schisms combined to give Holles an overwhelming majority in the first six months of 1647. Holles had not only won the support of approximately 125 recruiters as against an estimated 104 for the radicals, but could now count on some 35 former radicals. This substantiates Holles' assertion that the recruiting of the House, contrary to radical expectation, actually strengthened his hand, although original members still predominated among his followers. Among the radicals, on the other hand, the recruiters were in the majority by 1647. The result of these changes was that the moderates, in the period January–June 1647, had a maximum potential of 269 members as against 200 radicals of all descriptions.

The radical position was further weakened by internal dissension. One group numbering approximately 49 members either cooperated with Holles or remained passive. They included a high proportion of "old" radicals such as Cromwell himself, St. John, the two Vanes, Browne, and Pierrepont. The extent to which fear of the Levellers was a factor in bringing about a rapprochement is still a question, but at least one-third of these radicals had exhibited marked hostility to Lilburne and his cohorts.

By October 1647 the political situation, which was confused throughout the summer, had stabilized sufficiently to permit analysis. Cromwell could count on the support of some 128 members who were active to a greater or lesser degree. Of these, about 30 were usually absent from the House, and of the 98 more active members approximately 17 were moderates who were cooperating with Cromwell for religious or other reasons.[2] They included the genuine religious Presbyterians attracted by Cromwell's policy in this area. The figure for active Cromwellians accords closely with the maximum votes obtained by that group in divisions in the period. In the background were approximately 72 latent radicals, giving Cromwell a total potential strength of 200 members. The moderates in the same period had an estimated strength of 92 active members of whom approximately 50 were in regular attendance. In reserve were about 130 latent moderates to which may be added the 10 surviving expelled members for a total of 232.

Marten and his followers still constituted an important element in the political situation. Some 30 members can be tentatively identified as his supporters, and it is probable that he could sometimes attract 10 more. When Marten combined forces with the moderates, which he did occasionally in the fall of 1647, and also in the first six months of 1648, it was often enough to outnumber Cromwell's supporters, especially if on particular issues the moderates who were cooperating with him changed sides.

The political balance as it was in December 1647 remained substantially the same in the first quarter of 1648. With the outbreak of the second Civil War, the danger of a royalist restoration temporarily drove many moderates to a quasi-radical position. The resultant confusion and blurring of party lines make any clear analysis of the situation difficult if not impossible. By the autumn of 1648 the old party lines re-formed, and a situation somewhat analogous to that of the autumn of 1647 obtained, with many of the religious Presbyterians supporting essentially Cromwellian policies.

The last portion of the chart places the members in political categories as of December 1648. Here I must acknowledge a debt to the

2. The seventeen members were: Sir Nathaniel Barnardiston, Anthony Bedingfield, John Birch, Sir John Francklyn, Sir Gilbert Gerard, Edmund Harvey, William Jephson, John Maynard, Sir Richard Onslow, Arthur Owen, Henry Peck, Sir Robert Pye, Thomas Soame, John Swynfen, Zouch Tate, William Wheeler, Bulstrode Whitelocke.

close scholarship of David Underdown on this period. His work has enabled me to avoid making a number of errors and has greatly clarified the position of a number of members. There are, however, some significant differences of interpretation between Professor Underdown and myself with respect to the political significance of the purge and the events that followed. For reasons stated in the text, I view these events as essentially counterrevolutionary in character and am therefore very unwilling to treat a member's association with them as the criterion by which he is judged a revolutionary.

A wide difference of opinion is possible as to the identity of the revolutionaries of the Puritan Revolution. Arguing on the basis of those changes which were to be permanent, we might conclude that they were the men who effected the constitutional changes of the first six months of 1641. Again it could be contended that the true revolutionaries were those members who supported Pym in the course of action that converted a relatively peaceful revolution into a violent confrontation. If, however, a group of members can be identified who pursued consistently radical policies from 1640 to the purge, they have a strong claim to the title revolutionary whether or not they went along with Cromwell in the events subsequent to the purge.

I have, because of these considerations, employed the term "core Cromwellian" to designate those members who cooperated closely with Cromwell in the period immediately following the purge. Because in these matters the quest for objectivity can often distort rather than clarify, I have not adopted rigid criteria for determining whether or not a member should be included. The category applies to all members who signed the death warrant, as well as those with an average of five or more appearances in the Commons after December 6 or in January 1649, or who entered their dissent before February 15, or who were named to the Council of State without objecting to the oath justifying the execution of the King.

The category CR in December 1648 is reserved for members who entered their dissent before February 1, but who were otherwise inactive before and after the execution of the King, as well as persons named to the Council of State who objected to the oath or who had ten or more appearances in the Commons Journals before June 30, 1649. FR applies to those members who were active after the purge, but who had less than ten appearances in the Commons Journals between December 6, 1648, and June 30, 1649.

CM includes, but is not restricted to, members imprisoned at Pride's Purge. FM applies to those members who were either purged or ceased to sit and whose political record indicates moderate sympathies. Not all of those purged or who ceased to sit were moderates; a significant number had long radical records and were purged or withdrew because they balked at Cromwell's policies. They are designated by the letters SR (secluded radical) or RR (retired radical).

An important group of moderates who are not given a separate designation in the chart is the veteran element: those members who were consistent moderates from 1644 through 1647 and down to the purge. Some 60 members are of this type. Of this group, 30 were extremely inactive and of limited interest. The remaining 30, on the other hand, were the true leaders of the moderates and could be regarded as the moderate "hard core," if that is not a contradiction in terms.[3] In his recent work Underdown has arranged members in categories relating to wealth and social status. When these categories are applied to this group it can be seen to be homogeneous and one of marked wealth and social status. Of 30 members for whom information is available, fully 93.3 percent are in social categories other than "lesser gentry," and of 25 members whose income can be estimated, 23 (or 92 percent) are in the first two categories, having incomes in excess of £500 per annum.

A total of 76 members were CCs, of whom 37, or approximately 50 percent, were original members. Of this latter group, 32 were active radicals in 1644, of whom 25 were in the CR or PCR category.[4] With the exception of the temporary rapprochement with the moderates in the first half of 1647 all but one remained consistently radical throughout the five-year period. The exception, Michael Oldsworth, defected temporarily in the summer of 1647, but was radical thereafter. They were, moreover, among the most active committeemen of all the parliamen-

3. The thirty members were Sir Ralph Assheton, Sir Edward Ayscough, Sir Henry Cholmley, Sir John Clotworthy, Sir John Corbet, Sir Thomas Dacres, Sir Symonds D'Ewes, Sir Walter Erle, Sir John Evelyn of Surrey, John Glyn, Sir Harbottle Grimston, Sir Robert Harley, Denzil Holles, Sir Edward Hungerford, Sir Anthony Irby, William Jesson, Sir William Lewis, Sir Martin Lister, Walter Long, Sir Samuel Luke, John Maynard, Sir Dudley North, Henry Pelham, Sir John Potts, Richard Rose, Sir Benjamin Rudyard, Sir Philip Stapleton, Simon Thelwall, Richard Whitehead, Edward Wingate. Stapleton, of course, did not survive to the Purge, but no analysis of the moderate party leadership would be complete without him. For estimates of the status of Hungerford, Long, and Stapleton, I have depended on M. F. Keeler, *The Long Parliament, 1640–1641* (Philadelphia, The American Philosophical Society, 1954), pp. 225–226, 256–257, 348–349.

4. The thirty-two radicals were John Alured, John Blakiston, Denis Bond, Godfrey Bosvile, John Browne, William Cawley, Sir William Constable, Miles Corbet, Oliver Cromwell, Thomas, Lord Grey of Groby, John Gurdon, William Heveningham, Cornelius Holland, John Lisle, Sir William Masham, Sir Henry Mildmay, Gilbert Millington, John Moore, Michael Oldsworth, Peregrine Pelham, Isaac Pennington, Edmund Prideaux, William Purefoy, John Pyne, Alexander Rigby, Oliver St. John, Anthony Stapley, John Trenchard, John Venn, Robert Wallop, Valentine Walton, John Wylde. For material on Wylde and St. John, I have depended on Keeler, *Long Parliament,* pp. 330–331, 394.

tarians. Accordingly, they have a strong claim to be regarded as the hard-core revolutionaries of the original parliamentarians and are of peculiar interest in view of the controversies that have raged over the wealth and status of the prime movers of the Revolution.

When Underdown's categories of wealth and social status are applied to this group, we see that although the proportion of well-established persons was lower than the comparable group of veteran moderates, it was still remarkably high. Of 27 members for whom income information is available, 12 fall in the first category, 7 in the second, and 8 in the third. Thus some 70.3 percent were men of substantial means. A similar conclusion is reached when Underdown's categories of social status are applied. Of 32 members who can be categorized, 78.1 percent were in categories other than "lesser gentry," and only 4 are identified as belonging to declining families or seriously in debt. Whether or not these men were the makers of the Revolution is a matter of opinion. What seems beyond doubt is that they bear a much closer resemblance to the affluent objects of the late R. H. Tawney's ironic studies than to the rather threadbare squires presented to us by Professor H. R. Trevor-Roper.

It is fair to add that the picture is substantially different if the whole group of CCs is subjected to the same analysis. In this group the percentage of members who were other than lesser gentry drops to 71.1 percent, while the proportion of persons of substantial income drops to 56 percent, with 20.3 percent being in serious debt before the Revolution. This discrepancy simply emphasizes the contrast between the original members and the recruiters in the CCs. In the latter element, the percentage of lesser gentry rises from 21.6 percent in the original members to 35.8 percent. Even more striking is the contrast in financial status. The proportion of men of substantial means drops from 75 percent among the original CCs to 33.3 percent among the recruiters. The percentage of persons in serious debt rises from 15.6 percent among the original members to 25.9 percent among the recruiters.

Although almost exactly half of the CCs were recruiters, their political impact was not of proportionate significance. Fifteen (38.4 percent) of the group made only rare appearances in the Commons or on parliamentary committees before December 1648 and became active only after the purge.[5] They were prepared, at Cromwell's bidding, to come in, enter their dissent, go through the appropriate motions, and, in the main, return to the obscurity from which they came. It is true

5. The fifteen recruiters were Daniel Blagrave, Sir John Bourchier, John Carew, James Chaloner, Gregory Clement, George Fleetwood, John Fry, Augustine Garland, John Hutchinson, Richard Ingoldsby, Simon Mayne, James Temple, Peter Temple, Thomas Waite, Thomas Wogan.

that they played a part in the trial and execution of the King—no less than 13 of the 15 signed the death warrant—but they cannot be regarded as politically significant members of the Long Parliament, much less as architects of a revolution. To treat them for purposes of analysis on terms of equality with the truly influential and active members is to distort the picture.

It should be pointed out that my list of CCs differs from Underdown's Rs to a significant degree and that this has a bearing on the conclusions reached. There is a net difference of 21 names between the two lists. Twelve names excluded by Underdown are among my CCs, and 10 names that I do not include are in his lists. The significance of the first 12 may be seen when it is pointed out that 10 were original members, of whom 8 were either "greater" or "county" gentry and 9 were in either the first or second income category. Underdown has classified them as "Conformists" on the ground that they entered their dissent after January 31, 1649. As I have pointed out, I have not accepted the date of dissent as decisive in itself, and in any case at least 5 of the 12 actually took this step as early as February 1. The 10 original members were radicals of long standing with all the credentials for membership in the "hard core."

Among the secluded members, the most interesting group consists of those whose record was predominantly radical down to the autumn of 1648, but who suffered the consequences of opposition to the ascendancy of the military at that time. The list includes 25 names,[6] of whom 13 were original members and 12 were recruiters. Of the original members, 9 (75 percent) are in categories other than lesser gentry, and all 10 for whom information is available fall within the first two income categories. Thus it may be seen that if these 13 names are added to the 32 hard-core radicals already analyzed, the earlier conclusions with regard to their respectability and affluence would be further reinforced.

To do justice to the information contained in this table and the material upon which it is based would require a much more lengthy treatment than is possible here. It must suffice at this point to summarize the broad conclusions that it supports.

The table provides evidence indicating that the kind of continuity

6. The original secluded members whose record was predominantly radical were John Ashe, Richard Cresheld, Sir John Evelyn (Ludgershall), Nathaniel Fiennes, Sir John Hippisley, Thomas Hodges (Cricklade), Thomas Lane, Sir Marten Lumley, William Pierrepont, John Selden, Nathaniel Stephens, Sir Henry Vane, Sr., Samuel Vassall. It should be noted that not all of these have been listed as SR or RR in the chart. Lane, Lumley, and Vassall were probably supporting the moderates by late 1648.

and cohesion associated with the word "party" can be found in groups in the Long Parliament. It also provides evidence that the tendency, noted in other revolutions, for the original revolutionaries to become more conservative was markedly present. It confirms, too, that the slight preponderance enjoyed by the radicals in 1644 had disappeared by 1647 owing to the defection of substantial numbers to the moderates without a corresponding move in the opposite direction; that the recruiting of the Commons was at least as beneficial to the moderates as to the radicals; that the radical group was split into three groups in the first half of 1647 and that that division was only partly healed by by the autumn of that year; that a substantial group of radicals was secluded in December 1648; and that the final act in the drama was carried out by a combination of veteran hard-core radicals and relatively obscure individuals. Finally, I have emphasized the contrast in wealth and position between that hard core and the newer arrivals on the parliamentary scene, a contrast that is of vital importance in assessing the relative merits of the various theories that have been advanced concerning the sociological roots of the Puritan Revolution.

Table of Members' Activities, 1644, 1647, 1648
Abbreviations

CM	Core moderate
PCM	Probable core moderate
FM	Fringe moderate
PFM	Probable fringe moderate
LM	Latent moderate
PLM	Probable latent moderate
CR	Core radical
PCR	Probable core radical
FR	Fringe radical
PFR	Probable fringe radical
LR	Latent radical
PLR	Probable latent radical
MR	Marten radical
SR	Secluded radical
PSR	Probable secluded radical
CC	Core Cromwellian
SRy	Suspected royalist
Lds	Transferred to House of Lords
Out	Expelled
NI	No information
?	Insufficient information
Dec.	Deceased

Members' Activities, 1644, 1647, 1648

Member	Constituency	1644				1647				1648
		First quarter	Second quarter	Third quarter	Fourth quarter	First quarter	Second quarter	Third quarter	Fourth quarter	
Abbot, George	Tamworth	NI	NI	NI	NI	NI	NI	NI	?	PLM
Abbot, George	Guildford					Dec.				
Aldworth, Richard	Bristol	PFM	PLM	PLM	PLM	PFM	NI	PCM	PFM	FR
Alford, John	Shoreham	PFR	FR	PFR	PCR	PLM	PLM	PLM	?	LM
Allanson, Sir William	York					FR/FM	FR/FM	FM	FR	CR
Allen, Francis	Cockermouth					PFM	PLM	PFM	PFR	CC
Allen, Matthew	Weymouth & M.R.					PLM	PLM	CM	?	LM
Alured, John	Hedon	PLR	PLR	PLR	PLR	PLR	PLR	PFR	PFR	CC
Andrews, Robert	Weobley					PFM	?	NI	NI	PLR
Anlaby, John	Scarborough							FR	FR	CC
Annesley, Arthur	Radnorshire					PLM	PLM	CM	CM	CM
Apsley, Edward	Steyning					?	PLR	PLR	PLR	FR
Armine, Sir William, Bt.	Grantham	PCR	PLR	PLR	PLR	CR	CR	CR	CR	CC
Armine, William	Cumberland					?	CR	PLR	?	FR
Arthington, Henry	Pontefract					?	PLR	PLR	?	PLR
Arundell, John	W. Looe	NI	NI	NI	NI	PLM	PLR	?	?	LM
Arundell, Thomas	W. Looe	PCR	PCR	CR	PCR	PLM	PLM	?	NI	Dec.
Ashe, Edward	Heytesbury	PCR	PCR	PCR	PCR	PCR	PCR	?	PCR	FR
Ashe, James	Bath	CR	CR	NI	PCR	PLR	PCR	PLR	PLR	FR
Ashe, John	Westbury	NI	?	PLM	PFM		?	FM	FR	SR
Ashurst, William	Newton	PFM	PFM	PFM	PFM	FM?	FM?	PFM	PFM	PFM
Assheton, Ralph	Lancashire					FM?	FM	PLM	PFM	PFM
Assheton, Ralph	Clitheroe					PCM	PCM	CM	PCM	CM
Atkins, Thomas	Norwich	PFM	PFM	PFM	PFM	PFM	FM	FR?	PCR	CC
Ayscough, Sir Edward	Lincolnshire					FR/FM	PLM	PLM	PFM	FM
Ayscough, William	Thirsk					?	?	PLM	PLM	PLM
Bacon, Francis	Ipswich					PFM	PFM	PFM	PFM	FM

Name	Constituency				FR/FM			
Bacon, Nathaniel	Cambridge Univ.	PFR		FR?	PLR	PFR?	?	SR
Baker, John	E. Grinstead	NI	?		FR?	FR?	PLR	FR
Ball, William	Abingdon				PFM	CR	CR	Dec.
Bampfield, John	Penryn	PFR	PFR	PFR	PFM	CR	FR	PFM
Barker, John	Coventry	NI	?		PFR	NI	PFR	SR
Barnardiston, Sir Nathaniel	Suffolk	?		?	FM?	NI	PFR	PFM
Barnardiston, Sir Thomas	Bury St. Edmunds				PLM	PLM	?	LM
Barneham, Sir Francis	Maidstone	NI	NI	NI	Dec.			
Barrington, Sir John, Bt.	Newtown	NI			PLM	PLM	PFM	PFM
Barrington, Sir Thomas, Bt.	Colchester	FR	FR	Dec.	Dec.			PFM
Barrowe, Maurice	Eye	NI	PFR		PLM	PLM	PLM	PFM
Barwis, Richard	Carlisle	SRy	FM?		?	PLR	PLR	LR
Baynton, Sir Edward	Chippenham	CR	CR	NI	?	PLR	CR	FR
Baynton, Edward	Devizes	PFR	PFR	NI	CM	CM	Out	LM
Bedingfield, Anthony	Dunwich	NI	CR	CR	PFM	?	PFR	PFM
Bell, William	Westminster		PFR	PFR	PLM	PLM	PLM	PFM
Bellingham, James	Westmorland			PFM	SRy	PLM	PLM	LM
Bence, Alexander	Aldeburgh	PCR	PCR	?	PLM	NI	PLM	PFM
Bence, Squire	Aldeburgh	PCR	PCR	?	PLM	?	PLM	Dec.
Bennet, Robert	W. Looe				PLM	NI	PLM	PLR
Biddulph, Michael	Lichfield				FM?	PLM	PLM	LM
Bindlosse, Sir Robert, Bt.	Lancaster				PFM	PLM	PLM	LM
Bingham, John	Shaftesbury				PLR	CR	CR	FR
Birch, John	Leominster				CM	FR	FR	CM
Blagrave, Daniel	Reading				PLR	PLR	PLR	CC
Blake, Robert	Bridgwater	CR	CR		PLR	MR?	MR?	FR
Blakiston, John	Newcastle-on-T.	CR	CR	CR	MR?	MR?	MR?	CC
Board, Herbert	Steyning				NI	NI	?	Dec.
Bond, Denis	Dorchester				CR	CR	CR	CC
Bond, John	Weymouth & M.R.				PFM	PFM	PFM	PFM
Boone, Thomas	Dartmouth				PFR	PFR	PCR	CR
Boote, Edward	Portsmouth				?	NI	?	PLM
Booth, George	Cheshire				PCM	PCM	CM	CM
Boscawen, Hugh	Cornwall				?	NI	FM	PFM

Members' Activities, 1644, 1647, 1648 (cont.)

Member	Constituency	1644				1647				1648
		First quarter	Second quarter	Third quarter	Fourth quarter	First quarter	Second quarter	Third quarter	Fourth quarter	
Bosvile, Godfrey	Warwick	NI	PCR	CR	NI	MR?	MR?	MR?	MR?	CC
Boughton, Thomas	Warwickshire					CM	PCM	PLM	PCM	CM
Bourchier, Sir John	Ripon					PLR	PLR	PLR	PLR	CC
Bowyer, John	Staffordshire					CM	PCM	CM	PCM	PCM
Bowyer, Sir William	Staffordshire	Dec.								
Boynton, Sir Matthew, Bt.	Scarborough					NI	Dec.			
Boys, Sir Edward	Dover	?	?	NI	PFR	Dec.				
Boys, John	Kent					FM	FM	FM	PFR	SR
Brereton, Sir William, Bt.	Cheshire	CR	CR	CR	NI	CR	CR	CR	CR	CR
Brewster, Robert	Dunwich					PLR	PLR	PCR	PLR	FR
Briggs, Sir Humphrey	Much Wenlock					PLM	PFM	PFM	PFM	PFM
Brooke, Peter	Newton	NI				FM?	PLM	PFM	PFM	FM
Browne, Sir Ambrose, Bt.	Surrey	PFR	NI	NI	PLM	PLM	PLM	PLM	PLM	LM
Browne, John	Dorset	FM	PFR	PFR	PFR	PFR	PLR	PFR	PFR	CC
Browne, Richard	New Romney		FM	FM	FM	PLM	PLR	PFR	?	?
Browne, Richard	Wycombe					CM	CM	CM	PCM	CM
Browne, Samuel	Dartmouth	CR	CR	CR	PFM	FM?	FM?	?	PFR	?
Broxholme, John	Lincoln	PFM	PFM	PFM	PFM	Dec.				
Bulkeley, John	Newtown					?	CR	CR	CR	CM
Buller, Francis	E. Looe	PFR	PFR	PFR	PFR	PFM	PLM	PLM	PFM	CM
Buller, George	Saltash	PFR	PFR	PFR	PFR	Dec.				
Buller, Sir Richard	Fowey	Dec.								
Burgoyne, Sir John, Bt.	Warwickshire					PFM	PFM	FM	LM	FM
Burgoyne, Sir Roger, Bt.	Bedfordshire	PFM	PFM	NI		PLM	PLM	PLM	PLM	CM
Burrell, Abraham	Huntingdon					PLR	PLR	PLR	PLR	PFR
Button, John	New Lymington	PFM	PFM	NI	NI	PLM	PLM	PLM	PLM	LM
Bysshe, Edward	Bletchingley	PFM	PFM	NI	NI	PLM	PLM	PLM	PLM	LM

Name	Constituency									
Cage, William	Ipswich	PCR	PCR	FM?	PCR	Dec.	PLM	PLM	PLM	LM
Campbell, James	Grampound	PLM				PLM	NI	NI	NI	PLM
Campion, Henry	New Lymington	NI		PLM	NI	NI	PLR	PLR	PLR	FR
Carent, William	Milborne Port					PLR	PLR	PLR	PLR	CC
Carew, John	Tregony					PLR	PFM	CM		PCM
Carr, Charles, Lord	Mitchell						PLR	PCR	PCM	CC
Cawley, William	Midhurst					PLR			PCR	
Cecil, Charles, Viscount Cranborne	Hertford	?		NI	?		FM	CR?	PCM	CM
Cecil, Robert	Old Sarum	?	NI	PLM	NI	PFM	PLM	PLM	PLM	PLM
Ceeley, Thomas	Bridport					PLM	PLM	?	PLM	LM
Chaloner, James	Aldborough					FM	MR?	NI	PMR	CC
Chaloner, Thomas	Richmond					MR?	PMR	PMR	MR	CC
Charlton, Robert	Bridgnorth					PMR	PFM	PFM	PLM	PFM
Cheeke, Sir Thomas	Harwich	PFM	PFM	PFM	PFR	PFM	CM	CM	PFM	LM
Chettel, Francis	Corfe Castle					PLM	PFM	PFM	PFM	FM
Cholmley, Henry	New Malton	PCM	PCM	PCM	PCM	PLM	CM	PLM	CM	CM
Cholmley, Thomas	Carlisle					PLM	PLM	PLM	PLM	PLM
Clarke, Samuel	Exeter					PLM	PFM	SRy	PFM	PLM
Clement, Gregory	Fowey					PFM	PLR	PCM	PLR	CC
Clinton, Edward, Lord	Callington					PLR	PLM	PLR	PLM	LM
Clive, Robert	Bridgnorth					PLM	PFM	PLM	PFM	PFM
Clotworthy, Sir John	Maldon	CM	CM	CM	CM	PFM	CM	PFM	Out	CM
Coke, Sir John	Derbyshire	NI	FM	PFM	FM	CM	CM	CM	PFM	?
Constable, Sir William, Bt.	Knaresborough	PCR	NI	NI	NI	CM	PLM	PLM	PCR	CC
Cooke, Sir Robert	Tewkesbury	Dec.				PLM	CR/FM	CR		
Copley, Lionel	Bossinney	PCM	FM	PCM	PCM	CR/FM	CM	CM	Out	CM
Corbet, Sir John, Bt.	Shropshire	CR	CR	CR	CR	LM	PFM	PLM	PLM	PFM
Corbet, Miles	Great Yarmouth					PFM	CR	CR	CR	CC
Corbett, John	Bishop's Castle	NI	NI	NI	NI	CR	PCR	CR	CR	CC
Cowcher, John	Worcester	NI				PCR	NI	NI	?	?
Craddock, Matthew	London	Dec.				NI				
Crane, Sir Robert, Bt.	Sudbury	Dec.								
Cresheld, Richard	Evesham	?	PFR	NI	NI	?	NI	NI	PFR	PSR

Members' Activities, 1644, 1647, 1648 (*cont.*)

Member	Constituency	1644				1647				1648
		First quarter	Second quarter	Third quarter	Fourth quarter	First quarter	Second quarter	Third quarter	Fourth quarter	
Crewe, John	Brackley	CR	CR	CR	CR	FM	PFM	PFM	PFM	CM
Crimes, Elisha	Tavistock					PLM	PFM	PLM	PLM	LM
Crompton, Thomas	Staffordshire					PLR	PLR	PLR	PLR	PLR
Cromwell, Oliver	Cambridge	CR	CR	CR	CR	CR/FM	CR/FM	CR	CR	CC
Crowther, William	Weobley					PFR	PFR	CR	PCR	LR
Curzon, Sir John, Bt.	Derbyshire	CR	PCR	PFR	PFR	PFM	PFM	CM	CM	CM
Dacres, Thomas	Callington					PFM	PLM	SRy	PLM	LM
Dacres, Sir Thomas	Hertfordshire	PFR	PFM	CM	FR	PCM	CM	CM	CM	CM
Danvers, Sir John	Malmesbury					CR	CR	CR	MR?	CC
Darley, Henry	Northallerton	NI	?	NI	PCR	?	MR?	CR	PMR	LR
Darley, Richard	New Malton					PLR	PLR	PLR	PMR	FR
Davies, William	Carmarthen					FM?	PFM	?	?	PFM
Devereux, Sir Walter	Lichfield	Dec.								
Dewes, Sir Symonds	Sudbury	CM	CM	CM	CM	CM	CM	CM	CM	CM
Dixwell, John	Dover					PFR	PFR	FR	PCR	CC
Dodderidge, John	Barnstaple					?	PCR	FR	FR	FM
Dormer, John	Buckingham					PLR	PFR	PLR	PLR	PFR
Dove, John	Salisbury					PFR	PCR	PCR	PCR	CC
Dowce, Edward	Portsmouth	PFR	FR	PFR	PFR	?	PLR	NI	?	Dec.
Downes, John	Arundel	?	?	PLR	NI	PLR	PLR	PFR	PFR	CC
Doyley, John	Oxford	?	?	?	?	CM	CM	SRy	PLM	CM
Drake, Francis	Amersham	?	?	?	?	PCM	PCM	CM	PCM	CM
Drake, Sir Francis, Bt.	Berealston	Out	Out	Out	?	PFM	PFM	PLM	PFM	FM
Drake, Sir William	Amersham	PFR	PFR	PFR	NI	PLM	PLM	PLM	PLM	?
Dryden, Sir John, Bt.	Northamptonshire	FR?	PFR	PFR	FR?	?	PLR	PFR	PFR	PLR
Dunch, Edmund	Wallingford					PLR	PLR	CR	PCR	FR
Earle, Erasmus	Norwich					FR	PFR	?	PFR	SR

Name	Constituency										
Eden, Thomas	Cambridge Univ.	?				Dec.	PCR	CR	CR	CR	CC
Edwards, Humphrey	Shropshire					?	PLR	PLR	PLR	PLR	LR
Edwards, Richard	Christchurch					PCM	PCM	PCM	PCM	PFM	PFM
Edwards, William	Chester					PFM	PLM	PFM	PFM	PLM	LM
Egerton, Sir Charles	Ripon					PLM	PFM	PLM	PLM	PLM	LM
Elford, John	Tiverton					MR?	MR?	MR?	MR?	MR?	SR
Ellis, William	Boston	CR	CR	CR	CR	PFM	PFM	PLM	NI	NI	PFM
Ellison, Robert	Newcastle-on-T.	NI				PLM	PFM	PLM	PLM	PLM	LM
Erisey, Richard	St. Mawes	PFR	?	NI	PLM	PLM	PFM	PLM	PLM	PLM	PFM
Erle, Thomas	Wareham	FM	PFR	?	CM	CM	CM	CM	CM	CM	CM
Erle, Sir Walter	Weymouth & M.R.			CM	?	PLM	PLM	PLM	PLM	PLM	LM
Evelyn, George	Reigate	Out	Out	CR	CR	CR	CR	CR	CR	CR	SR
Evelyn, Sir John (Wilts.)	Ludgershall	Out	Out	PFM	FM	FM	PFM	PFM	PFM	PFM	FM
Evelyn, Sir John (Surrey)	Bletchingley	?	?	?	PLM	PLM	PLM	PLM	PLM	PLM	PFM
Exton, Edward	Southampton	?	?	?	PLR	CR	CR	PLR	CR	PLR	FR
Eyre, William	Chippenham	?	?	?	?	FM	FM	?	NI	FM?	FR
Fagge, John	Rye	NI	NI	NI	NI	PLR	PLR	PLR	PLR	PLR	Dec.
Fairfax, Ferdinando, Lord	Yorkshire	NI	FM	NI	NI	?	?	NI	NI	FM?	PLR
Fell, Thomas	Lancaster					PLR	PFR	PLR	PLR	PLR	FR
Fenwick, George	Morpeth	Out	Out	Out	Out	PFR	PFR	CR	CR	CR	FR
Fenwick, Sir John, Bt.	Northumberland	Out	Out	Out	Out	PFM	PLM	PLM	PLM	PLM	LM
Fenwick, William	Northumberland					PLM	PFM	PFM	PLM	PFM	PFM
Fiennes, James	Oxfordshire	?	PLM	PLM	PLM	FM?	PLR	FM	FM	FM	LM
Fiennes, John	Morpeth				PLR	PLR	PLR	CR	CR	NI	PSR
Fiennes, Nathaniel	Banbury	PLR	PLR	PLR	PLR	CR/FM	CR/FM	CR	CR	CR	SR
Finch, John	Winchelsea	Dec.	NI	PFM	?	CR	FM?	CR	NI	FM	FM
Fitzwilliams, William, Lord	Peterborough	?	NI	NI	NI	PLM	PLM	PLM	PLM	PLM	LR
Fleetwood, Charles	Marlborough			PFM	?	CR	FM?	CR?	?	MR?	CC
Fleetwood, George	Buckinghamshire					PLR	PLR	PLR	CR	PLR	CC
Fountaine, Thomas	Wendover	?	?	?	Dec.	Dec.	PFM	Dec.	Dec.	Dec.	Dec.
Fowell, Sir Edmund	Ashburton	FR?	?	?	FM?	FM?	PFM	PFM	CM	CM	PFM
Fowell, Edward	Tavistock				?	PFM	PFM	PFM	CM	PFM	PFM
Foxwist, William	Caernarvon					PFM	PFM	PLM	PLM	PFM	PFM
Francklyn, Sir John	Middlesex	?	FR?	?	FR?	CM?	CM?	PFM	PFM	CM/FR	Dec.

Members' Activities, 1644, 1647, 1648 (cont.)

		1644				1647				1648
Member	Constituency	First quarter	Second quarter	Third quarter	Fourth quarter	First quarter	Second quarter	Third quarter	Fourth quarter	
Francklyn, John	Marlborough	Dec.								
Fry, John	Shaftesbury					?	?	PLR	PLR	CC
Gardner, Samuel	Evesham							PFR	?	FM
Garland, Augustine	Queenborough									CC
Garton, Henry	Arundel	Dec.								
Gawdy, Framlingham	Thetford	NI	NI	NI	PLM	PLM	PLM	PLM	PLM	PFM
Gell, Thomas	Derby					PFM	PFM	FM	FM	PFM
Gerard, Francis	Seaford	Out	Out	Out	Out	FM	FM	PFM	PFM	CM
Gerard, Sir Gilbert, Bt.	Middlesex	PFR	FR	?	FM	PCM	CM	CM/FR	CM/FR	CM
Gewen, Thomas	Launceston					PCM	PCM	CM	CM	CM
Glyn, John	Westminster	CM	FM	?	FR?	CM	CM	CM	Out	FM
Godolphin, Francis	St. Ives	?	?	?	NI	PFM	PLM	PLM	PLM	PLM
Gollop, George	Southampton	PFM	PFM		NI	PLM	PLM	PLM	PLM	FM
Goodwin, Arthur	Buckinghamshire	Dec.								
Goodwin, John	Haslemere	PFR	NI	NI	?	PFR	PFR	PFR	PFR	CR
Goodwin, Robert	E. Grinstead	PFR	NI	?	PCR	CR/FM	CR	CR	MR?	FR
Gott, Samuel	Winchelsea					PCM	CM	CM	PCM	PCM
Gould, Nicholas	Fowey									CR
Grantham, Thomas	Lincoln	?	FR?	?	NI	PLM	PLM	PLM	PLM	PLM
Gratwick, Roger	Hastings	PFR	PFR	PFR	PFR	PLR	PLR	PLR	PLR	PFR
Green, Giles	Corfe Castle	PCR	PCR	PCR	PCR	PCM	PCM	CM	PCM	CM
Grey, Thomas, Lord, of Groby	Leicester	PFM	PFM	PFM	PFM	PCR	NI	CR	PLM	CC
Grimston, Sir Harbottle, Bt.	Harwich					PLM	PLM	PLM	CM	Dec.
Grimston, Harbottle	Colchester	CM	CM	PCM	PCM	CM	CM	CM	PFM	CM
Grove, Thomas	Milborne Port					PFM	FM	PFM		PFM
Gurdon, Brampton	Sudbury					PLR	PLR	PLR	PLR	LR
Gurdon, John	Ipswich	CR	CR	CR	CR	CR	CR	CR	CR	CC

Name	Constituency	1	2	3	4	5	6	7	8
Hallowes, Nathaniel	Derby	NI	?	FR?	?	?	CR	?	CR
Hampden, John	Buckinghamshire	Dec.							
Harby, Edward	Higham Ferrers			PCM	PLR	FR?	PFR	PLR	PFR
Harley, Edward	Herefordshire	PCM	PCM	PCM	CM	CM	CM	PCM	CM
Harley, Sir Robert	Herefordshire			PCM	PCM	CM	CM	CM	CM
Harley, Robert	New Radnor	NI	PFR	PCM	PLM	PLM	PLM	?	PFM
Harman, Richard	Norwich				PMR	PMR	PMR	PMR	CR
Harrington, Sir James	Rutland	Out	Out	PFR	PFR	PFR	PFR	PCR	PSR
Harrington, John	Somerset				PLM	PLM	PLM	PLM	PLM
Harris, John	Launceston	Out	Out		MR?	MR?	MR?	MR?	CC
Harrison, Thomas	Wendover			NI	CM	CM	CM/FR	PFR	CC
Harvey, Edmund	Great Bedwin	?	CR	CR	CM	CM/FR			
Harvey, John	Hythe	CR	NI	NI	Dec.				
Haselrig, Sir Arthur	Leicestershire	?	CR	CR	CR	CR	CR	CR	CR
Hatcher, Thomas	Stamford	CR	NI	NI	PCR	?	NI	?	FM
Hay, Herbert	Arundel	PFR			PFR	PFR	FR	PCR	SR
Hay, William	Rye	?	PLR	PFM	PLR	PLR	PLR	PLR	LR
Herbert, Henry	Monmouthshire	PFM	PFM		PLR	?	PFR	PLR	PFR
Herbert, James	Wiltshire				PLM	PCM	CM	PCM	CM
Herbert, John	Monmouthshire	NI		FM	PLM	PLM	CM	PLM	PFM
Herbert, Philip, Lord	Glamorganshire	FM	NI	PCR	PCM	CM	PCR	PLM	CM
Heveningham, William	Stockbridge	PCR	?	CR	PLR	PLR	FM/CR	PFR	CC
Heyman, Henry	Hythe	CR	CR		FM?	?		PFM	LR
Heyman, Sir Peter	Dover	Dec.							
Hill, Roger	Bridport	PCR	?	PCR	CR/FM	CR	CR	PCR	CR
Hippisley, Sir John	Cockermouth	PFR	PFR	PFR	?	PLR	PFR	PFR	SR
Hobart, Sir John, Bt.	Norfolk		PFM		NI	NI	NI	NI	Dec.
Hoby, Peregrine	Great Marlow	PFM	NI	PFM	PFM	?	PFM	PFM	PFM
Hodges, Luke	Bristol		PCR		PLR	PFR	PCR	PCR	CR
Hodges, Thomas	Cricklade	CR		PCR	FR/FM	PFR	CR	PFR	SR
Hodges, Thomas	Ilchester		PCR		PLM	PLM	?	PFM	PFM
Holcroft, John	Wigan				PLM	PLM	PLM	PFM	PFM
Holland, Cornelius	New Windsor	CR	CR	CR	CR	CR	CR	CR	CC
Holland, Sir John	Castle Rising	CR	*Leave of absence*		FM	PLM	PLM	PLM	?

Members' Activities, 1644, 1647, 1648 (cont.)

Member	Constituency	1644 First quarter	1644 Second quarter	1644 Third quarter	1644 Fourth quarter	1647 First quarter	1647 Second quarter	1647 Third quarter	1647 Fourth quarter	1648
Holles, Denzil	Dorchester	CM	CM	CM	CM	CM	CM	CM	Out	CM
Holles, Francis	Lostwithiel					PLM	PLM	PLM	PLM	PCM
Horner, George	Somerset					PFM	PFM	CM	PCM	PFM
Hoskins, Bennett	Hereford					FM?	PCM	SRy	PLM	PFM
Houghton, Richard	Lancashire					PFM	PFM	PLM	PFM	?
Hoyle, Thomas	York	PCR	PCR	CR	NI	?	PFR	PFR	MR?	PLR
Hungerford, Sir Edward	Chippenham	PFM	PFM	PFM	PFM	PLM	CM	CM	CM	CM
Hungerford, Henry	Great Bedwin					PFM	PLM	CM	FR?	FM
Hunt, Thomas	Shrewsbury					PFM	PFM	PLM	PFM	PFM
Hussey, Thomas	Whitchurch					PLR	PLR	?	PFR	LR
Hutchinson, John	Nottinghamshire					LR	LR	CR	LR	CC
Hutchinson, Sir Thomas	Nottinghamshire	Dec.								
Ingoldsby, Richard	Wendover								CR	CC
Ingram, Sir Arthur	Callington	Dec.								
Irby, Sir Anthony	Boston	FR?	FR?	PCM	PCM	PCM	CM	CM	PCM	CM
Ireton, Henry	Appleby	FR?	FR?	?	PFR	CR	CR	CR	CR	CC
Jenner, Robert	Cricklade	Dec.	?		PFR	PFM	FM	PFM	PFM	?
Jervines, Sir John	St. Albans	PFR		NI		PLM	PLM	PLM	PFM	PFM
Jennings, Richard	St. Albans	?	NI	NI	PLM	FM?	PFR	PFM	FR	FM
Jephson, William	Stockbridge	FR?	?	PFR	PFR	Dec.				
Jervoise, Richard	Whitchurch	NI	?	NI	NI	PLR	PLR	CR	PFM	PLR
Jervoise, Sir Thomas	Whitchurch	PFR	FR?	PFR	PFR	PCM	PCM	CM	CM	PCM
Jesson, William	Coventry	PFM	PFM	PFM	PFM	PLR	PLR	PLR	PLR	CC
Jones, John	Merionethshire					PCM	PCM	CM	CM	CC
Jones, William	Beaumaris					FM?	PFM	PLM	PFM	PFM
Kekewich, George	Liskeard					PLM	PLM	PLM	PLM	LM
Kemp, John	Christchurch					PFR	PFR	CR	CR	PLR

Name	Constituency								
Kirkham, Roger	Old Sarum	PFM	PFM	PFM	Dec.	Dec.	PLM	PLM	PLM
Knatchbull, Sir Norton	New Romney	PFR	PFR	PFR	PFM	PFM	CM	PFM	CM
Knightley, Richard	Northampton	NI	NI	NI	FM?	FM?	NI	NI	Dec.
Knollys, Sir Francis, Sr.	Reading	Dec.			NI	NI	NI	NI	PFM
Knollys, Sir Francis, Jr.	Reading	NI	NI	NI	PFM	PFM	PLM	PFM	CM
Kyrle, Walter	Leominster	PFR	PFR	FR?	PFM	PFM	FM?	CR?	PFM
Lane, Thomas	Wycombe				PFR	?	PLM	PLM	CR
Langton, William	Preston				PLM	PLM	PLM	?	PLR
Lascelles, Francis	Thirsk				PFR	PFR	CR	CR	
Lawrence, Henry	Westmorland				PFR	PFR			FR
Leach, Nicholas	Newport, Cornwall	Dec.					CM	PCM	PFM
Lechmere, Nicholas	Bewdley	PFM	PFM	PFM	PLM	PFM	PLM	PLM	PLM
Lee, Richard	Rochester	NI	NI	NI	PLM	PLM	FM	PCM	CM
Le Gros, Sir Charles	Orford				CM	CM	PLM	PLM	LM
Leigh, Edward	Stafford		?	NI	PLM	PLM	CR	CR	CR
Leigh, Sir John	Yarmouth, I.W.				PFR	PFR	NI	NI	LR
Leman, William	Hertford		?	?	?	FM?	?	?	FR
Lenthall, John	Gloucester				?	?	PLM	PLM	PFM
Lenthall, William	Woodstock		?	?	PLM	PLM	CM	Out	CM
Lewis, Lewis	Brecon	CM	CM	CM	CM	CM	?	CR	CC
Lewis, Sir William, Bt.	Petersfield	CR	CR	CR	CR/FM	CR/FM			
Lisle, John	Winchester	Dec.							
Lister, Sir John	Hull	PFM	PFM	PFM	PLM	PLM	PLM	PFM	CM
Lister, Sir Martin	Brackley				PLR	?	CR	PCR	CR
Lister, Thomas	Lincoln				PLM	?	PLM	PLM	PFM
Lister, Sir William	E. Retford				PMR	MR	MR	MR	CC
Livesey, Sir Michael, Bt.	Queenborough				NI	?	NI	?	PFM
Lloyd, John	Carmarthenshire				PLR	PCR	?	PFR	CR
Long, Lislibone	Wells	PCM	PCM	PCM	CM	CM	CM	Out	PLM
Long, Walter	Ludgershall				CR/FM	CR/FM	CR	CR	CC
Love, Nicholas	Winchester	NI	?	NI	PLR	PLR	PLR	PLR	FR
Lowry, John	Cambridge	NI	PFM	PFM	PFM	PLM	CM	PFM	PCM
Lucas, Henry	Cambridge Univ.								PFM
Luckyn, Capel	Harwich								PFM

Members' Activities, 1644, 1647, 1648 (*cont.*)

Member	Constituency	1644				1647				1648
		First quarter	Second quarter	Third quarter	Fourth quarter	First quarter	Second quarter	Third quarter	Fourth quarter	
Lucy, Sir Richard, Bt.	Old Sarum	Dec.				CM?	PCM	CM?	?	PLR
Lucy, Sir Thomas	Warwick					MR	MR	MR	MR	CC
Ludlow, Edmund	Wiltshire	Dec.								
Ludlow, Sir Henry	Wiltshire	Dec.								
Luke, Sir Oliver	Bedfordshire	PFM	PFM	PFM	PFM	PLM	PLM	PCM	PLM	PFM
Luke, Sir Samuel	Bedford	PFM	PFM	PFM	PFM	PCM	PCM	CM	CM	CM
Lumley, Sir Martin, Bt.	Essex	?	PFR	NI	PFR	PFR	PFR	?	FR?	FM
Luttrell, Alexander	Minehead	Dec.								
Lytton, Sir William	Hertfordshire	PFM	PFM	PFM	PFM	PLM	PFM	PLM	PFM	CM
Mackworth, Thomas	Ludlow					PLR	PLR	PLR	PLR	PFR
Marlott, William	Shoreham	?	NI	NI	NI	Dec.				
Marten, Henry	Berkshire	Out	Out	Out	Out	MR	MR	MR	MR	CC
Martyn, Christopher	Plympton Earl					?	PLR	PLR	PLR	LR
Martyn, Sir Nicholas	Devonshire					PFM	PLM	PLM	PLM	PLM
Masham, Sir William, Bt.	Essex	PCR	PCR	PCR	PCR	PCR	PCR	CR	CR	CC
Masham, William	Shrewsbury					PLR	PLR	?	?	FR
Massey, Edward	Wootton Bassett					CM	CM	CM	Out	Dec.
Master, Sir Edward	Canterbury	NI	NI	NI	PFM	PLM	PLM	PLM	PLM	CM
Mauleverer, Thomas	Boroughbridge	NI	NI	NI	PLR	PLR	PFR	PLR	PFR	PLM
Maynard, John	Totnes	CM?	CM	CM	CM	CM	CM	CM	FR?	CC
Maynard, Sir John	Lostwithiel					PCM	CM	CR	Out	CM
Mayne, Simon	Aylesbury					PLR	PLR	CM	PLR	CM
Meyrick, Sir John	Newcastle, Staffs.	?	?	CM	CM	PCM	PCM	CM	CM	CC
Middleton, Sir Thomas	Denbighshire	PFR	?	?	?	PCM	PFM	PFM	CM	CM
Middleton, Thomas	Flint					FM?	PFM	PFM	PLM	FM
Middleton, Thomas	Horsham	NI	PFM	NI	NI	PLM	PLM	PLM	PFM	LM
Mildmay, Sir Henry	Maldon	CR	CR	CR	CR	CR/FM	FM?	CR	PMR	FM

Name	Constituency								
Millington, Gilbert	Nottingham	PCR	CR	?	CR	?	PLR	PLR	PCR	CC
Montagu, Edward	Hunts.	?	Lds			PLM	PFM	CM?	PFM	PFM
Montagu, Edward	Huntingdon	PLM	PLM	PLM	PLM	PLM	PLM	CM?	NI	LM
Montagu, George	Huntingdon					Dec.				
Moody, Miles	Ripon	NI	PCR	NI	PCR	PCR	PCR	PLR	PCR	CC
Moore, John	Liverpool	?	NI	PFM	NI	PLM	PLM	PLM	PLM	FM
Moore, Poynings	Haslemere	?	NI	?	PLM	PLM	?	PLM	PLM	PFM
Moore, Thomas	Heytesbury	Dec.								
More, Richard	Bishop's Castle	NI	NI	NI	PFM	PLM	PLM	PLM	PLM	LM
More, Thomas	Ludlow					PLM	PLM	SRy	PFM	LM
Morgan, William	Breconshire	NI								?
Morice, William	Devonshire	Dec.	?	CR?	PCR	CR/FM	CR/FM	CR	MR?	CR
Morley, Herbert	Lewes	NI								CC
Moundeford, Sir Edmund	Norfolk	NI	NI	NI	NI	PLR	PFR	CR	PLR	PLR
Mounson, William, Viscount	Reigate	PFM	NI	?	NI	NI	NI	?	NI	PLR
Moyle, John	St. Germans	NI			NI	NI	NI	?	NI	LM
Moyle, John	E. Looe			NI	NI	PLM	PLM	PLM	PFM	PLM
Napier, Sir Robert, Bt.	Peterborough	PFM		NI	PLM	PLM	PLM	PLM	PLM	PLM
Nash, John	Worcester	NI				FM?	FM?	PFM	PLM	FR
Needham, Sir Robert	Haverfordwest					PLR	PLR	PFR	PFR	PCM
Nelthorpe, James	Beverley		PCR			PCM	PCM	CM	PCM	FR
Nelthorpe, John	Beverley	PCR	PCR	PCR	PCR	PCR	PLR	PLR	PCR	PLM
Nicholas, Robert	Devizes	?		PCR	PCR	PCR	PCM	CM	PLM	PFM
Nichols, Anthony	Bodmin					PFM	PLM	PLM	PLM	LM
Nixon, John	Oxford					PFM	PLM	PLM	PFM	FM
Noble, Michael	Lichfield	PFM	PFM	PFM	PFM	PCM	PCM	PLM	PFM	FM
North, Sir Dudley	Cambridgeshire	PCM	PCM	PCM	PCM	PFM	PFM			PFM
North, Sir Roger	Eye	PLM	?	?	?	FM	PFM	CR	PFM	CC
Northcote, Sir John, Bt.	Ashburton					PCR	PCR	PCR	PCR	PLR
Norton, Sir Gregory, Bt.	Midhurst					FM?	PFM	PCR	CR	PLR
Norton, Richard	Hampshire	PLR	PLR	PLR	PLR	NI	FM?	FM?		CC
Nutt, John	Canterbury	FR?	PFR	PFR						
Oldsworth, Michael	Salisbury		NI		?	FM?	FM?	CM	FM?	
Onslow, Arthur	Bramber	NI		NI	NI	PLM	PLM	PLM	PFM	PFM

Members' Activities, 1644, 1647, 1648 (cont.)

Member	Constituency	1644 First quarter	1644 Second quarter	1644 Third quarter	1644 Fourth quarter	1647 First quarter	1647 Second quarter	1647 Third quarter	1647 Fourth quarter	1648
Onslow, Sir Richard	Surrey	?	?	PFR	PFR	PFM	CM	?	PFR	CM
Owen, Arthur	Pembrokeshire	NI	NI	NI		PLM	PLM	PLM	FR?	LM
Owen, Hugh	Pembroke	Dec.			PLM	PLM	PLM	PLM	PLM	LM
Owfield, Samuel	Gatton									
Owfield, William	Gatton	NI	?	?	NI	PLM	PLM	PLM	PLM	PFM
Owner, Edward	Great Yarmouth					PLM	FM	CM	PLM	LM
Oxenden, Henry	Winchelsea					FM?	PLM	PLM	PFM	?
Packer, Robert	Wallingford					PLM	PLM	PLM	PLM	PFM
Palgrave, Sir John	Norfolk					PLM	PLM	PFR	PLM	PFM
Palmer, John	Taunton					?	PFR	PFR	PFR	CR
Parker, Sir Philip	Suffolk	?	NI	NI	NI	PLM	PLM	PLM	PLM	LM
Parker, Sir Thomas	Seaford	NI	NI	NI	SRy	PFM	PLM	PLM	PLM	LM
Parkhurst, Sir Robert	Guildford	NI	NI	NI	PLM	PLM	PLM	PLM	PLM	LM
Partridge, Sir Edward	Sandwich	?	NI	PFR	PFR	PFM	PFM	CM	PLM	PCM
Peard, George	Barnstaple	Dec.								
Peck, Henry	Chichester	NI				FM?	?	FR?	PFR	PFM
Pelham, Henry	Grantham		PFM	?		PCM	PCM	CM	CM	CM
Pelham, John	Hastings				NI	NI	NI	FR?	PFM	PFM
Pelham, Peregrine	Hull	PCR	PCR	CR	CR	PLR	PLR	PCR	PCR	CC
Pelham, Sir Thomas, Bt.	Sussex	?	NI	NI	PFM	PLM	PLM	PLM	PFM	FM
Pennington, Isaac	London	PCR	CR	CR	PCR	PCR	CR	CR	CR	CC
Penrose, John	Helston					NI	NI	?	PLR	PER
Perceval, John	King's Lynn	NI	NI	Dec.						
Perceval, Sir Philip	Newport, Cornwall					NI	SRy	CM	Dec.	
Pickering, Sir Gilbert	Northamptonshire	CR	PCR	PCR	PCR	?	?	NI	PFR	CR
Pierrepont, Francis	Nottingham					PCR	PCR	CR	PCR	LR
Pierrepont, William	Much Wenlock	PFR	PFR	PFR	CR	CR/FM	CR/FM	CR	PCR	SR

Name	Constituency									
Pigot, Gervase	Nottinghamshire	NI	NI			PLR	?	CR	PFR	PLR
Pile, Sir Francis, Bt.	Berkshire	NI	NI			PLR	PLR	PLR	PLR	SR
Playters, Sir William, Bt.	Orford	NI	PFM	PLM		PLM	PLM	PLM	PLM	PFM
Poole, Edward	Wootton Bassett			?		PLM	PFM	PLM	PFM	LM
Poole, Sir Neville	Malmesbury		PFM	?		NI	NI	NI	NI	FM
Pope, Roger	Merionethshire	PFR				PLR	PFR	PFR	PFR	Dec.
Popham, Alexander	Bath	PFR	?	PFR	?	NI		NI	FM?	CR
Popham, Edward	Minehead	Dec.				PFR?				LR
Popham, Sir Francis	Minehead	NI	NI	NI	NI	NI	NI	NI	NI	
Potter, Hugh	Plympton Earl	NI	NI	NI	FM	PLM	PLM	PLM	PLM	LM
Potts, Sir John	Norfolk		PFM	?		PLM	CM	PFM	PFM	CM
Povey, Thomas	Liskeard					PLR	PFR	PFR	PCR	PFM
Prideaux, Edmund	Lyme Regis	CR	CR	CR	CR	CR	CR	CR	CR	CC
Priestley, William	St. Mawes					NI	PFM	PCM	PFM	CM
Prynne, William	Newport, Cornwall					PLM	SRy	SRy	PLM	CM
Pryse, Sir Richard, Bt.	Cardiganshire	PCR	CR?	CR	CR	MR?	MR?	MR?	MR?	LM
Purefoy, William	Warwick	PCR	CR	CR	CR	?	PCR	PCR	CR	CC
Pury, Thomas	Gloucester	CR?				?	?	NI	?	CR
Pury, Thomas	Monmouth	NI	NI	PFM	PFR	PFM	PCM	CM/FR	PLM	PLR
Pye, Sir Robert	New Woodstock	Dec.		NI	PLM	PLM	?	PLM		CM
Pym, Charles	Berealston	NI			NI	PLR	PLR	PLR	PLR	LM
Pym, John	Tavistock		PCR			PMR	PMR	MR	MR	
Pyne, John	Poole	Dec.								CC
Rainsborough, Thomas	Droitwich		NI	NI	NI					CC
Rainsborough, William	Aldeburgh	?								Dec.
Ratcliffe, John	Chester			PLM		PFM	PFM	FM	PLM	PFM
Ravenscroft, Hall	Horsham	CM	CM	CM	?	PFM	PFM	PLM	PFM	PFM
Reynolds, Robert	Hindon		?	?	?	PFM	FM	FM	FM	FR
Rich, Charles	Sandwich	NI	NI	NI		?	NI	NI	?	CM
Rigby, Alexander	Wigan	NI		PCR	PCR	MR?	MR?	MR?	MR?	CC
Robinson, Luke	Scarborough					CR/FM	CR/FM	CR/FM	CR/FM	CC
Roe, Sir Thomas	Oxford Univ.	?	?	Dec.						
Rogers, Hugh	Calne	NI	NI	NI	NI	PLM	PLM	PLM	PLM	LM
Rolle, John	Truro	PFR	FR?	FR?	FR?	PFM	PFM	PFM	PFM	PFM

Members' Activities, 1644, 1647, 1648 (cont.)

Member	Constituency	1644				1647				1648
		First quarter	Second quarter	Third quarter	Fourth quarter	First quarter	Second quarter	Third quarter	Fourth quarter	
Rolle, Sir Samuel	Devonshire	NI	NI	PFR	FR?	FM?	NI	NI	?	Dec.
Rose, Richard	Lyme Regis	NI	PFM	PFM	PFM	PFM	PFM	CM	CM	PFM
Rossiter, Edward	Grimsby					CM	FM	NI	PCM	PCM
Rous, Francis	Truro	CR	PCR	?	?	PFR	FR/FM	CR	CR	FR
Rudyard, Sir Benjamin	Wilton	PCM	PCM	PCM	PCM	PCM	PCM	NI	PFM	CM
Russell, Francis	Cambridgeshire					PLR	PLR	CR	PFR	PLR
St. John, Sir Beauchamp	Bedford	PLM				PFM	PLM	PFM	PFM	PFM
St. John, Oliver	Totnes	CR	CR	CR	CR	CR/FM	CR/FM	CR	CR	CC
Salway, Humphrey	Worcestershire	CR?	?	PCR	CR	CR/FM	CR/FM	CR	CR	FR
Salway, Richard	Appleby					CR/FM	CR/FM	CR	PCR	CR
Sandys, Thomas	Gatton				PFR	PFM	PFM	NI	PFR	PFM
Say, William	Camelford	?	?	?	?		PCR	CR	PLR	CC
Sayer, John	Colchester					PLR	PFR	CR	PFR	PLR
Scawen, Robert	Berwick	PCR	PCR	PCR	PCR	CR/FM	PCR	CR	CR	RR
Scott, Thomas	Aldborough					PMR	PMR	MR	MR	Dec.
Scott, Thomas	Aylesbury					PMR	PMR	MR	MR	CC
Searle, George	Taunton	PLR	PLR	PLR	PLR	PLR	PLR	PLR	PFR	FR
Selden, John	Oxford Univ.	PCR	PCR	PCR	PCR	CR/FM	PFR	FR?	CR	SR
Seymour, Sir John	Gloucestershire					PFM	PFM	CM	PFM	PFM
Shapcote, Robert	Tiverton					PLM	PLM	PLM	PLM	LM
Shelley, Henry	Lewes	NI	NI	NI	NI	NI	NI	NI	?	?
Shuttleworth, Richard	Clitheroe	NI	NI	NI	NI	PLM	PLM	?	?	?
Shuttleworth, Richard	Preston	PLM	PLM	PLM	PLM	PLM	PLM	CM	PLM	PFM
Sidney, Algernon	Cardiff					PMR	PMR	PMR	PMR	FR
Sidney, Philip, Ld. Lisle	Yarmouth, I.W.	?	PFR	PCR	PCR	?	CR/FM	CR	PLR	CR
Skeffington, Sir Richard	Staffordshire					?	NI	NI	NI	Dec.
Skinner, Augustine	Kent	PFR	?	?	?	PFR	PLR	?	?	FR

Name	Constituency								
Skippon, Philip	Barnstaple				?	PFR	CR	PCR	CC
Skutt, George	Poole				PLM	PLM	PLM	PLM	LM
Smith, Henry	Leicestershire			PFR	PLR	PLR	CR	CR	CC
Smith, Philip	Marlborough	NI	NI	NI	PFR	PLR	CR	PFR	PLR
Snelling, George	Southwark	NI	PCR	PLM	PLR	PLM	PLM	PCR	LR
Snow, Simon	Exeter	NI	NI	?	FM?	PFM	CM/FR	PLM	LM
Soame, Thomas	London	PCR	PCR	?	PLM	PFM	PCM	PFR	CM
Spelman, John	Castle Rising				PFM	PFM	PLM	PFM	PFM
Spencer, Sir Edward	Middlesex					PLM	PLM	PLM	LM
Spring, Sir William, Bt.	Bury St. Edmunds				PLM	PLM	PLM	PLM	PFM
Springate, Herbert	Shoreham			PCR	PFM	PLM	PLM	PLM	LM
Spurstow, William	Shrewsbury	PCR	PCR	Dec.	Dec.			Dec.	
Standish, Thomas	Preston	Dec.				Dec.			
Stapleton, Brian	Aldborough				PMR	NI	PMR	PMR	RR
Stapleton, Henry	Boroughbridge	CM	CM	CM	MR?	NI	NI	NI	SR
Stapleton, Sir Philip	Boroughbridge	PCR	NI	NI	CM	CM	CM	Dec.	
Stapley, Anthony	Sussex	CM	CM	NI	PFR	PLR	PLR	PLR	CC
Starre, George	Shaftesbury	PFR	?	NI	?	?	NI	NI	Dec.
Stephens, Edward	Tewkesbury		?	?	PFM	PFM	CM	PLM	
Stephens, John	Tewkesbury		?	?	PFR	PCR	CR?	PFR	CM
Stephens, Nathaniel	Gloucestershire	PCR	PCR	PCR	CR/FM	FR?	FR?	PFR	PLR
Stephens, William	Newport, I.W.				PFR	PFR	PCR	PFR	SR
Stockdale, Thomas	Knaresborough				PFR	PCR	PLR	PLR	FR
Stoughton, Nicholas	Guildford				FR/FM	FR/FM	PLR	NI	LR
Strickland, Walter	Minehead	PCR	PCR		PFR	PFR	PFR	PCR	Dec.
Strickland, Sir William	Hedon	CR	CR	CR	CR	CR	PFR	PFR	?
Strode, William	Berealston				Dec.	PCM	PCM		
Strode, William	Ilchester				PCM	PCM	CM	FR	CM
Swinfen, John	Stafford				PFM	PFM	PCR	PCR	CM
Sydenham, William	Weymouth & M.R.				PLR	PFR	PFR	PCR	FR
Tate, Zouch	Northampton	CR	CR	CR	PFM	CM	CM	FR	CM
Temple, James	Bramber				PLR	PCR	CR	PFR	CC
Temple, Sir John	Chichester				PLR	PCR	CR	PFR	PCM
Temple, Sir Peter, Bt.	Buckingham	NI	?	PFR	PLR	PLR	PLR	PLR	LR

Members' Activities, 1644, 1647, 1648 (cont.)

Member	Constituency	1644				1647				1648
		First quarter	Second quarter	Third quarter	Fourth quarter	First quarter	Second quarter	Third quarter	Fourth quarter	
Temple, Peter	Leicester					PFR	PLR	CR	?	CC
Temple, Thomas	Mitchell					PLM	PLM	PLM	PLM	LM
Terrick, Samuel	Newcastle, Staffs.					PLM	PLM	PLM	PLM	PFM
Thelwall, Simon	Denbigh	PFM	PFM	PFM	PFM	PFM	PFM	PFM	PFM	PFM
Thistlethwaite, Alexander	Downton					PFM	FM	PLM	PFM	PFM
Thomas, Edward	Okehampton	?	NI	PLM	?	PLM	PLM	PLM	?	PLM
Thomas, Esay	Bishop's Castle					PFM	PFM	PFM	PFM	PFM
Thomas, John	Helston					FM?	NI	NI	PFR	LM
Thomson, George	Southwark					PFM	PFM	CM/CR	PCR	CR
Thornhaugh, Francis	E. Retford					PFR	NI	CR	PFR	Dec.
Thorpe, Francis	Richmond					CR/FM	PLR	PLR	PCR	CC
Thynne, John	Saltash					PFM	PFM	PFM	PFM	PFM
Toll, Thomas	King's Lynn	NI	NI	?	NI	PLR	PLR	PLR	PFR	FR
Tolson, Richard	Cumberland					PFM	PFM	CM	PCM	PFM
Trefusis, Nicholas	Cornwall					PFM	PFM	?	?	PFM
Trenchard, John	Wareham	PCR	PCR	PCR	PCR	CR/CM	CR/FM	CR	CR	CC
Trenchard, Sir Thomas	Dorset	PFR	CR?	CR?	PFR	PLM	PLM	PLM	PLM	PLM
Trevor, Sir John	Grampound					?	PFR	CR	?	LR
Trevor, John	Flintshire					PLM	PLM	PLM	PFM	PCM
Trevor, Sir Thomas, Bt.	Tregony					PLM	PLM	PLM	PLM	PCM
Tufton, Sir Humphrey	Maidstone	PFM	PFM	PFM	PFM	PLM	PLM	PLM	PLM	PFM
Twisden, Thomas	Maidstone					PFM	PFM	PLM	PLM	PCM
Uvedale, Sir William	Petersfield	PFM	NI	NI	PFM	PLM	PFM	PLM	PLM	PFM
Vachell, Tanfield	Reading					PFR	PFR	CR	PLR	PSR
Valentine, Benjamin	St. Germans	NI	NI	NI	?	FR/FM	FR/FM	FR?	PLR	PFR
Vane, Sir Henry, Sr.	Wilton	CR	CR	CR	CR	FR/FM	FR/FM	?	PFR	SR
Vane, Sir Henry, Jr.	Hull	CR	CR	CR	CR	CR/FM	CR/FM	CR	CR	CR

Vassall, Samuel	London	PCR	PCR	PCR	PCR	FM?	PFM	CM/FR	PFM	PFM
Vaughan, Charles	Honiton					PLM	PLM	PFM	PLM	CM
Vaughan, Edward	Montgomeryshire					PLM	PLM	PFM	?	CM
Venn, John	London	CR	PCR	PCR	PCR	CR/FM	CR/FM	CR	CR	CC
Waddon, John	Plymouth	PFM	PFM	PFM	PFM	FM?	FM?	PFM	CM	PFM
Waite, Thomas	Rutland					?	PLR	PLR	PFR	CC
Walker, Clement	Wells					PCM	PCM	CM	PCM	CM
Waller, Thomas	Bodmin									PFM
Waller, Sir William	Andover	CR	CR	CR	PCR	CM	CM	CM	Out	CM
Wallopp, Robert	Andover	PCR	PCR	PCR	PCR	PCR	PLR	PLR	PCR	CC
Walsingham, Sir Thomas	Rochester	PCR	PCR	PCR	PCR	PLR	PLR	PCR	PCR	FR
Walton, Valentine	Huntingdonshire	PCR	NI	PCR	PCR	PLR	PCR	PLR	PCR	CC
Wastell, John	Northallerton	NI	PFR	NI	NI	PFR	PLR	CR?	PFR	LR
Weaver, Edmund	Hereford					PLM	PLM	SRy	PLM	?
Weaver, John	Stamford					MR?	MR?	MR	MR	CR
Weaver, Richard	Hereford	Dec.								
Wenman, Thomas, Viscount	Oxfordshire	?	?	PCM	PCM	PFM	PFM	PLM	PCM	CM
Wentworth, Sir Peter	Tamworth	CR	CR	NI	CR	PMR	PMR	MR	MR	LR
West, Edmund	Buckinghamshire					FR/FM	FR/FM	PFR	PFR	LR
Weston, Benjamin	Dover	NI	NI	PFR	?	PLR	PLR	CR	PLR	FR
Weston, Henry	Guildford					NI	NI	NI	NI	LR
Westrow, Thomas	Hythe					FR/FM	?	PFR	PFR	PLR
Wheeler, William	Westbury	PCR	CR?	PCR	PFR	PCM	PCM	CM	CR?	CM
Whitaker, Lawrence	Okehampton	PFR	PFR	PFR	PFR	FR/FM	FR/FM	CR	PCR	CR
Whitaker, William	Shaftesbury	NI	NI	?	NI	Dec.				
White, John	Southwark	FR?	PFR	PFR	PFR	Dec.				
White, William	Pontefract					CR/FM	CR/FM	CR?	CR	LR
Whitehead, Richard	Hampshire	NI	PCM	PFM	PFM	PFM	PFM	PFM	PCM	PCM
Whitelocke, Bulstrode	Great Marlow	CM	CM	CM	CM	FR/FM	FR/FM	FR	FR	CR
Widdrington, Sir Thomas	Berwick	NI	PCR	PCR	PCR	CR/FM	CR	CR	CR	CR
Wills, Henry	Saltash					PLM	PLM	PLM	PLM	LM
Wilson, Rowland	Calne					NI	PFR	CR	PFR	CR
Wingate, Edward	St. Albans	PFM	PFM	PFM	PFM	PFM	PFM	?	PFM	FM
Winwood, Richard	New Windsor	PFM	PFM	PFM	PFM	PLM	PLM	PFM	PFM	FM

Members' Activities, 1644, 1647, 1648 (*cont.*)

Member	Constituency	1644				1647				1648
		First quarter	Second quarter	Third quarter	Fourth quarter	First quarter	Second quarter	Third quarter	Fourth quarter	
Wodehouse, Sir Thomas, Bt.	Thetford	?	?	?	PFR	PLR	PLR	PLR	PLR	PLR
Wogan, John	Pembrokeshire	Dec.								
Wogan, Thomas	Cardigan					PLR	PLR	PCR	PCR	CC
Wood, Richard	Anglesey					NI	NI	NI	NI	NI
Worsley, Sir Henry, Bt.	Newport, I.W.					PFM	PLM	PLM	PLM	PFM
Wray, Sir Christopher	Grimsby	PFM	PFM	PFM	NI	Dec.				
Wray, Sir John, Bt.	Lincolnshire	PCM	PCM	PCM	PCM	PLM	PLM	PLM	PLM	PFM
Wray, William	Grimsby	PCM	PCM	PCM	PCM	PLM	PLM	PLM	PLM	PFM
Wroth, Sir Peter	Bridgwater	?	Dec.							
Wroth, Sir Thomas	Bridgwater					CR/FM	?	PLR	MR?	CC
Wylde, Edmund	Droitwich					PLR	PLR	PLR	PLR	PFR
Wylde, John	Worcestershire	PCR	PCR	PCR	PCR	PCR	PCR	CR	CR	CC
Wynn, Sir Richard, Bt.	Liverpool	NI	NI	NI	NI	PLM	PLM	PLM	PFM	PFM
Wynn, Richard	Carnarvonshire					PFM	PLM	PFM	PLM	LM
Yelverton, Sir Christopher	Bossinney	?	?	PFR	?	FR/FM	FR/FM	NI	PFR	SR
Yonge, Walter	Honiton	PFR	PFR	PFR	PFR	NI	NI	NI	?	PLR
Young, Sir John	Plymouth	NI	NI	?	PLM	FM?	FM?	PLM	PFM	PFM

Index

Accomodation order: and Scots, 40, 42; and Separatists, 42n
Agitators in Five Regiments: approaches to, by Cromwell, 231, 233, 235; Putney debates, 235–236
Agitators: and Cromwell, 234
Agostini, Signor, Venetian ambassador, 12, 24, 26; defence of Essex by the moderates, 28; Lords' fear of Commons, 29; London Common Council pressure on radicals, 32; deposition of Charles I, 33; radical policies, 36, 51, 56, 59; and Scots, 49
Agreement of the People (First), 235, 243, 246
Agreement of the People (Second), 288, 290, 303, 313
Allen, Francis, 110, 230, 266
Allen, William, 182, 204
Alured, John, 322n
Anglicanism, 232, 240, 296
Antinomians, 40, 41
Argyle, Marquis of, *see* Campbell, Archibald
Armine, Sir William, 22, 142n
Army Remonstrance, 297, 300
Ashburnham, John, 213, 268, 269
Ashe, Edward, 293
Ashe, John, 214n, 324n
Ashurst, William, 215
Assheton, Sir Ralph (Clitheroe), 215n, 301, 322n
Atkins, Thomas, 285
Ayscough, Sir Edward, 322n

Bacon, Nathaniel, 162
Baillie, Robert, 13, 24, 35, 80, 87, 109, 127, 136, 280
Balmerino, Lord, *see* Elphinstone, John
Bamfield, Colonel Joseph: and radicals, 104, 139, 149–150; and royalists, 139; and moderates, 139, 202; and Charles I, 139, 190–191; King's negotiations with moderates, 184–186; disbanding of New Model, 184–185; and Cromwell, 185
Bampfield, Sir John: and Levellers, 246n
Barkstead, Colonel John, 297

Barnardiston, Sir Nathaniel, 52, 81
Barrington, Sir Thomas, 28n, 31n
Baynton, Edward, 25n, 28n, 215n
Beauchamp, Lord, 39
Bedford, Earl of, *see* Russell, William
Bellièvre, M. de: and moderates, 164, 186; and London, 167; and Holles, 186; Heads of Proposals, 207
Berkeley, Sir John: and Cromwell, 170, 241; Heads of Proposals, 213; and Charles I, 213, 241; and Ireton, 241; trial of the King, 241; Levellers, 241; Cromwell's abandonment of the King, 241–242, 248
Bishop's Castle, 101
Blagrave, Daniel, 323n
Blakiston, John: and Earl of Essex, 25n; House of Lords, 32; peace proposals, 47; and Charles I, 283; Levellers, 288n; "calling" of House, 289; "hard core" radicals, 322n
Blount, Mountjoy, Earl of Newport, 79
Bolingbroke, Earl of, *see* St. John, Oliver
Bond, Denis: and Earl of Essex, 25n, 40n; and Princes Rupert and Maurice, 48; trial of King, 294; "hard core" radicals, 322n
Book of Common Prayer: and moderates, 167; New Model, 179; abolition of, and radicals, 232, 250, 296; Hamiltonian Scots, 275
Bossiney, 101
Bosvile, Godfrey, 86, 322n
Bourchier, Sir John, 323n
Boys, John, 287
Brereton, Sir William, 54
Bristol, 102
Broghill, Lord, 242
Brooke, Peter, 216n
Browne, John, 322n
Browne, Major General Richard, 270
Browne, Samuel: and Earls of Essex and Holland, 20; and St. John, 20, 52; committee of both kingdoms, 22; Laud's trial, 52; Saville affair, 82; and Holles, 87; and Charles I, 121; and Scots, 121; Erastianism of, 124; re-